Promoting, Assessing, Recognizing and Certifying
Lifelong Learning

Lifelong Learning Book Series

VOLUME 20

Aims & Scope
"Lifelong Learning" has become a central theme in education and community development. Both international and national agencies, governments and educational institutions have adopted the idea of lifelong learning as a major theme in the coming years. They realize that it is only by getting people committed to the idea of education both life-wide and lifelong that the goals of economic advancement, social emancipation and personal growth will be attained.

The *Lifelong Learning Book Series* aims to keep scholars and professionals informed about and abreast of current developments and to advance research and scholarship in the domain of Lifelong Learning. It further aims to provide learning and teaching materials, serve as a forum for scholarly and professional debate and offer a rich fund of resources for researchers, policy-makers, scholars, professionals and practitioners in the field.

The volumes in this international Series are multi-disciplinary in orientation, polymathic in origin, range and reach, and variegated in range and complexity. They are written by researchers, professionals and practitioners working widely across the international arena in lifelong learning and are orientated towards policy improvement and educational betterment throughout the life cycle.

For further volumes:
http://www.springer.com/series/6227

Timo Halttunen • Mari Koivisto • Stephen Billett
Editors

Promoting, Assessing, Recognizing and Certifying Lifelong Learning

International Perspectives and Practices

 Springer

Editors
Timo Halttunen
Brahea Centre
University of Turku
Turku, Finland

Mari Koivisto
Brahea Centre
University of Turku
Turku, Finland

Stephen Billett
Education and Professional Studies
Griffith University
Brisbane, QLD, Australia

ISBN 978-94-017-8693-5   ISBN 978-94-017-8694-2 (eBook)
DOI 10.1007/978-94-017-8694-2
Springer Dordrecht Heidelberg New York London

Library of Congress Control Number: 2014932165

Printed on acid-free paper

Springer is part of Springer Science+Business Media (www.springer.com)

This book is dedicated to Vincent Merle (1950–2013) who played a central role in the French government's approach to vocational education and, most noticeably, introduced and guided the implementation of the Validation of Acquired Experience. He was a man much respected and admired by colleagues in vocational education and government.

About the Editors

Mr. Timo Halttunen is Development Manager at the University of Turku, Finland. He is the corresponding editor of this monograph.
timo.halttunen@utu.fi

Ms. Mari Koivisto is Education Coordinator at the University of Turku, Finland.
mari.koivisto@utu.fi

Dr. Stephen Billett is Professor of Adult and Vocational Education at Griffith University, Queensland, Australia.
s.billett@griffith.edu.au

Preface

This edited monograph addresses two central concerns in contemporary concerns about lifelong learning and lifelong education, and which are shared internationally. That is, firstly, the ways in which learning across life is directed towards and supportive of individuals' participation in and the achievement of goals associated with their working lives. At this time, a key imperative for nations, communities, workplaces and individuals is the capacity to secure and sustain employability beyond schooling and initial occupational preparation. The kinds of constant change that occur in work, work requirements, the kinds of occupations that are available and the means of undertaking work necessarily require that individuals are able to continue to learn in ways that sustain their employability through all of these changes. Featured here are accounts from a range of countries that offer conceptualisations, processes and approaches directed towards securing workers' lifelong learning.

Secondly, concerns about the ways in which this ongoing learning can be assessed, recognised and certified are also of concern to a range of countries who are seeking to identify and implement or improve practices that are broadly referred to as the recognition of prior learning. There are often significant equity goals associated with these processes, which like concerns about lifelong education seek to redress shortcomings and disadvantages of individuals' earlier education and work experiences. The perspectives here represent considerations of, approaches to and procedures for the effective recognition of individuals' ongoing learning across adult life.

These two sets of concerns are often correlated and, therefore, stand to be considered and advanced together. The contributions in this edited monograph bring insights from Australia, Belgium, Finland, France, Germany, Ireland, the Netherlands, Singapore, Sweden, Switzerland, the United Kingdom and the United States together in one volume. It is the diversity of these contributions that provides comprehension of how these two important issues can be understood and addressed more globally.

Turku, Finland   Timo Halttunen
Turku, Finland   Mari Koivisto
Brisbane, QLD, Australia   Stephen Billett
November 2013

Acknowledgements

This monograph has been produced in the framework of the European Social Fund – financed project Recognition of Prior Learning in Higher Education (Finland).

Turun yliopisto
University of Turku

European Union
European Social Fund

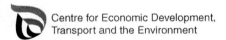

Centre for Economic Development,
Transport and the Environment

Leverage from
the EU
2007–2013

Contents

Part I
Promoting and Recognising Lifelong Learning: Key Concepts, Practices and Emerging and Perennial Problems

Chapter 1
Promoting and Recognising Lifelong Learning: Introduction

Timo Halttunen, Mari Koivisto, and Stephen Billett

1.1 Lifelong Learning and Employability

Currently, there is growing interest worldwide by governments, professional bodies, employers and workers in lifelong learning. This interest particularly relates to the ongoing learning beyond compulsory education and initial occupational preparation: across working life. Much of this interest is driven by key social and economic imperatives associated with sustaining individuals' employability in the context of changing requirements of work and working life (Billett 2010; Department of Education Science and Training 2002; Organisation for Economic Co-operation and Development 2010). This includes the significant transformations occurring within many occupations, and that all of these changes will continue to occur across lengthening working lives (Coffield 2000; Organisation for Economic Co-operation and Development 2006). Such demands to sustain employability are placing a premium on ongoing learning through and for work and emphasising the importance of the continuation of learning across working life (Field 2000). However, the concerns associated with lifelong learning are not restricted to work and working life, as there are also those associated with individuals being able to engage in learning about cultural knowledge and social roles and practices that they have not so far had the opportunity to engage with or because their interests have changed across adulthood. For instance, some adults have been disengaged from educational provisions during or on completion of their compulsory education because of unsatisfactory experiences in schools. Despite efforts of moving to a learner-centred approach in education, classroom-based approaches are not the optimal learning environment

T. Halttunen (✉) • M. Koivisto
Brahea Centre, University of Turku, Turku, Finland
e-mail: timo.halttunen@utu.fi; mari.koivisto@utu.fi

S. Billett
Education and Professional Studies, Griffith University, Brisbane, QLD, Australia
e-mail: s.billett@griffith.edu.au

T. Halttunen et al. (eds.), *Promoting, Assessing, Recognizing and Certifying Lifelong Learning: International Perspectives and Practices*, Lifelong Learning Book Series 20, DOI 10.1007/978-94-017-8694-2_1, © Springer Science+Business Media Dordrecht 2014

for these kinds of learners. Recognition of their learning from work experience may assist these individuals re-engage with ongoing education and empower to engage in continuing education and training. These kinds of learning are often seen as being beneficial to personal growth and well-being in retirement.

So, there is growing concern and action now being undertaken by global agencies, national governments, professional bodies, industry associations, workplaces, educational institutions and learners themselves about learning across the lifespan, with much of it associated with sustaining employability. Global agencies and national governments are making arrangements to organise and sustain continuing education and training (CET) to meet economic and social goals (Yacob 2009) through supporting individuals' learning. Professional bodies and industry associations are concerned about having effective and currently skilled workforces and are increasingly coming to share concerns about the need for CET for their sector and are effecting arrangements to require ongoing learning as a requirement for continuing occupational licensing. Many workplaces are also addressing concerns about skill shortages and ageing workforces (Tikkanen et al. 2002) through workplace-based continuing education provisions. For individuals now faced with maintaining employability across lengthening working lives, the ability to secure and sustain their occupational competence stands as a key personal and professional consideration (McNair et al. 2004). In the future, many of these individuals will likely make greater material and personal investments in sustaining that employability through learning across working life, as governments enable rather than support it directly (Field 2000). This also applies to those seeking outcomes associated with cultural and socially focused learning outcomes outside of working life. Recognition of prior learning as a practice of exercising self-regulation and metacognitive skills may lead to greater agency over individuals' learning processes. From individual's point of view, this capacity may provide for greater security and trust in the changing nature of working life. In particular, in small- and medium-sized companies, where human resource development is absent, this recognition may have a significant meaning to the success of the enterprises. At large, this form of agency may lead to increased physical and social mobility for these individuals in the labour market. In these ways, lifelong learning is now becoming an increasing area of focus for policy action by governments and global agencies, the enactment of mechanisms to monitor professional learning by professional bodies and initiatives by employers to sustain the skill levels in their workforces.

Moreover, for some circumstances and individuals, it is also important to understand how and implement by which means this learning can be assessed, recognised and certified. In particular, many in workforces across the world who have learnt much of the knowledge required to maintain their employability through that work have not had that knowledge assessed and certified (Billett 2005). Indeed, many of these workers are structurally disadvantaged because the means through which they have learnt their occupations did not lead to certification. Consequently, that learning and that competency remain without recognition and certification which can inhibit them seeking to either sustain their employability and advancement and/or extend their work into new occupations or workplaces. Whilst there are processes associated with the assessment of prior learning, not all of these are readily adaptable to all forms of work. In particular, in circumstances where there are no courses or benchmarks for those learnings to be equated against, there are no bases for the assessment leading to certification. Moreover, even where certification exists, this may not be seen as being as legitimate and valued as that which is acquired through participating in educational programmes. Indeed, despite the great interest in recognition of prior learning, not much attention has been paid to the very circumstances where learning from the experiences occurs and how this learning can be assessed and used for the benefit of personal growth. In many countries prior learning recognition has been undertaken within and largely directed towards vocational education and training and professionally oriented higher education. Consequently, again, individuals who have secured and had that knowledge recognised may still be subject to disadvantage because of the standing of their certification. Of course, as individuals have longer working lives, and confront changes in the occupations and may even be required to transfer to new occupations, the lack of certification can also render them at a disadvantage in securing ongoing employability. Hence, there are important issues associated with both policy and practice for not only understanding and supporting lifelong learning, but also how that learning can be assessed, certified and recognised in ways which meet the needs of individuals negotiating lengthening working lives and seeking to expand their interests and capacities outside of working life.

These concerns are those which are the focus of and shape the ordering of this monograph. It does so through the contributions within its three parts, which comprise: (1) *Promoting and Recognising Lifelong Learning: Key Concepts, Practices and Emerging and Perennial Problems*, (2) *Promoting Lifelong Learning for Economic, Social and Cultural Purposes* and (3) *Recognising and Certifying Lifelong Learning: Policies and Practices*. These contributors are from Australia, Belgium, Finland, France, Germany, Ireland, the Netherlands, Singapore, Sweden, Switzerland, United Kingdom and United States and provide a range of international perspectives on lifelong learning, its promotion and recognition.

1.2 Part I—Promoting and Recognising Lifelong Learning: Key Concepts, Practices and Emerging and Perennial Problems

In this part it is proposed that promoting and recognising lifelong learning now warrant significant attention within education policy and practice. It notes that there is considerable and growing interest in lifelong learning, worldwide, particularly as it relates to learning beyond the years of compulsory schooling and initial occupational preparation, which are usually the central focus of educational practices and policies. Instead, now it is necessary to consider how best to support and recognise individuals' learning beyond those initial phases of development that have traditionally been the dominant focus of national and global educational projects (i.e. national education systems, national curriculum, schools, colleges and universities). Much of this emerging interest is driven by key social and economic imperatives associated with the changing requirements of work and working life and the ongoing transformation of many occupations and lengthening working lives. There is a clear realisation from governments and global bodies that because of these changes and their ongoing nature, perhaps increasingly so, initial educational programmes and outcomes are unlikely to be effective in assisting individuals secure and sustain their employability across their working lives. At the same time, it is understood that merely recycling individuals through educational provisions on periodic bases is both impractical and unsustainable. All of this has led to an interest in finding ways to promote the continuation of learning across working life, with a growing realisation that much, if not most, of this learning will occur outside of educational institutions and programmes. Moreover, the promotion, recognition and certification of that learning whilst being essential may need to occur in circumstances that are quite different than when undertaken within educational programmes and within educational institutions. Often, much of this assessment and certification is currently addressed through the provision of educational courses and programmes. Indeed, some people view lifelong learning and lifelong education as being one and the same. However, they are not. The first is a fundamental human process that is ongoing across our lives: personal facts. The second is the provision of experiences with intentional learning outcomes and usually assessment of those outcomes: institutional arrangements. So, lifelong education is an element of lifelong learning. All of this suggests that there is a need for a considered critique of existing educational policies and practices that are centred on provisions of learning support and recognition that are centred within educational institutions. Instead, options, alternatives and approaches that sit outside of them need now to be considered.

So, the premises for a fresh appraisal of the promotion and recognition of lifelong learning are set out and then discussed through a consideration of the contributions of this monograph. Overall, it argues that a fresh element in the educational project is required. That is, one which is concerned primarily with the kinds of development that is required beyond initial educational provisions and needs to be supported in ways which are commensurate with individuals' needs across working lives, the kind of lives they lead and the kind of learning that they need and the most optimal ways in which that learning can be supported. Hence, it proposes setting aside presumptions and precepts associated with intentional learning being most optimally supported through experiences in educational institutions, although this may well be necessary and helpful. In addition, it suggests that fresh thinking and novel approaches are required to identify ways in which individuals' lifelong learning can be recognised and certified to assist supporting and sustaining their employability across lengthening working lives and potentially in competition with those who had more recent initial preparation.

This appraisal commences with Chap. 2, "Conceptualising lifelong learning and its recognition in contemporary times", by Stephen Billett. Although terms such as lifelong learning and the recognition of learning are well used and accepted within the educational discourse, the precision with which they are accused and the utility of that use is sometimes open to question. For instance, the term lifelong learning is quite commonly associated with continuing education or professional development programmes, which are educational provisions, whereas learning is something which people do both within such provisions, but also mostly outside of them. Moreover, even when considered as an ongoing process of learning, lifelong learning is often seen as being something which arises from specific kinds of experiences, rather than being an ongoing normal process of human cognition. Consequently, given that much of lifelong learning will inevitably occur outside of institutionalised arrangements such as those established and implemented to secure intentional learning outcomes (e.g. educational programmes), it is necessary to be clear about what constitutes lifelong learning. This clarification needs augmenting by understandings of how such conceptions of learning relate to important goals for individuals, their workplaces and societies such as learning across working life, securing and sustaining employability across lengthening working lives and the kinds of support that can promote that learning in ways which are accessible, helpful and enduring for individuals who will need to continue to learn across their working lives. Consequently, this chapter's first aim is to set out what constitutes 'lifelong learning' and how it might best be promoted across working lives, with the key focus on individuals' employability.

The related and second aim for this chapter is to elaborate what might constitute the means by which this learning can be recognised and certified. Securing this aim necessarily requires a consideration of the requirements for such recognition, the degree by which they will be taken as being legitimate and worthwhile and the kinds of frameworks and practices that will be required for assessment, recognition and certification. All of this needs to occur in ways that support individuals' employability as they work to secure employment, maintain that employment as work requirements change, and have a platform from which to seek promotion, extend the scope of their employment and, potentially, move to other forms of employment. Whilst it is necessary to address the tenets of assessment practices, broad policy and practice considerations associated with the recognition of skills across working life will be the key emphasis within the second focus of this chapter.

In their chapter, "New skills for new jobs: Work agency as a necessary condition for successful lifelong learning" (Chap. 3), Christian Harteis and Michael Goller argue that individuals are permanently exposed to changes in today's work environments due to strong economic competition and fast technological development. More and more frequently, employees face less job security, a higher need for flexibility, remarkable intensification of work and a strong demand for lifelong learning. In order to arrange daily working life self-dependently, individuals have to become active agents that do not passively react on the outcomes of such changes. From an educational viewpoint, it is important that individuals develop qualities to face future challenges that cannot be predicted during their initial occupational preparation. They have to be able to make decisions at any life stage that allow them to exert control over their professional work-life courses. Individuals have to develop appropriate self-concepts that ensure them independence from concrete conditions of current developments. Lifelong learning is a necessary part of such an endeavour. This contribution aims at introducing the concept of '*work agency*', which covers the personal capacity to cope with the stated challenges. Agency comprises the general capacity to make intentional choices, to initiate actions based on these choices and to exercise control over the self and the environment. Individuals are causal agents that deliberately affect both their own life trajectories as well as the general conditions of their environment (Billett 2008; Fenwick and Somerville 2006; Gecas 2006; Martin 2004; Watkin 2005; Smith 2006).

1.3   Part II—Promoting Lifelong Learning for Economic, Social and Cultural Purposes

The reasons for growing interest for lifelong learning do not limit to the transformation of professions. Economic, social and cultural changes behind these transformations have an impact on the very nature of work. Changes such as shift from industrial production to knowledge-based economy, challenges with ageing population and use of information and communications technology bring about reasons to governments and policy makers throughout the world for promoting lifelong learning and learning across working life. In this part lifelong learning is explored through economic, social and cultural purposes. In many societies people live longer and they are also expected to stay longer as productive members of the community. However, at the same time the character of employment has changed. Few people stay their entire career with the same employer. Many people will change their professions during their careers and spend shorter times with single employer. For an increasing number of individuals, alternating between employment and unemployment may become regular or even a choice, 'to be called to work when needed'. Despite this being welcomed flexibility for some, this new state of the art calls for support on assisting the ongoing process of learning. *The notion of lifelong employability has become ever more eminent in the discourse of lifelong learning.* Hence the importance of securing and sustaining employability and advancement across these lengthening and non-linear career paths has grown in the educational policies across the world. As this transformation goes on, a critical view on what comprises of learning has also emerged. The overlapping domains of education, work and leisure time call for a more varied view of learning, challenging the often presented categorisation of formal, non-formal and informal learning and the supposed differences these categories bring to learning of individuals. During the course of lifelong learning, these categories have always overlapped in the individual level. In the structural level education, work and leisure have also become closer to each other through introduction of, e.g., competency-based education and use of information and communication technology. The use of web-based social networks and games in learning has expanded the notion of learning environment outside of educational institutions. However, there are different and even contrasting views on how individuals learn and engage in the learning affordances at hand. The same goes with the definition of the 'workplace'. In the modern world more and more individuals carry out their work tasks in a networked environment, even with some distance to the actual physical workplace. Interaction between workers, managers and clients may be mediated by the use of information and communications technology.

During the last 20–50 years, individuals have come to face less job security and a higher demand for career management. This demand for flexibility and capability to construct professional identities during the course of working lives can be seen as exercising professional agency. Individuals come across learning affordances at work or during leisure time. Employers may even require learning at work in return for better salary or career advancement. Although learning at work is generally desired both by employees and employers, such learning opportunities that engage the individual in lifelong learning might not automatically be offered or arranged by the employer or education providers. Therefore, professional development calls for intentional construction of appropriate professional identities. In the changing landscape of labour and employability, individuals are not only expected to take part in upskilling their competencies in education but also to engage in the transformation of practices and conditions at work.

In Chap. 4, "Evaluating informal learning in the workplace", Karen E. Watkins, Victoria J. Marsick, and Miren Fernández de Álava introduce the particular challenges associated with evaluating informal learning in the workplace. Marsick and Watkins' model of informal and incidental learning is used as a framework for a conversation on how the nature of this learning makes assessment difficult, particularly due to the potential for error. Issues in determining what to assess in informal learning are discussed. A study of informal learning policies and assessment amongst communities of practice is used to illustrate some of the issues in assessing this learning. This approach is compared with current strategies to credential prior learning in the United States. Finally, a call for assessing open-ended learning in the workplace is offered, drawing again on research from participants in communities of practice. Surveys on participation in adult education suggest that many adults keep learning across the lifespan for economic and work-related reasons. At the same time, learning opportunities have expanded due to technology, globalisation and technology-driven social networking. Such learning is often informal, organic and based on intrinsic motivation and interests. The writers describe this kind of learning in organisations and raise questions on how to best support and link to desired performance and economic outcomes. To provide support for such learning, they examine the dynamics of this learning and the environment in which work and learning occur. The chapter will thus examine research on collective learning—still an emerging field—and identify how to guide organisations in supporting opportunities for collective learning linked to improved performance. The challenges of evaluating informal and incidental learning are presented through research on communities of practice (CoPs) in the public sector in Catalonia, Spain. The CoPs are explored with a critical insight whether informal and incidental learning can be evaluated for credentialing purposes. Drawing from the results of the case study, Watkins, Marsick and Fernández de Álava conclude the chapter with a discussion of the portability of skills an individual has gained through participation of a community of practice. The significance of the European case is weighed with the national movements currently rising in the United States towards credentialisation of experiential learning.

In Chap. 5, "Recognising learning and development in the transaction of personal work practices", Raymond Smith focuses on the transformational nature of work and its description and explanation as learning. Drawing on concepts of agency and Dewey's ideas of transaction, the chapter explores and discusses ways of making the transformational qualities of workers' personal work practices more visible as a means of understanding how change is enacted as learning through work and what changes are emergent as evidence of workers' learning. Sociocultural constructivist perspectives advance learning in and through work as the process and product of workers' situated participation in practice. Such participation is invariably interactive and personally enacted in the many ways workers' engage in the activities and events that characterise their practice. These discussions draw on data and findings from a research project that examined workers' personal work practices. The research focused on workers' self-description and explanation of the particular ways they went about their work, the purposes and outcomes accomplished through their personal practice and the kinds of personal and situational changes they accounted as evidence of their learning. From the findings of that research, the chapter elaborates three kinds of sets of transactions. They are: (1) transacting identity through forms of social engagement, (2) transacting goals as personal aspirations and shared purposes and (3) transacting the material as tools and procedures. These sets of transactions are advanced as possibilities for overcoming the limitations of interaction as the primary concept used to define the activities that underpin describing and explaining work learning as participative practice. Data samples from the interview transcripts of one of the three firefighters who participated in the research are used to illustrate the complex integration of personal and contextual factors that accomplish the transformations of person, place and practice that are the evidence of learning in and through work.

In Chap. 6, "Understanding work-related learning: The role of job characteristics and the use of different sources of learning", David Gijbels, Vincent Donche, Piet Van den Bossche, Peter Van Petegem, Ingrid Ilsbroux and Eva Sammels explore the relationship amongst job characteristics such as job demands, job control and social support and the learning that takes place in the workplace during internships. They start from an overview of recent research based on the Job-Demand-Control-Support (DCS) model (Karasek and Theorell 1990). The study exploring these relations took place in the context of internships of novice engineers. The students and their workplace supervisors were questioned by means of validated questionnaires (e.g. Gijbels et al. 2010). Whilst earlier studies used self-report of occurrence of work-related learning behaviours as operationalisation of workplace learning (e.g. Gijbels et al. 2010), the present study explores a wider perspective on workplace learning. From a process perspective, they used the framework of dynamic sources of regulation of student learning during internship (Oosterheert and Vermunt 2001). Different sources that can guide the learning of interns during work were investigated (Oosterheert and Vermunt 2001). Five such sources are distinguished: (1) external regulation, (2) self-regulation, (3) actively relating theory to practice, (4) collaboration with co-workers and (5) avoidance behaviour. From the outcome perspective, the writers looked at perceived competences reported by both the students and the supervisors in the companies. The results of regression analyses in the chapter support Karasek's learning hypotheses indicating that job demands, job control and social support influence the use of different learning resources in the workplace. In addition, the analyses show that high job demands and support by colleagues contribute to perceived competence. The chapter provides insight in workplace characteristics that affect learning during internships. Moreover, it disentangles different sources of learning regulation, hereby identifying different ways in which learning is shaped in the workplace. This suggests pathways to promote learning during internships.

In Chap. 7, "Experiential learning: A new higher education requiring new pedagogic skills", Anita Walsh introduces examples of practice in the area of recognition of prior learning in higher education and explores the pedagogic tensions which arise when combining knowledge from the academic disciplines and from experiential learning in the same curriculum. In 2009 Cedefop, the European agency with responsibilities for disseminating research findings and policy positions for vocational education, issued European guidelines for the validation of informal learning. Recent surveys of academic practice relating to the integration of experiential work-based learning in the business administration subject areas in the United Kingdom reveal that there are tensions between the pedagogies adopted to support experiential learning and those used in more conventional programmes. A consistent distinction is made between vocational and academic learning and is frequently reflected in policy, as with, for example, the Bologna process governing the area of higher education across Europe and the Copenhagen process of vocational education and training. Based on the examples from different fields, Walsh argues that high-level experiential learning can take place in a wide range of contexts, including the workplace, and it can be identified and assessed in a manner appropriate for inclusion in higher education awards. The knowledge production inside and outside university is evaluated towards the protocols and the pedagogies used in higher education institutions. Walsh concludes that the explored innovative pedagogic practice demonstrates an ability to address the need to use a more subtle conceptualisation of learning and skills which supports a wider range of curriculum delivery.

Scientific knowledge from different fields plays an important role in the development of emerging professional practices and emerging professions that are in many cases related to welfare societies' acute problems. In Chap. 8, "How expertise is created in emerging professional fields", Erno Lehtinen, Tuire Palonen and Els Boshuizen review research literature of the expertise formation in emerging professions and present data of their own empirical studies on the possibilities to integrate formal education and learning at work in new professional fields in which there are no established formal training. In their report 'The shape of future jobs to come', Talwar and Hancock (2010) analysed the changes in society, science and technology, resulting in a list of new jobs that might emerge due to these developments. They see number of global issues, i.e. 'change drivers', requiring co-ordinated global solutions, e.g. in the field of environment, finance and security. In these situations, the informal ways of knowing and authentic working-life practices develop in communities of practitioners, sometimes in cooperation with clients and/ or suppliers (Eraut 2004; Hakkarainen et al. 2004). Depending on the urgency or societal consequences of these new developments, the communities document their practices with certified knowledge. To support these processes, a better understanding is needed of the formal and informal learning that occurs through activities and interactions in the settings, in which occupational practices are undertaken. Based on Yielder's (2004) studies, Lehtinen, Palonen and Boshuizen define the elements that contribute in professional change processes. In the model presented expertise can be seen as a synthesis of a particular knowledge base and practitioners' cognitive processes, personality and internal integrative processes. Professional expertise builds on interpersonal relationships with other professionals through which it is expressed as an actual doing of professional practice. To better understand the variety and richness of the new jobs to come, the writers have created a classification of the reasons that are behind the change in professional practices in various domains.

An increasingly common means by which learning across working life is being promoted is through provisions of continuing education and training (CET) organised and enacted through partnerships between tertiary education systems and employers. Sarojni Choy, Ray Smith and Ann Kelly argue in their chapter "Continuing education and training at work" (Chap. 9) that greater consideration is required of processes and practices that are best suited to this provision of education and the needs and capacities of those who access and participate. Often, these provisions are seen as an extension or variation of initial occupational preparation, the main and core business of tertiary education institutions. However, as CET becomes an increasingly important component of tertiary education, this includes issues of access for individuals who are engaged in full-time employment whilst balancing family and other social commitments and the occupational capacities that employers seek and are interested to develop in their workers. This chapter reports the findings of a national project in Australia which examined the efficacy of existing CET provisions to identify and promote what a national CET provision might comprise. What the findings consistently indicate is that most likely this provision of education will need to be based in the circumstances of individuals' work and largely through their work practices, albeit augmented by assistance provided by more experienced co-workers and specialist trainers engaging with these workers in the circumstances of their work, and often, whilst engaged in work. This is not to deny the importance of and roles that specific training interventions (e.g. classroom events) can play in the overall provision of CET, but these largely augment what is made available and what occurs within individual's circumstance of practice. In all, a key contribution of this chapter is to set out the range of CET models and practices that will most likely be helpful for securing workers' continuing education and training at work in ways which will sustain their employability across lengthening working lives.

In Chap. 10, "Lifelong learning policies and practices in Singapore: Tensions and challenges", Magdalene Lin, Helen Bound and Peter Rushbrook provide an illustration of how practices, cultural ways of being and the framing of systems for developing a workforce to meet the challenges of globalisation mediate the formulation and implementation of a national approach to lifelong learning. Singapore's economic foci on productivity and innovation suggest that policy supporting lifelong learning has a principally economic intent. However, there are a number of initiatives that suggest Singapore is broadening its approach towards lifelong learning policy that supports greater inclusiveness and addresses social issues. However, when the writers delve into the policy and practice of learning programmes, their delivery and the enacted curriculum, they make visible the considerable tensions between the rhetoric and the desired intent. The chapter begins by describing the Singaporean continuing education and training landscape and the relevant economic and social policy, including recent policy changes. Lin, Bound and Rushbrook then draw on data from a number of research projects conducted by the Centre for Research in Learning at the Institute for Adult Learning, Singapore, to illustrate current practices. In all, the chapter provides illustrative accounts of how practices, cultural ways of being and framing of systems for developing a workforce to meet the challenges of globalisation mediate the formulation and implementation of lifelong learning.

1.4 Part III—Recognising and Certifying Lifelong Learning: Policies and Practices

The third and final part of the book provides a closer view on policies and practices related to recognising and certifying lifelong learning. Regarding support for learning at work during education, mentors are often used during internships as an external source to regulate the learning and assess learning outcomes. Mentors may be labelled as tutors, coaches or co-workers, and they are to help the individual in engaging in the learning affordances outside of the formal programme. Educators may include actors from the workplace during internships also in the assessment of learning and thus bring the notion of 'authenticity' in learning. However, job characteristics are interrelated to knowledge construction and regulation of learning. In addition, student characteristics probably play a role in knowledge construction and regulation of learning and influence the way an individual learns at the workspace, here defined as a specific learning environment during their education. Amongst the individuals already employed and engaged in learning at work, a similar variation is identified in the levels and directions of self-investment in transformation of work practices and working conditions. Workers may be sometimes effortfully engaged in the development of their job characteristics and at times seemingly indifferent to the requirements of work. Despite the fact that for many people work still secures life-wide and life-affirming significance for their roles and responsibilities in society, they may not find their work purposeful and meaningful. *When looking recognition of learning at workplace as a pedagogic space, one has to pay attention on the nature of the actions and engagement of individuals that make social activity as co-participation in the transforming collective practice.*

Recognition of prior learning has raised interest in educational policies. How can the various stakeholders in the world of work and in education make the many promises RPL beholds for lifelong learning a reality? Businesses should develop policies for ensuring the candidates for prior learning recognition with better job security and implement the use of RPL in their human resource development practices. In terms of developing policies into practices, further professionalisation of all stakeholders in the process is needed in order to help individuals get the most of their prior learning. To enhance the effectiveness of RPL supervision, learners ought to be tutored and mentored by expert members in their community of practice to make visible their prior learning and reflect on their experience. Supervisors should enhance their competencies in negotiating the knowledge, skills and attitudes presented in the accounts of those personal trajectories towards the institutional demands in higher education. To fully understand this learning process within RPL, learners and their tutors should explore more closely the cognitive processes and the individual agency and shaping of social settings. However, learners themselves are also shaped by interactive norms and resources embedded in their social settings. This interplay between the individual and the social structure is explored more closely in the third part of this book.

In addition to adopting a language of competency-based approach in curricula development and creating intended learning outcomes for education, the educators need to examine their ways of learning assessment. The scope of assessment of learning needs to be broadened to embrace learning outside of the classroom. A code of practice is required to ensure transparency and a minimum standard for the assessment procedures. Practice plays an important role in improving assessor skills. An assessor professionalisation and certification programme may help in creating a community of practitioners, contributing to the assessment procedure with specified knowledge from different fields of knowledge and disciplines. Assessment of learning may strengthen social integration and solidarity as well as develop personal identity. If the results of RPL processes and assessment are clearly communicated to learners, it may enable them to mobilise these learning experiences in new contexts and seek for career advancement. However, depending from national contexts, there are societal sentiments associated with different kinds of work, and some lines of work fall into the category of low status. Workers may find themselves in a situation where even an effective recognition and certification process will not result in progression of their status or career advancement.

The third part starts with Chap. 11, "Professionalisation of supervisors and RPL" by Timo Halttunen and Mari Koivisto, with a view on the supervision of learners with prior learning in higher education. In universities, learning that has taken place during work activities and leisure time has been far more challenging to recognise than learning in educational programmes. In their chapter the writers argue that in order to enhance the effectiveness of the recognition of prior learning, there is a need for more thorough support and guidance to facilitate this process in higher education institutions. The writers analyse the process of tailoring prior learning processes for higher education programmes and find it as a negotiation of accomplished and required expertise between the novice and expert members of a community of practice. In addition to an actual comparison of the learning from the experience and the learning stated in the official curricula, supervisors and learners should engage in a process of reflecting the construction of professional identities and professional agency. Great expectations lay on the shoulders of the learners in the process of recognition of prior learning. Adult learners may find difficulties in defining educational outcomes of this learning from experience. The attempts to match this contextualised learning with the learning appreciated in formal education are especially demanding in higher education. The chapter explores how students with prior learning should be supervised to optimise the recognition of their learning secured outside of educational programmes and how their supervisors are able to provide this support. The negotiations between the institutional demands and individual learning histories in the supervisors' work are seen as based on reflective processes, comprising a transformation of the professional identity and the exercise of their agency. The analysis is based on the data collected from the participants of a professional development programme for the recognition of prior learning in Finnish higher education.

In Chap. 12, "Securing assessors' professionalism: Meeting assessor requirements for the purpose of performing high-quality (RPL) assessments", Antoinette van Berkel addresses the question how assessor professionalism can be attained in a feasible and efficient manner. Over the past 10 years, the recognition of prior learning has gained increasing attention in the Netherlands. As a rule, in the Netherlands, RPL is carried out on the basis of a national competence or professional profile. An average RPL procedure consists of the following five phases: a preliminary interview, the compilation of a portfolio, a criterion-related interview, feedback and a preliminary judgment and, finally, an RPL report. In the Netherlands RPL providers must meet a national quality standard in order to be officially recognised and registered. Two different points of view with regard to the meaning of RPL in the Netherlands can be distinguished. Employers tend to look at it mainly as an employment instrument or a career tool. On the other hand, educational institutions, which carry out RPL procedures to provide exemptions for certain parts of degree programmes, regard RPL as a useful instrument for adults in lifelong learning. As the importance of diplomas and certificates is becoming increasingly important, the latter use of RPL is gaining ground. High-quality RPL assessments can best be performed if a number of preconditions are met, amongst which are the wide expertise and professional practice of assessors. These are basic assessor qualifications used for selection purposes. Furthermore, assessors are expected to acquire skills such as adequately applying interview techniques, constructing a well-founded judgment and giving development-focused feedback. An assessor training is a first step in the right direction, but it appears not to be enough. Therefore, a six-phase programme has been developed to enhance assessor professionalism, which will be explored in this chapter. Additionally, the lessons learned from 10 years of experience with conducting RPL procedures and contributing to assessor quality will be elaborated.

In his chapter, "Problems and possibilities in recognition of prior learning: A critical social theory perspective" (Chap. 13), Fredrik Sandberg argues for the importance of understanding recognition of prior learning (RPL) through the critical social theories of Jürgen Habermas and Axel Honneth. Using RPL for accreditation has for long been criticised for its instrumentalism and technical character. Results from a research project exploring RPL for the accreditation of prior experiential learning in the health-care sector in Sweden are used to develop the analysis. It is argued that RPL for accreditation could, by reflecting the results of Habermas' theory of communicative action, be a process that strengthens social integration and solidarity as well as develops personal identity. RPL as communicative action focuses on defining the situation of RPL through consensus and encourages mutual understanding between assessors and students, students and tutors and between students to enhance social integration, solidarity and the construction of personal identities, thus reproducing the lifeworld of caring practice instead of merely assimilating prior learning into the system through grades or certificates. RPL could encourage critical learning in the lifeworld of education through reflections on prior learning, experiences and knowledge gained in work. It is important that the results of the RPL process and assessment are clearly communicated. This would enable these experiences to be mobilised when students move on and use these learning experiences in new contexts. Honneth's recognition theory can further help us understand what kind of an impact the recognition in RPL could have for an individual's self-esteem development and how RPL processes can support self-realisation.

In their chapter, "Changing RPL and HRD discourses: Practitioner perspectives" (Chap. 14), Anne Murphy, Oran Doherty and Kate Collins study aspects involved in leading and responding to change in discourses related to RPL and human resource development (HRD). The chapter discusses discourses of recognition of prior learning within meta human resource development and qualification frameworks contexts at the global level. In addition, a brief narrative and analysis of RPL in Ireland is offered with three examples of RPL for human resource development in enterprises and in labour market activation initiatives. The writers then return to the issue of competing RPL and HRM discourses and their implications for RPL practitioners who operate within them. The chapter is written from the perspective of RPL practitioners in higher education who are intimately involved in work-related learning and recognition of prior learning as researchers, policy experts and practitioners. The authors bring their collective experiences together to offer case studies of RPL in practice both in private, commercial companies and in higher education itself as an employment sector, supported by analysis of research data and of policy literature.

The French experience of validating the knowledge, skills and competences acquired through informal and non-formal learning is unique in the world. In their chapter, "French approaches to accreditation of prior learning: Practices and research" (Chap. 15), Vanessa Remery and Vincent Merle argue for the singularity of this experience in France. They first review the beginnings of APL movement, from the early experiments until its current modes of functioning. The chapter shows in particular how the implementation of APL introduced a significant break in the French educational model that attaches great importance to diplomas obtained within the school system. APL radically transformed the landscape of classic means of certification. It established a strong distinction between diplomas and pathways to gain certification by recognising the formative dimension of work experience. The raised issue concerns not only the recognition of knowledge, skills and competences that have been acquired at work, but also the means by which the recognition can be operationalised within the programme itself. Remery and Merle focus, therefore, on the methodological resources provided to support candidates and to assist the complex process by which they are expected to put into words their work experience. To do so, they discuss recent research conducted in France in the field of psychology and educational sciences that investigate the counsellors' activities. The writers argue that results from these research threads open up interesting perspectives in terms of training and professionalisation in the field of APL.

Stephen Billett, Helen Bound and Magdalene Lin conclude the book with their chapter, "Recognising and certifying workers' knowledge: Policies, frameworks and practices in prospect: Perspectives from two countries" (Chap. 16). Outside of participation in education programmes, there is always a range of practicalities, barriers, imperatives and sensitivities associated with recognising and certifying workers' knowledge. The particular country and institutional context often shape many of these factors, such as the standing of the work, its affiliation with other kinds of work, the status of workers, their need for recognition and certification, the kinds of institutions that provide assessment processes and the degree by which there are bases for workers' knowledge to be recognised and certified. These factors play out in different ways for particular kinds of workers. Perhaps there is no cohort of workers for whom the recognition and certification of knowledge is more important than those who lack them and employed in low status work. Yet, at the same time, there are often greater barriers for these kinds of workers to having their skills assessed and recognised. For instance, the very benchmarks required for recognising and certifying the kinds of skills which have been learnt wholly through work and outside of educational provisions may not exist. Then, there can be the societal sentiments associated with different kinds of work and views that such work is of low worth. And, even if recognised and certified in some way, this work may still remain largely unworthy, and perhaps barely legitimate. In addition, such workers often find themselves in circumstances in which few, if any, organisations or agencies will promote their interests, let alone push for effective recognition and certification of their skills. Billett, Bound and Lin consider how these factors play out in particular national contexts and how the practicalities, barriers, imperatives and sensitivities associated with recognising and certifying workers' knowledge might be confronted and redressed. They identify means by which the recognition of such workers' knowledge might progress in situations where many workers lack that certification and remain disadvantaged in some ways by that situation. Yet, beyond the mechanisms considered for providing such recognitions, there are broader issues associated with the relative societal standing of occupations that also shape the worth of these mechanisms and the recognitions they can provide.

References

Billett, S. (2005). Recognition of learning through work. In N. Bascia, A. Cumming, A. Datnow, K. Leithwood, & D. Livingstone (Eds.), *International handbook of educational policy* (Vol. 2, pp. 943–962). Dordrecht: Springer.

Billett, S. (2008). Learning through work: Exploring instances of relational interdependencies. *International Journal of Educational Research, 47*, 232–240.

Billett, S. (2010). *Promoting and supporting lifelong employability for Singapore's workers aged 45 and over*. Singapore: Institute for Adult Learning.

Coffield, F. (2000). Lifelong learning as a lever on structural change? Evaluation of white paper: Learning to succeed: A new framework for post-16 learning. *Journal of Education Policy, 15*(2), 237–246.

Department of Education Science and Training. (2002). *Employability skills for the future*. Canberra: Department of Education Science and Training, Commonwealth of Australia.

Eraut, M. (2004). Informal learning in the workplace. *Studies in Continuing Education, 26*(2), 247–274.

Fenwick, T., & Somerville, M. (2006). Work, subjectivity and learning: Prospects and issues. In S. Billett, T. Fenwick, & M. Somerville (Eds.), *Work, subjectivity and learning* (pp. 247–265). Dordrecht: Springer.

Field, J. (2000). Governing the ungovernable: Why lifelong learning promises so much yet delivers so little. *Educational Management and Administration, 28*(3), 249–261.

Gecas, V. (2006). Self-agency and the life course. In J. T. Mortimer & M. J. Shanahan (Eds.), *Handbook of the life course* (pp. 369–388). New York: Springer.

Gijbels, D., Raemdonck, I., & Vervecken, D. (2010). Influencing work-related learning: The role of job characteristics and self-directed learning orientation in part-time vocational education. *Vocations and Learning, 3*, 239–255.

Hakkarainen, K., Palonen, T., Paavola, S., & Lehtinen, E. (2004). *Communities of networked expertise: Educational and professional perspectives*. Amsterdam: Elsevier.

Karasek, R., & Theorell, T. (1990). *Healthy work. Stress productivity and the recognition of working life*. New York: Basic Books.

Martin, J. (2004). Self-regulated learning, social cognitive theory, and agency. *Educational Psychologist, 39*(2), 135–145.

McNair, S., Flynn, M., Owen, L., Humphreys, C., & Woodfield, S. (2004). *Changing work in later life: A study of job transitions*. University of Surrey, Centre for Research into the Older Workforce.

Oosterheert, I. E., & Vermunt, J. D. (2001). Individual differences in learning to teach: Relating cognition, regulation and affect. *Learning and Instruction, 11*(2), 133–156.

Organisation for Economic Co-operation and Development. (2006). *Live longer, work longer: A synthesis report*. Paris: OECD.

Organisation for Economic Co-operation and Development. (2010). *Learning for jobs*. Paris: OECD.

Smith, R. (2006). Epistemological agency in the workplace. *Journal of Workplace Learning, 18*(3), 157–170.

Talwar, R., & Hancock, T. (2010, January). *The shape of jobs to come. Possible new careers emerging from advances in science and technology (2010–2030)*. Final report. Fast Future Research.

Tikkanen, T., Lahn, L., Ward, P., & Lyng, K. (2002). *Working life changes and training of older workers*. Trondheim: Vox.

Watkin, C. (2005). *Classrooms as learning communities*. London: Routledge.

Yacob, H. (2009). *Welcome address*. Paper presented at the IAL symposium, adult learning: Emerging challenges and opportunities, Singapore.

Yielder, J. (2004). An integrated model of professional expertise and its implications for higher education. *International Journal of Lifelong Education, 23*, 60–80.

Chapter 2
Conceptualising Lifelong Learning in Contemporary Times

Stephen Billett

2.1 Learning Across Working Lives

Concerns about sustaining individuals' employability across their working lives have emerged in recent years as a priority for governments, industry, workplaces and professional groups. Much of this concern is premised upon the emerging consequences of the changing demands for occupations (e.g. skills currency), requirements for sustaining the capacities for performance within those occupations, transforming needs of workplaces, licensing authorities and those brought about by emerging technologies and workplace practices. All of these changing requirements for work emphasise that initial occupational preparation will be insufficient for sustaining employability and occupational competence across lengthening working lives. Instead, the ongoing development of workers' capacities – learning across working lives – is now required. Concomitantly, there is also a growing governmental emphasis on educational provisions that can support this ongoing learning. The need for what is referred to as 'lifelong learning' has become widely used in everyday and governmental discourses to describe this requirements for ongoing development (Organisation for Economic Co-operation and Development 2010). This term is now accepted within the educational discourse, yet often with a lack of precision and much ambiguity (Billett 2010).

For instance, there is often confusion between, on the one hand, the ongoing human process of learning and development (i.e. lifelong learning) and, on the other, the provision of educational programmes and experiences to meet needs across lives (i.e. lifelong education). This confusion is exemplified prominently in a recent government-funded report on lifelong learning that was intended to shape the policies in practice in the United Kingdom for the foreseeable future (Schuller and Watson 2009). A fundamental category error was made within this report. It confuses lifelong learning with lifelong education and suggests they are one and

S. Billett (✉)
Education and Professional Studies, Griffith University, Brisbane, QLD, Australia
e-mail: s.billett@griffith.edu.au

T. Halttunen et al. (eds.), *Promoting, Assessing, Recognizing and Certifying Lifelong Learning: International Perspectives and Practices*, Lifelong Learning Book Series 20, DOI 10.1007/978-94-017-8694-2_2, © Springer Science+Business Media Dordrecht 2014

the same. The outcome is that this report and its recommendations offered narrow prescriptions of how lifelong learning might be considered, supported and the range of provisions supporting it (i.e. through lifelong education). This erroneous categorisation distorts understandings about and means by which ongoing learning across life and the recognition of that learning is considered and supported. For instance, not only in the above-mentioned report, but elsewhere, the term 'lifelong learning' has quite commonly associated with continuing education courses or professional development programmes. That is, lifelong learning has become associated with individuals' participation in educational provisions, when these are just one set of experiences through which individuals learn across their adult lives. Moreover, these educational provisions are quite procedurally and conceptually distinct from individuals' acts of learning and development across their lives that occur through everyday activities and interactions, including their workplaces. The former (i.e. educational programmes and workplace provisions) are institutional or societal facts (i.e. they arise through social forms, norms and structures). However, learning through these experiences and others are personal facts (i.e. they arise through personal processes and means, albeit shaped by social and physical world) (Billett 2009a). Hence, categorical errors are made, which restrict considerations of lifelong learning (i.e. something that largely happens through courses). Also, it suggests that the learning occurring through these programmes is privileged over other kinds of experiences and is usually accompanied by the certification of what has been learnt, whereas other experiences are not. All of this has implications for the standing and recognition of learning arising from experiences outside of those programmes. Indeed, ultimately lifelong education is a subcategory of lifelong learning.

When lifelong learning is considered in this way as an ongoing process of learning and development across people's lives, it can only really be seen as something arising in person-particular ways from the particular sets of experiences individuals encounter and their engagement with those experiences. Hence, when conceptualising lifelong learning, there is a need to place centre stage the entire range of individuals' experiences and their responses to them. This conception necessitates accounting for the combination of individual attributes, particular experiences and the ongoing legacies arising through those experiences (i.e. micro-genesis or moment-by-moment learning) across individuals' lives. This consideration also need to include these legacies in terms of their being shaped by but also contributing to individuals' development across their personal histories (i.e. ontogenesis – development across life histories). This learning and development, therefore, can only be fully understood through considering individuals' personal histories and their bases for construing and constructing (i.e. learning) from what they experience. As much of this learning across life courses inevitably arises through experiences outside of institutional arrangements (e.g. educational institutions), both micro-genesis and ontogenetic development are not confined to those kinds of experiences. Likely, the vast majority of learning and development across adults' life course occurs outside of experiences comprising intentionally organised and implemented education programmes aiming to secure learning outcomes that have been pre-specified for those programmes. It is, therefore, necessary to be both clear and inclusive about what constitutes and contributes to individuals' lifelong learning and on what basis it can be promoted.

Here, it is proposed that this clarification can be advanced through discussing how such conceptions of learning and development relate to important goals for personal, professional, workplace and societal purposes, such as learning across individuals' working life. This work-lifelong project comprises individuals securing and sustaining employability and advancement across lengthening working lives. It, therefore, needs to consider and account for the kinds of support assisting that ongoing process of learning. This assistance needs to be exercised in ways that are accessible, helpful and enduring for individuals who now need to continue to learn for work longer than their predecessors, as retirement ages and pension entitlements in many countries move into the late 60s and possibly 70 years.

Consequently, this chapter aims to set out what constitutes 'lifelong learning' and how it might best be promoted across working lives, with the key focus on individuals' employability. The central case made here is that, ultimately, individuals' learning constitutes personal facts. That is, they are shaped by and arise through individuals' history of activities and interactions engaged in across their lives (Goodnow and Warton 1991; Rogoff 2003). These activities and interactions are shaped by both institutional (i.e. those of society) (Searle 1995) and brute (i.e. those of nature) facts both as attributes within individuals and also as contributions and reactants beyond individuals. Their contributions comprise the suggestions projected by both the brute and social world. Yet, ultimately, individuals mediate what they experience and from which they subsequently construe and construct knowledge (Billett 2009b). Indeed, it is the intersection between the personal facts and those representing and projected by the social and brute worlds that occurs constantly (i.e. microgenetically) as individuals engage in everyday activities (Rogoff and Lave 1984) and interactions that is central to understanding the process of individuals' lifelong learning or ontogenetic development.

It follows then that such an account is not one that distinguishes between individual and social contributions per se. This is not the least, because the personal is inherently social. There is nothing more social than the individual. Social and brute facts both shape and are themselves shaped by a lifetime of experiences, including how individuals come to interact and engage with the world beyond them, but also through maturation (Billett 2009a). As noted, those worlds project what individuals experience comprising both the suggestions of nature and society. Proposed here is a consideration of lifelong learning being ultimately a personal fact that arises through engagement and negotiations with what is experienced and how we mature over time. In making its case, this chapter proposes that lifelong learning is necessarily a personally mediated process (i.e. a personal fact), albeit shaped by brute and institutional facts and conceptions. Consequently, a clear distinction is drawn between the provision of experiences as in educational programmes (e.g. lifelong education) or those in workplaces as institutional facts and individuals' learning and development, which are personal facts. Then, it is proposed that because of these misunderstandings, the purposes of lifelong learning and education have become distorted. Moreover, to overcome the misrepresentation of lifelong learning as lifelong education that has been embraced by governments, global agencies and employers as well as uninformed academics, it is necessary to discuss the provision of courses (i.e. institutional facts comprising taught processes) in terms of how they can meet the needs of lifelong learning as personal facts, leading to a set of propositions about how lifelong education might be considered and promoted across working lives.

2.2 Lifelong Learning: Personal Facts

There are myriad references to and uses of the term 'learning' and all of these do not make easy the task of considering what constitutes lifelong learning and how it best might be promoted. Reference is often made, for instance, to 'learning organisations', which is a problematic concept, proposing that organisations learn and those within them are part of that learning. Certainly, organisations such as workplaces have norms and practices that change over time and these are institutional facts. However, the cause or volition for these changes is not derived from the consciousness, neural, sensory and procedural capacities of the 'organisation' because it does not have them, but rather from those who work within them. Then, terms such as e-learning are used to refer to a different kind of institutional fact – the provision of learning experiences mediated electronically through text, symbolic and images. Elsewhere, the term 'informal learning' is frequently used to describe learning occurring outside of educational programmes (Marsick and Watkins 1990). Yet, when considered this conception from the view that it is people who learn, it implies that a particular mode of learning (i.e. construal, construction) is being engaged with labelled informal or non-formal in these settings. However, there is no evidence to suggest that how individuals deploy the processes of construing and constructing knowledge (i.e. learning) is qualitatively distinct ways across different kinds of social settings. Instead, it is most likely to be the degree by which individuals engage with what is afforded them through their experiences in each of these settings that is central to their learning (Billett 2001) not ascribing a particular modes of thinking and acting occurring across different kinds of setting (i.e. informal or formal). What is probably intended here is a reference to formal and informal educational provisions (i.e. institutional facts).

Moreover, there can be no guarantee that what is intended through such provisions will be learnt. Hence, claiming specific kinds of learning arising from particular experience is overly ambitious. Educational provisions are nothing more or less than invitations to change. As such, these provisions are dependent upon how students themselves elect to take up the invitation which is afforded to them (i.e. activities and interactions). So, it needs to be remembered that learning is something that humans do albeit mediated by personal, social and brute facts. This is because learning requires consciousness, a sensory system and cognition including the capacity to construe experiences and construct knowledge (Barsalou 2008, 2009; Reber

1989) from them, thereby utilising what we know and change both what we know and how we know. Yet, these processes are person-particular and outcomes cannot be guaranteed.

Indeed, this learning is a necessary imperative for humans so they can make sense of what is experienced and be reflexive about it. Sharing what we know with others and across generations reflexively is central to our existence and continuity as a species (Taylor 1985). Moreover, if humans were able to simply appropriate what is suggested to them by the social and brute worlds, there would be little need for communication for sense-making (Cronick 2002). In these circumstances, interpersonal interaction would largely be unnecessary because the suggestion from the world beyond us would be unequivocal and unambiguous. However, this is not the case and these suggestions are often ambiguous and unclear (Newman et al. 1989). As noted, social institutions, such as workplaces, have norms and practices that change overtime and in response to changing demands. Humans need to comprehend and understand these changes premised on the processes of perception, cognition and action. Hence, for both individual development and societal progression, we need to learn both new knowledge and develop further what we know (Billett 2009a). Moreover, learning is something that humans inevitably do continuously and across our lives (microgenetically and ontogenetically) (Billett 2003) to make sense of what we experience. So, we are all and have to be lifelong learners. As processes such as maintaining equilibrium (Piaget 1971), ontological security (Giddens 1991) and viability (Van Lehn 1989) suggest, we have no option than to attempt to make sense of what we experience. The necessity for this continuous learning includes completing the tasks we require, simply, to live connected, effective and worthwhile lives. So, this learning is an inherent feature of our working lives as directed by our individual needs and intentionalities and as mediated by our capacities and interests and shaped by imperatives and contributions that are external to us.

In these ways, learning is held to be very much a personal process directed by our capacities, interests, circumstances and personal histories as engaged with by our minds, bodies and consciousness. It is a lifelong occurrence as we engage in activities and interactions in our homes, with our families, with our friends and acquaintances, not to mention our work or our workplaces, in our community engagements and in the everyday tasks in which we engage. Also, through participation in them, learning also arises through participation in educational programmes (e.g. courses). Yet, far from being dependent upon these kinds of experiences, learning arises in all social settings, not just those settings of which activities are directed to particular kinds of intentions (i.e. lifelong education). Moreover, the learning of rich (i.e. adaptable) knowledge is not privileged by experiences in these kinds of settings and through these kinds of programmes, as it also arises through practice experiences, for example, as well as through educational experiences (Ericsson and Lehmann 1996; Raizen 1989; Scribner 1984). Hence, learning is not 'determined' by what is suggested through interactions with external sources. Instead, we learn inevitably across our lives when engaging in the range of circumstances that comprise of what we encounter across our lives and that learning progresses in ways which are inherently person specific.

There is another dimension to this ongoing process of learning that is significant for societies and institutions. As individuals engage in this ongoing learning, they are also participating in the process of remaking the social and cultural practices in which they engage (Billett et al. 2005; Giddens 1991). That is, the norms and practices that are central to institutions such as workplaces, families, schools, colleges and universities are remade and sometimes transforming through individuals enacting them. As this learning involves engaging in societally derived activities and interactions at particular points in time and for particular purposes, it is central to the process of remaking and transforming these practices. At any moment in time, individuals engaged in occupations such as caring for others, teaching, legal work, construction and manufacturing are doing so as directed towards particular goals and purposes in particular circumstances and at particular points in time using an array of resources that are available and responding with what they know and can do. As Braudel (1981) claims, this societal advancement occurs through significant innovations, but also:

> The slow improvements in processes and tools, and those innumerable actions may have no immediate innovating circumstance, but which are the fruits of the accumulated knowledge: the sailor rigging his boat, the miner digging a gallery, the peasant behind the plough or the smith at the anvil (sic) (1981: 334)

Through this process of everyday and ongoing learning, these societal norms and forms are made and transformed iteratively and continuously by individuals within and across their working lives, for instance. So, societal continuity and transformation co-occurs with individuals' lifelong learning. All of this suggests that occupations, occupational practice and workplace norms are remade and transformed concurrently with individuals learning across their working lives.

2.3 Purposes and Processes of Lifelong Learning

There are a range of purposes to which individuals will direct that learning and with varying degrees of interest, engagement, intentionality and effort (Malle et al. 2001). These purposes include learning to communicate with others, engaging with social partners and developing the capacities to engage in socially valued activities, one of which is work. It also includes continuing to develop those capacities across working life including learning how to engage in new occupational activities across working life. Yet, in addition, there is also learning associated with roles that emerge across our lives, to be a son or daughter, brother, sister, twin, partner, parent and carer for parents, etc. (Billett 1998a). Both the processes of and outcomes of this learning are deemed by individuals themselves or others as being either effective or less than effective for these roles, because these processes can include effortful engagement. This personal appraisal is particularly the case for learning that is personally transformative (Allan 2005; Perkins et al. 1993; Tobias 1994). Likely, when learning new knowledge, as well as being effortful, it also involves monitoring and self-regulation (Cavanagh 2008; Rohrkemper 1989). Indeed, it is difficult to find an informed account of human learning that does not position the individual centrally in directing the process of their learning. Behaviouralist and socio-determinant (Ratner 2000) accounts may be the exception here. Even theories explicitly advancing the social contribution to knowledge acknowledge the role of the personal in these processes (Berger and Luckman 1967; Valsiner and van der Veer 2000). However, most contemporary accounts of learning and development, particularly constructivist ones, in different ways and by degree emphasise the importance of humans as active meaning makers who shape the direction and intensity of learning processes. The key difference amongst various accounts of human learning is the degree by which that learning is also shaped by the world beyond the individual, but in which they engage.

So, beyond individuals' contributions to their learning, much of the effectiveness of human learning can be attributed to the kinds of guidance and support we are able to secure with which we engage. Much of this guidance and support arises from engaging with other people either directly (Rogoff 1995) or, perhaps more commonly, indirectly through observing them, listening to them (Billett 2001), undertaking the activities they suggest (Pelissier 1991), reading what they have written or engaging with what they have produced. These kinds of engagements and activities are important because much of the knowledge needed to fulfil our roles and direct our energies towards the tasks we need to undertake are derived from the social world (Billett 1998b; Rogoff 1990; Scribner 1985). So, across individuals' lives, their learning is supported and mediated by parents, siblings, friends, family members, interlocutors at school, work, in community activities as well as those whose role is to help us learn (e.g. teachers, trainers, mentors). Consequently, all lifelong learning is a socio-personal process as individuals negotiate their thinking, acting and doing across a lifetime of engaging in activities and interactions.

However, in 'schooled societies', with their universal compulsory education and extensive provision of tertiary education and where the discourse of schooling is strong, it is often assumed that the learning arising from activities and interactions in educational institutions is privileged or is more legitimate and worthwhile that these experiences constitute the major contribution to our learning. Yet, there is little evidence to support the first assertion and the latter most likely applies to those whose experiences are dominated by school settings (i.e. school-age children in boarding schools). Indeed, the era of schooled societies is relatively recent and represents only a small fraction of human history. Before the era of schooling and schooled societies, what we refer to as teaching, seemingly, was rarely practised (Billett 2011a). Instead, more likely, for the vast majority of individuals, securing the knowledge required for that work and across their lives was premised upon their active learning processes, rather than being taught. Exemplifying this process of learning was a set of occupational practices that learners needed to understand and engage in to appropriate the kinds of knowledge required for them to practice their occupations and then go on to learn more about them. Much of this learning appears premised upon individuals' personal epistemologies and sets of pedagogic practices which were largely vested in the actions of learners whilst engaged in the circumstances of practice.

It would also be quite incorrect to assume that the kinds of conceptual and symbolic knowledge required in contemporary times are wholly dependent upon teaching processes. Certainly, many of the forms of knowledge that are now required to be learnt may need assistance of some kind to be learnt. However, it would be erroneous to assume that before the era of schooling, such forms of knowledge were not required to be learnt and that, in the absence of teaching processes and educational institutions, this learning did not progress. So it is not helpful to view individuals' learning as something that is held wholly captive to physical and social circumstances in which individuals engage. Instead, it is necessary to view physical and social settings as providing contributions and mediational means (i.e. ways of making that knowledge accessible) for individuals' learning and development.

Importantly, this set of propositions is not to deny or downgrade the contributions of experiences in educational institutions or the efforts and activities of teachers, trainers and mentors, which are often invaluable and sometimes indispensable. Moreover, they are often needed to assist, prepare and support individuals as independent and agentic learners. However, it is particularly important to be reminded in an era of schooling that there are a range of experiences and activities that can be accessed outside of those provided by educational programmes and that many of our requirements for lifelong learning cannot be realised through educational provisions or even direct teaching. There are some kinds of experiences that have to be engaged with authentically, albeit forming partnerships, and negotiating the end of relationships, becoming a parent, developing occupational capacities, etc. That is, there are many things that have to be learnt and not taught. Moreover, it is not possible or desirable that lifelong learning becomes dependent on access to educational provisions, because learning of necessity, both in the form of new learning and refining what is known, typically arises through everyday experience as people engage in every aspect of their lives: during work, leisure, domestic activities, cultural pursuits, when travelling, etc. (Billett 2009a).

In sum, processes of ongoing learning across individuals' lifespans (i.e. lifelong learning) are worthy of the kinds of considerations advanced above because it is of salience to individuals, their families, communities, work and workplaces. When we learn, we not only develop capacities to fulfil our societal and economic roles, but we also have an important role in the remaking and transforming those social and economic activities (Billett et al. 2005). Consequently, lifelong learning is essential not only to ourselves and those close to us, but also through the remaking and transformation of the society in which we live (Giddens 1991).

2.4 Interests in Lifelong Learning and Their Reconciliation

Given the importance of this learning and processes of remaking and transforming societal and cultural practices, it is not surprising that others become interested in seeking to organise, direct and realise these outcomes, and in particular ways. Principally, national governments have long sought to direct and support learning for particular purposes (Greinert 2002). The advent of mass compulsory education and the provision of vocational education were largely focused on attempts by nation states to direct the interests and energies of its citizens as to achieve its social and economic goals which arise from a more broadly and specifically educated population (Gonon 2009). Hence, powerful social institutions and societal agencies have been developed for these purposes (i.e. bureaucracies, educational sectors, national and international agencies) with their own norms and practices and discourses that seek to direct, promote, support, capture and secure particular kinds of learning across individuals' lives. Historically, there are very few educational institutions that were established and directed by individual teachers or individuals with particular educational philosophies and purposes in mind (Skilbeck 1984). Instead, it has been the state, social and religious institutions that have largely founded and sustained educational institutions and ordered the kinds of intended educational outcomes to be achieved and the kinds of experiences that are selected to secure these outcomes. For instance, many definitions of curriculum emphasise achieving the goals of the school (Glatthorn 1987; Marsh and Willis 1995). In more recent times, global agencies (Organisation for Economic Co-operation and Development 2006; Organisation of Economic and Cultural Development (OECD) 1996) as well as national governments (Department of Education Science and Training 2002; Department of Innovation Universities and Skills 2008; Working Group on 14–19 Reform 2004) have come to emphasise and attempt to capture or mobilise (Edwards 2002) lifelong learning, principally for achieving economic purposes, enterprise, industry or national competitiveness. This shift has led to the appropriation of the term lifelong learning not only for economic purposes (Edwards 2002; Field 2000), but also to be seen as something equated with an educational provision and, usually, through taught courses (i.e. lifelong education). This change in emphasis from a personal process of learning (i.e. personal fact) to one in which institutional imperatives and goals are strongly promoted can be seen as a means of largely about securing institutional imperatives.

Of course, individuals need to engage in learning particular kinds of knowledge to secure the capacities they need to sustain their employability across working lives. This need necessitates them engaging with social institutions and norms, forms and practices. So, there is nothing particularly novel here. What is perhaps insidious in seeking to understand and discuss learning across working lives is that within schooled societies – where the educational discourse is powerful and extends to the administration and sponsorship of support for learning that educational provisions become overly privileged – conceptions of personal learning and development occurring outside of educational provisions are viewed as inherently inferior. Part of this repositioning is achieved through the labelling, ordering and conceptualising of educational arrangements and developmental goals which are shaped and defined more in terms of institutional facts than those associated with individuals.

There may be tensions arising between the kinds of provisions that aimed to intentionally promote and support particular kinds of learning and the interests and intentionalities of those who learn (e.g. Hodges 1998). The focus on the content of highly regulated courses do not always meet the needs of those who they are intended to assist, sometimes because nobody has bothered to ask them (Billett 2000). Instead, privileged others who are remote from those who are to participate in such programmes usually make decisions about what they should comprise and how they should progress. Often, in contemporary times, it is the voices and opinions of employers who are canvassed for their advice which are privileged in such processes. There is habitually a lack of consensus across the requests of those who employ and the preferences of those who are employed. In a recent study, for instance, it was found that managers and employers' view of continuing education and training (CET) were premised upon educational provisions (e.g. attendance in courses), whereas workers' emphasis was on processes of learning occurring in and through their work practices and how that learning can be supported (Billett et al. 2012a). Hence, whereas managers referred to the importance of educational programmes, workers referred to the importance of learning processes. Similarly, it is often reported that those who own or work in small businesses claim that their needs and concerns are not met within national curriculum provisions that reflect the form and interests of large enterprises (Coopers and Lybrand 1995). In these ways, efforts by government and key agencies in seeking to control and regulate what individuals learn, may not always be successful and may even be counter to the very goals they wish to realise.

Further, the imperatives of key central government agencies can do much to change the language, or the discourse of how this learning is conceptualised, and should be progressed and for what purposes. Many governments have adopted a particular view of what constitutes competency, usually in highly measurable and behavioural forms. These forms then come to constitute what passes as the requirements for vocational education to prepare individuals for and sustain their competence as workers, regardless of whether such measures capture the intentions (i.e. goals, aims, objectives) for the organisation, teaching and assessment of learning for occupations. Moreover, the espoused purposes of learning throughout our lives can be reshaped and re-privileged in particular ways by such key agencies. For instance, as a result of the OECD's year of lifelong learning in 1996, the key focus for this learning is now seen as being primarily about achieving economic purposes, and in which, individuals have to take a key role (Organisation of Economic Cooperation and Development 2000). So, there are, on the one hand, individual and personal purposes and processes (i.e. personal facts) that constitute lifelong learning which are as necessary as they are important for individuals, their communities, countries and humankind. Then, on the other hand, there are the important and necessary purposes for and contributions to that learning from the activities and interactions (i.e. institutional facts) in which they engage. As noted, these educational provisions and their purposes have often and over time reflected the interests of privileged others rather than those who are positioned as learners (Billett 2011b). Yet, it is the balance and reconciliation amongst the needs and the imperatives of individuals, their communities, workplaces and country and individuals themselves that is central to considerations of what constitutes the purposes, assesses and outcomes of individuals' lifelong learning and how this might be supported through lifelong education.

So, contemporary accounts of lifelong learning deserve to be informed by inquiry and clear consideration to the processes that underpin them and avoid the imposition of concepts and propositions that are erroneous and unhelpful. The importance of these considerations is that, outside of wartime, there has probably never been a time in human history when the requirements for work are changing at such an intense pace and with such scope. Consequently, if we are to assist individuals to maintain their occupational competence and secure their advancement across working lives and their further development as adults, clear understandings about the process of human learning and development are essential for informed policy and directed practice for promoting individuals' lengthening working lives. Certainly, the available literature is extensive and considerations within it are not constrained by institutional imperatives, such as those that seek to primarily understand learning as arising through participation in schools, vocational education and higher education.

2.5 Lifelong Education

Given global concerns about lifelong employability, the lengthening of working lives and the need for ongoing learning across working lives as necessitated by the changing nature of work requirements, the promotion and support for adults' learning across their lifespans is now essential for achieving key economic and social goals. Indeed, ageing populations in most countries with advanced and developing economies make this focus on adults' development a global concern. Many groups in the community stand to benefit from enhanced opportunities for supporting that learning, including participation in educational programmes. In particular, these programmes can assist the kinds of learning which would otherwise be unavailable to adults. For instance, although workplace-based experiences may be the most effective for sustaining currency of skills within a particular workplace setting, these environments may well not be the best ones in which to learn the knowledge required for alternative forms of work or assisting new directions for individuals' career paths. So, provisions of continuing education (i.e. lifelong education) are important in their different forms and means and can realise forms of ongoing learning that might not be accessible elsewhere. Those easily identifiable include those individuals seeking to participate more fully in working life because they have been outside of the work force, perhaps caring for their children, the unemployed or those have been unwell. This listing extends to those who want to secure transitions from their current circumstances to other or more productive ones, including those who are currently marginalised or restricted in their current employment (Billett et al. 2012b). So, there are a range of important purposes, focuses and goals for the promotion and support of lifelong education across working lives as directed to promoting ongoing employability. Also, because its provisions extend to forms of learning support outside of educational institutions, in community and workplaces settings, for instance, these forms of learning support need to be more fully acknowledged, and the learning arising through them recognised and certified through worthwhile and legitimating processes.

Hence, a comprehensive consideration of lifelong education needs to embrace, legitimate and extend the range of activities both within and outside of educational institutions that support individuals' learning and development across their lives. Moreover, coming to understand, identify purposes for, then organise and implement such educational provisions need to be accommodating of the range of intentions individuals have for engaging in such provisions. Therefore, offering a systems approach to meet the needs of learners across the lifespan as do Schuller and Watson (2009) can be an unhelpful return to directive models that have failed in the past. They propose an age-related scheme for organising learning support ignoring criticism of earlier models such as Erickson's account of development across the life he identified in Middle America in the 1950s. As commentators have observed and is reflected in the vignettes' in their own report, contemporary life is not about a linear progression through societally ordered stages. Instead, in contemporary times people often need to change occupations, and forms of employment. They also experience redundancy and periods of unemployment and at different point in their life histories. There are also life-influencing events such as divorce, relocation, as well as caring for wayward parents and children. Consequently, instead of a view of lifelong education system based on categorises of age and attempts to characterise learner needs at particular age stages, such commentators might point to the need for educational arrangements focusing on initial preparation for occupational and societal roles, transitions across roles, management of disappointment, processes of revitalisation of self and providing bases for overcoming gender, age or racial discrimination. Hence, an age-based categorisation of learner needs ignores the failings of staged development theories and offers an account of development as a linear progression with predictable needs at particular needs. In its place, a more localised socio-personally centred approach to lifelong education is likely required. Such an approach is outlined in the following five distinct considerations.

2.6   A Framework for Lifelong Learning and Education

Five distinct considerations are advanced here in proposing how a framework for lifelong education might be conceptualised, ordered and best progressed. In preview, these are (1) a central emphasis on individuals' learning, (2) a more inclusive accounting of the circumstances where that learning arises, (3) that this learning arises continuously across (working) lives, (4) that mechanisms for recognising and certifying this learning need to accommodate the diverse circumstances of this learning (i.e. not through educational programmes alone) and (5) that this learning should be promoted in and through the broad array of circumstances in which individuals participate.

Firstly, a provision of lifelong education should be premised upon a consideration of individuals' learning, in all its complexities, contributing factors, individual differences, etc., including the circumstances associated with how that learning progresses. That is, it should promote lifelong learning. By only focusing on and having a starting point as a provision of courses developed by others, the process of lifelong learning is misinformed, misrepresented and skewed. That is, principally it is a personal fact. For instance, one of the most common elements of something seen as synonymous with the institutionalised concept of lifelong learning is the provision of taught courses. These are easily and greedily embraced by an institutional and educational discourse that wants to organise an ordered individuals' learning, even though founded on limited precepts, and that this can be best achieved through such ordered and pre-specified processes. Institutionally, these arrangements lend themselves to administration based on institutional imperatives (e.g. numbers of participants, length of courses, assessments against intended outcomes) rather than individuals' learning. Often absent here are considerations of the very bases by which lifelong educational provisions should be considered and conceptualised. The premises for an effective lifelong learning pedagogy and curriculum should not be constrained by these kinds of institutional arrangements and should be extended to include those appropriate for and exercised in practice settings (Billett et al. 2012b). Central to these is the importance of learners' personal epistemologies.

Secondly, building upon these concerns, there needs to be a broader consideration of the circumstances of learning and the forms of support which can promote lifelong learning. So, rather than being restricted to a consideration of lifelong learning as being supported by the provision of courses, a consideration of experiences arising in a range of settings and by a range of institutions needs to be accounted for. Moreover, more than being a taught process, greater emphasis needs to be given to learning through the range of imperatives and circumstances that arise across adult life. The processes of negotiating changing work requirements stand as being powerful platforms for individuals' construal and construction of what they experience and their need for guidance and direction in these processes. Moreover, these processes are not restricted to work life, as expectations and demands of becoming a parent, caring for elderly parents, managing financial matters in an era in which individuals are held to be responsible for their own post-retirement income and making informed decisions about health care, purchases and the balance between work and other forms of daily commitments become essential features of adult life. Indeed, looking across these examples, one might conclude that these kinds of learning are unlikely to be effectively realised through taught processes and enrolments in courses. That is, the most common sites and settings for learning that occur throughout everyday thinking and acting largely sit outside experiences provided by taught courses, yet these rarely feature in structured responses from workplaces and governmental agencies, where administrative imperatives are often positioned as being more important than the goals they seek to achieve.

Thirdly, there is a need for a greater acceptance of and use of the outcomes of informed enquiries into learning through and across working life and other forms of everyday practice, when converted into helpful and practical processes. Much research in this field has been funded and undertaken, and although some findings are highly descriptive and not readily applicable, there is much that can be used to advance adult's learning across working lives. For instance, the constant emphasis on learner agency, sense of self and subjectivity arising across these studies reinforces the importance of emphasising personal facts and not just institutional ones. Also, those researching and informing learning across lives and, in particular, working lives need to focus their efforts on the kinds of curriculum, pedagogies and personal practices which are likely to be effective for supporting this lifelong learning.

Fourthly, there needs to be processes for the recognition and certification of learning outside of educational institutions given that so much learning across working life occurs outside of educational programmes and institutions. There is an increasing demand for credentials and certification of learning that privileges the assessment and recognition of learning. Yet, largely these are only provided as a result of participating in educational programmes and in educational institutions. All of this tends to deny the worth, legitimacy, richness and adaptability of the knowledge that is learnt outside of those circumstances. Hence, there needs to be a broader perspective on and more accessible provisions for the assessment and recognition of learning that embraces the recognition of prior learning and also extends to ongoing learning across working lives. There is nothing particularly difficult about this, except the current vesting of processes of assessment and certification within educational institutions.

Fifthly, there is a need for broader action on the part of workplaces, educational institutions and government agencies to more broadly embrace and support lifelong learning. As has been proposed above, there probably has never been an era in which the requirements for lifelong learning have been so intense. Not only are the requirements for sustaining employability across lengthening work lives intense, but also workplaces are increasingly reliant upon older workers and those with diverse forms and levels of readiness to direct their own intentional learning to secure their employability across working lives. Whether referring to women returning to the work force having been the principal caregiver to their children or individuals who by circumstances of birth or education are not well equipped to engage effectively with the changing requirements of work, considered and specific initiatives are likely to be required for these individuals. Again, there is nothing particularly new here, except that with a consideration of lifelong learning comes a focus upon the individuals themselves, their readiness and capacities and how they might best be provided with experiences which can support their learning and development in ways which will allow them to participate more fully in work and civic life.

It follows from this listing that a framework for lifelong learning needs to be inclusive of the entire scope of purposes and experiences that shape the personal fact of ongoing learning. These intents and these circumstances can then be considered in terms of their effectiveness, completeness and how they might be improved. In particular, consideration might be given to what kinds of experiences can likely achieve particular learning goals and where these experiences might be best located and enacted. Part of this consideration is also how government imperatives associated with inclusivity, continuity of development and the maintenance of lifelong employability can best be realised for individuals. Such a framework might also be premised upon the kinds of goals and transitions that individuals will need to secure in their lifelong learning project. So, rather than a system of support for learning being premised on categories of age, other kinds of categories might be far more useful. As foreshadowed, these categories might include focusing on initial preparation for occupational and societal roles, transitions across roles, management of disappointment, revitalisation and bases for overcoming gender, ages or racial discrimination. In all and in sum, lifelong education should be shaped by considerations of lifelong learning, not simply confused for and with it.

References

Allan, J. K. (2005). Farmers as learners: Evolving identity, disposition and mastery through diverse practices. *Rural Society: The Journal of Research into Rural and Regional Social Issues for Australia and New Zealand, 15*(1), 4–21.

Barsalou, L. W. (2008). Grounded cognition. *Annual Review of Psychology, 59,* 617–645.

Barsalou, L. W. (2009). Simulation, situated conceptualisation, and prediction. *Philosophical Transactions of the Royal Society B, 364,* 1281–1289.

Berger, P. L., & Luckman, T. (1967). *The social construction of reality.* Harmondsworth: Penguin.

Billett, S. (1998a). Ontogeny and participation in communities of practice: A socio-cognitive view of adult development. *Studies in the Education of Adults, 30*(1), 21–34.

Billett, S. (1998b). Situation, social systems and learning. *Journal of Education and Work, 11*(3), 255–274.

Billett, S. (2000). Defining the demand side of VET: Industry, enterprises, individuals and regions. *Journal of Vocational Education and Training, 50*(1), 5–30.

Billett, S. (2001). Learning through work: Workplace affordances and individual engagement. *Journal of Workplace Learning, 13*(5), 209–214.

Billett, S. (2003). Sociogeneses, activity and ontogeny. *Culture and Psychology, 9*(2), 133–169.

Billett, S. (2009a). Conceptualising learning experiences: Contributions and mediations of the social, personal and brute. *Mind, Culture, and Activity, 16*(1), 32–47.

Billett, S. (2009b). Personal epistemologies, work and learning. *Educational Research Review, 4,* 210–219.

Billett, S. (2010). The perils of confusing lifelong learning with lifelong education. *International Journal of Lifelong Education, 29*(4), 401–413.

Billett, S. (2011a). Learning in the circumstances of work: The didactics of practice. *Education and Didactique, 5*(2), 129–149.

Billett, S. (2011b). *Vocational education: Purposes, traditions and prospects.* Dordrecht: Springer.

Billett, S., Smith, R., & Barker, M. (2005). Understanding work, learning and the remaking of cultural practices. *Studies in Continuing Education, 27*(3), 219–237.

Billett, S., Choy, S., Tyler, M., Smith, R., Dymock, D., Kelly, A., et al. (2012a). *Refining models and approaches in continuing education and training.* Adelaide: National Centre for Vocational Education Research.

Billett, S., Henderson, A., Choy, S., Dymock, D., Beven, F., Kelly, A., et al. (2012b). *Change, work and learning: Aligning continuing education and training.* Adelaide: National Centre for Vocational Education Research.

Braudel, F. (1981). *The structures of everyday life* (Vol. 1). New York: Harper & Row.

Cavanagh, J. (2008). Women auxiliary workers' learning and discovering 'self' through work. In S. Billett, C. Harties, & A. Eteläpelto (Eds.), *Emerging perspectives of learning through work* (pp. 67–82). Rotterdam: Sense Publishing.

Coopers & Lybrand. (1995). *Small business: A review of training evaluation and effectiveness' in enterprising nation (Research report volume 2). Industry task force on leadership and management skills.* Canberra: AGPS.

Cronick, K. (2002). Community, subjectivity and intersubjectivity. *American Journal of Community Psychology, 30*(14), 529–547.

Department of Education Science and Training. (2002). *Employability skills for the future.* Canberra: Commonwealth of Australia.

Department of Innovation Universities and Skills. (2008). *Higher education at work: High skills: High value.* Sheffield: Department of Innovation, Universities and Skills.

Edwards, R. (2002). Mobilizing lifelong learning: Governmentality in educational practices. *Journal of Education Policy, 17*(3), 353–365.

Ericsson, K. A., & Lehmann, A. C. (1996). Expert and exceptional performance: Evidence of maximal adaptation to task constraints. *Annual Review of Psychology, 47*, 273–305.

Field, J. (2000). Governing the ungovernable: Why lifelong learning promises so much yet delivers so little. *Educational Management and Administration, 28*(3), 249–261.

Giddens, A. (1991). *Modernity and self-identity: Self and society in the late modern age.* Stanford: Stanford University Press.

Glatthorn, A. (1987). *Curriculum leadership.* Glenview: Scott Foresham.

Gonon, P. (2009). *The quest for modern vocational education: Georg Kerschensteiner between Dewey, Weber and Simmel* (Vol. 9). New York: Peter Lang.

Goodnow, J. J., & Warton, P. M. (1991). The social bases of social cognition: Interactions about work and their implications. *Merrill-Palmer Quarterly, 37*(1), 27–58.

Greinert, W.-D. (2002). *European and vocational training systems: The theoretical context of historical development.* Paper presented at the towards a history of vocational education and training (VET) in Europe in a comparative perspective, Florence.

Hodges, D. C. (1998). Participation as dis-identification with/in a community of practice. *Mind, Culture, and Activity, 5*(4), 272–290.

Malle, B. F., Moses, L. J., & Baldwin, D. A. (2001). Introduction: The significance of intentionality. In B. F. Malle, L. J. Moses, & D. A. Baldwin (Eds.), *Intentions and intentionality: Foundations of social cognition* (pp. 1–26). Cambridge, MA: The MIT Press.

Marsh, C., & Willis, G. (1995). *Curriculum: Alternative approaches, ongoing issues.* Englewood Cliffs: Merill.

Marsick, V. J., & Watkins, K. (1990). *Informal and incidental learning in the workplace.* London: Routledge.

Newman, D., Griffin, P., & Cole, M. (1989). *The construction zone: Working for cognitive change in schools.* Cambridge: Cambridge University Press.

Organisation for Economic Co-operation and Development. (2006). *Live longer, work longer: A synthesis report.* Paris: OECD.

Organisation for Economic Co-operation and Development. (2010). *Learning for jobs.* Paris: OECD.

Organisation of Economic and Cultural Development (OECD). (1996). *Lifelong learning for all.* Paris: OECD.

Organisation of Economic Cooperation and Development. (2000). *Economics and finance of lifelong learning.* Paris: OECD.

Pelissier, C. (1991). The anthropology of teaching and learning. *Annual Review of Anthropology, 20*, 75–95.

Perkins, D., Jay, E., & Tishman, S. (1993). Beyond abilities: A dispositional theory of thinking. *Merrill-Palmer Quarterly, 39*(1), 1–21.

Piaget, J. (1971). *Structuralism* (C. Maschler, Trans. and Ed.). London: Routledge & Kegan Paul.

Raizen, S. A. (1989). *Reforming education for work: A cognitive science perspective.* Berkeley: National Centre for Research in Vocational Education.

Ratner, C. (2000). Agency and culture. *Journal for the Theory of Social Behaviour, 30*, 413–434.

Reber, A. S. (1989). Implicit learning and tacit knowledge. *Journal of Experimental Psychology, 118*(3), 219–235.

Rogoff, B. (1990). *Apprenticeship in thinking – Cognitive development in social context.* New York: Oxford University Press.

Rogoff, B. (1995). Observing sociocultural activity on three planes: Participatory appropriation, guided participation, apprenticeship. In J. W. Wertsch, A. Alvarez, & P. del Rio (Eds.), *Sociocultural studies of mind* (pp. 139–164). Cambridge: Cambridge University Press.

Rogoff, B. (2003). *The cultural nature of human development*. Oxford: Oxford University Press.

Rogoff, B., & Lave, J. (Eds.). (1984). *Everyday cognition: Its development in social context*. Cambridge, MA: Harvard University Press.

Rohrkemper, M. M. (1989). Self-regulated learning and academic achievement: A Vygotskian view. In B. J. Zinnerman & D. H. Schunk (Eds.), *Theory, research and practice: Progress in cognitive development research* (pp. 143–168). New York: Springer.

Schuller, T., & Watson, D. (2009). *Learning through life: Inquiry into the future of lifelong learning*. Leicester: National Institute of Adult Continuing Education.

Scribner, S. (1984). Studying working intelligence. In B. Rogoff & J. Lave (Eds.), *Everyday cognition: Its development in social context* (pp. 9–40). Cambridge, MA: Harvard University Press.

Scribner, S. (1985). Vygostky's use of history. In J. V. Wertsch (Ed.), *Culture, communication and cognition: Vygotskian perspectives* (pp. 119–145). Cambridge: Cambridge University Press.

Searle, J. R. (1995). *The construction of social reality*. London: Penguin.

Skilbeck, M. (1984). *School based curriculum development*. London: Harper and Row.

Taylor, C. (1985). *Human agency and language: Philosophical papers 1*. Cambridge: Cambridge University Press.

Tobias, S. (1994). Interest, prior knowledge, and learning. *Review of Educational Research, 64*(1), 37–54.

Valsiner, J., & van der Veer, R. (2000). *The social mind: The construction of an idea*. Cambridge: Cambridge University Press.

Van Lehn, V. (1989). Towards a theory of impasse-driven learning. In H. Mandl & A. Lesgold (Eds.), *Learning issues for intelligent tutoring systems* (pp. 19–41). New York: Springer.

Working Group on 14–19 Reform. (2004). *14–19 curriculum and qualifications reform: Final report of the working group on 14–19 reform*. London: Department for Education and Skills.

Chapter 3
New Skills for New Jobs: Work Agency as a Necessary Condition for Successful Lifelong Learning

Christian Harteis and Michael Goller

3.1 Introduction

In the last 20–50 years, the world has been experiencing a range of economic and social developments that have had crucial impacts on labour markets, the world of work and life in general (e.g. Billett 2009; Green 2007). Educational policy in Europe focuses on the support of lifelong learning in order to cope with these developments. This chapter discusses the concept of work agency which is an educational approach explaining fostering and hindering influences on lifelong learning. The concept is construed as individual level construct; however, this decision for a specific analytic perspective does not neglect its interrelatedness with situational and social conditions. Before explaining work agency in detail, this chapter will lay out three crucial economic and social developments and their effects on the "new" jobs in the European labour market as well as on the associated "new" skills employees have to hold.

First of all, a major shift in the general economic structure of the most of the western countries could be observed. Whereas the primary and secondary sectors have been constantly shrinking, the tertiary and quaternary economic sectors have been growing. Along with these developments, the demand for manual work has been decreasing in favour of the so-called knowledge work (CEDEFOP 2010). Consequently, the unemployment rate of low-skilled workers has been constantly higher than for better-skilled individuals (OECD 2012a). This employment gap has further increased in the face of economic crises. Low-skilled workers have been especially likely to lose their jobs due to recent economic recessions (OECD 2012b). But even in employment, low-skilled workers are financially worse off compared to their better-skilled counterparts. A large income gap can especially be observed

C. Harteis (✉) • M. Goller
Institute of Educational Science, University of Paderborn, Paderborn, Germany
e-mail: Christian.Harteis@upb.de; michael.goller@upb.de

between employees with and without postsecondary education (OECD 2012a). Hence, pursuing higher educational levels as well as acquiring skills for new jobs in the tertiary and quaternary sector adds significantly to the individual economic welfare in the long run.

Second, the combination of exponentially growing and rapidly accumulating technological knowledge with a high level of global competition leads to steadily decreasing product and process life cycles (Green 2007). Consequently, work is becoming less routine, and employees need a higher capability to adapt to new work processes including new work-related tools (Billett 2009). Work-related change can therefore be characterised as a rule rather than an exception. It is therefore no surprise that employers prefer employees that are able to adapt to these and other unforeseen developments (CEDEFOP 2010). For individuals, it takes a combination of a certain amount of flexibility and the willingness and capacity for learning to manage substantial changes.

Third, traditional paternalistic employer-employee relationships that guaranteed individuals long-term employment contracts with one single employer are less and less common (Fugate et al. 2004; Hall 1996). Such organisational careers where the psychological contract between employer and employee ensured the exchange of commitment and hard work on the employee side for job security and a reward structure on the employer side (Cullinane and Dundon 2006) have been replaced with a more "protean"-type career model (Hall 1996, 2002). Individuals nowadays need to self-manage their careers within their current organisations and at the labour market in general (Battilana and D'Aunno 2009). Although this might open up opportunities for some employees, especially for low-skilled workers, the loss of such a psychological contract might bring serious threats. For example, on the background of current economic instabilities, many employers hire new personnel only on short-term basis. Other employers even tend to subcontract their personnel using labour leasing agencies (OECD 2012a). For employees, both strategies result in precarious employment conditions, frequent job changes and/or high job insecurities.

The briefly outlined developments describe the range of possible features that characterise the so-called "new" jobs of the new millennium. A common issue of those megatrends is a constantly growing uncertainty regarding work conditions and prospective employment situations. These uncertainties require employees to continuously develop their work-related knowledge, skills and competences. In order to secure current employment and to open up new employment opportunities, employees cannot only rely on their competences and on their qualifications obtained in their initial vocational education. They are rather requested to engage in lifelong learning endeavours that allow ongoing employability under the changing requirements of the labour market. Although desirable from the employee point of view, such learning opportunities might not always be automatically offered and arranged by the employer or external institutions (Strategy Group 2011). It therefore takes both the motivation and the capacity of the employee to actively seek out learning opportunities. Individuals have to engage in certain self-management behaviours that allow them to cope with ambiguous situations. They have to be able to make decisions at any life stage that allow them to exert control over their professional work-life courses. Individuals have to develop appropriate identities that ensure them independence from concrete conditions of current developments. This may not only comprise lifelong learning activities but also the bottom-up development or transformation of work practices and work conditions.

This chapter aims at introducing the concept of *work agency*, which covers the personal capacity to cope with the stated challenges. The concept describes on an individual level the prerequisites to cope with the challenges described above. This contribution is based on the following line of thought: The second paragraph develops the understanding of work agency as well as conceptualises and defines the concept. Then, the third paragraph links this understanding of work agency with the issue of lifelong learning, in order to argue how work agency contributes to the development of expertise and, thus, to the "new" skills the European agenda claims for the "new" jobs at the European labour markets. The chapter ends with the development of a research agenda for educational research.

3.2 Work Agency

From an educational science perspective, it is important that individuals develop qualities to face the upcoming challenges connected to ambiguous and uncertain developments. Such qualities comprise the individual competences to ensure them independence from concrete conditions of current employment and to apply self-directed vocational flexibility and mobility through lifelong learning. Individuals need not only to be able to seize available opportunities potentially leading to further personal development but also to actively shape current work conditions. This way, individuals are not only reacting to change but rather deliberately initiate change from the bottom-up. In the following discussion, the capacity to make such work-related decisions and to act on these choices will be comprised in the concept *work agency*.

The idea of *agency* is not an entirely new one. Its roots can at least be traced back to Kant's idea of enlightenment (cf. Ecclestone 2007) and the historical debate about determinism versus free will (cf. Wehmeyer 2004). In general terms, agency is connected to the idea that human beings are indeed in possession of a free will and that they use this will to make decisions and choices regarding their own lives (Wehmeyer 2001). They are perceived as self-determined agents that have the fundamental capacity to take initiatives, to control and to willingly change their life situations as well as to resist external forces (Eteläpelto et al. 2012).

In the last decades, the agency concept has been widely used in different research disciplines with a broad variety of meanings and interpretations. However, there is no well-established and widely shared understanding of this concept. Based on their research, Eteläpelto et al. (2012) could identify four different lines of theoretical discussions on agency. Within the *social sciences* agency mainly comprises intentional and goal-directed processes at the individual level (e.g. Giddens 1984).

The concept is often implicitly or explicitly used as a notion of human freedom or individual volition within a given social structure (Hitlin and Elder 2007). Agency concerns the initiation of human actions. It can be understood as the self's executive function to make choices, take responsibilities and exert control over the environment (Baumeister 1999; Gecas 2003). Research in organisational behaviour, for example, discusses agency in the concepts about self-started behaviour at work (e.g. personal initiative and job crafting behaviour; e.g. Bindl and Parker 2010; Frese and Fay 2001; Wrzesniewski and Dutton 2001). In contrast, the *post-structural* discussion is strongly rooted in social-constructionist ideas. In radical post-structural discussions, agency is almost exclusively manifested at discursive and collective levels. Agency is a social rather than an individual phenomenon. More intermediate post-structural notions on the other hand see agency as "a key mediating category through which the inter-connections between cultural and economic forces, identity formations and social structures can be examined" (McNay 2004, p. 177). In subject-oriented *sociocultural* discourses on the concept, individuals are understood as agentic actors within a social world. Agency is strongly related to subject's professional identities and subjectivities (e.g. Holland et al. 2003; Billett 2006). Those might be manifested as decisions to participate in or rejections of certain practices (e.g. Billett 2004). The focus of the *life course and identity* discussion on the other hand lies on choices and actions that influence individuals' life courses. Agency describes the active construction of one's own life course within the given historical and social circumstances (e.g. Gecas 2003; Elder 1995). Prototypical examples for agency in this discussion are decisions concerning the transition from one educational stage to another or vocational and career-related choices.

In our understanding agency comprises the general capacity and disposition to make intentional choices, to initiate actions based on these choices and to exercise control over the self and the environment (see for similar conceptualisations Eteläpelto et al. 2012; Martin 2004; Watkin 2005). In order to exercise agency, individuals have to set personal goals, to decide to pursue those goals and to show commitment and willingness as well as resilience to actually reach those goals in cases of drawbacks and obstacles. Such individuals perceive the locus of control within themselves (Rotter 1966). Hence, they have a self-concept of being an active individual with opportunities to influence their own development and to tune environmental components in favour of their own goals. The opposite of agency would be a rather reactive behaviour. Instead of trying to make intentional choices that lead to the engagement in self-started activities, individuals practising this passive or undeveloped agency tend to react and comply with external forces and conditions. Such individuals may either not have the capacity to make intentional choices or do not succeed to act on their choices. In either way, such individuals are highly dependent on other people and experience themselves being non-effective on their own development and environment in comparison to causal agents that have control over their lives.

It might be clear that individuals cannot be characterised as either fully agentic or completely reactive. The proposed dichotomy between *developed* and *undeveloped* agency is only used for analytical reasons to separate different qualities of agency. Both categories should be understood as ideal end points of a continuum with many possible manifestations between them.

It can be assumed that human beings have a natural propensity to exercise developed agency because they either have the need to experience causation and control (deCharms 1968) or the need to be self-determining (Deci 1980; Deci and Ryan 1985). Both needs describe a basic human urge to be a cause of one's own actions. However, not all individuals are able to satisfy those needs in the same way and to the same extent. The reasons for this might interdependently be found in situational and/or individual factors.

Any kind of agency is always at least somehow bounded by opportunities and constraints defined by the environment and the situation in which the individual tries to act (Evans 2007; Silbereisen et al. 2007). To give an example, consider a school dropout that decides to take up his educational trajectory by enrolling at a university at a certain point after leaving school. Usually this will not be possible since universities demand certain entry requirements that the described individual cannot provide. However, the same individual may have the opportunity to obtain such requirements through evening classes. After having acquired the necessary qualifications, the individual is consequently free to pursue his/her initial aim. This example should have illustrated that agency cannot be understood as the freedom to act in an unrestrained way, regardless of social and structural circumstances. External conditions and circumstances always inherit the potential to enable and also constrain the exercise of agency. One can also say that agency is always at least somehow partially socioculturally mediated (Ahearn 2001; Hitlin and Elder 2007).

Although the social structure both constraints and enables human actions to a certain point, behaviour is not a simple function of social and physical conditions. Different individuals interpret external factors in particular ways based on their prior experience. Such a perception of concrete circumstances then affects the human goal-setting process and the motivation to pursue those goals. Both the antic-ipated outcome of an action and the expected consequences of these outcomes are taken into account into the decision whether to act or not to act (Vroom 1964). Although to a certain point externally defined, the expectation about outcomes and consequences depends also on the individual's beliefs about his/her personal capacity to influence the results of his/her own actions. The actual decision to engage in certain activities that ought to reach certain goals is highly dependent on the belief that one is personally capable of the intended actions (Bandura 1982, 2001). Such self-efficacy beliefs affect the perception of external factors and subjec-tively define whether they are construed to enable or constrain planned actions.

Whether an individual develops high or low self-efficacy beliefs in a certain domain depends on biographical incidents (Gecas 2003). Individuals that could experience situations where they caused actions and where the consequences of those actions lead to desired outcomes are more likely to have higher self-efficacy beliefs than individuals who could not make such experiences. On the other hand, frequent experiences of failures can easily lead to low self-efficacy beliefs

(Bandura 1977, 1997). This, for example, explains why some people are reluctant to engage in formal learning settings. Although they might experience the need to update their competences in a certain domain, they believe that they are not capable to do so because of negative school or similar experiences (Brookfield 2006). However, low self-efficacy beliefs may also result of not being able to exercise agency in the past. If an individual is constantly deprived of being a cause in certain situations, he/she might learn to be helpless under similar circumstances (Seligman 1972). In extreme cases, individuals learn to be passive and reactive rather than to exercise any kind of agency. In either way, low self-efficacy beliefs and learned helplessness lead to situations where individuals fail to exercise agency even though the opportunities for agentic actions are widely present.

Although self-efficacy is often conceptualised as general belief, there is many evidence that the beliefs of being capable to act and to reach goals differ between tasks and domains for single individuals (e.g. Bandura 1997; McAvay et al. 1996; Skaalvik and Skaalvik 2004). This might be best explained through the individuals' prior biography and his/her past opportunities to successfully exercise agency in certain life domains (e.g. work, education, love life).

Based on this insight, one can argue that individuals with the general capacity and prosperity to exercise agency direct their agentic energy towards certain domains. This agency channelling depends upon the perception of current opportunities and/or constraining factors for agentic actions as well as past domain-specific experiences. An individual, for example, might not show any kind of agency at work but acts highly agentic as the trainer of a local sports team in his/her leisure time. The agentic engagement in such voluntary work might be chosen over the work life because past external conditions did not allow exercising agency in the workplace. In such a case, he/she appears unlikely to develop work-related self-efficacy beliefs. On the other hand, the voluntary work might have allowed a range of agentic actions that led to the development of self-efficacy beliefs as well as a certain kind of individual fulfilment.

Within a certain domain, individuals may exercise agency in a wide range of concrete actions. What kinds of agency expressions are finally exercised will depend upon domain-specific individual goal orientations as well as possible opportunities or constraints. It is therefore indispensable for any empirical investigation on agency to explicitly define the domain of analysis as well as the type of agency expression that the study wants to focus on. In order to stimulate further empirical research, the discussion on agency will now be limited to agentic actions concerning the domain of work.

The concept *work agency* can be understood as a facet of agency that is directed towards the individual's working life. Thus, agentic individuals are causal agents that deliberately affect both their own work-related life trajectories and/or the general conditions of their work environment. Exercising agency at work or in relationship to work-related affairs is a fundamental precondition to manage the challenges connected to the economic and social developments outlined at the beginning. Although work agency can be manifested in different ways, we will now constrain our analyses on two relevant expressions of agency that are deeply connected with lifelong learning as well as the handling of work-related uncertainties. In order to concretise our understanding of both expressions, the following examples shall be used for illustrative purposes.

The first example is a car mechanic that just started to work for a new employer. In her previous employment, a tight reward system was introduced that ultimately lead to reduced repair quality. At first, she tried to address this matter to her employer but did not succeed. For her, high quality standards are highly important because they are necessary requirement for the passengers' safety. Since she could not change the situation at her old employer, she decided to look for a new job that complies better with her work philosophy. Apart from the better employee-employer fit, she perceives her new job as a new challenge with high learning potentials. She constantly uses every opportunity to repair cars with problems yet unknown to her. She both wants to further develop her skills and also to be better prepared for new situations where her skills are needed. The second example is about a teacher working in a school for mentally and physically handicapped children. She constantly reflects about the current and future situation of the students and is especially concerned about possible employment chances that follow compulsory education. In order to improve the employment chance of her protégés, she deliberately looks for well-suited training material. A role player game simulating application processes and early employment years met her criteria, and she started to use it at her school. For every student cohort, she invests a lot of her spare time to organise and prepare this role player game. Usually, the games are a big success in terms of preparing students for the time after school as well as student satisfaction during the activity. Although she does not get the recognition of her supervisors and colleagues she would like to get, she launches the game again every new year.

Both cases can be used to illustrate two analytical separate but not fully disjunct expressions of work agency. The two analytical categories refer to the goal orientation of exercising agency: There is work agency that is predominately oriented towards outcomes on the individual level. Such *individual-oriented work agency* can best be described as making a difference in or for the self. Individuals exercising this kind of work agency pursue a personal curriculum at work. In our example, the car mechanic might best fall into this category. The agentic action is mainly directed at the improvement of the own person-environment fit by either changing individual or situational characteristics. Typical expressions for this kind of developed work agency is the deliberate engagement in learning and development activities as well as a strive to shape one's own career trajectory. Individuals that exercise an undeveloped work agency, on the other hand, tend to comply with existing career pattern that are externally provided or they accept other's definition of self and role. In comparison, the other orientation of work agency comprises actions directed towards changing the situation of others or towards making differences to current work practices (*externally oriented agency*). It is not the individual himself/herself that is the focus of change and improvements but rather situational characteristics. In our examples, the teacher might be an instance for this kind of behaviour. Individuals express this kind of work agency by addressing tensions in work practice, by creating new work practices and/or by the transformation of already existing work practices.

Table 3.1 Conceptualisation of both dimensions of agency

Orientation	Developed	Undeveloped
Individual-oriented agency	Intentional activity to make a difference in or for the self, e.g.: Deliberately pursue learning and development activities Shaping one's own career Improving the person-environment fit	Tendency to: Comply with existing career patterns Accept other's definitions of self and role Accept given work conditions
Externally oriented agency	Intentional activity to make a difference in the current work practice, e.g.: Develop or transform work practices Create new work practices Address tensions in work practices	Tendency to: Overlook tensions in work practices Protect existing work practices even if problems are obvious

Less agentic individuals, for instance, tend to overlook tensions in work practices by not addressing them. Table 3.1 summarises the conceptualisation of both expressions of work agency in combination with the earlier introduced categories of developed and undeveloped agency.

3.3 Lifelong Learning and Its Interdependence with Work Agency

Education and lifelong learning are indispensable contributions to individuals' access to labour markets, to economic growth and competitiveness and to social cohesion in Europe. In times of permanent change, top-down-oriented educational policy cannot be sufficient and must be complemented by bottom-up educational activities. The concept of work agency describes individuals' capacity to make intentional choices and to act on these choices in ways that make a difference in their professional lives. Such an understanding of agency comprises individual skills, attitudes and beliefs which generates individual independence from concrete workplace conditions. Maintaining competent agency implies strategies of advancing and renewing an individual's skills and competencies. This requires individuals at their workplaces to enrol in knowledge cultures and disciplines. Work life is understood as participation in a community which enables individuals to advance knowledge and skills to be able to raise crucial questions, identify opportunities and engage in learning activities.

In general, lifelong learning describes the economic demand and the political invitation for learning that comprises all phases of the human lifespan (European Commission 2000). It implies that learning does explicitly not end with the completion of compulsory education or the achievement of a professional qualification. Learning must not only be perceived as a means to enter the labour market. Work or nonwork-related learning has to continue to assure both the long-term employability of individuals and their social and cultural participation. Learning is hereby not restricted to educational settings provided by educational institutions like community colleges or training suppliers. It rather also includes learning through the participation and reflection in day-to-day activities at the workplace or the family life (Fischer 2000).

A key feature of lifelong learning described by the OECD (2004) is the motivation to learn. After finishing compulsory education, the further development of skills and knowledge requires both a certain desire and willingness for learning and progression. Apart from few legal obligations in some professions (e.g. teaching, law, medicine), the participation in institutionalised learning programmes is usually not mandatory. The same applies for the utilisation of less institutionalised learning opportunities. Professional magazines, for example, might be available at workplaces, but employees are usually not formally required to read them. It is therefore absolutely necessary that individuals build up intentions to seize available learning opportunities or to initiate conditions that open up new learning potentials. These intentions have then to be translated into appropriate actions that allow skill and knowledge development.

Work agency can therefore be understood as a necessary precondition for successful work-related and nonwork-related lifelong learning. Individuals have to make choices regarding their learning and to act on these choices in order to create and pursue a personal learning curriculum. A passive approach to lifelong learning entails the risk to slow down or to actually stop professional development processes. Especially for low-qualified employees, corporate organisations seem to be reluctant to provide training and development opportunities in an adequate extent (Asplund and Salverda 2004). Thus, especially those kinds of employees are at risk for not being able to adequately handle work-related changes that result out of the megatrends described in the first paragraph. Without taking an active approach towards lifelong learning by proactively demanding learning opportunities, certain employees end up being excluded from further professional development and therefore lose their employability in the long term.

However, even when learning opportunities are provided by the employer, a passive approach may lead to the instrumentalisation of learning processes. By relying only on learning opportunities that are readily available and/or somehow compulsory, individuals give up the control of their professional development. Consequently, learning programmes will not always meet individuals' concrete needs. Rather contrary, organisations will use the provision of learning opportunities to pursue an agenda that is directed towards corporate objectives that may not always overlap with the goals of their employees. Ashton (2004), for instance, reports that companies use trainings not for professional development and educational purposes. The main reason behind the company's training efforts was to increase staff flexibility in order to guarantee that internal vacancies can be filled up on very short notice. In the long run, such human resource development strategies can systematically be used to make personnel redundant (Bratton and Gold 1999). Training and development programmes may also be used to reproduce and to reinforce hierarchical inequalities at the workplace. Employees at lower levels of the organisational hierarchy tend to gain access only to training that aims at skills and knowledge which are directly applicable in their current workplace. Training on knowledge that can be generalised and transferred between different workplaces and organisations, on the other hand, is often reserved for employees on higher hierarchical levels (Rainbird 2000).

In general, individuals only exercising an undeveloped agency are restricted to a smaller variety of learning opportunities in comparison to more agentic individuals. Although the access to learning experiences is often limited, Bryson et al. (2006) found evidence that employees could create development opportunities by taking initiative in otherwise rather restrictive work environments. The described employees proactively asked and sought out for both on-the-job learning affordances and institutionalised training opportunities which are usually not automatically provided to them. Other workers used their leisure time to deliberately engage in activities that provided positive spill overs to their daily work activities. In a similar manner, Evans et al. (2004) as well as Evans and Kersh (2006) report about employees that did not wait till their employer provided further training. These employees rather took a chance to proactively negotiate with their employers in order to get access to further learning opportunities. Both studies showed that an active approach to one's own professional development can open up new learning potentials that would not be available without exercising work agency. Employees have to deliberately invest time and energy into their professional development. Without making active choices to show a certain commitment and resilience, their extended access to new learning opportunities would be limited or in the worst case not exist at all.

Exercising work agency may not only be important in terms of increasing the variety of learning opportunities that individuals have access to. Research on expertise shows that individual-oriented agency is also strongly connected to the quality of development processes. Extensive experience is a necessary requirement for expertise development in all kind of domains (Gruber 2001). However, not all individuals that spent the same time span engaging with activities of their domain eventually reach expert status (Ericsson 2006). The plain engagement in routine and mundane activities that are already well known and mastered to a certain point has only very restricted learning potential. In order to further improve particular aspects of performance, individuals have to engage in activities that are still outside their current performance. Such activities range from new tasks that have not been mastered yet to activities that help to understand why past actions did not lead to outcomes that have been expected. Ericsson et al. (1993) describe this kind of behaviour in the concept deliberate practice. Central characteristics are for those activities that they have usually not perceived as something pleasant but rather wearisome and unpleasant. Consequently, individuals have to actively decide to engage in these kinds of activities and to show willingness and resilience to successfully pursue them. Again, this is the core of individual-oriented agency as defined in the second section.

So far, the discussion has been predominately focussed on the relationship of individual-oriented agency with certain aspects of lifelong learning. Although not that obvious, exercising externally oriented agency can also be connected to lifelong learning processes of the agentic individual as well as related others (e.g. colleagues, subordinates).

Vähäsantanen et al. (2009) studied vocational teachers visiting the workplaces of their students during a workplace learning programme. Apart from supporting the workplace learning process of their students, teachers were also responsible to assist organisational staff acting as trainers in the workplace. However, many teachers perceived the practitioners seeing them to be rather incompetent in terms of their daily work routines. For some teachers, this led them to be only passive observers that are not allowed to criticise or question current workplace practices. On the contrary, other teachers showed a more extensive agentic approach by actively indicating improper work routines using their own professional knowledge. This way, exercising agency started learning processes for all participants and eventually led to improved work practices.

Rainbird et al. (2004) report about a female supervisor in cleaning work showing extensive individual-oriented agency that later on led to agentic actions on a more collective level. The woman managed to get a supervisor position in order to obtain more job autonomy and to make her job more interesting. Using the new position, she introduced a new system to assign workers to units and developed new routines to organise work in general. Furthermore, she used her supervision duties to teach others correct cleaning methods. The reported case shows that a new job position that was established through the exercise of individual-oriented agency opened up opportunities for externally oriented agency. By exercising this externally oriented agency, the supervisor did not only change current practices but also stimulated the learning of her subordinates.

In a study on hospital cleaning staff, Wrzesniewski and Dutton (2001) describe a group of very agentic cleaners. Members of this group perceived their work tasks as a critical part of the patients healing process. Based on this interpretation, the cleaners discretionarily tried to time their regular cleaning in order to avoid disturbance of care procedures carried out by medical staff. They furthermore deliberately added new tasks that were outside their formal job description. They showed visitors around or cheered up patients by talking to them. Again, the described cleaners exercised externally oriented agency and managed to change both their own and other's current practices. However, successfully establishing the targeted results of such job crafting requires significant analyses of work procedures in general and work tasks of other employees. In other terms, the agentic cleaners had to establish work-related knowledge that surpassed the knowledge that is usually required to do cleaning job.

Summarising this understanding of work agency, it should have become obvious that agency is construed in a sense that it mediates and shapes individuals' capabilities to be successful in developing a self-directed, self-responsible career and life path during their work life and beyond. This implies that the exercise of work agency not only refers to the creation of learning opportunities. It implies further that the exercise of agency also results in the realisation of learning experiences after creating opportunities. Such an understanding of agency raises various research options for empirical investigations.

3.4   Research Agenda

In order to develop research further, a multi-perspective research approach appears appropriate. Literature on agency and lifelong learning represents different paradigmatic and methodological approaches which yet are not well connected to each other (e.g. for research on agency; Eteläpelto et al. 2012). The proposed research agenda suggests investigating effects of individual as well as social influences on the exercise of agency and how the concept is related to engagement in formal, flexible and instant learning processes. The agenda also proposes to investigate how lifelong learning investments are related to the development of work agency and how they contribute to growth and competitiveness. Such a research programme requires the application of different paradigms and research methods. The comparison of findings among these approaches will provide strong empirical evidence (1) on how best to support the development of work agency, (2) on its effects on lifelong learning and (3) on how agentic lifelong learning affects societal and economic outcomes. The different paradigmatic and methodological approaches can be distinguished as follows.

3.4.1 Large-Scale Approach

The core of such an approach is focusing on the developmental trends of the effectiveness of lifelong learning activities in Europe from the point of view of work careers, employment and productivity. The top-down implemented educational systems and policies of different European countries differ in many respects. This reflects partly deeper differences in the societies and economic structures as well as demographic features of the populations. Studies also show that the economic impact of education varies in different EU countries (e.g. Temple 2001). Such research aims at analysing educational trajectories on different levels of education and in different sectors, dropout rates, exclusion, transition periods (from education to work, from one workplace to another and from work back into the educational system), social well-being, gender and work career and employment rate. Demographic data of different countries could be used as important basis for the detailed analyses of the efficacy of lifelong learning, e.g. follow-up and secondary analyses of the database of the Hungarian Educational Longitudinal Project (HELP). There are data of the educational achievements of ca. 4,000 students for the first eight grades of primary school. Their future expectations and career plans may be connected to their educational history. Similar data exists for 3,000 students for their high-school career (grades 8–12). Comparable databases exist or are being currently build in various European countries (e.g. NEPS in Germany; Blossfeld et al. 2011) and could be object of a large-scale approach. Those analyses would reveal how exactly and which types of lifelong learning policies are most conducive to innovation, competitiveness and growth. Furthermore, more individual-based analyses could concentrate on the identification of individual variables that explain agentic participation in lifelong learning.

3.4.2   Cognitive Approach

Applying a cognitive approach means to operationalise singular variables for empirical measurement. The cognitive research approach focuses on the mental states and individual perceptions of working life; data collection will comprise questionnaires and interviews. Within the cognitive research approach, following selection of variables would be appropriate objects of investigation of the development as well as the effects of work agency:

- *Individual self-perception.* The Self-Determination Theory of Motivation (Deci and Ryan 1985) can be considered as a crucial indicator of the agentic self-perception of individuals. The experience of autonomy, competence and social embedding enables individuals to perceive themselves as subject of their work and learning biography (Harteis et al. 2004; Ryan and Deci 2000).
- *Behavioural aspects of agency.* Instead of just focussing on individuals' perception of their agentic nature, measurements about the individual expressions of work agency are indispensable. At this time, no explicit questionnaires on work agency exist. However, an adaption of the job crafting scale (Tims et al. 2012) could be used to measure individual-oriented work agency.
- *External conditions.* A crucial issue of external conditions is shaped by the workplace environment and its opportunities and restrictions for individual agentic work behaviour. There are questionnaires available for grasping employees' opportunities for participation and responsible work behaviour (Festner et al. 2007; Harteis 2012).
- *Individual biography.* We have argued that past experiences affect the individual's capacity to exercise agency (Sect. 3.2). As prior learning is an important individual influence on each learning process, investigations of emotional experiences particularly regarding learning success and failures (Cannon and Edmondson 2001; Harteis et al. 2008), domain experience and expertise (i.e. procedural knowledge, routines, intuition) appear appropriate (e.g. Boshuizen et al. 2004; Gijbels et al. 2010; Harteis and Billett 2013).
- *Internal aspirations.* Internal aspirations (e.g. short- and long-term objectives) should be grasped in order to comprehend the subjects' educational and occupational career, their biography and their further ambitions in these areas. In addition, measurements indicating subjects' self-efficacy (Bandura 1997) and epistemic beliefs (Schraw et al. 2002; Harteis et al. 2010) are strongly connected to goal-setting processes and should therefore also be collected.
- *Effects on individual level.* Interviews can reveal subjects' creativity and flexibility in working contexts, can grasp issues of well-being by covering happiness and can finally discuss individual perceptions of labour market access (i.e. appropriate work alternatives and perception of competition). Questionnaires could be used to measure subjects' job satisfaction (Brayfield and Rothe 1951). Those measurements could be used to explain both the development and the effects of work agency.

- *Effects on social (i.e. company or societal) level.* Interviews will cover the subjects' view on the labour market situation and will explore the big issues of societal being, as they are equality (e.g. discrimination experiences), welfare (e.g. work-life balance) and social cohesion (e.g. participation on societal events).

3.4.3 Relational Approach

The relational approach of investigation focuses on the question how work agency is developed and sustained collaboratively in everyday practices in different and shifting organisational settings. Project work might be an appropriate kind of work organisation for analysing interindividual relations. In the global knowledge, economy knowledge-intensive work has become a key factor (Sect. 3.1) and is increasingly organised as project work (Ettlinger 2003; Midler 1995; Lindkvist 2004). Project work takes different forms within stable and dynamic contexts (Grabher 2003). One common feature, however, is that project work demands work agency as people collaborate in shifting context, around shifting tasks and within different organisations. To establish and maintain work relationships, necessary competencies include making one's own competence relevant for the tasks at hand and learning from others, as well as to identify competencies critical for the performance of the team. Several studies have pointed to the need for such competencies (Eklund et al. 2010; Guile 2011; Ó Riain 2000). Research has also shown that knowledge-intensive project work presupposes collective as much as individual modes of activity (Guile 2010; Børte and Nerland 2010). However, little is known about how project work and its related demands differ between stable and dynamic contexts or about how these competencies are oriented to, developed and sustained.

To fill this gap, research is necessary to follow the question (a) how specific organisational settings support or discourage the development of work agency, (b) how work agency is developed and sustained within different organisational boundaries through collaboration and (c) how work agency facilitates individuals' and groups' capacities to evolve and/or transform professional and workplace practice. Such research attempts to contribute to identifying critical competencies and their support mechanisms that may enhance individuals' employability and organisations' competitiveness in a global knowledge economy.

3.4.4 Ethnographic Approach

This approach presupposes that human beings have different kinds of relations to the world representing (1) discursive, (2) practical and (3) embodied levels (e.g. Archer 2003). These have all been taken into account when addressing how work agency is practised in the sociocultural and material conditions of the workplace. These kinds of studies can be conducted within an *ethnographic framework*

(Hammersley and Atkinson 2007). An ethnographic approach is necessary for the elaboration of work-community social processes, including current work practices, power relations and dominating discourses, plus the subject positions available in the workplace. At the initial stage of the ethnographic data collection, research shall focus on these contextual conditions, since one needs to have a comprehensive view of the sociocultural contexts before suggesting any interventions. A *longitudinal strategy* will be needed for collecting data on dynamic processes and on the influences of interventions. After the first intervention, previous data will be utilised at each stage in the planning of subsequent interventions. Collin et al. (2010) – for example – developed a method of collective ethnography within the hospital context.

Since the data is mainly qualitative in nature, the validity and credibility of analysis will be enhanced through *researcher and methods triangulation.* Researcher triangulation means that at all stages of the analysis, at least two researchers will collaborate in conducting the data analysis (Patton 2002). Methods triangulation implies that different aspects of the phenomenon and contexts will be taken into account in putting together different data sets (from observations and interviews). Methods triangulation is used to increase the internal validity of data analysis and to create a multilevel understanding of the phenomenon investigated.

3.5 Summary

This contribution introduced the concept work agency. Work agency has been defined as the general capacity and disposition to make intentional choices, to initiate actions based on these choices and to exercise control over the self and the environment in relation to work-related matters. It has been made clear that the exercise of work agency is indispensably related to lifelong learning as well as the general capacity to manage uncertainties in the context of work. Since (empirical) research on work agency and its relationship to lifelong learning is still scarce, a possible research agenda was set up. The proposed research agenda takes stock of recent research activities on professional VET and lifelong learning in European contexts and implies a considerable progress beyond the state of the art:

- Maintaining competent work agency implies the individual to find, develop and adopt strategies of advancing and renewing specific skills and competencies. The enrolment in knowledge cultures and disciplines or vocations, hereby, is an important requirement for competence-oriented work agency. Participating in communities enables individuals to advance their knowledge and skills to express a critical personality, to identify chances and opportunities and finally to get socially engaged in an explorative manner.
- Contemporary societal and economic developments prepare the ground and circumstances for the creation of highly professional jobs for which nowadays no institutional graduation or apprenticeship programme exists. Research, therefore, should address the importance of lifelong formal, non-formal and informal

learning for adequately preparing individuals for these new jobs' demands. Ensuring the individual's capability to identify and start such a new job is an important task and contribution for sustaining employability and better jobs in the twenty-first century.

- There are diverse requirements for vocational, occupational and professional transformations across varying industry and service sectors or lines. Whereas in some areas transformation is necessary as the industry goes down (e.g. coal mining), other areas transform due to general societal, macroeconomic or environmental changes (e.g. increase of relevance in vocational education and training, teacher education and workplaces in the logistic area).

To sum up, researching the concept of work agency has the potential to enhance a progress beyond the state of the art in scientific as well as in practical respects. The parallel application of different theoretical and methodological approaches on a commonly shared research issue, the comparison of findings and their merging are extraordinary ways of conducting research. One reason is that this procedure demands a critical mass of research resources which are difficult to provide on national levels. Another reason is that scientific discourses of professional and work-related learning often remain within their own paradigmatic community (Harteis and Billett 2008). The proposed agenda transcends these paradigmatic borders. Furthermore, it allows developing educational interventions for all protagonists of societal outcomes: workforce (employees), employers, stakeholders and politicians. By that, the agenda focuses crucial topics raised in the new EU Framework Programme Horizon 2020 (European Commission 2011).

References

Ahearn, L. M. (2001). Language and agency. *Annual Review of Anthropology, 30*(1), 109–137.
Archer, M. (2003). *Structure, agency and the internal conversation.* Cambridge: Cambridge University Press.
Ashton, D. N. (2004). The impact of organisational structure and practice on learning in the workplace. *International Journal of Training and Development, 8*(1), 43–53.
Asplund, R., & Salverda, W. (2004). Introduction: Company training and services with a focus on low skills. *International Journal of Manpower, 25*(1), 8–16.
Bandura, A. (1977). Self-efficacy: Toward a unifying theory of behavioral change. *Psychological Review, 84*(2), 191–215.
Bandura, A. (1982). The self and mechanisms of agency. In J. Suls (Ed.), *Psychological perspectives on the self* (Vol. 1, pp. 3–39). Hillsdale: Erlbaum.
Bandura, A. (1997). *Self-efficacy: The exercise of control.* New York: Freeman.
Bandura, A. (2001). Social cognitive theory: An agentic perspective. *Annual Review of Psychology, 52*, 1–21.
Battilana, J., & D'Aunno, T. (2009). Institutional work and the paradox of embedded agency. In T. B. Lawrence, R. Suddaby, & B. Leca (Eds.), *Institutional work. Actors and agency in institutional studies of organizations* (pp. 31–58). Cambridge: Cambridge University Press.
Baumeister, R. F. (1999). The nature and structure of the self: An overview. In R. F. Baumeister (Ed.), *The self in social psychology* (pp. 1–20). New York: Taylor & Francis.

Billett, S. (2004). Workplace participatory practices. Conceptualising workplaces as leaning environments. *Journal of Workplace Learning, 16*(6), 312–324.

Billett, S. (2006). Relational interdependence between social and individual agency in work and working life. *Mind, Culture, and Activity, 13*(1), 53–69.

Billett, S. (2009). Changing work, work practice: The consequences for vocational education. In R. Maclean & D. Wilson (Eds.), *International handbook of education for the changing world of work* (Vol. 1, pp. 175–187). Dordrecht: Springer.

Bindl, U. K., & Parker, S. K. (2010). Proactive work behavior: Forward-thinking and change-oriented action in organizations. In S. Zedeck (Ed.), *APA handbook of industrial and organizational psychology* (Vol. 2, pp. 567–598). Washington, DC: American Psychological Association.

Blossfeld, H. P., von Maurice, J., & Schneider, T. (2011). The National Educational Panel Study: Need, main features, and research potential. *Zeitschrift für Erziehungswissenschaft, 14*(2), 5–17.

Børte, K., & Nerland, M. (2010). Software effort estimation as collective accomplishment. An analysis of estimation practice in a multi-specialist team. *Scandinavian Journal of Information Systems, 22*(2), 71–104.

Boshuizen, H. P. A., Bromme, R., & Gruber, H. (Eds.). (2004). *Professional learning: Gaps and transitions on the way from novice to expert.* Dordrecht: Kluwer.

Bratton, J., & Gold, J. (1999). *Human resource management. Theory and practice.* London: Erlbaum.

Brayfield, A., & Rothe, H. (1951). An index of job satisfaction. *Journal of Applied Psychology, 35*, 301–311.

Brookfield, S. D. (2006). *The skillful teacher: On technique, trust, and responsiveness in the classroom.* San Francisco: Jossey-Bass.

Bryson, J., Pajo, K., Ward, R., & Mallon, M. (2006). Learning at work: Organisational affordances and individual engagement. *Journal of Workplace Learning, 18*(5), 279–297.

Cannon, M. D., & Edmondson, A. C. (2001). Confronting failure: Antecedents and consequences of shared beliefs about failure in organizational work groups. *Journal of Organizational Behavior, 22*(2), 161–177.

CEDEFOP. (2010). *Skills supply and demand in Europe. Medium-term forecast up to 2020.* Luxembourg: Publications Office of the European Union.

Collin, K., Paloniemi, S., & Mecklin, J.-P. (2010). Manifesting interprofessional team work and learning – The case of surgical operating theatre. *Journal of Education and Work, 23*, 43–63.

Cullinane, N., & Dundon, T. (2006). The psychological contract: A critical review. *International Journal of Management Reviews, 8*(2), 113–129.

DeCharms, R. (1968). *Personal causation: The internal affective determinants of behavior.* New York: Academic.

Deci, E. L. (1980). *The psychology of self-determination.* Lexington: D. C. Heath (Lexington Books).

Deci, E. L., & Ryan, R. M. (1985). *Intrinsic motivation and self-determination in human behaviour.* New York: Plenum Press.

Ecclestone, K. (2007). An identity crisis? Using concepts of "identity", "agency" and "structure" in the education of adults. *Studies in the Education of Adults, 39*(2), 121–131.

Eklund, A.-C., Mäkitalo, Å., & Säljö, R. (2010). Noticing the past to manage the future: On the organization of shared knowing in IT helpdesks. In S. Ludvigsen, A. Lund, I. Rasmussen, & R. Säljö (Eds.), *Learning across sites. New tools, infrastructures and practices* (pp. 122–137). Oxford: Pergamon Press.

Elder, G. H. (1995). Life trajectories in changing societies. In A. Bandura (Ed.), *Self-efficacy in changing societies* (pp. 46–68). Cambridge: Cambridge University Press.

Ericsson, K. A. (2006). An introduction to the Cambridge handbook of expertise and expert performance: Its development, organization, and content. In K. A. Ericsson, N. Charness, P. J. Feltovich, & R. R. Hoffman (Eds.), *The Cambridge handbook of expertise and expert performance* (pp. 3–19). Cambridge: Cambridge University Press.

Ericsson, K. A., Krampe, R. T., & Tesch-Römer, C. (1993). The role of deliberate practice in the acquisition of expert performance. *Psychological Review, 100*(3), 363–406.

Eteläpelto, A., Vähäsantanen, K., & Hökkä, P. (2012). Towards a reconceptualization of professional agency at work. In *Conference proceeding in professions and professional learning in troubling times: Emerging practices and transgressive knowledge* (pp. 1–13). Stirling: Conference CD.

Ettlinger, N. (2003). Cultural economic geography and a relational and microspace approach to trusts, rationalities, networks, and change in collaborative workplaces. *Journal of Economic Geography, 3*, 879–909.

European Commission. (2000). *A memorandum on lifelong learning* (SEC(2000) 1832). Brussels: EC.

European Commission. (2011). *Horizon 2020 – The framework programme for research and innovation*. Brussels: EC.

Evans, K. (2007). Concepts of bounded agency in education, work, and the personal lives of young adults. *International Journal of Psychology, 42*(2), 85–93.

Evans, K., & Kersh, N. (2006). Learner biographies, workplace practices, and learning. In K. Evans, P. Hodkinson, H. Rainbird, & L. Unwin (Eds.), *Improving workplace learning* (pp. 68–94). London: Routledge.

Evans, K., Kersh, N., & Sakamoto, A. (2004). Learner biographies: Exploring tacit dimensions of knowledge and skills. In H. Rainbird, A. Fuller, & A. Munro (Eds.), *Workplace learning in context* (pp. 222–241). London: Routledge.

Festner, D., Harteis, C., Kyhä, H., & Tuominen, T. (2007). Participation as predictor of responsibility in working life. In H. Gruber & T. Palonen (Eds.), *Learning in the workplace – New developments in the relation between learning and working* (pp. 65–90). Turku: Finnish Educational Research Association (FERA).

Fischer, G. (2000). Lifelong learning – more than training. *Journal of Interactive Learning Research, 11*(3/4), 265–294.

Frese, M., & Fay, D. (2001). Personal initiative: An active performance concept for work in the 21st century. *Research in Organizational Behavior, 23*, 133–187.

Fugate, M., Kinicki, A. J., & Ashforth, B. E. (2004). Employability: A psycho-social construct, its dimensions, and applications. *Journal of Vocational Behavior, 65*(1), 14–38.

Gecas, V. (2003). Self-agency and the life course. In J. T. Mortimer & M. J. Shanahan (Eds.), *Handbook of the life course* (pp. 369–388). New York: Springer.

Giddens, A. (1984). *The constitution of society: Outline of the theory of structuration*. Cambridge: Polity Press.

Gijbels, D., Raemdonck, I., & Vervecken, D. (2010). Influencing work-related learning: The role of job-characteristics and self-directed learning orientation in part-time vocational education. *Vocations and Learning: Studies in Vocational and Professional Education, 3*, 239–255.

Grabher, G. (2003). Learning in projects, remembering in networks?: Commonality, sociality, and connectivity in project ecologies. *European Journal of Regional Studies, 11*, 103–120.

Green, F. (2007). *Demanding work. The paradox of job quality in the affluent economy*. Woodstock: Princeton University Press.

Gruber, H. (2001). Acquisition of expertise. In J. J. Smelser & P. B. Baltes (Eds.), *International encyclopedia of the social & behavioral sciences* (pp. 5145–5150). Oxford: Elsevier.

Guile, D. (2010). *The learning challenge of the knowledge economy*. Rotterdam: Sense.

Guile, D. (2011). Interprofessional activity in the 'space of reasons': Thinking, communicating and acting. *Vocations and Learning: Studies in Vocational and Professional Education, 4*, 93–111.

Hall, D. T. (1996). Protean careers of the 21st century. *Academy of Management Executive, 10*(4), 8–16.

Hall, D. T. (2002). *Careers in and out organizations*. Thousand Oaks: Sage.

Hammersley, M., & Atkinson, P. (2007). *Ethnography: Principles in practice* (3rd ed.). Milton Park: Routledge.

Harteis, C. (2012). When workplace learning fails: Individual and organisational limitations – Exemplarily demonstrated by the issue of responsibility in work life. *International Journal of Human Resources Development and Management, 12*, 92–107.

Harteis, C., & Billett, S. (2008). The workplace as learning environment: Introduction. *International Journal for Educational Research, 47*, 209–212.

Harteis, C., & Billett, S. (2013). Intuitive expertise: Theories and empirical evidence. *Educational Research Review, 9*, 145–157.

Harteis, C., Bauer, J., Festner, D., & Gruber, H. (2004). Self-determination in daily working life. In M. Radovan & N. Dorderic (Eds.), *Current issues in adult learning and motivation. 7th Adult Education Colloquium* (pp. 212–221). Ljubljana: Slovenian Institute for Adult Education.

Harteis, C., Bauer, J., & Gruber, H. (2008). The culture of learning from mistakes: How employees handle mistakes in everyday work. *International Journal for Educational Research, 47*, 223–231.

Harteis, C., Gruber, H., & Hertramph, H. (2010). How epistemic beliefs influence e-learning in daily work-life. *Journal of Educational Technology & Society, 13*, 201–211.

Hitlin, S., & Elder, G. H. (2007). Time, self, and the curiously abstract concept of agency. *Sociological Theory, 25*(2), 170–191.

Holland, D., Lachicotte, W., Skinner, D., & Cain, C. (2003). *Identity and agency in cultural worlds.* Cambridge, MA: Harvard University Press.

Lindkvist, L. (2004). Governing project-based firms: Market-like processes in hierarchies. *Journal of Management and Governance, 8*, 3–25.

Martin, J. (2004). Self-regulated learning, social cognitive theory, and agency. *Educational Psychologist, 39*(2), 135–145.

McAvay, G. J., Seeman, T. E., & Rodin, J. (1996). A longitudinal study of change in domain-specific self-efficacy among older adults. *Journal of Gerontology, 51*(5), 243–253.

McNay, L. (2004). Agency and experience: Gender as a lived relation. *The Sociological Review, 52*, 173–190.

Midler, C. (1995). "Projectification" of the firm: The Renault case. *Scandinavian Journal of Management, 11*(4), 263–275.

Ó Riain, S. (2000). Net-working for a living: Irish software developers in the global workplace. In M. Burawoy, J. A. Blum, S. George, Z. Gille, T. Gowan, L. Haney, M. Klawiter, S. H. Lopez, S. Ó Riain, & M. Thayer (Eds.), *Global ethnography: Forces, connections, and imaginations in a postmodern world* (pp. 175–202). Berkeley: University of California Press.

OECD. (2004). Lifelong learning. *OECD Policy Brief*, 1–7.

OECD. (2012a). *Education at a glance 2012: OECD indicators.* Paris: OECD Publishing.

OECD. (2012b). *OECD employment outlook 2012.* Paris: OECD Publishing.

Patton, M. Q. (2002). *Qualitative research and evaluation methods.* Thousand Oaks: Sage.

Rainbird, H. (2000). Skilling the unskilled: Access to work-based learning and the lifelong learning agenda. *Journal of Education and Work, 13*(2), 183–197.

Rainbird, H., Munro, A., & Holly, L. (2004). Exploring the concept of employer demand for skills and qualifications: Case studies from the public sector. In C. Warhurst, I. Grugulis, & E. Keep (Eds.), *The skills that matter* (pp. 91–108). Basingstoke: Palgrave.

Rotter, J. B. (1966). Generalized expectancies for internal versus external control of reinforcement. *Psychological Monographs: General and Applied, 80*(1), 1–28.

Ryan, R. M., & Deci, E. L. (2000). Intrinsic and extrinsic motivations: Classic definitions and new directions. *Contemporary Educational Psychology, 25*, 54–67.

Schraw, G., Bendixen, L. D., & Dunkle, M. E. (2002). Development and validation of the Epistemic Belief Inventory (EBI). In B. K. Hofer & P. R. Pintrich (Eds.), *Personal epistemology. The psychology of beliefs about knowledge and knowing* (pp. 261–275). Mahwah: Erlbaum.

Seligman, M. E. P. (1972). Learned helplessness. *Annual Review of Medicine, 23*, 407–412.

Silbereisen, R. K., Best, H., & Haase, C. M. (2007). Editorial: Agency and human development in times of social change. *International Journal of Psychology, 42*(2), 73–76.

Skaalvik, E. M., & Skaalvik, S. (2004). Self-concept and self-efficacy: A test of the internal/external frame of reference model of subsequent motivation and achievement. *Psychological Reports, 95*, 1187–1202.

Strategy Group. (2011). *National strategy for higher education to 2030.* Dublin: Government Publications Office.

Temple, J. (2001). Generalisations that aren't? Evidence on education and growth. *European Economic Review, 45*, 905–918.

Tims, M., Bakker, A. B., & Derks, D. (2012). Development and validation of the job crafting scale. *Journal of Vocational Behavior, 80*(1), 173–186.

Vähäsantanen, K., Saarinen, J., & Eteläpelto, A. (2009). Between school and working life: Vocational teachers' agency in boundary-crossing settings. *International Journal of Educational Research, 48*, 395–404.

Vroom, V. H. (1964). *Work and motivation*. New York: Wiley.

Watkin, C. (2005). *Classrooms as learning communities*. London: Routledge.

Wehmeyer, M. L. (2001). Self-determination and mental retardation. In L. M. Glidden (Ed.), *International review of research in mental retardation* (Vol. 24, pp. 1–48). Hillsdale: Erlbaum.

Wehmeyer, M. L. (2004). Beyond self-determination: Causal agency theory. *Journal of Developmental and Physical Disabilities, 16*(4), 337–359.

Wrzesniewski, A., & Dutton, J. E. (2001). Crafting a job: Revisioning employees as active crafters of their work. *Academy of Management Review, 26*(2), 179–201.

Part II
Promoting Lifelong Learning for Economic, Social and Cultural Purposes

Chapter 4
Evaluating Informal Learning in the Workplace

Karen E. Watkins, Victoria J. Marsick, and Miren Fernández de Álava

4.1 Evaluating Informal Learning in the Workplace

In this chapter we take up the particular challenges associated with evaluating informal learning in the workplace, given that such learning typically occurs in the context of real work and not in a classroom. We introduce an informal and incidental learning model developed to recognise and support natural learning outside the classroom. We preface the model discussion by examining the complementary, yet competing, pragmatic and sociocultural theory perspectives that differently conceptualise the interaction of individuals and their social environments in shaping workplace learning. In the middle section of the chapter, we illustrate the challenges of evaluating informal and incidental learning through research on communities of practice (CoPs) in the public sector in Spain. We discuss dilemmas that arise from this case for evaluating workplace learning and conclude with implications for credentialing.

K.E. Watkins (✉)
Department of Lifelong Education, Administration and Policy,
The University of Georgia, Athens, GA, USA
e-mail: kwatkins@uga.edu

V.J. Marsick
Department of Organization and Leadership, Teachers College,
Columbia University, New York, NY, USA
e-mail: marsick@tc.columbia.edu

M.F. de Álava
Department of Applied Pedagogy, Autonomous University of Barcelona, Barcelona, Spain
e-mail: Miren.Fernandez@uab.cat

T. Halttunen et al. (eds.), *Promoting, Assessing, Recognizing and Certifying Lifelong Learning: International Perspectives and Practices*, Lifelong Learning Book Series 20, DOI 10.1007/978-94-017-8694-2_4, © Springer Science+Business Media Dordrecht 2014

4.2 Comparing Sociocultural and Cognitive Perspectives on Workplace Learning

Marsick and Watkins' model discussed below grew out of interest in understanding naturally occurring learning at work—outside structured education and training—that at the time was not adequately understood or taken into account in the USA. Over time—likely because of shifts toward knowledge work and globalisation, as well as intelligent technology—this imbalance has shifted as the new norm involves ongoing learning from and through experience. (See, e.g. Marsick and Watkins 2014, and McCauley et al. 2014). Hence, this is an opportune time to examine learning at work in its many forms and formats, whether or not it is facilitated by an "educator".

Two different streams of research on workplace learning grow out of different underpinnings: sociocultural theory and cognitive psychology (Marsick and Watkins 2014). Billett (1996) linked the two views theoretically by identifying common ground: "Both refer to the manipulation or transformation of knowledge, and whereas one focuses on the internal process the other details the negotiated nature of the reciprocal transformation with social partners and sources" (p. 265). Billett identified six bridging areas of complementarity between cognitive and sociocultural theory:

> (i) expertise is domain-specific; (ii) knowledge is constructed through problem solving; (iii) compilation is negotiated in social circumstances; (iv) transfer is a socially and culturally constructed [sic]; (v) individuals' efforts are relational to social practice; and (vi) socially determined dispositional factors are relational to cognitive structures and activities. (Billett 1996, p. 266)

Billett identified problem-solving "through interaction with social sources" (p. 267) as common ground, though how each perspective understands this process reflects their respective emphases. The two different views of how knowledge and learning take place, nonetheless, share focus on "goal-directed activity" through which individuals "access, manipulate and transform cognitive structures which are socially sourced resulting in the construction and organisation of knowledge" (p. 271).

Both theories take problem-solving as a starting point. The model that Watkins and Marsick developed originates in Dewey's pragmatism. It honours the social construction of reality but emphasises inner cognitive processes and the *individual agency and shaping* of social settings. Billett, by contrast, works from sociocultural theory that emphasises *collective agency and shaping* of individuals through interactive norms and resources embedded in social settings. In this model, Watkins and Marsick start with ways that individuals frame and use social circumstances to meet their *own* goals and intentions. Sociocultural theory, by contrast, dwells on "the defining and negotiation which occurs within a particular social situation which makes it problematic to separate individuals' performance of tasks from the social process of defining and negotiating the task and its goals" (Billett 1996, p. 271).

Billett's (1996) reconciliation of the two helps to better understand the value each view brings and "provides a means by which arrangements for learning can be deliberated upon and evaluated" (p. 277). It draws attention to workplace climate, cultures, structures, practices, power dynamics and politics. Although Marsick and Watkins' model does not problematise the social setting in the way that Billett and others have done through their research, their model discussed below recognises the way individuals can interpret or misinterpret the social context, the nature of problems, implementation options, resource constraints and unrecognised consequences—often due to cognitive selectivity, error and bias. Cseh's research in Eastern Europe (Cseh et al. 2000) using this model brought social context to the fore and led to its revision, strengthening its understanding of social settings. Watkins and Marsick also examine social setting through parallel research on learning culture as a critical success factor using the Dimensions of a Learning Organization Questionnaire (Marsick 2013; Watkins and Dirani 2013).

Marsick and Watkins' model likely reflects the national cultures in which this work has originated—as affirmed by Hofstede and Hofstede's (2005) extensive (though critiqued) research on national culture values that shape work. The US workplace is distinctly individual in its orientation with learning and development mandated to develop knowledge and skills that improve performance and boost organisational productivity. Even with changes due to globalisation and the knowledge era, individual achievement is still celebrated.

We turn now to Marsick and Watkins' model of informal and incidental learning.

4.3 Marsick and Watkins' Theory of Informal and Incidental Learning

How does learning occur in the ordinary course of doing one's work? Most workplace learning occurs when something comes up for which an individual does not have the necessary knowledge or skills. They do not get the results they expected, a new initiative is launched, they are promoted to a new position that demands new skills, or a similar problem or opportunity jolts them into a learning cycle. Marsick and Watkins' (1990) model of informal and incidental learning depicts how learning outside the classroom can occur when situated within work.

Marsick and Watkins (1990) defined informal and incidental learning by contrasting them with formal learning:

> Formal learning is typically institutionally-sponsored, classroom-based, and highly structured. Informal learning, a category that includes incidental learning, may occur in institutions, but it is not typically classroom-based or highly structured, and control of learning rests primarily in the hands of the learner. Incidental learning...is defined by Watkins as a by-product of some other activity, such as task accomplishment, interpersonal interaction, sensing the organisational culture, trial-and-error experimentation, or even formal learning. Informal learning can be deliberately encouraged by an organisation or it can take place despite an environment not highly conducive to learning. Incidental learning, on the other hand, almost always takes place although people are not always conscious of it. (p. 12)

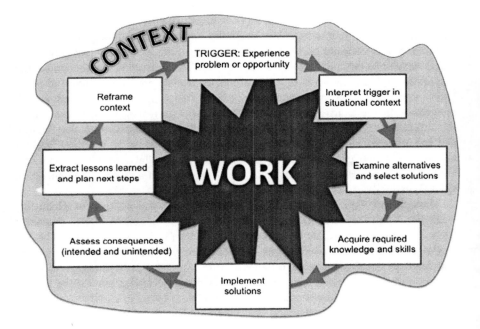

Fig. 4.1 Marsick and Watkins' informal and incidental learning model (Marsick et al. forthcoming. Adapted from Marsick et al. 2009)

In an extensive review of the literature on informal learning, Livingstone (2001) uses a definition of informal learning from the Centre for Education and Work (2004): "Learning resulting from daily life activities related to work, family, or leisure. It is not structured in terms of learning objectives, learning time or learning support and typically does not lead to certification" (p. 3). Informal learning is often intentional, though not always related to specific objectives, but much learning, as Livingstone further asserts, "is non-intentional, incidental or random (Ibid.)".

Marsick and Watkins (1990) propose an informal learning model that is based on the problem-solving cycle. They propose that people learn from their experience when they face a challenge or problem that is new to them in some way, triggering a fresh look at their situation, followed by a search for alternative responses, action and evaluation of results. Learners are constrained in their ability (1) to make meaning of the experience by their framing of the situation, (2) to enact the solutions they envision and (3) to interpret lessons learned. Drawing on six learning theories, Watkins and Marsick (1997) identified characteristics of informal and informal learning. Characteristics include (1) internal or external triggers causing reinspection of "givens" or taken for granted "truths", (2) an openness to new information and interpretations and (3) a resolution, ideally at a higher level of understanding, competence and/or maturity. Figure 4.1 depicts their model of informal and incidental learning.

Billett (2002) critiques the idea of categories of formal and informal learning, seeing more of a continuum and considerable overlap between the two ideas. He argues that there is formal and informal *education*—but that learning is much more protean and the learners' meaning making is similar whether learning occurs in a more formal setting and structure. Marsick and Watkins hold that learning is indeed constructed in both settings but that the degree of variability of the outcomes, the depth of learning and the potential for both serendipitous and errorful learning increase in more informal settings (Marsick and Watkins 1990; Marsick et al. 2002).

Marsick and Watkins' (1990) model is an empirically derived understanding of *how people learn* using informal approaches in the workplace. In practice, individuals may not set out explicitly to accomplish particular ends through pre-planned means. Often, their choices evolve from interaction with others in the midst of work activities. Sometimes people are conscious of these choices; at other times, they remain unaware. Reflection is needed, not only to make more effective use of informal and incidental learning but, more importantly, to unearth erroneous assumptions and mistakes, forestall unintended negative consequences and even achieve learning-propelled transformation. Frequently, an outsider or a disinterested third party serves to prompt and facilitate the reflection, or reflection occurs in groups such as action learning groups or communities of practice.

The strongly interpersonal nature of this learning is evident at each stage of the process. This leads Fenwick (2003) to rethink experiential learning entirely. Drawing on the notion of co-emergence in complex adaptive systems, Fenwick notes:

> A workplace project, for example, is a collective activity in which interaction both enfolds and renders visible the participants, the objects mediating their actions and dialogue, the problem space that they define together, and the emerging plan or solution they devise. As each person contributes, she changes the interactions and the emerging object of focus; other participants are changed, the relational space among them all changes, and the looping-back changes the contributor's actions and subject position within the collective activity. (p. 7)

This co-emergence demonstrates the essential interactive nature of learning in the workplace and the importance of the context (Cseh et al. 2000). Similarly, Gherardi (2013) focuses on learning in and through practice and how it leads to an awareness that "Learning and practice and learning a practice enables us to focus on the fact that, in everyday practices, learning is not an activity separate from others; it instead takes place in the flow of experience, with or without our being aware of it" (p. 30). Gherardi (2009) makes clear that the flow of experience is social, in relationship to other people and a particular context, "To know is to be capable of participating with the requisite competence in the complex web of relationships among people, material artifacts and activities. Acting as a competent practitioner is synonymous with knowing how to connect successfully with the field of practice…" (p. 118).

Indeed, we might reconceptualise the social nature of informal and incidental learning as depicted in Fig. 4.2.

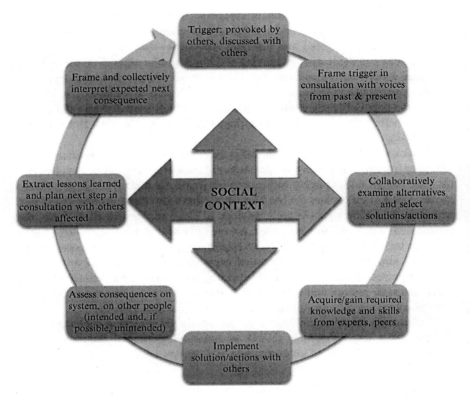

Fig. 4.2 Marsick and Watkins' model adapted to reflect social nature of informal and incidental learning

Scholars note that this learning is omnipresent in the workplace, most estimating as much as 80 % of workplace learning *to be* informal (Bruce et al. 1998; Leslie et al. 2003; Lowenstein and Spletzer 1999; McCall et al. 1988; Zemke 1985). Paradoxically, 70 % of learning is estimated to be informal, but in contrast, 70 % of resources are spent on formal training and education (Cross 2007). Informal learning can be planned but includes incidental learning that is not designed or expected. Writers often intermingle the terms "informal and incidental learning", presenting a challenge to the researcher who would tease them apart. For example, in an investigation of the Teaching Firm, Bruce et al. (1998) seemed to ignore the concept of incidental learning. However, they included within informal learning the "acquisition and application of skills and knowledge; movement along the continuum from inexperience to confidence; and maturity and expertise in regard to specific tasks, skills, and knowledge... [in a learning process that] is neither determined nor designed by the organisation" (p.15). The authors also highlighted the critical role of contextual factors in informal workplace learning, and they listed intrapersonal and interpersonal skills as well as cultural assimilation among the participants' learning.

Marsick and Watkins (1990) define incidental learning as "a by-product of some other activity, such as task accomplishment, interpersonal interaction, sensing the organisational culture, trial-and-error experimentation or even formal learning" (p. 12). Thus, all human experiences—including intentional learning activities, both formal and informal—are potential settings for incidental learning.

Moreover, Marsick and Watkins (1990) agree with Fenwick (2006) that informal learning that is prompted by the needs of the organisation, and sometimes direct command or request of powerful others, may differ considerably from learning for one's own purposes. People do pursue their own learning, but the research shows that the natural work groups and communities of practice through which they learn influence the learning process and outcomes (Billett 2002). Indeed, Billett (1994) argues that learning arrangements situated in a culture of practice must be embedded in the social relational context of that practice for optimal learning to occur. The organisational context is thus a powerful mediator of an individual's learning. In organisations, learning typically occurs in groups who have a life together outside of the classroom, one which is continuous over a long period of time. These people share norms, a culture and meanings that are so mutually reinforced that individuals may seldom consider the possibility that other meanings are thinkable. So the social nature of informal learning is a critical aspect and affects what is learned. One form of informal learning that examines the social nature of this learning and fits well with the concept of co-emergence is that of communities of practice.

Communities of practice (CoPs)—in their original conceptualisation—are naturally occurring, emergent groups at whose core are interdependent, usually practical interests (Wenger 1998). Lave and Wenger (1991) refer to groups of individuals who come together to share their knowledge of practice in stories. These stories become a repertoire of the know-how of expert practice, a constantly evolving "database" passed on over the water cooler, through blogs, through professional groups, both at and away from work. Brown and Duguid (1991), for example, focus on what and how people learn while collaborating to solve problems. Indeed, they contend that learning is closely intertwined with work practice in that it is:

- Narrative, serving as both diagnosis and repository of accumulated wisdom
- Collaborative, crossing administrative boundaries and pervading all phases of life
- Socially constructed, building identity and membership as problems are solved

A case study of CoPs illustrates how these entities might lead to both formal assessment and credentialing of informal learning. But it also raises more questions. The Catalan case was selected, even though occurring in a European context, because it illustrates challenges experienced in similarly hierarchical organisations in the USA as well—especially when organisations seek to "control" and "manage" what is essentially an organic, self-directed learning phenomenon. It could be argued that intrinsically motivated learning that occurs naturally in CoPs should not be evaluated externally by the organisation. Yet as discussed here, CoP members might seek recognition for their accomplishments—posing the question of how such evaluation can best be framed and carried out, which is what the research investigated. The two examples in the case provide rich description in order to shed light on the way each social context and workplace culture differently affects learning—even though both agencies are part of the same overall government initiative to encourage collaborative knowledge sharing.

4.4 Communities of Practice in Public Administration in Spain

The CoPs described here were catalysed by a change process in the Directorate General for Citizen Attention (DGAC) in 2004 that was designed to replace a traditional hierarchy for a horizontal structure based more on collaborative knowledge sharing among professionals. To achieve this goal, the DGAC established an online collaborative working environment, e-Catalunya (http://ecatalunya.gencat.cat), for all the staff of the Catalan Public Administration: both substitute/temporary staff and civil servants with career job security based on competitive examinations.

DGAC CoPs are designed differently but generally include (a) participants who are more or less actively engaged in activities based on interests and other factors, (b) moderators who drive the learning and work process, (c) discussion and debate on topics using the *e-Catalunya* tools such as forums or wikis and (d) end products, the creation of which often merits recognition in the form of a certificate of participation.

Questions arose in two departments—the Department of Justice (DJ) and the Health Protection Agency (ASPCAT, is the Spanish and/or Catalan acronym)—about how CoPs can count toward satisfying a collective agreement, in the Catalan Public Administration, for professionals to participate, annually, in a maximum of 40 h of training as part of their work schedule. The first option, more widely selected, is formal training—activities of 20 h, divided in sessions of 4 h. The second option is informal learning by participating in a CoP and two face-to-face meetings. Formal training was counted through class hours, but it was less clear how participants in CoPs would be assessed to meet annual professional development requirements.

Informal learning always varies with the context in which it occurs, so descriptions are included here for CoPs in each agency.

The Department of Justice. The Centre for Legal Studies and Specialized Training (CEJFE) in the DJ provides specialist training to all members of the DJ. In 2005, the CEJFE launched *Compartim* (*let's share,* in English) to promote personal and professional development and to improve quality and organisational results. Members of these CoPs work, for example, in juvenile justice, prisons and judicial libraries.

Characterised by intensive use of technology, although there are also face-to-face meetings, these CoPs use the *e-Catalunya* tools. The moderator is central to these CoPs. He/she creates a pleasant climate, encourages motivation, builds morale and structures all generated knowledge. A new topic is selected each year by the organisation, and a small group of active participants join in discussion and debate. Once debate is concluded, the moderator shapes and publishes contributions in the form of leaflets, papers, manuals, etc. for widespread dissemination—providing access to both active and less active CoP participants. They are uploaded on the DJ web page so that everyone in the department can access results.

Over the past 8 years, approximately 1,400 professionals have worked on different topics, such as ICT in prisons, interventions on suicidal behaviours, ethical issues for technical advice with children and legal information dissemination services, among others.

The Catalan Health Protection Agency. The Health Protection Agency (ASPCAT)'s purpose is to protect the public from food- and drink-related health hazards, to integrate health protection services and activities and coordinate with other agencies. ASPCAT health professionals work in slaughterhouses, health inspection and the food industry. In 2007—modelled after the experience of the DJ—the ASPCAT launched its own CoPs.

However, unlike the DJ, CoPs did not qualify for meeting the 40-h annual training requirement. CoPs were attractive because many ASPCAT employees work individually in isolated circumstances. The ASPCAT set out to replace these circumstances with collaborative teamwork and learning. Members, for their part, were attracted by the opportunity to solve challenging problems in conversation with others and to gain new skills or upgrade existing capabilities. The CoP was expected to stimulate internal promotion, promote informal learning and strengthen training across public health disciplines and functions.

In 2008, the ASPCAT developed six CoPs involving 76 members. Their success led to form, in 2009, a knowledge management team and to approve a plan aimed at creating a knowledge sharing culture and at creating horizontal networks to encourage informal learning and professional development to meet organisational requirements. Each year new topics are addressed. So far, these CoPs have involved 382 employees who have worked on topics such as chemical dangers related to sunflower oil, water not suitable for human consumption, and health education in schools (food hygiene), among others.

Research on DJ and ASPCAT CoPs. Fernández de Álava researched these CoPs in 2012–2013 as part of a doctoral thesis through a R&D project of the Ministry of Economics and Competitiveness entitled "Knowledge Creation and Management in Online Communities of Professional Practice" (EDU2010-18506). Her study focuses on describing these CoPs and finding out how professionals in both agencies preferred their participation in CoPs to be recognised and certified. Case studies were carried out using multiple data collection methods: survey, interviews (with CoP managers, participants and moderators), observation and document analysis. The information discussed in this chapter derives from all of these sources.

Surveys were designed to elicit information about members' professional background (31 items), the organisational culture and environment (9 items), informal learning (36 items) and evaluation and certification of informal learning experienced in the CoPs (27 items). Items were developed based both on the literature and on field work in the agencies as a first step in the research. The online survey was administered to a total population in both the DJ and ASPCAT at the time of study of 108 participants in, and moderators of, these CoPs. Reliability analysis, T-tests, Z-tests and descriptive statistics were conducted on 81 usable questionnaires ($n = 48$ from DJ, $n = 33$ from ASPCAT).

Evaluation-related items are here considered for both agencies taken together. However, interviews also shed light on differences in the social context that affected the ease or difficulty with which participants in each agency engaged. A key difference is that CoPs in the DJ were proposed by management to encourage employees to learn in these new ways, whereas at the ASPCAT, CoPs grew out of the isolation of some health-care professionals, such as those engaged in inspecting cattle destined for slaughter, environmental protection workers, and those addressing various forms of addiction treatment. Data were not collected specifically on intrinsic vs. extrinsic motivation, but interviews indicate that CoPs at the ASPCAT may have been driven by high need to learn in the face of isolating work circumstances and the nature of the challenges encountered on the job. CoP participation enabled helpful social exchange and problem-solving. Both CoPs were designed as horizontal networks, yet they were differently managed. In the ASPCAT, any professional could take on the role of moderator, whereas at the DJ, the moderator was designated by management. CoPs in ASPCAT thus solved problems of greatest interest to many members.

Survey items related specifically to evaluation and certification of the informal learning derived from the CoP probed views on the following: (1) evaluation of participation in CoP, (2) methodologies for evaluation, (3) perception of certification, (4) importance of certification and (5) influence of certification.

Key findings from the survey data indicate that:

- 91 % of CoP participants felt that organisations should evaluate the utility of the newly acquired competencies in daily practice.
- 80 % believe that organisations should evaluate transfer to other contexts of what is learned in CoPs.
- CoP participants agreed most with the statements that informal learning certification emphasises the role that this learning plays and it gives importance to the learning that derives from daily practice.
- CoP participants felt most strongly that recognising informal learning acknowledges the organisation as a place of continuous learning, promotes a knowledge sharing culture and has a positive effect on the organisation.

Interviews related to evaluation and certification of informal learning derived from the CoP focused on the following questions: "It appears that participation in a CoP is recognised as training, but a high percentage of participants believe that there is no recognition. Do you agree? If no, what type of recognition is used? If yes, what strategies could be followed to ensure that participants feel recognised for their participation in the CoP? How should these strategies be applied?" Finally, an open-ended question was included that requested interviewees to rate items that seem associated with recognition due to "immobility in the status of career staff". All of the interviews were transcribed and analysed using qualitative data analysis software Atlas Ti 5.0.

Findings: The Paradox of Extrinsic Mandates vs. Intrinsic Motivation. As noted earlier, civil servants have job security; that is, barring a serious mistake or error, they hold their jobs until they retire, so they do not fear job loss or demands that they certify their knowledge and experience in career-related advancement. However, there is a need to update knowledge and skills in order to adapt to a continuously changing environment (Delors 1996). Research on intrinsic motivation suggests that rewards and recognition for intrinsically motivated learning are very different than those needed for learning based on extrinsic motivation (Deci et al. 2001). Professionals may well be intrinsically motivated to learn in CoPs. However, the externally regulated collective agreement still requires civil servants to undertake a maximum of 40 h of training. While DJ members can elect participation in a CoP *instead of* training, ASPCAT members who participate in CoPs must *also* take 40 h of training. It could be paradoxical to reward professionals with certificates for sitting in training for 40 h, whether or not the topic is relevant or learning is optimal, but *not* reward or value intrinsically motivated work and learning on authentic work-based questions and challenges.

Findings: Dilemmas Surrounding Certification. Some dilemmas regarding certification were uncovered through the interviews that differed by agency. Participants in the DJ CoPs can engage during their work hours, and if they participate actively, they receive a certificate validating the required hours. However, not all participate actively, and hence, do not receive certification. DJ members noted, for example, "Recognition exists only if you demonstrate active participation … If participation is based on reading, you do not receive the certificate". Another member also noted that "people who have followed the programme and apply the knowledge in the workplace do not receive any certificate".

For some DJ CoP members, even though participation is recognised, managers do not respect or credit their accomplishments. The training mentality has to change, as one person puts it: "There are still managers who think that training is [only] in a class, with a teacher and a blackboard". At the same time, peers recognise the value of the learning products. A moderator described an email from an educator who used materials on a programme of sexual-affective education who used and valued the programme. The moderator contrasted this peer recognition with that of managers for whom recognition "depends on the centre [government]".

For the ASPCAT, participation in CoPs is not included in their work schedule, so they learn in their leisure hours. Recognition comes only from the CoP's participants and other colleagues and, externally, from other departments that request and value the end products developed. As members explained:

We participate in the CoP [because] we believe in what we are doing and because we think that our profession can make progress that way.

For me there is, at least, recognition within your working group … of the work done, of your implications, and that recognition enriches you.

From the outside they recognise the value of our work, but on the other hand, our managers put the brakes on the CoP.

Dilemmas such as these raise the following questions for ASPCAT participants and moderators: Do I have to participate in a CoP in order to improve my knowledge without any formal recognition and through investing much of my leisure time (more than 40 h) to successfully complete the work involved? Or should I simply attend some formal lessons, courses, seminars, etc. that, automatically, entail a certificate even though they are not related to my workplace?

Findings: Assessment Preferences. Because participants value the CoP and want it to be sustained, they are willing to find various ways to validate informal learning in their agencies. Survey results indicate that, however, there is little consensus on the actual means of evaluating learning in CoPs with 65 % preferring to write a personal development portfolio and 55 % preferring observation in the workplace by an assessor. In addition:

- 50 % (DJ) and 42.4 % (ASPCAT) accept being interviewed by an assessor to explain the learning process and the newly acquired competences.
- 70.8 %5 (DJ) and 39.4 % (ASPCAT) agree to write a portfolio with all the contributions made in the CoP and a summary of lectures.
- 72.9 % (DJ) and 57.6 % (ASPCAT) approve preparing a personal development portfolio; that is, they will describe their initial knowledge when beginning investigation of a topic as well as the final knowledge gained as a result of participation.
- 56.3 % (DJ) and 54.5 % (ASPCAT) agree to be observed in their workplace, i.e., in the presence of an assessor, to prove application of newly acquired competence on the job.

On the one hand, it is encouraging to see the level of interest in evaluation of learning in the CoPs in this study. On the other hand, the pressure exerted by formal evaluation policies as to what can or cannot be counted toward a training requirement may have affected attitudes toward evaluation of knowledge gains. Job security, however, makes public service positions attractive and might mitigate against job dissatisfaction from other sources. Other sources of recognition for performance could also have been considered in these CoPs, though they go beyond the research project's focus on learning in CoPs—for example, career advancement, allocation of desirable work assignments, changes to scope of work and other job-based beneficial adjustments to one's role or tasks.

Critique from Perspective of Communities of Practice. This case demonstrates the potential of CoPs to generate significant learning in the workplace. Much has been written about whether or not CoPs can achieve the potential for which they have been lauded. Given the highly centralised context in the two agencies in this study prior to introducing CoPs, the move in each agency toward greater decentralisation and collaborative knowledge sharing appeared to be a step toward improved learning and knowledge sharing. On the other hand, much is not known about the nature of participation among members. Hodges (1998), for example, explores the ways "a community of practice is organized … [that] make participation contingent on identifying, or dis-identifying, within ideological constructs" embraced by powerful discourse within the community in ways that may require members to "practice the suppression of difference" in order to embrace membership (p. 289). Power dynamics—reinforced within organisations by sanctioned structures and practices—can be coercive rather than liberating.

At the same time, the case thus illustrates common concerns about CoPs as an informal learning strategy. Since learning is situated within a particular work context, the degree to which that context is learning rich has the potential to facilitate or constrain what is learned. Edwards (2005) also argues that CoPs focus on what is known, and are less useful for learning something new, and that they are more focused on what is done than what is actually learned. Roberts (2006) adds that CoPs are affected by power dynamics, levels of trust and "path-dependent" habits of mind that limit what is learned. She concludes that despite its limitations, however, a CoP "approach does provide us with a means to explore the transfer of tacit knowledge in a social context" (p. 637).

In this section, we explored CoPs as one form of informal learning that is particularly social and that might be amenable to credentialing. At the same time, we have noted that this approach has certain inherent limitations that make assessment problematic. We see a number of dilemmas that spring as much from the idea of certification as from the nature of informal and incidental learning that affect whether or not this learning can be evaluated for credentialing purposes.

4.5 Dilemmas in Assessing Informal Learning

There are many dilemmas in assessing informal learning, some of which relate to a clearer understanding of what it is that should be evaluated in experience-based learning. Fenwick (2003), for example, critiques the excessive emphasis in much theory on reflection and rationality in scholarship and practice at the expense of embodied learning that leads to an emphasis on conceptualised lessons of experience but not their embedded in the situations and conditions in which human beings struggle. What becomes assessed and rewarded then, argues Fenwick, becomes patterned toward decontextualised products of learning.

Another dilemma in assessing informal learning is the ubiquitous, self-directed nature of that learning. How does one capture and codify something so omnipresent, individually tailored, emergent and so invisibly conducted? And should one do so? Bell et al. (2009) recognise that the contextual, learner-centred and social nature of informal learning is not captured in most individual learning outcomes: "Other important features of informal environments for science learning include the high degree to which contingency typically plays a role in the unfolding of events—that is, much of what happens in these environments emerges during the course of activities and is not prescribed or predetermined" (p. 56). Livingstone (2001) summarises research on assessing informal learning and focuses on core dilemmas that assessment will introduce rigidity to an inherently creative process and that learners do not necessarily know what they have learned or cannot articulate it. He quotes, "Furthermore, many experts have great difficulty articulating complex knowledge they have acquired through informal learning because it has become so integrated into what they do that it is no longer easily accessible to conscious description (Kercel et al. 2005)" (Livingstone 2001, p. 31).

Even though assessment is a faulty process, in US workplaces that are biased toward instrumentality, to *not* assess outcomes may be a disservice to employees. It is perhaps just that possibility that drove interest in evaluation among members of CoPs in the government agencies in Spain described above.

Perhaps because it is so difficult to assess, informal and incidental learnings are typically not certified in the USA, whereas structured learning can be assessed through class hours, through examinations or through an independent credentialing body. Lack of assessment, with corresponding lack of uniformity in meaningful criteria for interpreting competence, creates a lack of portability of skills. Given that employees today seldom work in the same organisation throughout their working lives—a condition that did not pertain in the CoPs in the government agencies in Spain—how can competence and expertise be recognised without reducing it to a lowest common denominator? How does one translate knowledge gained informally through work and learning experiences into transportable, meaningful "credentials"? Do credentials need to be uniformly meaningful to all parties engaged in assessment? Or can there be agreement as to some threshold of competence without closing off appreciation for, and access to, a range of embodied experience-based learning outcomes that can contribute to a rich learning environment in workplaces joined by new employees with these capabilities? Evidence to support this view can be garnered from accounts of ways that individuals draw upon their rich personal life experience, as well as earned qualifications, when solving problems or generating new ideas to address nonroutine challenges that call for innovation at work.

One way to think about assessment is the practice of professional associations that provide continuing education units via providers that have met standards developed by each profession. The American Society for Training & Development, for example, will certify trainers after participation in activities they offer based on evidence of performance to standard in the specified area [see http://www.astd.org/Certification]. Certification carries many benefits, not the least of which is protection for those who use a learner's products or services and the learners themselves who can point to external certification of knowledge and skills to current and future employers. In an age when people frequently change jobs, by necessity or choice, certification provides a way to document skills to new employers making the learning gained transparent and portable.

Gorard et al. (1999) argue that credentialing privileges learning in some domains, most notably job-related, over other important areas for enrichment. Based on analysis of participation in learning in South Wales, they show that, while not easily identified and rewarded, many kinds of informal learning on the job are essential to a well-functioning organisation as well as being important to a person's lifelong needs and development. They reviewed 3,787 work episodes in the work histories of 1,104 respondents. They found that work-related formal training has either not increased, or is on the decline, and is biased toward shorter episodes, frequently targeted in the earlier years of work and often in areas of legal compliance or risk such as health and safety. Such learning is often mandatory, not certified, not transferable and paid for by government agencies. "The relative lack of substantive training in work episodes suggests that informal learning still has a key role for individuals adapting to new work situations, and that this may be becoming more important but probably less highly regarded" (p. 443). The authors found that many interviewees valued learning informally, within or outside of work, but the kind of learning that is funded and made available is learning that is credentialed and related to vocational improvement. Moreover, many instances of valuable informal learning in the workplace are not readily supported because they are hard to measure.

Support for the need to document and credential informal learning is offered by Scully-Russ (2005) who notes: "Some of the negative impacts on low-wage workers because of frequent job changes might be mitigated if workers could carry with them traditional tenure-based benefits—wage increases, skill recognition, social capital, portable benefits—as they move between firms" (p. 272). In an increasingly competitive global economy, workers are advantaged when their knowledge is portable. Hence, there is growing interest by some unions, professional associations, educational providers and employment specialists in finding ways to award certificates that testify to the gaining of expertise in performance-related skills.

Governments in Europe seek ways to document capabilities over one's lifetime. For example, Norway's Realkompetanse Project is designed to "give adults the right to document their non-formal and informal learning without having to undergo traditional forms of testing" (Vox 2002, p. 5).

Numerous approaches have been attempted to "formalise" informal learning so that it could be both assessed and used either for credentialing or for certification of continuing education. One approach developed by Watkins and Wiswell (1987) resulted in a "Learning Practices Audit" that identified formal, informal and incidental learning approaches. Respondents indicated the number of hours per month they spent engaging in each activity. Hours were the metric that allowed us to equate informal learning to the approach used in the USA to measure continuing education units—ten hours of seat time equals one CEU [continuing education unit]. The organisation primarily sets expectations, creates opportunities, provides resources and supports learners through its culture. For example, Watkins and Cervero (2000) were asked to provide expert testimony regarding the informal learning of two accounting firms. The question was whether or not the learning provided was sufficient and equivalent. So Watkins developed an audit of formal, informal and incidental learning practices in an accounting firm, and they assessed both degrees of participation by the individuals involved and whether or not the learning practice was available at each firm. They concluded there was no difference in either participation rates or learning available to the accountants in either firm. What made this study of particular interest was the inclusion of the idea that an organisation might be held accountable for how "learning rich" it was in making informal and incidental learning available.

They developed and used a checklist to assess organisational capacity to support individual participation in professional development activities that lists formal, informal and incidental learning opportunities. Individuals checked whether or not each option is available at their organisation and whether or not they participated in that activity during the last year. Using the checklist may enhance individual and organisational awareness of learning opportunity availability and utilisation.

4.6 Implications for Credentialing Informal and Incidental Learning

We have concentrated our discussion on the learning individuals undertake as part of their work. The larger question of how their work and learning experiences might translate into creditable, credentialed learning is more complex. Work by the Council for Adult and Experiential Learning and the American Council on Education in the USA has focused on translating learning at work and in life into college credit. This approach, like that in Europe, focuses on the competencies and courses associated with certain training and degree programmes. While the USA does not have the workforce qualifications specified as they are in Europe, they do have the College Level Examination Program [CLEP], Advanced Placement examinations [AP], ACE credit equivalencies and prior learning assessments. In a study of prior learning assessment in the community college, researchers at CAEL found that of 88 community colleges who responded to the online survey:

- 64 % offer portfolio assessments
- 90 % accept CLEP exam credit
- 93 % accept AP exam credit
- 85 % offer challenge exams
- 82 % use the ACE Guides to award credit to students with military transcripts (Brigham and Klein-Collins 2010, p. 2)

At the CAEL website, http://www.learningcounts.org, individuals can enrol in courses to complete portfolios for up to 12 college credits for less than the cost of one credit at many colleges and universities. Emphasis is both on valuing individuals' prior learning at work, in the military and in life and on decreasing the time and cost of a college degree.

These movements have had mixed success in the USA. Lacking a national system of qualifications and consensus on competencies, credentialing of prior learning has focused on core disciplines [e.g. French], general education courses [Mathematics, English] and known equivalents where some standardisation has occurred [e.g. some in-company engineering training to a standard, leadership experience in the military and union apprenticeship programmes] rather than the more common forms of informal job-related learning.

Mandatory continuing professional education has acknowledged informal learning. For example, for CFAs (Certified Financial Analysts), individuals can document self-study, in-house training and sponsored training to the extent that it fits a global body of investment knowledge identified by members of the CFA Institute [http://www.cfainstitute.org/learning/continuinged/mce/Pages/index.aspx].

The American Bar Association has mandatory legal education standards for each state, and participants document their participation with most states allowing some forms of independent and self-study. These efforts approximate the interest in documenting vocational qualifications in Europe. However, in Europe, legislation has permitted development of both more standardised models of qualifications but also advances in means of assessing experiential learning.

It is clear that there are a number of very decentralised examples in the USA of movement in the direction of credentialing experiential learning, yet it is also evident that the lack of either national policy or sufficient employer interest means that efforts to evaluate and give credit for prior learning will remain underutilised and undervalued. The study from Catalan offers evidence that individual informal learners may be more receptive to receiving such credit.

References

Bell, P., Lewenstein, B., Shouse, A. W., & Feder, M. A. (Eds.). (2009). *Learning science in informal environments: People, places, and pursuits. Committee on Learning Science in Informal Environments.* Washington, DC: National Academies Press.

Billett, S. (1994). Situated learning – A workplace experience. *Australian Journal of Adult and Community Education, 34*(2), 112–130.

Billett, S. (1996). Situated learning: Bridging sociocultural and cognitive theorizing. *Learning and Instruction, 6*(3), 263–280.

Billett, S. (2002). Critiquing workplace learning discourses: Participation and continuity at work. *Studies in the Education of Adults, 34*(1), 56–67.

Brigham, C., & Klein-Collins, R. (2010). *Availability, use and value of prior learning assessment within community colleges.* Chicago: Council for Adult and Experiential Learning.

Brown, J. S., & Duguid, P. (1991). Organizational learning and communities-of-practice: Toward a unified view of working, learning, and innovation. *Organization Science, 2*(1), 40–57.

Bruce, L., Aring, M. K., & Brand, B. (1998). Informal learning: The new frontier of employee & organizational development. *Economic Development Review, 15*(4), 12–18.

Centre for Education and Work. (2004). *Learning at work: Workplace appraisal of informal learning.* Winnipeg: Centre for Education and Work.

Cross, J. (2007). *Informal learning: Rediscovering the natural pathways that inspire innovation and performance.* San Francisco: Pfeiffer.

Cseh, M., Watkins, K., & Marsick, V. (2000). Informal and incidental learning in the workplace. In G. Straka (Ed.), *Concepts of self-directed learning* (pp. 59–74). Bremen: Waxmann.

Deci, E. L., Koestner, R., & Ryan, R. M. (2001). Extrinsic rewards and intrinsic motivation in education: Reconsidered once again. *Review of Educational Research, 71*(1), 1–27.

Delors, J. (1996). *La educación encierra un tesoro.* Paris: Santillana, Ediciones UNESCO.

Edwards, A. (2005). Let's get beyond community and practice: The many meanings of learning by participating. *Curriculum Journal, 16*(1), 49–65.

Fenwick, T. (2003). Reclaiming and re-embodying experiential learning through complexity science. *Studies in the Education of Adults, 35*(2), 123–141.

Fenwick, T. (2006). Tidying the territory: Questioning terms and purposes in work-learning research. *Journal of workplace learning, 18*(5), 266–278.

Gherardi, S. (2009). Introduction: The critical power of the "practice lens". *Management Learning,* *40*(2), 115–128.

Gherardi, S. (2013). Is organizational learning possible without participation? In S. M. Weber et al. (Org.), *Organisation und Partizipation in Organisation und Pädagogik, 13* (pp. 29–43). Wiesbaden: Springer Fachmedien Wiesbaden. doi: 10.1007/978-3-658-00450-7.

Gorard, S., Fevre, R., & Rees, G. (1999). The apparent decline of informal learning. *Oxford Review* *of Education, 25*(4), 437–454.

Hodges, D. C. (1998). Participation as dis-identification with/in a community of practice. *Mind,* *Culture, and Activity, 5*(4), 272–290.

Hofstede, G., & Hofstede, G. J. (2005). *Cultures and organizations: Software of the mind.* New York: McGraw-Hill.

Kercel, S. W., Reber, A. S., & Manges, W. W. (2005). Some radical implications of Bach-y-Rita's discoveries. *Journal of Integrative Neuroscience, 4*(4), 561–565.

Lave, J., & Wenger, E. (1991). *Situated learning: Legitimate peripheral participation.* New York: Cambridge University Press.

Leslie, B., Aring, M. K., & Brand, B. (2003). Informal learning: The new frontier of employee and organizational development. *Economic Development Review, 14*(4), 12–18.

Livingstone, D. W. (2001). *Adults' informal learning: Definitions, findings, gaps and future* *research* (WALL Working Paper No. 21-2001). Toronto: Centre for the Study of Education and Work & Ontario Institute for Studies in Education of the University of Toronto.

Lowenstein, M. A., & Spletzer, J. R. (1999). Informal training: A review of existing data and some new evidence. *Research in Labor Economics, 18*, 402–438.

Marsick, V. J. (2013). The Dimensions of a Learning Organization Questionnaire (DLOQ): Introduction to the special issue examining DLOQ use over a decade. *Advances in Developing* *Human Resources, 15*(2), 127–132.

Marsick, V. J., & Watkins, K. E. (1990). *Informal and incidental learning in the workplace.* London: Routledge.

Marsick, V. J., & Watkins, K. E. (2014). Informal learning in learning organizations. In R. Poell, T. Rocco, & G. Roth (Eds.), *Routledge companion to HRD* (pp. xx–xx). New York: Routledge.

Marsick, V., Watkins, K., & Wilson, J. (2002). Informal and incidental learning in the new millennium: The challenge of being rapid and/or accurate. In M. Pearn (Ed.), *Individual differences* *and development in organisations: A handbook in the psychology of management in organizations* (pp. 249–266). Chichester: Wiley.

Marsick, V. J., Watkins, K. E., Callahan, M. W., & Volpe, M. (2009). Informal and incidental learning in the workplace. In M. C. Smith & N. DeFrates-Densch (Eds.), *Handbook of research on* *adult learning and development* (pp. 570–600). New York: Routledge.

Marsick, V., Nicolaides, A., & Watkins, K. (forthcoming). Adult learning theory and application in human resource and organization development. In N. Chalofsky, T. Rocco, & L. Morris (Eds.), *The handbook of HRD: Theory and application* (pp. 40–63). San Francisco: Jossey-Bass.

McCall, M., Lombardo, M. M., & Morrison, A. M. (1988). *Lessons of experience: How successful* *executives develop on the job.* New York: Lexington Books.

McCauley, C. D., Derue, D. S., Yost, P. R., & Taylor, S. (2014). *Experience-driven leader development: Models, tools, best practices, and advice for on-the-job development.* New York: Wiley.

Roberts, J. (2006). Limits to communities of practice. *Journal of Management Studies, 43*(3), 623–639.

Scully-Russ, E. (2005). Agency versus structure: Path dependency and choice in low-wage labor markets. *Human Resource Development Review, 4*(3), 254–278.

Vox, Norwegian Institute of Adult Education. (2002). *Validation of nonformal and informal learning in Norway: The Realkompetanse Project 1999–2002.* Oslo: VOX on the Instructions of the Ministry of Education.

Watkins, K., & Cervero, R. (2000). Organizations as contexts for learning: A case study in certified public accountancy. *Journal of Workplace Learning, 12*(5), 187–194.

Watkins, K. E., & Dirani, K. M. (2013). A meta-analysis of the dimensions of a learning organization questionnaire: Looking across cultures, ranks, and industries. *Advances in Developing Human Resources, 15*(2), 148–162.

Watkins, K. E., & Marsick, V. J. (1997). *Dimensions of the learning organization.* Warwick: Partners for the Learning Organization.

Watkins, K., & Wiswell, B. (1987). Incidental learning in the workplace. In H. Copar (Ed.), *Proceedings of the human resources management and organizational behavior western regional conference.* Virginia Beach: Virginia Association of Human Resources Management and Organization Behavior.

Wenger, E. (1998). *Communities of practice: Learning, meaning, and identity.* Cambridge: Cambridge University Press.

Zemke, R. (1985). The Honeywell studies: How managers learn to manage. *Training, 22*(8), 46–51.

Chapter 5
Recognising Learning and Development in the Transaction of Personal Work Practices

Raymond Smith

5.1 Work-Learning Perspectives

Social constructivist perspectives of learning, and particularly those based on sociocultural and cultural-historic theories of practice, focus on personal action and collective activity as foundation of the description, analysis and explanation of the human order and endeavour that is learning. It is examining and interpreting what people 'do' and how their 'doing' is ineluctably interconnected with others that can illuminate and substantiate understandings of learning and its legacies. Notable within this 'doing' are developing personal and occupational identities, that is, establishing and negotiating understandings of who one is and what one does, who others understand one to be and how these understandings change through the development process that is living in society. Concomitant within this identity development are knowings of the values, priorities and aspirations that bring meaning to identity and the skills, capacities and attitudes that enable the enactment of what one knows and does with all the others that populate experience. All these 'doings' are elements of learning in social practice, inseparable from it and, thereby, defined as one of the many social relations among people (Lave and Wenger 1991). Work, of course, is one of the many things people do and, paid or unpaid, is a central feature of social activity. Therefore, work-learning (learning in, through and for work) is particularly significant as an illustrative and examinable form of the social practice that is learning. This significance is evidenced by the vast resources contemporary knowledge economies invest in schooling, training and workforce development (OECD 2010); the necessity of working, particularly paid employment, as the primary source of personal wellbeing and social transformation (Edgell 2012); and the nature of work and workplaces as sites where social structures and cultural

R. Smith (✉)
School of Education and Professional Studies, Griffith University, Brisbane, QLD, Australia
e-mail: raymond.smith@griffith.edu.au

T. Halttunen et al. (eds.), *Promoting, Assessing, Recognizing and Certifying Lifelong Learning: International Perspectives and Practices*, Lifelong Learning Book Series 20, DOI 10.1007/978-94-017-8694-2_5, © Springer Science+Business Media Dordrecht 2014

norms are personally and organisationally enacted, in often quite unique ways, as learned occupational practices (Nijhof and Nieuwenhuis 2008).

Considerate of the action and activity that is 'doing' work and accommodative of the multitude of mediating factors that comprise the circumstances of its enactment, constructivist researchers and theorists define work-learning as the socio-personal process and product of workers' situated and relational participation in practice (e.g. Lave and Wenger 1991; Engeström 2001; Fuller and Unwin 2004; Billett 2006). The range of differing emphases and understandings amalgamated in such a unifying definition include disciplines of anthropology and concepts of communities of practice and situated learning (Lave and Wenger 1991); social psychology and concepts of co-participation, relational interdependence (Billett 2006), knotworking and expansive learning (Engeström 2001, 2008); sociology and concepts of structuration (Giddens 1991); philosophy and concepts of lifelong learning (Bagnall 2004) and multidisciplined orientations including concepts of learning environments (Fuller and Unwin 2004) and concepts of the learning society (Jarvis 2006). The salient feature common to this rich set of understandings is participation.

Workers' participation in work is always active, by varying degrees of intensity and intentionality that represent levels or kinds of engagement in the joint activities and events that characterise practice (Billett and Smith 2006). For example, workers can be sometimes effortfully engaged and at other times seemingly indifferent to the requirements of work (Billett 2001). Equally, workers may vigorously pursue improved working conditions and yet can often resist the introduction of changes that support improved working conditions (Kvande 2013). Similarly, workers may find little meaning and purpose in their general work and yet secure life-wide and life-affirming significance through aspects of the roles and responsibilities they enact. Equally, workers may or may not find salient synergies and alignments among their personal occupational goals and those of their workplace (Noon and Blyton 2007). So, the nature of workers' engagement in work can vary greatly as the levels and directions of their self-investment in occupational practice strengthen and weaken through the altered circumstance of their experience.

Further, a fundamental characteristic of work practice is transformation: nothing remains the same (Wertsch 1998) as the constant state of flux that is human activity traverses the moments of time, space, purpose and method in and by which it is enacted. At its simplest, work is seemingly reconstructive of occupational practice. As such, work-learning can be considered a remaking process, a transforming of current circumstances to approximate or secure expected and familiar practice. For example, novice's learning can be considered to be focused on the necessity of learning to do things as they should be done (Smith 2006). When more complex, work can be innovative and creative of new outcomes and new ways of accomplishing them and, thereby, redefining of occupational practice. In such circumstances, work-learning is a genuine making process, a generative rather than reproductive form of transformation. So, whether distinguishably new or familiar and routine, workers are always in the transformational state of doing something; variably, relationally and simultaneously engaging in working, learning, (re)making practice and occupational identity (Billett et al. 2008). It is this 'doing', this socio-personal practice of engagement in work that can be described and explained as learning through the many personal, material, cultural and social changes work accomplishes. The enduring complexities and continuities of these accomplishments are the relational bases from which further activity proceeds. They may be seen as the fundamentals and necessities of lifelong learning. In schooling, in family, in friendships and in work particularly, the transformations that characterise engagement in social activity and the learning that enables them are constituted in the actions (e.g. negotiations, collaborations, transactions, systemic procedures, etc.) that make social activity visible as co-participation in collective practice.

From within this sociocultural and constructivist participation and practice perspective, this chapter focuses on the transformational nature of work and its description and explanation as learning. More specifically, the chapter explores and discusses individual workers' work-learning as the transaction of personal practice. It considers that within the activities of occupational practice, some elements of human agency (i.e. individuals' distinctly personal contributions to collective practice) and the transactions that enable and identify these practices can remain hidden and, thereby, unaccountable as significant resources brought to, generated by and enacted within work. Failure to acknowledge and account for these resources can reduce the capacity of the sociocultural perspective of work-learning to sufficiently describe and explain such learning as co-participative practice. Similarly, such failure can mask salient transformations of person and practice and reduce opportunities to more fully understand how individuals contribute to the collective practices in which they are engaged. Simply put, the chapter contends that making the transactions that characterise workers' personal enactment of work more visible is necessary to understanding work-learning as co-participative practice.

The argument is progressed through the following sections. From this introduction, the conceptual bases of human agency and transaction are outlined. These conceptual bases were foundational of ethnographic research conducted with twelve workers from four different work places and across a range of occupational practices. Findings from the research drawing on specific data illustrative of the personal work practices and experiences of one of the workers are outlined. Three kinds of sets of transactions are elaborated. They are (1) transacting identity through forms of social engagement, (2) transacting goals as personal aspirations and shared purposes and (3) transacting the material as tools and procedures. The chapter concludes in discussion of these findings as indicative of how acknowledging and accounting for the transactions and transformations enacted in work can enhance sociocultural constructivist understandings of work-learning.

5.2 Human Agency

Generally, human agency is the essential quality of activity that simultaneously endorses individuality as both a personal and a collective sociocultural practice. 'I' and 'you' and 'we' are analytically distinct categories of personhood yet remain inseparable in social practice. 'I' am always your 'you' and 'you' are always other and the separation this implies is manifest in the 'we' that unites us as other for each other. Together, 'I' and 'you' and 'we', both personally and collectively, engage in the actions, activities and events that identify us as social beings. And that being, that activity, has impact. We influence experience. Our being in the world identifies us as people who 'have the powers of critical reflection upon their social context and of creatively redesigning their social environment, its institutional or ideational configurations, or both' (Archer 2000, p. 308). It is this influence, the impact it generates and the analytic distinction of 'I' and 'we' that enables others' simultaneous attribution of these powers to individuals and collectives or groups as personal agency.

From the 'I' perspective, personal-individual agency conceptualises the enactment of the self-in-action and the capacities and impacts such actions generate as evidence of individuals' accomplishing some control and influence over what they do and how they do it. At work this enactment is always a collective practice and, therefore, a social accomplishment as individual workers' efforts and intentions, however significant or effective, cannot be considered outside the context in which they are enacted (Eteläpelto and Saarinen 2006; Edwards 2005). Workers, no matter how isolated, self-reliant or individually engaged, are always in relationship with the mediating artefacts of their practice and, therefore, cannot be separated from the social production of their actions. Nevertheless, and as Archer (2000) notes, individuals' capacities and efforts, based in powers of reflection and manifest as redesigning, evidence the person-specific and productive qualities of personal agency. As we intuitively and experientially know, no two are alike (Harris 2006).

From the 'we' perspective, personal-collective agency conceptualises joint-activity as the coming together of resources that accomplish what individuals alone cannot. As solidarity, community and collaboration or as partiality, fragmentation and conflict, the processes and outcomes of shared endeavour shape the relationships from which activity progresses. At work, the team or group is only as productive as its membership cohesion enables, the project only as good as the resources and support it can secure, and the system, its structures and performance only as effective as its interdependencies hold and integrate the procedures and resources by which it operates (Webber and Donahue 2001; Evans and Davis 2005). So, just as the individual cannot act on their world without the necessary involvement of being in and of a context that constitutes them in relationship with others, likewise, the collective (small or large) cannot enact its influence (for better or worse) without the relationships and facilities that connect, first, member with member and, second, members with their context. Equally, that context (i.e. the organisational or social press) cannot accomplish its purposes without the interdependent actions of the individuals and groups by which it is comprised.

Hence, workers' agency is relational and interdependent (Edwards 2005; Billett 2006), emergent in the push and pull of competing and collaborating personal and social preferences and presses to action. Such agency is bounded by its being situated in the specificities of the relations and interdependencies enacted (Evans 2007). Equally, workers' agency is promising of the new, the innovative and the different, as the possibilities inherent in every moment (Wertsch 1998) manifest as 'improvisations [that] are the openings by which change comes about' (Holland et al. 1998, p. 18). Therefore, workers' agency, as it may be identified in the personal actions of any individual worker, is contingent on and enacted in the negotiations among (1) the occupational or vocational norms and expectations of a situated practice that defines specific work; (2) the colleagues, tools and systems that enable and support that work and (3) the person of the worker who activates that work as personal practice.

As Wertsch (1998) asserts, action is influence – it mediates what is to come and is mediated by what has been. That is, to act is to contribute to the way things are and thereby change things from what they were. As such, all action is transformative. Personal-individual agency is the concept that captures and locates this form of trans-formative power, whether weak or strong, within the individual and their practices. To examine this form of agency in and for work is to examine individuals in action and so become engaged in at least three fundamental and concurrent considerations. They are: 'who' is the individual worker and 'how' is their individuality enacted through 'what' they do. These considerations raise issues about understanding the 'self' as a personal and social being who is engaged in the pursuit of substantiating themself and the cultural experience in which they are participating (Holland et al. 1998). These issues go to questions about the multiple and simultaneous subjectivities of the agent (e.g. their roles, identities, aspirations, continuities of personhood, etc.), the relational properties of all the negotiations among these aspects of self (e.g. one is now col-league, also friend, then spouse, once novice, now more expert, still learning, etc.) and the realisation of these properties in enactments of self (e.g. that are variously pur-poseful, indifferent, unintentional, etc.). These are issues about the person and praxis of self. Here, such issues are captured in the conception of worker as individual and agentic 'self-in-action', an experience that is enacted socially. The individual worker is a unique human being, who is always, as Jarvis (2006, p. 5) confirms, in a state of 'becoming ... never unchanging and always social' (Jarvis 2006, p. 5). So, the self-in-action is a socio-personal being, uniquely enacting themselves (and all this entails) in and through the collective activities in which they participate, not as passive represen-tations of a social position, but as agentic transformers of the practices that identify them (Smith 2008). Understanding what initiates and directs workers' learning in par-ticipative practice will be enhanced when more of those practices are visible and open to the scrutiny of reflection and analysis.

5.3   Transaction

Making more visible the properties and qualities (e.g. motivations, subjectivities and relationships) that identify workers in action requires critically examining the nature of their participation. How is participation enacted and what elements and aspects of engagement contribute to and can be considered as learning practices? For many work-learning theorists, such questions are addressed through concepts of interaction. Hence, workers enact their personal work and learning practice as participants in the numerous forms of interaction required of their occupational practice. For example, through cooperating and/or competing for access to resources, through reluctantly or willingly engaging with others and through being coerced, guided or invited into the learning opportunities enabled by their particular circumstances, workers may be viewed as co-participants (Billett 2001). Their interaction is co-participative as, one among many, they co-generate the press for action. From another perspective, workers enact their practice through 'knotworking' (Engeström 2008). That is, workers interact collaboratively as team members bringing their respective inputs to the task at hand. In such interactions the responsibilities for and coordination of the integrated tasks that constitute their work-learning are shared to the point of all participants, if only temporarily, being accountable for the outcomes of their collective efforts. And from yet another perspective, workers negotiate the meaning of their practice as they make the arrangements, debate the understandings and generate the purposes that are foundational of their activities and all across domains ranging from immediate task requirements to life-wide identity formation (Wenger 1998). These forms of interaction (i.e. co-participation, knotworking and negotiation) enable different perspectives and emphases on how workers are connected and disposed to the multiple resources (e.g. people, processes, materials, tools, etc.) that comprise their work practices. However, the concept of interaction, in as much as it can account for the purposeful connection among resources bound in activity, implies their separation outside the activity that brings them together. The concept of interaction is, essentially, a concept of separation. It offers opportunity to describe and explain something of how resources are brought together and what can generate from their connection, but its focus is always on the mechanisms, the procedures and relationships that 'bring' together rather than the understanding that these resources are already in relationship, already together and already transforming each other, if not visibly so.

Further, interaction conceptualises individuals' connection with others, with materials, with the context in which they are situated, that is, with elements of their social environment. However, more than this, individuals' engagement with their environment is a practice of environment and as such cannot be separated from it. That is, practice does not mediate between the person and the environment. Rather, practice is the evidence of the unity that is person-environment, a unity that Dewey and Bentley (1975, p. 109) describe as 'the organism-in-environment-as-a-whole'. In the circumstances of work, that unity can be described as the unity of person, place and practice that is work and which is made visible as the self-in-action and evidenced by their personal practices. So, workers are more than engaged in their work or connected to the resources that comprise their work context or environment. Rather, they are always of their environment: not simply active or interactive within it, but inseparably part of the activity that is them and their environment. And that environment, constituted by the activity that defines it, is always in transformation.

For Dewey and Bentley (1975), the concept that characterises the unity of the environment and its continuous transformation is transaction. That is, all action is transaction. Transaction is the transformative process by which humanity, as knowledge and meaning, as culture and activity, as person and identify, is enacted as change. This experiential state of constant flux can be illustrated through the familiar purchase or commercial transaction.

> ... a trade, or commercial transaction ... determines one participant to be a buyer and the other a seller. No one exists as buyer or seller, save *in and because of* a transaction in which each is engaged. Nor is that all; specific things *become* goods or commodities because they are engaged in the transaction ... Moreover, because of the exchange or transfer, both *parties* (the idiomatic name for *participants*) undergo change; and the goods undergo at the very least a change of locus by which they gain and lose certain connective relations or "capacities" previously possessed. (Dewey and Bentley 1975, p. 270, Italics in the original)

So, through the social transaction of purchase (buying and selling), what belonged to one, now belongs to another, what was valued by one has now been re-valued by the other and each of these others has also been transformed through the transaction that identifies their activity. For example, a bottle of wine that sits as inventory on the shop shelf is transformed to become the celebratory drink at the wedding and the buyer is now owner just as the seller is now no longer able to sell that particular bottle of wine. Similarly, human action, in all its forms, generates and creates the transformations identifiable as new or different ideas, relationships and resources. In the case of the occupational practice of farming wheat, the transaction of tilling turns the ground into a cultivated field, the transaction of planting turns the cultivated field into a crop, the transaction of harvesting turns the crop into grain and the transaction of milling turns the grain into flour that will in turn become bread as the transaction of baking brings yet other actions and different resources to the making of food, to the transformation of all that is transacted. Just as transaction transforms the resources of activity, so it transforms those who enact these activities, for they are also resources, enmeshed with all resources in the dynamic flux of experience. Farmers, like all workers, are multiply engaged in multiple transactions through their enactment of their practice. Now engaged in machinery maintenance, in animal husbandry, in parental duties and in monitoring the latest market fluctuations, the farmer is continually enacting engagement in the multiple transactions that constitute their participation in work, in family, in location, in an agricultural industry sector, in a national economy, etc.

So the meanings of workers; their positionings in activity and the relationships these account for; their things, understandings and purposes; and their bases of entering into subsequent and future activities are enacted in the transactions by which they are transformed. As in the example above, from purchaser to owner, from owner to seller to now holder of other assets that were previously more liquid, less liquid, differently valued or utilised, whatever the case may be, individuals and their practices are identifiable in the nature of their transactions. In the circumstances of work, through practices of learning through participation, as in all activity,

> from birth to death every human being is a *Party*, so that neither he nor anything done or suffered can possibly be understood when it is separated from the fact of participation in an extensive body of transactions – to which a given human being may contribute and which he modifies, but only in virtue of being a partaker in them. (Dewey and Bentley 1975, p. 271)

So, making the transactions that characterise work and learning practices more visible can assist understandings of learning as participative practice by illuminating what and how the transformations that characterise learning are accomplished. Equally, accounting for the personal contributions and transformations enacted in these transactions can assist understandings of learning as a lifelong socio-personal practice.

In summary, the concepts of agency and transaction enable a focus on workers' engagement in work that can illuminate how they invest themselves (intentionally or incidentally) in the activities that constitute their practice and how those investments, or personal contributions, can be accounted as some of the resources transacted and transformed through that engagement. Such a focus is on the person of the worker, not as sovereign individual, but as salient locus of the learning that can be identified through the changes of which they are part. Addressing such issues can support better understandings of what Engeström (2001) defined as fundamental questions any social learning theory must consider, namely, who is the learner and how do they learn. Equally, considering such issues enables ways of viewing what Billett (2006) described as the relational interdependencies that characterise co-participation. So considerations of the characteristics of the relationships enacted in work and the nature of the personal and contextual factors mediating these relationships are supported. In addressing such issues and concerns, the nature of work-learning as change is elaborated in ways that view change as a holistic phenomena that unify work, workplaces and workers in on-going processes of multiple and simultaneous transformations that are reflected in and generative of workers' personal practice.

5.4 Exploring Workers' Personal Practices

Through semi-structured interviews and in-work observations over 18 months, 12 workers discussed their work and learning practices and the many changes and influences they experienced and accounted as significant contributions to how and why they enacted their work in the ways they did. The 12, each engaged in different occupational practices and holding different status and authority positions, were three from each of a restaurant, a fitness centre, an information technology support group and a fire station. The ethnographic research sought to examine the simultaneity of work and learning. The focus was on learning as it may be considered part of work practice, part of workers' engagement in the routine activities of their work, rather than an educational intervention as might be typical of training where intents of specific instruction are enacted. A particular focus throughout was the personal perception of change (organisational, procedural, personal, etc.) and the ways in which such changes could be identified and accounted as emergent from personal practice and consequential of personal effort, intention and preferences (i.e. agency).

The extensive data collection (18 months) and substantial interview periods (from 60 to 90 min each) enabled workers and researchers to witness and reflect on an extensive range of factors that shape the conduct and meaning of personal practice at work. In the findings discussion that follows three kinds of sets of transactions is elaborated. As noted earlier, they are: (1) transacting identity through forms of social engagement, (2) transacting goals as personal aspirations and shared purposes and (3) transacting the material as tools and procedures. These sets of transactions are not offered as definitive or complete. Nor are they discrete. They are interrelated and co-constitutive. They are advanced as some of the kinds of transactions in which workers are engaged and elaborated as possibilities for overcoming the limitations of interaction as the meta-concept that unites the resources of work-learning in participative practice. Data samples from the interview transcripts of Hugh, one of the three firefighters who participated in the research, are utilised. They illustrate the complex integration of personal and contextual factors that accomplish the transformations of person, place and practice that are the substance and gravitas of learning in and through work. Hugh's experience of work and the transactions that identify his personal practice and learning may be considered representative of the kinds of personal identity, goals and material elements of practice enacted by the 12 participants. Each of them was engaged in negotiating and renegotiating their meanings (Lave and Wenger 1991) of themselves and their work practices through transactions related to who they understood themselves to be, what they wanted to do and how they could enact their work, both personally and collectively.

5.5 Transacting Identity Through Forms of Social Engagement

The immediacy of the self-in-action, that is, the sheer presence of being in work (before considerations of choices made or actions taken) carries more than a position in activity and an expectation of what should happen given the social roles and norms that identify position. This fact is often made visible as the source of ironic or slapstick humour in popular culture as when the clearly identified occupational practitioner (usually in a uniform of one type or other) fails to enact their practice as expected (check any Abbott and Costello movie for humorous illustration of how not to be a builder, a policeman, etc.) The individual worker uniquely personalises any social or occupational position by their 'who' that embodies and enacts that position (Harris 2006). Equally, the person, more than their position, activates the response(s) necessitated by their presence. Enacting this immediacy is a person-dependent practice that enables a diverse range of personal and social possibilities (i.e. responses). These enactments and possibilities (potential or actual) are the evidence, substance and influence of the person in and through the contexts and events in which they are engaged. In short, simply being present in activity evidences personal agency and initiates the transactions of self, identity and practice that follow.

To illustrate: Hugh is a firefighter. He works in a large city-based fire station as a full-time employee of the State Fire and Rescue Services. He has not come to this current work as a raw recruit. Rather, he has migrated from his country of birth where he had previously worked as a firefighter after working some years as a slate tile roofer. Hugh is a large and physically powerful man who, on arrival in this country, took employment with a furniture removal company for a few years before applying and successfully joining the state fire and rescue service. As a means of securing extra income, Hugh still works part-time with the removalist company when his firefighting shift rotations permit. In responding to questions about his declared love of the job and the kinds of explanations he has for this, he stated in some of the interviews,

> I enjoy being in the Fire Service because of the actual work, the variety of it, but also the respect that comes with the position. I mean, I first noticed it back home in my local pub. When I was just a roofer the old fellas at the top end of the bar wouldn't particularly speak to me because I was just one of the village boys, you know, but as soon as I joined the Fire Service they all wanted to talk to me, sit down, have a pint, they would all tell me their World War stories. (Int#2)
>
> If I'm at a BBQ and to answer someone asking me what I do, I say, I'm a furniture removalist, they walk away. When I say I'm a fire fighter, then oh man, that's interesting and they start telling you their story – because everyone's got a fire story. They want to talk. (Int#3)
>
> I've had 10 years experience now ... and it's up to me what I say about me and the job. It's a job a lot of people think they could do but no they can't. I can say what I want but you've got to be careful, and I think – oh, I've seen this before, I could say this, I could say that. You can tell by the reactions when they don't know what's happening ... There aren't many people you can talk to about being a firey. (Int#5)

In these brief excerpts, Hugh is acknowledging something of the social origins and meanings of his work: meanings that identify him as the embodiment of a familiar and highly respected social position/occupation. Further, he reveals his personal construal of these meanings in everyday social situations away from work where his occupational practices as a firefighter are enacted as personal social practice. When Hugh enters into these situations, he enters as firefighter, as roof tiler, as furniture removalist, as BBQ guest, as bar patron – as full participant in the occasion. It is not simply the case that a firefighter has entered. Rather, it is the case that Hugh, the person, the unique self-in-action with all his history and legacy of past and current engagement in social activity has entered. His presence in these situations generates transactions of self and occupational identity, transactions over which he has some personal control, particularly in terms of directing the possibilities related to his work. So, some of these possibilities are realised as inclusion and sharing, and a conferred status of respect and interest as he reveals himself as firefighter. Similarly, these possibilities can be realised as exclusion and isolation as he reveals himself to be a furniture removalist. Yet, in as much as these possibilities attach to the diverse social positions Hugh embodies, they remain his to enact within the transactions underway. He knows, from experience both in and out of work, that there is much that could be said about 'who he is' and 'what he does' and how the complexities of these understandings intersect and collide with those outside his immediate work experience.

At other times throughout the interviews, Hugh comments on the often incomprehensibility of the destruction and distress his work experience entails and how discussing such things is both difficult and often inappropriate. He talks about how, increasingly, the work of firefighters is less about emergency responses to fires and more about attending motor vehicle accidents where witnessing human tragedy as loss of life and limb demands very different personal responses than is the case when only buildings are damaged and destroyed. His comments from Int#5 above hint at the tension he contends with as personal practice when the romance of firefighters as social heroes (as might be discussed at social gatherings like BBQs) needs to be tempered by the harsh realities of the tragedies he confronts as part of his work. One conclusion is clear, despite the many who want to talk about his work, Hugh knows there are few he can genuinely talk to about his occupational practice as it is actually and personally enacted.

So, the trajectory and legacy of such transactions wait on the choices and decisions participants will enact as personal practice and, in Hugh's case, additional occupational practice. We can only speculate on what Hugh will discuss with the old fellows at the top of the bar. We can, however, be certain that Hugh's personal presence has generated this particular interaction made all the more salient by his having previously been just another labouring lad in the village. And similarly, at the next BBQ, will Hugh choose to identify himself as a firefighter or a furniture removalist and what factors will influence this decision? These become important considerations because Hugh's occupational practice is transacted in these seemingly casual encounters as he negotiates the terrain of his, others' and society's understandings of the work and position of firefighters.

Firefighters, like furniture removalists, like roof tillers, like guests at a BBQ, are guided by personal, occupational and social norms and expectations (Holland et al. 1998). These elements of sociocultural activity are, like persons and their practices, resources that are being transacted through the flow of activity that identifies them. Hugh transacts these resources through his enactment of them. He may not be completely the subject of his practices (Bourdieu 1998), but he is always the complete personification of them because only he practices the way he does, only he changes the way he does. Hugh enacts his personal practice in ways that derive from his personal construal of what it means to be and work as a firefighter, whether at the bar, at BBQs or at work. It is in all these sites of practice that Hugh transacts his personal and occupational identity through the highly personal practices he multiply enacts as part of the extensive body of transactions through which he and his work are being transformed. Such transactions are learning practices.

5.6 Transacting Goals as Personal Aspirations and Shared Purposes

Hugh is keen to continue working at the large city-based fire station, instead of one of the smaller suburban stations. The constant activity of the larger city stations (there are only two) motivates him to work to secure his position both within his crew and within the station. Generally speaking, a four-member crew operates the standard pump appliance vehicle (i.e. fire truck) that attends to emergency call-outs. Each of the four crew members has specific tasks and responsibilities that can be identified by the seating position each takes in the vehicle. Firefighters, through the normal course of their progression in the service, become senior firefighters who have attained sufficient training qualifications and experience to assume any role and therefore seating position within the vehicle crew. Hugh, who has not attained this rank as yet, is limited to filling position number three in the crew, and there are only two such number three positions available within the station – one per day and evening shift. To secure his place at the station and avoid transfer to a less active suburban station means making himself more flexible within the workplace. This equates to qualifying himself to take on other roles additional to the number three position. This is a difficult task given his official junior status. Hugh explains,

> I want to stay at this station and the only real way to do that is to become an all car driver. It's something I want, so I'm pursuing it.
>
> Yeah well – as it is at the moment, due to my lower rank and limited time in the Fire Service, there's only a number of places I can ride machines. In the back of a pump you get a number one and a number three ... I can't ride as number one. I can only ride as a number 3 and I've not made driver yet, so I can't drive any of the vehicles apart from the control unit, Tango – that's a Mercedes Sprinter van. So that at least allows me 2 positions that I can ride. The more positions you ride the more useful you are to the shift. So I'm pushing now to get made up on second car, Bravo, and then it'll just be experience driving that for a few months before going up to the heavier ones. It's just flexibility – the more useful you are, the easier it is to keep you here because they can slot you in with someone and just move you around – and it also helps the boys. If you've only got two blokes on the shift that drive one particular machine, well it's only ever going to be either of those driving it – and they get stale or they might drive the same thing for months in the same position, doing the same job every day. Well some blokes don't mind it, but some find it a bit limiting. Especially when you get a run of good fires and they're not in a position to be wearing breathing apparatus – actually getting in there, squirting water around – they're back from it a little bit. You start to lose why you joined the job – you know? So it's a combination of making yourself more useful, more flexibility and more change. (Int#5)

Hugh's aspirations (and their interdependence within the structural constraints and affordances of his work) are clear as he 'pushes' to take advantage of the opportunities the station supports. He is not content to hold position number three with its guarantee of 'getting in there' and directly fighting fire: something he could sustain if he accepted being sent to one of the suburban fire stations, that unfortunately for Hugh, do not engage in as many emergency responses as the city stations. So, he must secure his position at the city station by being able to perform other duties. Driving the two smaller control vehicles, Tango and Bravo (vehicles that are equipped with the command and communications facilities necessary for managing larger emergency responses) are not tasks that will get Hugh into the action of directly fighting fires. For Hugh, *actually getting in there* and fighting fires is his primary reason for being a firefighter. The fundamental importance of this is constant throughout Hugh's discussion of his work. However, and importantly for Hugh, becoming a designated driver of these two vehicles is a negotiated opportunity to secure a station position by enabling his greater capacity to be deployed across other essential work tasks and roles. His increased utility may mean being in position three less often and being more valuable at the station, more easily deployed and thereby less likely to be rostered to less active suburban stations.

Hugh's actions and motivations for seeking to stay at the city station evidence a range of transactions of practice through which he measures and evaluates his agency. For example, he explains himself as *pushing* for what is relationally possible as he transacts his aspirations. Similarly, he views himself as relatively successful following his qualifying to drive Tango, the smaller of the two control vehicles. For Hugh, *pushing* means finding time in a busy daily work schedule to devote to driver training without detracting from other duties, not least being ready to attend emergency call-outs. Throughout the interviews, he discusses how he must continually initiate requests for training opportunities that will support his aspirations to remain at the station. Pushing means badgering senior station officers to set aside time, to organise contingencies and to allocate appropriately qualified staff to supervise driver training. It means being diplomatic in all of this, being careful to balance personal priorities with the capacities and interests of colleagues and work requirements. Pushing means being successful, knowing that the right balance of enacted personal and organisational objectives can secure an outcome that fits with greater personal plans. So, *pushing* is a relational measure, a self-appraisal of himself-in-action that confirms a relatively high measure of personal agency that achieves personal success. This high level of agency equates to purposeful, directed personal practice that is negotiated through personal goals transacted as organisational goals. What Hugh wants and pursues is personally apprehended as what the fire service needs and affords. He transacts his personal practice through these negotiations and is transformed by the actions he takes and the accomplishments achieved. As is the fire service that now has a number three who can be additionally deployed on each of the control cars when required.

Hugh's transaction of his personal practice, purposeful and directed by his agency, is premised primarily on the positive resonance between his intentions and the chances of their being realised within a context of high command and control protocols that resemble the strong authority structures of military culture. His practice, like that of the fire service, is transformed by transactions that identify the relationship between what he wants, what he perceives the fire service wants and how effectively his actions can secure parity between the two. Hugh knows this to be true because, among other things, the 'boys', that is his colleagues, are supported by his aspirations to remain at the station. A personal-collective agency is enacted. His aspirations help the boys and evidence the shared purposes he transacts in pursuing his goals.

5.7 Transacting the Material as Tools and Procedures

The diverse work of firefighters sometimes involves attending emergency situations in support of police. Often, these situations do not involve fire or accident but require the firefighters' skills of entering locked premises quickly and securing the safety of trapped or disabled inhabitants. There are different pieces of equipment that make up the firefighters 'kit' in such situations. These include battering rams, heavy levers and hydraulic spreaders used to quickly remove or simply smash in doors. The most commonly used tool is the heavy hammer or sledgehammer. Hugh explains, '*at the end of the day a few good smacks with a heavy sledge hammer and most household doors come off*' (Int#4). In an interview, Hugh described an incident where such circumstances and expectations applied. He recounted how he approached the entrance of a private home where police officers stood waiting for him to do what firefighters do, hammer the door down. He stated:

> I carry a piece of milk carton plastic in my kit – no one else does. When you have to gain access – I've used it where there was an elderly person on the floor, there's no damage. I've had the policemen look at me strangely when I've actually pulled it out of my pocket and popped the lock in front of them – they were gob smacked. (Int.#4)

Hugh's personal presence at the door, in full emergency response uniform and carrying the familiar sledgehammer, the usual 'kit', carries all the social press of standard roles and expectations. The interaction generated by his presence in this typical work scenario is both immediate and seemingly predictable. However, from the immediacy of his presence emerges a different set of possibilities, not because a firefighter is on the job (although this is plainly the case), but because Hugh is on the job. He does what he is supposed to do, that is gain access, and so confirms the social norms of firefighters and their occupational practice. Additionally and most saliently, he personalises the role through his personal practice of using a piece of flexible plastic to open the door. In doing so, Hugh transacts his personal practice in ways unfamiliar to the attending police. His knowledge and use of specific density plastics for tripping particular locks, a skill learned in earlier days, stands as a person-specific aspect of Hugh's occupational practice and the transacted transformation of milk bottle into firefighting and rescue tool.

5.8   Recognising Learning Through the Transactions of Work Practice

In terms of the sociocultural constructivist perspective, there are a range of perspectives that offer description and explanation of Hugh's work-learning practices. For example, from the perspective of Holland et al. (1998), Hugh is 'figuring' his occupational world through personal agency enacted from a supported position within it. Workers, like all in social activity, 'figure' who they are and how they accomplish this developing self and occupational knowing through what they do. What they are doing is 'figuring' how to relate to others and the requirements of their contexts in ways that will enable them to organise and be organised in meaningful and acceptable activities. These activities are already socially constructed as the figured worlds people populate and perpetuate through interactive processes. Through his work, Hugh has entered the figured world of the fire and rescue service, and just as he participates in his other worlds of furniture removals and BBQ guest, he will learn who he is as a firefighter and how to do this through the processes of participation open to him in the activities organised by this strongly figured world. From Billett's (2006) perspective, Hugh's choices and decisions (i.e. the exercise of his personal agency) progress from a base of relational interdependence between his personal aspirations and the affordances of his work. Where congruities are evident or emerge through practice, Hugh will positively construe his connection with his workplace and the opportunities it affords him. This congruity may lead to Hugh's engagement in more demanding or more personally aligned work activities and this engagement may support (or hinder) his work-learning that will include developing and constructing occupational skills and subjectivities. From the perspective of Lave and Wenger (1991), Hugh's development of these occupational skills will strengthen his engagement in the activities that characterise his community of practice and this, in turn, will cement his participation in that community as a more central and influential member of its defining practices. Engeström (2001) would argue that such membership assists defining more fully the objects of his learning practices (e.g. his occupational identity, the tasks he undertakes, the successes and failures of the emergency responses he and his crew attend, his efforts to secure an all car driver position, etc.) as collaborative achievement. And Jarvis (2006) would claim that Hugh experiences his work as the personal transformation of becoming more knowledgeable about who he is and how and why he does what he does. From such sociocultural and constructivist perspectives, Hugh's work and learning practices are illuminated as both personal and social accomplishments, enacted and secured (for better or worse) through the interactive processes of engaging with others in occupational practice.

The concepts of personal agency and transaction, as outlined earlier, enable an extension of the sociocultural participation and practice paradigm and its basis in activity. These concepts can illuminate more fully the relational and transformational qualities of Hugh's work-learning practices. Hugh the person, primarily as a firefighter but also as furniture removalist, BBQ guest, etc., is engaged in an extensive range of simultaneous transactions that comprise his occupational practice. These include the transactions of personal agency, social position, occupational and personal identity, expertise and skill development, aspirational career planning and tool making. And, as demonstrated through the many hours of interviews conducted, none of this wealth of activity, except the specific training directed at becoming an *all car driver,* is personally construed as learning. Rather, it is simply accounted as *doing my job.* For Hugh, his learning to enact his work the way he does, his learning transacted in personal practice, is predominantly invisible, not tacit, but masked by the demands of work.

There are, however, some clearly visible aspects of this learning – and they are the transformations observed in and following from the transactions enacted. Hugh notices and continues to notice the changes, in himself, others and his work, *as soon as* he becomes a firefighter. The old men at the bar change, they all wanted to talk. The guests at the BBQ change and the policemen change and become *gobsmacked* as they and Hugh transact the personal, social and occupational practice of a firefighter. Hugh's being there brings an immediate personalisation, a unique self-in-action, with a range of possibilities that go beyond the press of social roles and expectations. Hugh demonstrates that from what could be done, whether hidden in personal potential or obvious in predictable behaviour, the self-in-action is transformed and transforming through the transactions enacted.

Describing and explaining work-learning as participation in activity requires understanding how workers engage in the transactions that constitute their personal practice of work. The few illustrations of Hugh's work practices above offer some insights into how he does what he does in work. When these transactions are made more visible, that is, open to the awareness of those involved, the transformations being experienced may become equally open to awareness as an evidence of learning rather than an illustrative example of simply having done something. Hence, learning, as the process and product of that experience, becomes recognisable as a certain kind of transaction, a visibility generating transaction, perhaps. That is, learning as the transaction of personal practice makes visible the transformations of person, place and practice by which it is characterised. The concepts of interaction do not accomplish this 'making visible'. Rather, it waits on the generation of the object that will become the evidence of learning. In this way, interaction fails to recognise the altered relationships and simultaneous transformations initiated by the transaction already underway.

These suggestions, following from the agency and transaction understandings advanced here, offer a means of clarifying and elaborating a fuller subject-centred perspective of work-learning from within the sociocultural perspective that predominantly draws on social and contextual resources to describe and explain learning in practice. In doing so, the chapter highlights that the relationship between workers and their work is more than a practice-mediated interaction that can be labelled as learning through participation. That is, work-learning is more than emergent from the coming together of sets of personal (worker) and contextual (work) resources. Rather, work-learning may be better understood when more fully encompassing a subject-centred view that workers are simultaneously transforming of and transformed by the personal practices in which they are engaged through work. These practices are the multiple transactions that constitute work. Workers' engagement in them is both the beginning and the evidence of the transformations that can be identified as work-learning.

References

Archer, M. (2000). *Being human: The problem of agency*. Cambridge: Cambridge University Press.

Bagnall, R. (2004). *Cautionary tales in the ethics of lifelong learning policy and management: A book of fables*. Dordrecht: Kluwer.

Billett, S. (2001). *Learning in the workplace: Strategies for effective practice*. Sydney: Allen & Unwin.

Billett, S. (2006). Relational interdependence between social and individual agency in work and working life. *Mind, Culture, and Activity, 13*(1), 53–69.

Billett, S., & Smith, R. (2006). Personal agency and epistemology at work. In S. Billett, T. Fenwick, & M. Somerville (Eds.), *Work, subjectivity and learning* (pp. 141–156). Dordrecht: Springer.

Billett, S., Barker, M., & Smith, R. (2008). Relational interdependence as means to examine work, learning and the (re)making of work as cultural practices. In W. Nijhof & L. Nieuwenhuis (Eds.), *The learning potential of the workplace* (pp. 99–116). Rotterdam: Sense.

Bourdieu, P. (1998). *Practical reason: On the theory of action.* Stanford: Stanford University Press.

Dewey, J., & Bentley, A. (1975). *Knowing and the known.* Westport: Greenwood Press.

Edgell, S. (2012). *The sociology of work: Continuity and change in paid and unpaid employment.* London: Sage Publications.

Edwards, A. (2005). Relational agency: Learning to be a resourceful practitioner. *International Journal of Educational Research, 43*(3), 168–182.

Engeström, Y. (2001). Expansive learning at work: Toward an activity theoretical reconceptualisation. *Journal of Education and Work, 14*(1), 133–156.

Engeström, Y. (2008). *From teams to knots: Activity-theoretical studies of collaboration and learning at work.* Cambridge: Cambridge University Press.

Eteläpelto, A., & Saarinen, J. (2006). Developing subjective identities through collective participation. In S. Billett, T. Fenwick, & M. Somerville (Eds.), *Work, subjectivity and learning* (pp. 157–178). Dordrecht: Springer.

Evans, K. (2007). Concepts of bounded agency in education, work and the personal lives of young adults. *International Journal of Psychology, 42*(2), 85–93.

Evans, W., & Davis, W. (2005). High-performance work systems and organizational performance: The mediating role of internal social structure. *Journal of Management, 31*(5), 758–775.

Fuller, A., & Unwin, L. (2004). Expansive learning environments: Integrating organisational and personal development. In H. Rainbird, A. Fuller, & A. Munro (Eds.), *Workplace learning in context* (pp. 126–144). London: Routledge.

Giddens, A. (1991). *Modernity and self identity: Self and society in the late modern age.* Cambridge: Polity Press.

Harris, J. (2006). *No two alike: Human nature and human individuality.* New York: Norton and Company.

Holland, D., Lachicotte, W., Skinner, D., & Cain, C. (1998). *Identity and agency in cultural worlds.* Cambridge: Harvard University Press.

Jarvis, P. (2006). *Lifelong learning and the learning society. Vol. 1: Towards a comprehensive theory of human learning.* London: Routledge.

Kvande, E. (2013, June 11–14). *Changing world of work: The Nordic model under pressure.* Key note address at the International Helix Conference – Innovative practice in work, organisation and regional development: Problems and prospects. Linkoping University, Sweden.

Lave, J., & Wenger, E. (1991). *Situated learning: Legitimate peripheral participation.* Cambridge: Cambridge University Press.

Nijhof, W., & Nieuwenhuis, L. (2008). *The learning potential of the workplace.* Rotterdam: Sense.

Noon, M., & Blyton, P. (2007). *The realities of work: Experiencing work and employment in contemporary society.* New York: Palgrave Publishers.

OECD. (2010). *OECD reviews of vocational education and training: Learning for jobs.* http://www.oecd.org/edu/skills-beyond-school/oecdreviewsofvocationaleducationandtraining-learningforjobs.htm. Accessed 4 Oct 2013.

Smith, R. (2006). Epistemological agency: A necessary action-in-context perspective on new employee workplace learning. *Studies in Continuing Education, 28*(3), 291–304.

Smith, R. (2008). Negotiating engagement: The personal practice of learning at work. In S. Billett, C. Harteis, & A. Eteläpelto (Eds.), *Emerging perspectives of workplace learning* (pp. 199–213). Rotterdam: Sense.

Webber, S., & Donahue, L. (2001). Impact of highly and less job-related diversity on work group cohesion and performance: A meta-analysis. *Journal of Management, 27*(2), 141–162.

Wenger, E. (1998). *Communities of practice: Learning, meaning and identity.* Cambridge: Harvard University Press.

Wertsch, J. V. (1998). *Mind as action.* New York: Oxford University Press.

Chapter 6
Understanding Work-Related Learning: The Role of Job Characteristics and the Use of Different Sources of Learning

David Gijbels, Vincent Donche, Piet Van den Bossche, Ingrid Ilsbroux, and Eva Sammels

6.1 Introduction

Higher education has been criticised for not developing the competencies students need to be successful in professional practice (Boyatzis et al. 2002; Segers et al. 2006; Tynjälä 2008). At the same time, workplace learning has been praised for facilitating transfer of learning – i.e. applying what has been learned in professional practice (Billett 2004; Eraut 1994). Everyday work practice is full of potential learning processes. These learning activities during work can be very effective and necessary for the purposes of becoming more expert in a profession (Billett 2004; Eraut 1994). In many professional fields, internships are provided as an indispensable part of the education towards professional competence. It is argued that internships have a distinctive contribution to professional education. It is suggested that the confrontation with the workplace triggers learning. These learning activities during work can be very effective and necessary for the purposes of becoming more expert in a profession (see, e.g. Dochy et al. 2011). Despite the theoretical reasoning, research on work-related learning and its antecedents has however remained rather scarce. This chapter presents a study that, on the one hand, questions antecedents of workplace learning by studying job characteristics and, on the other hand, unravels work-related learning during internships. In the next paragraphs, we discuss the most important variables that were included in the study.

D. Gijbels (✉) • V. Donche • P. Van den Bossche
Institute for Education and Information Sciences, University of Antwerp,
Antwerpen, Belgium
e-mail: david.gijbels@ua.ac.be; vincent.donche@ua.ac.be; Piet.VanDenBossche@ua.ac.be

I. Ilsbroux • E. Sammels
Group T – International Enterprising Engineering School, University of Leuven,
Leuven, Belgium

T. Halttunen et al. (eds.), *Promoting, Assessing, Recognizing and Certifying Lifelong Learning: International Perspectives and Practices*, Lifelong Learning Book Series 20, DOI 10.1007/978-94-017-8694-2_6, © Springer Science+Business Media Dordrecht 2014

6.1.1   Job Characteristics

To investigate the influence of job characteristics, the present study relied on the Demand-Control-Support (DCS) model (Johnsen and Hall 1988; Karasek 1979; Karasek and Theorell 1990). This model stresses the important role of job characteristics such as job demands, job control and social support on the learning in the workplace during internships. Job demands refer to stress factors which are present in the work environment. Within the DCS model a demanding job means that someone has to complete a great deal of work within a limited space of time (De Witte et al. 2005). Job control refers to the opportunities with which an employee has to satisfy these job demands. These opportunities are represented by the scope the employee has for taking decisions (De Witte et al. 2005). Social support refers to the existence of good relations with colleagues, being able to rely on others, obtaining accurate information via others, as well as gaining actual help, understanding and attention when difficulties are encountered (De Jonge et al. 2003). In the present study, both the quality and the quantity of the feedback from both co-workers and supervisors are taken into account as an indicator of social support (see, e.g. Steelman et al. 2004; Van der Rijt et al. 2012). The most favourable effects *on work-related learning* are expected with a combination of high job demands (but not overwhelmingly), high job control and high social support. This expectation is also known as Karasek's learning hypothesis.

6.1.2   Work-Related Learning

In earlier studies, we used self-report of occurrence of work-related learning behaviours as an operationalisation of workplace learning, and we did not succeed in confirming the learning hypotheses (e.g., Gijbels et al. 2010, 2012a, b). In the chapter by Gijbels et al. (2012b), we compared the results from a study on the work-related learning of low-qualified students in part-time vocational education with the results from a study on the work-related learning of highly qualified ICT workers. Both the results from the part-time vocational students and the ICT workers pointed in the same direction: when taking the self-directed learning orientation of workers into account, no link could be established between job characteristics of the workplace and the work-related learning of students from the part-time vocational education sector and of ICT employees working within an information service company. This was not what was expected and one of the possible explanations that can be given for this unexpected result relates to the relatively weak way in which work-related learning was operationalised in these studies: the respondents were only asked about the frequency with which they had actually participated in certain work-related learning activities during the past year. In the present study we therefore want to go beyond the reporting of participation in work-related activities as a proxy for work-related learning and measure the diverse learning activities that students undertake during internships.

6.1.3   Learning Activities During Internships

Within the current study, we will focus on the learning activities students undertake during their internship, more specifically cognitive and regulative learning activities will be investigated. The framework we use is developed by Oosterheert and Vermunt (2001) and was based on research that focused on how student teachers learn, starting from the assumption that student teachers do not only learn by studying course materials but also from the experiences they have during internships in which different sources of regulation are present such as learning from peers and colleagues at the workplace. Although this framework has been solely addressed in student teacher learning contexts, five distinguished learning dimensions in this framework can be assumed to have potential grounding to investigate learning during internships in also other educational contexts. We briefly sketch below this selection of five dimensions of knowledge construction and regulation as it has been distinguished in former research in the context of learning to teach.

The first dimension pertains to a 'proactive, broad use of the mentor'. This dimension entails all student actions in terms of asking for practical suggestions, interpreting lesson situations and evaluating the student teachers' performance. This dimension captures students' use of the mentor as an external source to regulate their own learning. In most internship contexts, mentors are present, often differently labelled as tutors, coaches or co-workers who are responsible for both coaching the learning process and judging students' performances. The second dimension focuses on the extent students engage in self-initiated or 'independent search for conceptual information' when being confronted with a specific problem or issue at the workplace. Students search for answers themselves and examine various information sources outside of the formal programme. This dimension has many characteristics in common of more self-regulated learning as it tries to capture what happens when students are confronted with challenges or questions during internship which triggers this learning activity. A third dimension is entitled 'actively relating theory to practice' and refers to the deliberate use of conceptual information to reflect on one's teaching experiences and improve one's teaching. One of the aspects this dimension aims to capture is if students when confronted with new questions or challenges at the workplace also use information of knowledge at the workplace which has been provided in formal learning contexts. The fourth dimension pertains to the relation of student teachers with their colleagues. This fourth dimension encompasses all student activities that involve intentionally approaching experienced colleagues for both practical suggestions and developing ideas/views about teaching. The scale focuses on how knowledge construction during internships takes place through interaction with co-workers. Whereas the first dimension focuses on the mentor and the second on the individual learner, the fourth dimension concentrates on the extent students cooperate and interact with their colleagues to further develop their understanding of a phenomenon at the workplace or a practical solution for a problem they come across. The fifth dimension focuses on maladaptive learning behaviour as represented in the dimension of 'avoidance of learning'.

Former research showed that some student teachers do not reflect on their own roles after having been faced with bad teaching experiences or lessons that went wrong (Oosterheert et al. 2002). They were not all intended to take lessons from these experiences for further performance improvement. Other students did find this an important event as it triggers to think about alternative ways of dealing with these less comfortable teaching situations. A recent study among teachers at the workplace indicated that avoidance of learning was also negatively correlated with experimentation and informal interaction and can be also viewed as a negative learning activity (Van Daal et al. 2013).

Until now, the framework of Oosterheert and Vermunt (2001) to understand student teacher learning and follow-up studies has predominantly been used to capture how pre-service and in-service teachers learn during internships but opens a perspective for use in other educational contexts (Endedijk et al. 2013). In the present study, we take a first step in this direction, as we will explain in the next paragraph.

6.2 The Present Study

The aim of the present study is to go beyond the investigating of self-report measurements of occurrence of work-related learning. Through the lens of the framework of Oosterheert and Vermunt (2001), we aim to deepen how students learn during internships and which differences in student learning are present. Although in this study also an initial validation takes place of a contextualised version of an existing self-report measurement to tap differences in student learning, we expect to find in the data a baseline distinction between learning activities aiming to increase knowledge construction through the means of different sources of regulation and maladaptive learning activities in which avoidance behaviour regarding learning is present.

Next, we aim to examine how these differences in student learning during internships are associated with the job characteristics in the internship context outside the domain of learning to teach. The study is conducted in the context of internships in engineering education.

In order to investigate *the learning hypothesis* more thoroughly, we deliberately chose an internship context in which variation of internship tasks is assumed to be present in a context in which knowledge construction and learning gains are also expected as important learning outcomes. This research context shares a lot of conditions which are also present in student teacher internships: (1) the internship period is a substantial part of the curriculum in which students are expected to actively participate in processes at the workplace; (2) the presence of sources of regulation such as the important role tutors play in the internship context; (3) students are confronted with new challenges which will trigger their prior knowledge of a problem or conceptual understanding; and (4) interaction and collaboration with peers is deemed important at the workplace, in view of both knowledge construction and performance.

Although no previous empirical studies have been reported so far, we have some theoretical assumptions that are guiding our study and which are based on the *learning hypothesis*. First, we expect that learning dimensions will be differently associated with job characteristics. We expect that job control and job demands will be respectively more positively and negatively related to the learning dimensions.

In order to further explore the relationship between student learning and learning outcomes, we measured students' perceived competence at the end of the internship from both the students' and the supervisors' perspective. Previous research already pointed at important associations between differences in learning at the workplace and a closely related construct of perceived competence, namely students' self-efficacy (Thoonen et al. 2011; Van Daal et al. 2013).

6.3 Method

A convenience sample of 117 third year engineering students of a university college participated in this study. Students' learning activities during a long-term internship were measured by means of a contextualised version of the Inventory Learning to Teach Process (ILTP, Oosterheert et al. 2002). Based upon the validated Flemish version of the questionnaire (Donche and Van Petegem 2005), 5 out of 10 scales of the ILTP questionnaire were selected and slightly adapted to the specific context of learning during engineering internships. This has led to changes in the wording of the scales and items.

The resulting questionnaire (engineering version) consisted of statements which were entered on a Likert scale from 1 (entirely disagree) to 7 (entirely agree). To check the construct validity of the questionnaire, a principal components factor analysis with varimax rotation was conducted, and an inspection of the scree plot was carried to determine the number of factors to be retained. The analyses yielded five reliable factors with acceptable eigenvalues (ranging from 6.740 to 1.073) and with a factor solution accounting for 64.63 % of the total variance. However, the scree plot indicated 4 instead of 5 factors, and based upon further content inspection of the items and scales, the 4-factor solution was preferred for further analyses. The resulting scales, number of items for each scale and an illustrative item for each scale and the Cronbach's alpha score for each scale are summarised in Table 6.1.

To measure the job characteristics, job demands and job control, we used existing and validated questionnaires that were used in the study by Gijbels et al. (2010). Job control is measured as the amount of say an employee has in his job (decision authority). The respondent is asked about the extent to which the job that the students perform at their learning workplace provides them with the opportunity to 'stop working when they like' or 'to determine their own way of working'. Job demands are measured by means of statements such as 'My job requires that I work very hard' (see also Table 6.2). Social support was measured based on existing and validated questionnaires that were earlier used in the study by Van der Rijt et al. (2012) and was operationalised in terms of the quality and quantity of feedback that was received

Table 6.1 Dimensions of knowledge construction and regulation

Scale	Item example	Alpha
External-regulated knowledge construction ($N=4$)	I ask my mentor what (s)he doesn't like about my work during internship	.76
Self-regulated knowledge construction through self-regulated information seeking and actively relating theory and practice ($N=7$)	I try to find answers to my questions about my work during internship by consulting the literature on my own	.76
Shared regulation of knowledge construction of workplace experiences through contacting and being involved in discussions with peers ($N=5$)	Through discussion with experienced colleagues, I further develop my ideas about working as an engineer	.85
Avoidance of learning (recoded $N=4$)	I search for the cause of a bad work experience during internship	.85

Table 6.2 Job demands, job control, social support and perceived competence

Scale	Item	Alpha
Job demands ($N=10$)	My job demands from me to solve work-related problems within a limited timeframe	.79
Job control ($N=10$)	To what extent do you have the ability to: decide on the sequence of your tasks, decide when to interrupt your tasks	.86
Quality of feedback supervisor ($N=4$)	I find the feedback of my supervisor very useful	.94
Availability of feedback supervisor ($N=4$)	My supervisor is too busy to provide me with feedback (recoded)	.81
Quality of feedback co-workers ($N=4$)	The feedback that I receive from experienced colleagues is useful for my job	.94
Availability of feedback co-workers ($N=4$)	I have daily contact with experienced colleagues during my job	.79
Perceived competence by student ($N=5$)	I am satisfied about my competencies as an engineer	.93
Perceived competence supervisor ($N=5$)	I am confident that I have enough knowledge to start working as an engineer	.96

from both co-workers and supervisors. As a performance indicator, students' perceived competence was measured in two ways. We composed a self-report measure, to capture students' own perceptions of their general engineering competence. The items used were inspired by former research and instruments used to measure self-efficacy (Pintrich et al. 1993) and perceived competence (Ryan and Deci 2000) but were adapted to the context of this study. Next, we also questioned the tutors/mentors at the workplace to fill in the same set of items for the students they supervised.

For all scales, items were measured on a 7-point Likert scale ranging from 1 = 'totally disagree' to 7 = 'totally agree'. The scales, the number of items for each scale, an illustrative item for each scale and the Cronbach's alpha score for each scale are summarised in Table 6.2.

6.4   Results

6.4.1   *Differences in Learning During Internships*

Table 6.3 provides an overview of the descriptive data and the interrelatedness of the different dimensions of knowledge construction and regulation. The significant internal correlations vary on average from .22 to .59 which mainly shows that the scales measure different aspects of student learning during internship. The higher correlations among the scales 'external regulation' and 'co-regulation' may be an indication that there is a degree of overlap with what the scales measure which is not theoretically unsound. Both scales seem to tap different aspects of external sources of regulation which is different than the self-regulation dimension. The intercorrelations point at the discriminant value of the scale measuring maladaptive learning and confirm prior expectations. The scale 'avoidance of learning' generally shows a lower average score. The results indicate that during the internship context, students in general apply self-regulatory learning activities and knowledge construction by actively relating theories they have learned in formal learning contexts in practice placement and are less prone to avoid learning and take difficulties they come across during internship as learning opportunities.

From Table 6.4 it becomes clear that the feedback context matters for the use of different sources of regulation and knowledge construction: the quality and availability of feedback from co-workers is related to more external regulation of knowledge construction, more self-regulation of knowledge construction, more use of others and less to avoiding learning opportunities. As far as the feedback from the supervisor is concerned, both the quality and the availability of feedback are significantly and positively related to external regulation of knowledge construction whereas only the quality of the feedback from the supervisor is significantly and negatively related to the avoidance of learning opportunities. Job control is negatively related to external regulation of learning but not to any other dimension of knowledge construction and regulation, whereas job demands are positively related to both self-regulated knowledge construction and learning from others and negatively to the avoidance of learning.

From the results in Table 6.5, it becomes clear that supervisors perceive those students as more competent that are working in jobs that are perceived (by the students themselves) to have high job demands and in which the students are relying

Table 6.3 Mean scale scores, standard deviations and correlations between learning scales

		Mean	SD	1	2	3	4
1.	Self-regulated	4.89	.76	1			
2.	External regulated	4.55	1.08	.367	1		
3.	Shared regulated	4.53	1.20	.412	.576	1	
4.	Avoidance	2.89	1.12	−.444	−.469	−.383	1

Note: All correlations are significant

Table 6.4 Correlations between the different job-related variables and the dimensions of knowledge construction and regulation

		Self-regulated	External regulated	Shared regulation	Avoidance of learning
1.	Job control	.137	**−.197**	−.017	−.111
2.	Job demands	**.236**	.109	**.288**	**−.433**
3.	Quality feedback supervisor	.171	**.389**	.109	**−.191**
4.	Availability feedback supervisor	.119	.226	.130	−.139
5.	Quality feedback co-workers	**.397**	**.409**	**.583**	**−.418**
6.	Availability feedback co-workers	**.202**	**.366**	**.546**	**−.215**

Note: Significant correlations are marked in bold

Table 6.5 Correlations between job-related variables, dimensions of knowledge construction and perceived competence

	Perceived self-competence	Competence as perceived by supervisor
Job control	**.183**	.082
Job demands	**.363**	**.348**
Quality of feedback supervisor	.088	.041
Availability of feedback supervisor	.129	−.016
Quality of feedback co-worker	**.197**	−.031
Availability of feedback co-worker	.140	.055
Self-regulated	**.252**	*.261 (p = .057)*
External regulated	.132	.129
Shared regulation	**.290**	.237
Avoidance of learning	**−.277**	−.143

Note: Significant correlations are marked in bold

on self-regulated sources of learning and knowledge construction. It should be remarked that the latter correlation is only 'nearly' significant ($p = 0.057$). Students perceive themselves as more competent workers during the internship in workplaces that are perceived as jobs with higher job control and higher job demands and when they receive qualitative feedback from their co-workers. Students perceive themselves more competent when they self-regulate their knowledge construction during their internships and relate on others. Finally (and not surprisingly), avoidance of learning is negatively correlated with the score for perceived self-competence.

6.5 Conclusions and Discussion

The aim of the present study was to go beyond the use of self-report measurements of occurrence of work-related learning when investigating antecedents of learning during internships. Through the lens of the framework of Oosterheert and Vermunt (2001), we aimed to deepen how students learn during internships and which differences in student learning are present and how these differences are associated with job characteristics such as job demands, job control and the quality and quantity of feedback received from co-workers and the supervisor. A final aim was to probe into the relationship between, on one hand, differences in student learning (measured as dimensions of knowledge construction and regulation) and job characteristics and, on the other hand, the learning outcomes as measured by the perceived self-competence and the competence as perceived by the supervisor.

The study was conducted in the context of an engineering education programme. Four different dimensions of knowledge construction and regulation during these internships could be distinguished in our sample: (1) external-regulated knowledge construction, (2) self-regulated knowledge construction through self-regulated information seeking and actively relating theory and practice, (3) shared regulation of knowledge construction of workplace experiences through contacting and being involved in discussions with peers and (4) avoidance of learning. The results of the correlational analyses indicate that the context of the internship does matter and is related to the learning that takes place during internships. In short the results show that especially high job demands and supportive feedback from the supervisor and especially from co-workers are related to more self-regulated knowledge construction, more shared regulation of knowledge, less avoidance of learning and higher perceived self-competence. Supervisors seem to perceive those students as more competent that are working in jobs that are perceived to have high job demands and in which the students are relying on self-regulated sources of learning and knowledge construction. When (re)considering workplaces for learning during internships, high job demands and a supportive feedback climate seem to be important factors to take into account. This confirms partially the learning hypotheses as formulated by Karasek (1979) and opens opportunities to further explore the value of high demanding jobs for internships and of peer feedback on the workplace in further research (see also Van der Rijt et al. 2012). The results of the present study further indicate that the framework of dimensions of knowledge construction and regulations adapted from Oosterheert and Vermunt (2001) seems to be worthwhile to explore in further research on workplace learning, especially during internships.

Although some valuable conclusions can be drawn based on the results of this study, we should acknowledge some limitations of the present study that warrant us to be careful in our interpretations of the results. Most important to acknowledge is probably that this study was a cross-sectional one and that therefore no inferences based on these data can be made on the direction of influence. Future research using a repeated measurement or other longitudinal research design could provide us with such insights. Second, it would be worthwhile to complement future quantitative research with more qualitative data (based on, e.g. interviews or observations) to triangulate the results and to enrich the interpretation of the means and relationships between the variables under study. Next, and in line with the previous remark, all data collected in this study was based on perception measures. Although we did not only take students' self-perceptions into account and also took the supervisors' perceptions of students' competences into account, other performance indicators such as persistence and dropout are important to further take into account as well as to explore the predictive validity of the knowledge construction and regulation scales. Finally, not only job characteristics but also student characteristics have been indicated to have explanatory value to explain differences in learning at the workplace (e.g. Gijbels et al. 2010).

Despite these limitations, the present study provided some useful insights in workplace characteristics that can affect learning during internships. The study disentangled different dimensions of knowledge construction and regulation during internships and identified different ways in which learning is shaped in the workplace. The suggested pathways to promote learning during internships will need to be elaborated in further research.

References

Billett, S. (2004). Workplace participatory practices: Conceptualising workplaces as learning environments. *Journal of Workplace Learning, 16*, 312–324.

Boyatzis, R. E., Stubbs, E. C., & Taylor, S. N. (2002). Learning cognitive and emotional intelligence competences through graduate management education. *Academy of Management Learning and Education, 1*, 150–162.

De Jonge, J., Bakker, A., & Schaufeli, W. (2003). *Psychosociale theorieën over werkstress* [Psychological theories about work stress]. Houten: Bahn Stafleu van Loghum.

De Witte, H., Verhofstadt, E., & Omey, E. (2005). *Testing Karasek's learning and strain hypothesis on young workers in their first job.* Working paper, Faculty of Economics and Business Studies, Ghent University.

Dochy, F., Gijbels, D., Segers, M., & Van den Bossche, P. (2011). *Theories of learning for the workplace: Building blocks for training and professional development programs.* London: Routledge.

Donche, V., & Van Petegem, P. (2005). Assessing preservice teachers' orientations to learning to teach and preferences for learning environments. *Scientia Paedagogica Experimentalis, 42*(1), 27–52.

Endedijk, M., Donche, V., & Oosterheert, I. D. (2013). Student teachers' learning patterns in school-based teacher education programmes: The influence of person, context and time. In D. Gijbels, V. Donche, J. T. E. Richardson, & J. D. Vermunt (Eds.), *Learning patterns in higher education: Dimensions and research perspectives.* London: Routledge.

Eraut, M. (1994). *Developing professional knowledge and competence.* London: Farmer Press.

Gijbels, D., Raemdonck, I., & Vervecken, D. (2010). Influencing work-related learning: The role of job characteristics and self-directed learning orientation in part-time vocational education. *Vocations and Learning, 3*, 239–255.

Gijbels, D., Raemdonck, I., Vervecken, D., & Van Herck, J. (2012a). Understanding work-related learning: The case of ICT-workers. *Journal of Workplace Learning, 24*(6), 416–429.

Gijbels, D., Raemdonck, I., Vervecken, D., & Van Herck, J. (2012b). What keeps low- and high-qualified workers competitive: Exploring the influence of job characteristics and self-directed learning orientation on work-related learning. In P. Van den Bossche, W. Gijselaers, & R. G. Milter (Eds.), *Learning at the crossroads of theory and practice: Research on innovative learning practices* (pp. 53–72). Dordrecht: Springer.

Johnsen, J., & Hall, E. (1988). Job strain, work place social support, and cardiovascular disease: A cross-sectional study of a random sample of the Swedish working population. *American Journal of Public Health, 78*(10), 1336–1342.

Karasek, R. A. (1979). Job demands, job decision latitude, and mental strain: Implications for job design. *Administrative Science Quarterly, 24*, 285–308.

Karasek, R., & Theorell, T. (1990). *Healthy work. Stress, productivity and the reconstruction of working life*. New York: Basic Books.

Oosterheert, I. E., & Vermunt, J. D. (2001). Individual differences in learning to teach: Relating cognition, regulation and affect. *Learning and Instruction, 11*(2), 133–156.

Oosterheert, I. E., Vermunt, J. D., & Denessen, E. (2002). Assessing orientations to learning to teach. *British Journal of Educational Psychology, 72*, 41–64.

Pintrich, P. R., Smith, D. A. F., Garcia, T., & McKeachy, W. J. (1993). Reliability and predictive validity of the motivated strategies for learning questionnaire (MSLQ). *Educational and Psychological Measurement, 53*, 801–813.

Ryan, R. M., & Deci, E. L. (2000). Self-determination theory and the facilitation of intrinsic motivation, social development and well-being. *The American Psychologist, 55*, 68–78.

Segers, M., Nijhuis, J., & Gijselaers, W. (2006). Redesigning a learning and assessment environment: The influence on students' perceptions of assessment demands and their learning strategies. *Studies in Educational Evaluation, 32*, 223–242.

Steelman, L. A., Levy, P. E., & Snell, A. F. (2004). The feedback environment scale: Construct definition, measurement and validation. *Educational and Psychological Measurement, 64*(1), 165–184.

Thoonen, E. E. J., Sleegers, P. J. C., Oort, F. J., Peetsma, T. D. D., & Geijsel, F. P. (2011). How to improve teaching practices: The role of teacher motivation, organizational factors, and leadership practices. *Educational Administration Quarterly, 47*(3), 496–536.

Tynjälä, P. (2008). Perspectives into learning at the workplace. *Educational Research Review, 3*, 130–154.

Van Daal T., Donche V., & de Maeyer S. (2013). The impact of personality, goal orientation and self-efficacy on participation of high school teachers in learning activities in the workplace. *Vocations and learning*, 1–20. http://dx.doi.org/doi:10.1007/s12186-013-9105-5

van der Rijt, J., van de Wiel, M., Van den Bossche, P., Segers, M., & Gijselaers, W. (2012). Contextual antecedents of informal feedback processes in the workplace. *Human Resource Development Quarterly, 23*(2), 233–257.

Chapter 7
Experiential Learning: A New Higher Education Requiring New Pedagogic Skills

Anita Walsh

7.1 Introduction and Background

In 2009, Cedefop, the European Centre for the Development of Vocational Training, issued European guidelines for the validation [recognition] of informal learning. Informal learning was defined as 'learning resulting from daily activities related to work, family or leisure. It is not organised or structured in terms of [learning] objectives, time or learning support. Informal learning is mostly unintentional from the learner's perspective' (p. 74). Informal learning is therefore learning that occurs incidentally through other activities, when the learner is not intentionally engaged in a learning experience. It is the learning that 'takes place in the spaces surrounding activities and events with a more overt formal purpose, and takes place in a much wider variety of settings than formal education or training' (Eraut 2004, p. 247). Cedefop, which defines its own role as 'the European Union's reference centre for vocational education and training', reports that, 'More European countries are emphasising the importance of making visible and valuing learning that takes place outside formal education and training institutions, for example, at work, in leisure time activities and at home' (2009, p. 11). Furthermore, Cedefop argues that, 'Across a country this [informal learning] represents a vast untapped resource of invisible knowledge and skills and, in addition to the rights [of learners] to have their learning recognised, its increased visibility could lead to significant economic and social benefits for individuals, communities and countries' (2009, p. 11). Berglund and Andersson (2012) point out that, 'since its introduction into European Union debates in the 1990s, traditional RPL [recognition of prior learning] has been recognised as a powerful tool for articulating informal (and non-formal) learning in the workplace' (p. 81).

A. Walsh (✉)
School of Business, Economics and Informations, Birkbeck,
University of London, London, UK
e-mail: a.walsh@bbk.ac.uk

T. Halttunen et al. (eds.), *Promoting, Assessing, Recognizing and Certifying Lifelong Learning: International Perspectives and Practices*, Lifelong Learning Book Series 20, DOI 10.1007/978-94-017-8694-2_7, © Springer Science+Business Media Dordrecht 2014

Research by Eraut (2004) indicates that the majority of knowledge used in the workplace comes from learning that takes place in a workplace context and would be defined as informal learning by Cedefop. The Recognition of Prior Learning (RPL) and the integration of experiential work-based learning into academic programmes offer a valuable opportunity for a wide range of higher-level learning to be formally recognised and to contribute to higher education qualifications.

In the UK, there is a longstanding tradition of the inclusion of a period of work experience in academic awards within some disciplines – for example, in the form of time spent in the workplace between periods of academic study on 'sandwich' degrees in a range of undergraduate programmes. On such courses, students are taught theory in the university and get experience of workplace practices through their practice placement. Where practice placements are included in programmes leading to a statutory licence to practise, for example, in nursing or teaching, the learning required in a practice context is tightly defined. Indeed, the degree of control exercised by the professional body over the intended learning taking place in the workplace is equivalent to the control exercised in lecture theatres by academic experts, which means that the primacy of the expert model in not challenged (Walsh 2003). That is, a learning situation where the student is the novice in both contexts – being inculcated into an academic discipline in the context of the university and into appropriate professional practice in the context of the hospital or school. In other placements, historically, while direct experience of the workplace was recognised to be of value, frequently the learning gained from such an experience was not clearly identified (Walsh 2006, p. 2). It was often assessed only through a report written by the student to cover a period of work experience of between 6 months and 1 year and the employer's judgement that the performance of the student was satisfactory. As specific learning outcomes from the work experience had not been identified, students were not required to demonstrate particular learning or to relate their work experience to a body of academic literature. This provided a strong contrast to the more formal academic assessment, which was usually based on academic literature and took the form of academic essays and unseen examinations. This illustrates the claim made by Boud and Solomon (2001) that, 'The more typical workplace learning episodes, such as professional placements ... usually sit discretely within conventional course structures and understandings about academic knowledge and learning' (p. 24). In addition, although learning outside of the university was identified as a necessary element of an academic award and students were required to pass a placement/internship in order to gain the award, it was treated differently to learning acquired inside the university. In contrast to the use of a range of either grades or marks used to evaluate academic work, the use of a pass/fail grading to evaluate learning in the workplace meant that performance in practice could not be included in consideration for classification of the award. When evaluating the quality of a student's degree, only the work with marks or grades allocated could be included in the calculation of overall student achievement, thus maintaining the perspective that 'real' learning takes place inside the university (Walsh 2008, p. 10).

More recently, the design of academic programmes in terms of learning outcomes (i.e. what the student will learn) has put the focus on the students and the outcome of a learning experience rather that tutor inputs (what the lecturer will teach). In addition, the development of an academic credit framework has facilitated the formal recognition of a wider range of learning and, through a framework of levels, enabled equivalence to be drawn between learning in different contexts. These developments have supported the identification of specific learning outcomes from work experience and the design of more formal assessment for this experiential work-based learning. In addition, the recent emphasis on employer engagement and workforce development – for example, through the Higher Education Funding Council for England (HEFCE) funded Employer Engagement projects – has also extended practice in this area. More broadly across Europe, Cedefop claims that, 'Expansion and diversification of education and training policies towards a broader, lifelong learning perspective, widens the focus from the delivery of qualifications by formal education and training institutions to include other, more flexible routes to qualification. These are sensitive to different ways in which people have developed their knowledge and skills and the way they live their lives' (2009, p. 16). Discussions of experiential work-based learning often locate recognition of such learning in the context of the knowledge economy and of the importance of continuing professional development as a way of ensuring currency of high-level knowledge and skills (Portwood and Costley 2000, p. 9). The recognition of experiential learning, whether through RPL or through experiential work-based learning, is also presented as a more effective response from the university to the need for higher-level skills in the workplace. Since the inception of workplace experience as part of higher education activities in the 1950s, the approach has shifted from one which emphasises the use of workplace experience as an enhancement to academic learning to one which supports the use of assessed high-level learning from workplace experience as an integral part of academic programmes (Walsh 2011b, p. 5).

There is now a wide range of academic practice in the UK relating to the recognition and assessment of learning in the workplace, which can either enhance the employability of full-time students or provide a more flexible response to part-time learners who are working. The Quality Assurance Agency (QAA – the body responsible for assuring the academic standards of UK higher education) has issued a Code of Practice relating to work-based and placement learning which defines work-based learning as 'learning that is integral to a higher education programme and is usually achieved and demonstrated through engagement with a workplace environment, the assessment of reflective practice and the design of appropriate learning outcomes' (QAA 2007, p. 4). This definition was deliberately broad as QAA was concerned that a 'formal definition [of work-based learning] might even be counter-productive and act as a constraint to the further development of innovative practice in this area' (ibid, p. 4). The QAA document makes clear the experiential base of such learning, adding that 'Institutions can draw upon and make use of … accreditation of prior experiential learning (APEL)' (ibid, p. 4).

The innovative work relating to supporting and assessing experiential work-based learning can be seen as part of the more flexible and responsive approaches in higher education, which have been student-centred and have emphasised the importance of experience for learning. It is probably useful here to highlight the distinction between recognising that workplace experiential learning has a value which complements academic learning (the 'sandwich' degree model of higher education) and recognising that high-level experiential learning can take place in a wide range of contexts, including the workplace (Walsh 2011a, b), that it can be identified and assessed in a manner appropriate for inclusion in higher education awards, and given an equivalent weighting to academic learning. Those academic practitioners involved with experiential work-based learning fall into the second group and take pedagogic perspectives which draw on a constructivist approach to learning, offering a valuable enhancement to current practice related to learning and teaching in higher education. Such perspectives emphasise active learning and the creation of knowledge in context. For example, Wenger (1998) questions the assumption that learning takes place through the dissemination of subject content; he argues that, 'required learning takes place not so much through the reification of a curriculum as through modified forms of participation that are structured to open the practice to non-members' (p. 100). This perspective is echoed by Biggs (2003) who claims that it is not what the teacher teaches, but 'what the learner has to *do* to create knowledge [that] is the important thing', emphasising the importance of students' active engagement in learning (p. 12). These views emphasise the fundamental importance of students' active participation to learning, not the context in which the learning takes place, enabling parallels to be drawn between learning inside and outside the university. In addition, there is an ongoing debate about the nature of knowledge produced in the context of the workplace, one example of this being Gibbons et al.'s (2000) categorisation of mode 1 and mode 2 knowledge – the former being produced according to academic protocols, the latter being constructed outside the university to address particular issues in context (p. 3). The distinction made here is between knowledge production in the university, which follows specific protocols set down by the academic disciplines, and knowledge production outside the university – for example, in research units and other workplaces – which, although taking a stringent and organised approach to knowledge production, are approaching particular problems to attempt to develop solutions. As Gibbons et al. point out, 'When knowledge is actually produced in the context of application, it is not applied science, because discovery and applications cannot be separated' (2000, p. 4).

These debates have very real implications for the recognition of experiential work-based learning and for the structuring of the learning experience on higher education programmes. It is, perhaps, worth reminding ourselves that it is not experience per se, but the learning from that experience which is under consideration. Dewey (1997) claims that experience is the basis for all learning but he does not believe that all experiences are equally educative, and he argues that the educator's role is to design learning based on experience which will develop the learner and enable them to carry such learning forwards. The importance of shaping experience to provide learning is also emphasised by Brookfield (1993) who argues that 'experience without critical analysis can be little more than anecdotal reminiscence' (p. 23), and by Hensman (2001) who claims that learning takes place when 'knowledge is created through the transformation of experience' (p. 45). The pedagogic approach adopted for the transformation of experience into learning and the translation of learning outside the academy into a format appropriate for academic assessment usually draws heavily on reflective practice and is quite different to that used in what Biggs terms the 'transmission model' of higher education.

7.2   Current Context

There is some evidence that pedagogic perspectives influenced by constructivism and the importance of situated learning are beginning to be fully integrated into higher education programmes and that elements of programme design are being designed on this basis (Walsh 2011a, b). The recent surveys of experiential work-based learning funded by the Higher Education Academy (HEA) and undertaken by Pierce (2011) and by Walsh on behalf of the Learning From Experience Trust (LET) indicate the extent to which such learning has become an integral part of the higher education curriculum. The surveys were small scale and offer an insight into practice, rather than a clear indication of scale of provision within the sector. Nevertheless, the findings indicate that, while still a relatively minor element of the undergraduate and postgraduate curriculum (respondents reported that assessed experiential work-based learning accounted for between 10 and 15 % of the assessed learning in the awards concerned), there is now an established range of pedagogic practice which draws directly on students' experience for learning. Learning gained through work-place experience is clearly identified through learning outcomes and demonstrated via formal assessment. It is also the case that, in contrast to the previous situation whereby work/practice placements, while being a necessary element of an academic award, were marked on a pass-fail basis, much of the assessment of experiential work-based learning is now awarded a grade or mark (i.e. an indication of standard of student achievement). This is an important development, because it means that such learning now contributes towards the classification of an award in the same way as learning achieved in the university, giving it equal status in this context.

The small studies were undertaken at a time of change and uncertainty in higher education. They specifically considered subjects where, although direct experience of practice was desirable, it was not by definition required, because the areas involved did not confer a statutory competence to practise. This is an important aspect of the programmes which were considered, because often, when colleagues are exploring the recognition of experiential work-based learning, the model drawn on is that used in areas such as Education, Nursing and Social Work. All these areas relate to occupations which require a licence to practise and full recognition by a professional body. There is therefore tight control over intended practice learning, and considerable resources are devoted to both supporting learning in the workplace and assessing performance in context. In contrast, the subject areas studies – those in the Business, Management, Accountancy and Finance (BMAF) subject area and in the Hospitality, Leisure, Sport and Tourism (HLST) subject area – are providing higher education for a range of occupations which are emerging as professions and for which no licence to practise is required, which means that there is no single professional body to influence curriculum content. There university, therefore, has the freedom to determine what the content of the academic programme is and can include experiential work-based learning should it choose to do so.

The small qualitative studies critically reviewed the integration of experiential work-based learning into both the undergraduate and postgraduate curriculum. The aims of the study were to identify the range of practice relating to academic recognition of experiential work-based learning and to examine how this informs curriculum design, particularly with regard to modes of assessment. The intention was to identify examples of effective practice and also to explore any particular challenges during programme design and development relating to the integration of experiential work-based learning into the curriculum.

The respondents to the surveys were specifically selected on the basis of having pedagogic practice relating to experiential, work-based learning. Therefore, all respondents had current direct involvement in learning, teaching and assessment activities which drew directly on experiential work-based learning and worked with students who use their workplace experience for learning and professional development. As assessment is fundamental for the academic recognition of learning, considerable attention was paid to assessment, although this was fully contextualised in a broader consideration of overall programme design. The surveys, therefore, offer an insight into a range of approaches to this area, together with practitioners' view on what challenges need to be addressed when designing programmes and assessments which can demonstrably meet the standards required by higher education. As Tynjälä points out, 'Although the knowledge-transmission paradigm and the behaviourist view of learning have been replaced by different constructivist approaches in research on learning, education practitioners have been much slower to change' (1999, p. 425). Respondents to the survey are among those academic colleagues who have chosen to change their practice and to engage more actively with experiential work-based learning in higher education. Responses to the survey therefore provide an insight into how different institutions have facilitated the development of pedagogic practice which supports the recognition of experiential work-based learning and its integration into the higher education curriculum. In addition, respondents' comments give an indication of how academic colleagues who remain embedded in the mainstream academic disciplines view experiential work-based learning.

7.3   Tensions Experienced

Brennan and Little (1996) point out that the established order for undergraduate education in the twentieth century is, '(i) induction into a discipline, leading to (ii) the development of the mind...' (p. 32). In addition, as Biggs (2003) states:

> The view of university teaching as transmitting information is so widely accepted that delivery and assessment system the world over are based on it. Teaching rooms and media are specifically designed for one way delivery. A teacher is the knowledgeable expert who expounds the information the students are to absorb and report back accurately. (p. 127)

The dominance of the culture of the academic disciplines and of Gibbons et al.'s mode 1 knowledge means that, 'Many academics continue to express the notion that 'applied' learning represents training and theoretical learning represents 'education' – the old 'hand versus head' division of industrial forms of labour. This sees Work-Based Learning as a 'lesser and weaker' form of learning and as a 'watering down' of the true nature of the University' (Wagner and Childs 2001, p. 333).

Given existing distinctions between academic and vocational learning and between theory and its application, it may not be surprising that recent surveys of academic practice relating to the integration of experiential work-based learning in the Business Administration subject areas in the UK reveal that there are tensions between the pedagogies adopted to support experiential learning and those in use in more conventional programmes. As will become apparent later in the chapter, the tensions arise because of the perceived challenge to existing 'mainstream' practice which is provided in the pedagogic approach adopted. When discussing the curriculum with respect to the integration of experiential work-based learning into academic programmes, Raelin (1998) states that, 'Unfortunately, classroom and real world development experiences are usually provided independently as if there were no need to merge theory with practice' (p. 280). In 2009 he refers to the 'rather dramatic non-use of practice based pedagogical strategies, particularly in formal academic programmes of management, in spite of significant theorizing and evidence of value' (p. 401). Raelin argues that there has been a 'practice turn away', and that colleagues are still wedded to the practice of transmitting information to students, and claims that, 'The passivity of the learner is reinforced by the longstanding assumption that the role of the teacher is to rescue learners from their state of "not knowing"' (p. 408).

Certainly when reporting their experience of developing and establishing the integration of experiential work-based learning into higher education programmes, work-based learning practitioners cited their awareness that they were often challenging colleagues' widely held views of what higher-level learning is and what it should be. Despite their own conviction that experiential work-based learning offers transformative learning to their students, many respondents were also aware that this was not a conviction which was shared by colleagues who used an approach based on established pedagogic practice.

When asked about the challenges they had come across in their own practice, respondents to the survey referred to:

- The extent to which the authority awarded to theoretical knowledge by the academic disciplines meant that other 'knowledges' were disadvantaged and perceived to be inferior.
- The inappropriateness of the didactic teaching model for many students, particularly those students who had already had high-level professional experience, in that it tended to treat all students as novices and tutors as experts.
- The reluctance of colleagues to make space for experiential learning in a 'crowded curriculum', i.e. the emphasis on the primary importance of theoretical knowledge leading to a concern to ensure wide coverage of disciplinary content and a reluctance to cut content to accommodate other approaches to learning.

- The lack of familiarity with other workplaces of those academic colleagues whose careers began immediately after their academic studies. Having not worked outside of a university context, they were unaware of the rich variety of learning experiences available there and found it difficult to conceive that appropriate learning opportunities existed.
- Colleagues' and institutions' preference for conventional assessments such as unseen examinations (i.e. time-constrained assessments which require students to answer a number of questions, none of which have been seen prior to the beginning of the examination), which are often seen as the appropriate form of assessment for higher-level learning. This placed a considerable constraint on those colleagues assessing experiential learning and required them to design a 'compromise' assessment in order to meet institutional requirements.
- More than one respondent referred to the lack of familiarity with the more complex pedagogy required to support experiential work-based learning and to the fact that people embedded in the pedagogic approaches of the academic disciplines 'aren't always tuned in' to the required approach. It was also pointed out that, if academic colleagues who were unconvinced of the value of experiential learning were involved in delivering an experiential work-based learning module, the approach taken was usually unsuccessful in terms of creating a positive learning experience.
- The lack of familiarity with both the modes of delivery and of assessment of experiential work-based learning led to academic colleagues in the disciplines expressing a lack of confidence in the academic rigour of this area.
- The constraints impost by the dominant tradition of higher education, both in terms of the organisation and the dissemination of knowledge were also cited as an impediment to the effective engagement with employers and work-based learners. One example given was that the structuring of teaching, learning and assessment into academic terms, which governed assessment boards, etc., was not easily understood by people who worked and whose organisational systems were designed to function all year.

All the points relating to curriculum design and pedagogy made above reinforce the claim made by Gibbons et al. that, 'Disciplinary boundaries matter far more in education than in research. They are more important in the university than outside' (2000, p. 148). The studies undertaken indicate the extent to which curriculum design is dominated by a conventional perspective of the academic disciplines, often to the exclusion of more responsive pedagogies which can more effectively meet student needs. This is demonstrated by the emphasis on the importance of disciplinary content and the reluctance to reduce this to allow for the inclusion of experiential elements in the curriculum. Tutors' preference for conventional pedagogic approaches which treat learners as novices, even when those learners are highly experienced professionals, and for familiar assessments such as examinations, regardless of the type of learning being assessed, is also consistent with established disciplinary practice. It is, perhaps, not surprising that those colleagues whose only workplace has been a university should be unfamiliar with the wide range of learning opportunities available in many other workplaces. In addition, the lack of familiarity with the complex pedagogies required to support effective experiential work-based learning may well be the reason that a lack of confidence is expressed in the academic rigour of such learning. However, it is also possible that colleagues unfamiliar with other workplaces and with experiential learning are only willing to recognise academic rigour if it is displayed in a manner with which they are already familiar. The findings from the surveys suggest a situation in the UK which is relatively unchanged from when Trowler, who investigated practice relating to the recognition of prior experiential learning, made his claim that, 'These interviews suggest that academics on the ground still tend to defend the epistemological battlements of their disciplines and domains against attacks upon them ... with the traditional weapons of 'the essay' and 'the literature'' (1996, p. 22). Overall, the points made indicate that mainstream practice in the university has an inward focus, emphasising knowledge and practices which are important to the academic disciplines, but being less willing to recognise and engage with forms of knowledge and practice outside the institution.

7.4 Solutions Adopted

As work-based learning practitioners who did engage with different forms of knowledge, respondents to the surveys were very much aware of the attitudes of their colleagues to experiential work-based learning and of the general nervousness of colleagues in terms of the appropriateness of its inclusion in programmes of higher education. When developing parts of the curriculum using experiential work-based learning, they recognised the need to demonstrate the academic validity of their practice. All respondents were quite clear that they had made explicit attempts to address the lack of academic confidence when designing their modules/programmes. There was a consistent emphasis on their own recognition that experience alone was not sufficient for higher-level learning and that any experiential learning had to be related to a relevant theory to meet the required academic standards. This is illustrated by the following quotes:

> We went quite hard on the learning outcomes relating to theory
> We are explicitly including critical analysis/integration of theory
> We've linked theory to practice
> The experience must dialogue with the literature
> Students compare their experience to the theory
> Students draw on experiential learning theory but focus on the topic that is important to them

The level of engagement with theory was not the same as that in a conventional theory-led module or programme, but engagement with theory was perceived to be a necessary aspect of experiential learning. It can be useful to distinguish between theory-driven modules, whose content is defined by the requirements of an academic discipline, and experience-driven modules, whose content is based on experience in the workplace which is theoretically informed. In the latter, it is the requirement of the practice/experience which indicates relevant theory. This is entirely consistent with Brookfield's claim that 'experience without critical analysis can be little more than anecdotal reminiscence' (1993, p. 23) and with the recognition that learning takes place when 'knowledge is created through the transformation of experience' (Hensman 2001, p. 45). It is through the adoption of a pedagogy based on facilitating reflection and the use of theory as a lens through which to examine practice that such a transformation can take place.

Respondents to the surveys emphasised the fact that assessment 'measured' experiential work-based learning rather than workplace performance per se. This is an extremely important aspect of work-based learning and one which needs more exploration, particularly in the context of employer assessment, but is not an issue which will be pursued further here. In addition, there was an insistence that assessment, although taking a less familiar shape than the widely used essay and examination, was entirely 'fit for purpose'.

This approach is consistent with Biggs' (2003) emphasis on the importance of active engagement for learning and his argument that higher education programmes should aim to develop functioning knowledge in students. He claims that functioning knowledge is the kind of knowledge professionals use in context and thus the kind of knowledge that students will need to be successful in their chosen profession. He points out that functioning knowledge combines declarative theoretical knowledge, process knowledge (the practice knowledge integrated in many professional programmes) and conditional knowledge. Biggs (2003) argues that the transmission model of higher education is very good at disseminating declarative knowledge, and fairly good at providing process knowledge, but that students are often left to develop conditional knowledge (i.e. the awareness of when to use declarative and process knowledge) after graduation. When discussing his approach of constructive alignment, which he defines as aligning teaching and assessment with the learning required of students, he also emphasises the importance of designing assessment which will effectively 'measure' the desired learning, pointing out that students learn what they think they will be tested on. Examinations are a form of assessment which is good at measuring declarative knowledge, but assessment of function knowledge requires 'performance assessment'. Many of the modes of assessment used with experiential work-based learning could be seen to be performance assessments, in that they often assess processes rather than disciplinary content. The focus on process, which requires students to analyse and evaluate their workplace experiences and identify their learning, means that a wide range of content is accommodated in contrast to the defined content of more conventional learning delivery.

There has been a tendency for the assessment of experiential learning in the UK and elsewhere to be consistently linked with the portfolio as a mode of assessment (see Romaniuk and Snart 2000; Brown 2001, 2002; Conrad 2008). Portfolios have often been used as an element of practice assessment and as 'evidence' for claims of prior experiential learning – a factor which has sometimes been claimed to have inhibited more effective recognition of experiential learning, due to the fact that portfolios can be very time-consuming to assess. However, although the portfolio was one element of assessment referred to in the survey, it was by no means the predominant mode of assessment. Respondents in these studies used a wide range of innovative and responsive modes of assessment to assess their students' performance. Requiring the integration of both academic and experiential work-based knowledge, the range of assessments in use includes:

Consultancy proposal/project proposal/bid for client – where these were used as modes of assessment the student was working with a live client or organisation and was required to meet appropriate professional standards. Any proposal or bid needed to be deemed satisfactory by the client, as well as meeting the required academic standards.

Live case studies – these could be used by students who were working either as employees or as placement students in particular organisations. The case studies could be used to explore a particular issue or problem for the organisation concerned.

Presentations are seen to be an important element of professional practice and are used quite widely – sometimes for formative feedback, sometimes as part of the formal assessment of learning. In one particular instance, academics, employers and students were all involved in presentation assessment (the weighting of the marks allocated was 50 %, 25 % and 25 %, respectively) with briefing sheets being issued to provide guidance.

Peer assessment of work in groups was also used – sometimes the marks awarded by other students were moderated by a tutor, sometimes they were not.

Applied research projects were used quite widely. The research report was required to include a coherent academic literature review. Often this project would address a real workplace problem and make recommendations for its solution. In one case, the focus of the research was agreed with the Head of Training in the organisation so that the outcome could be used to inform strategic decisions.

A critically reflective narrative on professional practice was also often used. This is a formal first person narrative which draws on relevant theory and/or on experiential learning theory and which explicitly combines elements from academic literature with experiential learning. There is frequently a requirement to keep a professional journal during the duration of the module. Such journals are not usually assessed, but they are seen as an important element of 'data capture' in terms of learning experience through the duration of the modules.

Essays are used to a limited extent, but reliance on more conventional modes of academic assessment is low.

It is apparent from the foregoing that, in designing experiential work-based learning modules and their assessment, respondents to the surveys explicitly attempted to address the concerns of fellow academics while balancing this with the requirements of their own pedagogy. The assessments used indicate that the link between assessment of experiential learning and portfolios has been loosened and the modes of assessment listed above could be argued to be closer to established academic assessments such as essays and examinations than the portfolio. Unless specifically required by institutional regulations, the range of assessments in use excludes the unseen examinations which are a familiar feature on most programmes.

One interesting point made by a respondent to the undergraduate survey was that, although students are familiar with examinations and essays, they usually have not come across the newer forms of assessment which are used to assess experiential learning. They therefore need specific guidance on the format of these less familiar forms of assessment. This guidance usually needs to be provided by the tutor, since, as one respondent pointed out, although there is a considerable literature giving guidance on the more established modes of assessment, little literature is available to guide students in preparing assessments which are designed specifically to assess experiential learning.

When discussing assessment, respondents to the LET studies also emphasised the need for transparency of process, so that 'justice could be seen to be done' during the assessment process. This was felt to be a way in which academic confidence could be built in this area. Generic frameworks and assessment criteria, which could be applied to both academic and experiential work-based learning, were seen as a particularly helpful aspect of curriculum design in terms of demonstrating appropriate standards. It was also pointed out that in conventional academic courses examinations are seen as an important way of minimising plagiarism, but that there is evidence that individually designed assessment also reduces the risk of plagiarism. As the content, which is drawn on in the assessment of experiential work-based learning, is necessarily individual and usually contextualised, it is difficult to envisage plagiarism being an issue.

When designing both learning experience and assessment, respondents to the surveys were very much aware that, 'the crux of the issue is academic credibility and quality – the extent to which institutions and other accrediting bodies can feel confident that credit gained through work can be reliably assessed, and is of equivalent standard to that deriving from more established modes of learning' (Lush and Gomez 2002, p. 154). Great care was taken to demonstrate that an appropriately academic stance was being taken to the experience used for learning, and there was a keenness to achieve the transparency of process which would show the value of experiential learning. It is easy to discern an element of persistence against attitudes which are at best apathetic to, and at worst devaluing of, experiential work-based learning.

7.5   Benefits Reported

All those colleagues directly involved with facilitating experiential work-based learning expressed their enthusiasm for the positive learning experience and for the transformative nature of experiential work-based learning for a range of reasons. They emphasised the rich benefits of a 'real-life, real-time' learning experience, explaining that it enhanced the educational benefits of higher education by providing a different and complementary form of learning. The following benefits were claimed:

- The ability to give students an insight into the range of pressures on performance in the workplace. One respondent, when contrasting real work experience with simulation inside the university, gave the example of the difference between changing a wheel in an engineering workshop and changing a wheel in the rain during a pit stop in a race. He pointed out that the experience of the student was quite different in the two contexts and that the impact of contextual factors on performance was important.

- The challenging intellectual experience and increase in confidence which arose from managing and structuring one's own learning in context.
- The development of the ability to explicitly identify learning and skills. This is an integral part of the reflection on learning which is an important element of pedagogy in this area and is also a valuable way of enhancing performance at job interviews, in that students have already had to identify specific learning and achievement.
- The autonomy in learning which developed from a more collaborative learning experience where, in contrast to working with specific academic content, students are involved in deciding the content of their study.
- An enhanced recognition of links between academic knowledge and workplace knowledge through the requirement to negotiate the interface between the two cultures and explicitly link them.
- A raised awareness of the difference between theory and practice and of the way theory can facilitate insights through providing a framing for workplace experience.
- The enhanced employability which comes from increased familiarity with the requirements of workplace practice.

The benefits listed above all derive from direct involvement in workplace experience and from being exposed to the pedagogy used to support effective learning in context. These findings support Raelin's claim that, while using simulations and case studies in the classroom may be a useful way to begin relating theory and practice, 'it is not sufficient as a holistic form of learning, which can take account of such real-time and relational contingencies as unplanned disturbances, non-deliberative coping strategies, defensive routines, or just plain failures and surprises' (2009, p. 403). The integration of the innovative practice which has been developed to integrate 'real-life, real-time' experiential learning into more conventional academic programmes can be seen as a successful exercise in developing more responsive and relevant higher education programmes and in developing learning which is student-centred. The academic practice which supports such learning and whose pedagogy draws on a constructivist model of learning offers a valuable enhancement to the more traditional approaches to learning and teaching in higher education. In addition, colleagues involved with experiential work-based learning are convinced that the curriculum which combines experiential work-based learning with learning in the disciplines is of demonstrable benefit to students. However, the tensions with existing approaches to higher education pedagogy are inhibiting the more extensive use of the 'new pedagogies', despite the growing body of literature which evidences their effectiveness in assessing learning in context. Laycock points out that, 'In all work-based learning there is a serious challenge to the dominant discourse of higher education, to what counts as a legitimate site of learning, to what counts as legitimate knowledge' (2003, p. 127). It is also the case that, 'To the extent that a particular way of producing knowledge is dominant, all other claims will be judged with reference to it' (Gibbons et al. 2000, p. 1). Respondents to the surveys were well aware of this, and the way they approached module and assessment design reflects this, yet they were very conscious that many of their colleagues had not really engaged with the pedagogic discourses which demonstrated the academic validity of experiential learning.

7.6   Reconciling Approaches to the Higher Education Curriculum

Earlier in the chapter, reference was made to the difference between the mode 1 knowledge which is produced through the practice of the academic disciplines and the mode 2 knowledge which is knowledge produced in context. The two different knowledges are produced in two different contexts – one inside the academy and one outside it in 'think tanks, consultancy agencies, non-governmental organisations, professional societies, governmental and corporate R&D (sic) laboratories' (Delanty 2001, p. 109). This is not the case for the pedagogies which are used to support learning in the academy and learning in context – both these are present in the higher education curriculum, and, where experiential learning is included in academic programmes, students often experience the two differing approaches to pedagogy side by side. It is, therefore, important that the principles underlying both approaches are clearly understood – rather than the dominant approach which emphasises the primary importance of decontextualised theoretical knowledge being accepted as the norm and the experiential work-based learning approach being perceived to be 'deviant'.

A fundamental aspect of the debate here is that of academic coherence, i.e. the decision about what contributes to a programme making academic sense and having academic validity – until relatively recently the only voice which defined academic coherence was that of the academy. However, more recently, other influences have been recognised in terms of curriculum design. Muller (2009), when discussing organising principles for the higher education curriculum, drew on the distinction made by Chisholm et al. (2000) to distinguish between conceptual coherence and contextual coherence. He gives the following definitions:

> conceptual coherence curricula, have, what Merton calls, high codification; they presume a hierarchy of abstraction and conceptual difficulty. Contextual coherence curricula, on the other hand, are segmentally connected, where each segment is adequate to a context, sufficient to a purpose. Here, adequacy is externally guaranteed, often by a profession or professional statutory body, where in the former, adequacy is internally guaranteed.

Conceptually coherent curricula are entirely familiar in higher education – they are the curricula which are developed and designed by the academic disciplines. Contextually coherent curricula, as Muller (2009) defines them, are those curricula which are influenced by the needs of professional practice. Muller goes on to point out that there is a 'tension between a more conceptual and a more contextual form of disciplinary practice' (2009, p. 217). Although frequently no professional body is involved in defining the design of experiential work-based learning modules, it could be argued that experiential work-based learning is a 'more contextual' form of academic practice, in that it is formed by the requirements of external factors and is designed to respond to needs outside the academy. It is, therefore, likely that the tension which is experienced between conceptually coherent curricula and contextually coherent curricula will arise also in this area.

Muller (2009) refers to the UK Higher Education Framework (sic) distinguishing between 'two modal types of curriculum and qualification: one that aims to produce disciplinary adepts, and is thus formative or research-based; the other that aims to produce knowledgeable professionals, and is thus oriented more to the demands of the workplace' (2009). It could be argued that the integration of experiential work-based learning into the higher education curriculum falls into the second category and supports the development of 'knowledgeable professionals'. The challenge to existing academic practice comes from the fact that the difference in pedagogic practice between the two approaches – that of the academic disciplines and that of experiential work-based learning – is marked. In contrast to the focus on theoretical disciplinary content which is the fundamental element of pedagogic debates within the academic disciplines, colleagues involved with experiential work-based learning emphasised the need for students to develop high-level generic skills. Staff referred to the need for applied research skills, the ability to integrate theory with practice and the autonomy required to manage independent learning in the workplace and to undertake critical reflection on professional practice so that they can evidence the ability to monitor and evaluate their professional performance. Supporting the development of these higher-level skills through the facilitation of experiential work-based learning demands a different pedagogy from that used for the delivery of disciplinary content and requires different pedagogic skills from those academics involved. As Boud and Tennant (2006) point out, academic colleagues need to move 'from seeing themselves as persons who induct students into a disciplinary culture to one in which they accept a role as learning consultants, actively engaged in mediating work, context and academic expectations'(p. 302). This is because, in contrast to a subject curriculum which contains defined disciplinary content, 'In work-based learning, research and development and reflective practice are located within a real social and work-based community that gives them meaning, rather than illustrated through hypothetical or devised examples' (Portwood and Costley 2000, p. 31). Curriculum content for experiential work-based learners is drawn from their work roles, with the effect that such learning 'redraws the epistemological map of higher education because the boundaries of disciplines are at most partly relevant' (ibid, p. 17). This does not represent a rejection of theoretical disciplinary knowledge, but rather the recognition that, in a workplace context, it is 'used selectively on a 'fitness for purpose' basis' (Portwood and Costley 2000, p. 125). Therefore, academic practice which involves supporting experiential work-based learning moves the academic from their role as the disciplinary expert introducing an academic discipline to those who are unfamiliar with it, towards a more collaborative role of working with students (and sometimes with employing organisations) to support higher-level learning which is based on knowledge created outside the academy. The role is one that is new to academic staff, and there are indications from the reviews undertaken that it is not currently fully recognised or understood. There is some indication from the relatively widespread adoption of references to reflection and to reflective practice in conventional curricula that such approaches to learning are seen as relatively straightforward. However, as Ryan (2012) argues, 'attempts to include reflection in assessment tasks with little or no pedagogical scaffolding generally results (sic) in superficial reflections that have virtually no impact on learning or future practice' (2012, p. 44). She goes on to point out that, 'Critical reflection is not an intuitive skill, and competence in different levels of reflection … cannot be taken for granted' (2012). Colleagues responding to the surveys were very much aware of this, but had also observed the transformative learning which resulted from engagement with experiential learning. This is consistent with Mezirow's (1991) claim that, 'When students are provided with opportunities to examine and reflect upon their beliefs, philosophies and practices in relation to the contextual conditions of their field, they are more likely to see themselves as active change agents and lifelong learners within their profession' (cited in Ryan 2012). The powerful educative effect of experiential work-based learning may explain why, on more than one occasion, respondents identified themselves as 'evangelising' for experiential work-based learning with their academic colleagues and as championing a richer form of learning for higher education. However, co-existing with their commitment to experiential work-based learning was the recognition that vocational and applied learning of any sort was still frequently seen to be inferior to the more general academic education and that experiential learning was still a contested area in many contexts. The view was expressed that explicit reference to experiential learning in the curriculum was becoming 'more naturally accepted', but the point was made that, with regard to the recognition of experiential work-based learning, there was still 'some way to go', particularly in some subject areas and some institutions.

It is perhaps worth briefly considering the context in which higher education is currently operative in the UK when considering the likelihood that this mode of learning will be actively extended. There is now a range of evidence of the successful integration of a variety of pedagogic practice relating to experiential work-based learning in higher education, and there is also increasing pressure on higher education to demonstrate the added value it offers in terms of enhanced employability or of a real contribution to continuing professional development. It is, therefore, timely to consider the wider integration of experiential work-based learning into the higher education curriculum. The reviews recommended the following as relatively straightforward ways that this could be done:

- By ensuring that the full range of experiential learning is used as the basis for assessment. Increasingly students are working to support their studies, they are undertaking internships or placements, or being given experiences to support the development of an entrepreneurial approach. These are opportunities for learning outside the academy which already exist and the experiences they provide can be examined to ensure that the learning gained from them is fully utilised.

- Through exploration of the extent to which credit volumes from the assessment of experiential work-based learning could be increased. The current level of around 10 % of the assessed learning for an Honours Degree is low, and it is often the case that students undertake considerable experiential learning assessment for a limited volume of credit. In one instance, an optional placement extended an academic programme by 6 months while the assessed learning from it would enable a student to gain approximately 12 % of the credits required for the award. Had the 6 months been spent studying in an academic context, it is likely that the student would gain approximately 30 % of the required credits.
- By reviewing modes of assessment to ensure that they are 'fit for purpose' and avoiding the imposition of traditional forms of assessment (e.g. examinations) in a context where performance assessment of some sort would be more suitable.
- Through raising colleagues' awareness of the pedagogic debates relating to the use of reflection as a fundamental aspect of experiential work-based learning so that they are aware that a formal educational process is involved in the identification and assessment of such learning.

All the above points could be addressed in the course of curriculum development and review and could be included in the discussions relating to learning, teaching and assessment which occur during that process. There would be no requirement for major revisions to pedagogic approaches overall, and such curriculum amendments could extend the innovative and responsive practice outlined here so that it offered a greater complement to more formal disciplinary studies. This would provide a reasonably straightforward way to introduce direct and individual relevance for students into the curriculum. However, as has been indicated earlier, curriculum change in the area of recognition of experiential learning has been slow. The progress outlined here, although valuable in gaining greater validity for such learning, has been limited in scope.

Generally speaking, respondents to the surveys were of the view that national developments in the context of higher education were helping to change attitudes to experiential work-based learning. Economic and social pressures are pushing towards a higher education that is responsive to a much broader range of students. In addition, particularly in England, the cost of higher education is considerable and it is in this context that recognition of experiential work-based learning has a contribution to make. However, since the tradition is of awarding higher status to theory than to practice, often little effort is made to explore the academic principles involved with experiential work-based learning. In the absence of familiarity with the pedagogy, further development of the area in such a context could be dismissed as a pragmatic response to demands for 'bums on seats' and the need for funding. It is therefore important to engage with the social and pedagogic arguments for change and to ensure that the social and academic rationales for the greater recognition of experiential learning are clear. Annette (2007) quotes Newby (2004) arguing that, 'as higher education moves from being a "once in a lifetime" opportunity to a lifelong requirement which needs to be refreshed and updated across a lifetime, so it needs to be delivered in a more student-centred form – part-time as well as full-time, in the workplace, online, via distance learning and so forth' (2007, p. 19). Annette (2007) continues that, 'The idea of a lifelong learning curriculum is both a normative ideal and the basis for practically re-organising the curriculum. This (sic) requires us to think not only about how we teach but also about when we teach, where we teach, and importantly what we teach' (p. 19). He claims that a real commitment to lifelong learning will entail a shift to 'a much wider range of curriculum delivery, from the traditional liberal education to more employer-based and community-based learning opportunities' (2007, p. 19). This stance is reinforced by the recent Wilson Review of Business and University Collaboration, whose author challenges the established academic vocational divide, and argues that, 'we need a more nuanced way of thinking about knowledge and skills in higher education, rather than claiming a divide and value differential between the two' (2011).

There is some indication that the stark distinction between knowledge and skills has been influential in slowing the pace of development in the area of experiential work-based learning. As early as 1992, the Department of Employment in the UK was claiming that, 'the straightforward assumption that what can be learnt at work is as valid as that which can be learnt in the lecture theatre, and that it is worthy of academic recognition. This is a concept which, whilst still challenging for many academics, is beginning to win acceptance in higher education' (cited in Ebbutt 1996). Although some progress has made, this statement could be said to still apply today. Yet, as Boud and Symes (2000) point out, 'Universities were always to a degree vocational institutions, particularly in terms of the high status professions such as medicine and law, but in the last few years this vocationalism has become more pronounced, reflecting the growth in knowledge-based employment sectors' (p. 18). In addition, there is now a considerable range of effective pedagogic practice to draw on in extending the recognition of experiential learning. The innovative pedagogic practice explored in these reviews demonstrates an ability to address the need to use a more subtle conceptualisation of learning and skills which supports a wider range of curriculum delivery. The practice outlined shows that it is possible to be considerably more responsive to learners while at the same time using appropriate pedagogy for higher education and maintaining academic standards. In supporting the explicit recognition of knowledge in practice, higher education will be more effectively preparing students for professional life and helping them to build their professional expertise. Eraut (2004) states that, 'the research literature on expertise consistently finds that the distinguishing feature of experts is not how much they know but their ability to use their knowledge, because that knowledge has been implicitly organised as a result of considerable experience for rapid, efficient and effective use' (p. 254). In considering the use of knowledge in the workplace, Eraut (2000) argues that, 'Even in well-theorised areas of practice, the interpretation of theory is problematic and requires further learning from experience' (p. 125). Moreover, he challenges the distinction often made between formal and informal learning, explaining that, 'It is hard to imagine a formal learning context in which only explicit learning of explicit knowledge takes place' (Eraut 2000, p. 131). (Those with experience of Gender Studies would recognise the 'hidden curriculum' as an example of informal learning in a formal situation, where implicit messages about gendered behaviour are conveyed at the same time as formal subject content.) In engaging our students with the different types of knowledge that are used in real-life, real-time practice, we will be enhancing their future professional performance. It is also important to keep in mind that, although the structuring and supporting of experiential work-based learning is arguably a more responsive and egalitarian exercise than focusing purely on the teaching of disciplinary content, the relationship between university and learner is never an equal one. The learner has to complete assessment which is judged satisfactory by the university and marked according criteria agreed with the institution. Thus, although the facility to undertake a 'translation' from the discourse of the workplace to the discourse of the university allows for a wider recognition of learning, it is still the university which decides whether the translation submitted is acceptable or not. Therefore, although the innovative practice relating to experiential work-based learning challenges some existing academic practices, the maintenance of academic standards is not one of them – the location of that practice remains where it has always been – within the institution.

References

Annette, J. (2007). Lifelong Learning, research-based academic disciplines and the undergraduate curriculum. *Academy Exchange, 6*(7), 18–19.

Berglund, L., & Andersson, P. (2012). Recognition of knowledge and skills at work: In whose interests? *Journal of Workplace Learning, 24*(2), 73–84.

Biggs, J. (2003). *Teaching for quality learning at university* (2nd ed.). Maidenhead: SRHE/OU Press.

Boud, D., & Solomon, N. (Eds.). (2001). *Work-based learning: A new higher education?* Buckingham: SRHE/OU Press.

Boud, D., & Symes, C. (2000). Learning for real: Work-based education in universities. In C. Symes & J. McIntyre (Eds.), *Working knowledge: The new vocationalism and higher education*. Buckingham: SRHE/OU Press.

Boud, D., & Tennant, C. (2006). Putting doctoral education to work: Challenges to academic practice. *Higher Education Research and Development, 25*(3), 293–306.

Brennan, J., & Little, B. (1996). *A review of work-based learning in higher education*. London: Department for Education and Employment.

Brookfield, S. (1993). Through the lens of learning: How the visceral experience of learning reframes teaching. In D. Boud, R. Cohen, & D. Walker (Eds.), *Using experience for learning*. Buckingham: SRHE/OU Press.

Brown, J. O. (2001). The portfolio: A reflective bridge connecting the learner. Higher education and the workplace. *Journal of Continuing Higher Education, 49*(2), 2–13.

Brown, C. (2002). Electronic portfolios in pre-service education – distinguishing between process and product. In D. Willis et al. (Eds.), *Proceedings of society for information technology and teacher education international conference* (pp. 539–545). Chesapeake: AACE.

Cedefop. (2009). *European guidelines for validating non-formal and informal learning*. Luxembourg: Office for Official Publications of the European Communities.

Chisholm, L., Volmink, J., Ndhlovu, T., Potenza, E., Mahomed, H., Muller, J., Lubisi, C., et al. (2000). *A South African curriculum for the twenty first century*. Pretoria: Department of Education.

Conrad, D. (2008). Building knowledge through portfolio learning in prior learning assessment and recognition. *Quarterly Review of Distance Education, 9*(2), 139–150.

Delanty, G. (2001). *Challenging knowledge: The university in a knowledge society*. Buckingham: SRHE/OU Press.

Dewey, J. (1997). *Experience and education*. New York: Touchstone (originally published 1938).

Ebbutt, D. (1996). Universities, work-based learning and issues about knowledge. *Research in Post-Compulsory Education, 1*(3), 357–372.

Eraut, M. (2000). Non-formal learning and tacit knowledge in professional work. *British Journal of Educational Psychology, 70*(1), 113–136.

Eraut, M. (2004). Informal learning in the workplace. *Studies in Continuing Education, 26*(2), 247–274.

Gibbons, M., Limoges, C., Nowotny, H., Schwartzman, S., Scott, P., & Trow, M. (2000). *The new production of knowledge: The dynamics of science and research in contemporary societies*. London: Sage.

Hensman, C. (2001). Context based adult learning: The new update on adult learning theory. *New Directions for Adult and Continuing Education, 89*, 43–52.

Laycock, M. (2003). *Work-related learning: Notes for guidance for higher education delivery*. Work-Based Learning Opportunities for Lifelong Learning: Conference Proceedings of the Work-Based Learning Network of the Universities' Association for Continuing Education.

Lush, D., & Gomez, S. (2002). *Managing the diversity of bioscience placements for credit accumulation via the web*. Knowledge, Work and Learning: Conference Proceedings of the Work-Based Learning Network of the Universities' Association for Continuing Education.

Mezirow, J. (1991). *Transformative dimensions of adult learning*. San Francisco: Jossey-Bass Publishers.

Muller, J. (2009). Forms of knowledge and curriculum coherence. *Journal of Education and Work, 22*(3), 205–226.

Newby, H. (2004). *Doing widening participation: Social inequality and access to higher education*. The Colin Bell Memorial Lecture given on 30 March 2004.

Pierce, D. (2011). *A critical review of contemporary practice: Experiential and work-based learning in hospitality, leisure, sport and tourism*. Higher Education Academy (final report of review undertaken on behalf of the Learning from Experience Trust).

Portwood, D., & Costley, C. (2000). *Work-based learning and the university: New perspectives and practices*. Birmingham: SEDA.

Quality Assurance Agency. (2007). *Code of Practice for the assurance of academic quality and standards in higher education. Section 9: Work-based and placement learning*. Gloucester: Quality Assurance Agency for Higher Education.

Raelin, J. (1998). Work-based learning in practice. *Journal of Workplace Learning, 10*(6/7), 280–283.

Raelin, J. (2009). The practice turn-away: Forty years of spoon feeding in management education. *Management Learning, 40*(4), 401–410.

Romaniuk, K., & Snart, F. (2000). Enhancing employability: The role of prior learning assessment and portfolios. *Journal of Workplace Learning, 12*(1), 29–34.

Ryan, M. (2012). The pedagogical balancing act: Teaching reflection in higher education. *Teaching in Higher Education, 18*(2), 144–155.

Trowler, P. (1996). Angels in marble? Accrediting prior experiential learning in higher education. *Studies in Higher Education, 21*(1), 17–30.

Tynjälä, P. (1999). Towards expert knowledge? A comparison between a constructivist and a traditional learning environment in the university. *International Journal of Educational Research, 31*, 357–442.

Wagner, R., & Childs, M. (2001). Work-based learning as critical social pedagogy. *Australian Journal of Adult Learning, 42*(3), 314–334.

Walsh, A. (2003). *Academic recognition of work-based learning: A paradigm revolution?* Paper presented at the Universities' Association for Continuing Education Work-Based Learning Network Annual Conference Work-Based Learning: Opportunities for Lifelong Learning.

Walsh, A. (2006). *Pragmatism or principle? Academic recognition of work-based learning*. Paper presented at the Society for Research into Higher Education Annual Conference.

Walsh, A. (2008). What is distinctive about work-based knowledge and learning? In *Work-based learning – workforce development: Connections, frameworks and processes*. York: Higher Education Academy.

Walsh, A. (2011a). *A critical review of experiential work-based learning in the postgraduate curriculum in the subject areas of business, management, accountancy and finance and hospitality, leisure, sport and tourism*. Higher Education Academy (final report of review undertaken on behalf of the Learning from Experience Trust).

Walsh, A. (2011b). *A critical review of experiential work-based learning in the undergraduate curriculum of the business, management, accountancy and finance subject area*. Higher Education Academy (final report of review undertaken on behalf of the Learning from Experience Trust).

Wenger, E. (1998). *Communities of practice: Learning, meaning and identity*. Cambridge: Cambridge University Press.

Wilson, T. (2011). *Reflections on knowledge and skills*. Thinkpiece written as part of the Review of Business and University Collaboration: The Wilson Review. http://www.wilsonreview.co.uk/blog/2011/10/18/70/. Accessed 12 Nov 2011.

Chapter 8
How Expertise Is Created in Emerging Professional Fields

Tuire Palonen, Henny P.A. Boshuizen, and Erno Lehtinen

8.1 Introduction

In this chapter, we outline future developments in the formation of expertise, especially in relation to emerging professions, and how educational systems are prepared for educating experts in new or rapidly growing occupational fields. In their report, 'The Shape of Future Jobs to Come', Talwar and Hancock (2010) analysed the forces of change influencing society and key trends on the science and technology horizon, resulting in a list of new occupations that might arise because of these developments. However, as helpful as their analyses are for comprehending the opportunities and chances for work in the future, they are not finely grained enough to describe the evolution and creation of occupations in the present and near-future society. Englund (1996), among many other researchers, referred to the concept of professionalism when explaining the development of work practices. Professional groups have diverse means of reaching their standards for recognition. These standards are rooted in shared values. Examples of such means are attending conferences, writing for and reading journals and participating in programmes offered by training institutes that together build a shared body of professional knowledge. Professional communities can also regulate their standards by requiring registration and certification. Yet, there are also personal dimensions within most professions. Certainly, being a professional of a certain kind goes beyond the delivery of professional quality and maintaining professional conduct but also involves a shared occupational identity where working and learning are co-constructed through

T. Palonen (✉) • E. Lehtinen
Centre for Learning Research, University of Turku, Turku, Finland
e-mail: tuire.palonen@utu.fi; erno.lehtinen@utu.fi

H.P.A. Boshuizen
Welten Institute – Research Centre for Learning, Teaching and Technology, Open Universiteit in the Netherlands, Heerlen, The Netherlands
e-mail: Els.Boshuizen@ou.nl

T. Halttunen et al. (eds.), *Promoting, Assessing, Recognizing and Certifying Lifelong Learning: International Perspectives and Practices*, Lifelong Learning Book Series 20, DOI 10.1007/978-94-017-8694-2_8, © Springer Science+Business Media Dordrecht 2014

co-participatory practices. Transformations in the workplace are not conceivable without individuals' active involvement and engagement. Changing practices that occur in workplaces are thus products of relational interactions between the socially derived activities, technologies and individuals. Identity formation is part of individuals' roles in transforming work and work requirements (Billett and Somerville 2004). However, not all new jobs will be classified as professions, and even for those that will, this recognition can take a long time. Medicine and law have had a long tradition of being accepted as professions, whereas health and social care and teaching started to develop their profiles as professions much later.

Hargreaves (2000) conducted an analysis of the development of the teaching profession and discerned four 'ages' of professionalisation. For teachers, firstly, the pre-professional age 'was seen as managerially demanding but technically simple, its principles and parameters were treated as unquestioned common sense' (p. 156). Individuals learned through practical apprenticeship and honed and developed further using trial-and-error strategies. Secondly, during the age of the autonomous professional, individual experts 'had the right to choose the methods they thought best' (p. 162). At the age of the collegial professional, the strong autonomy is traded for a division of labour due to the increased complexity of the work. Regarding the fourth age, Hargreaves speculated whether that would be more like a post-professional or postmodern age. Teachers' professional expertise becomes institutionalised and their individually acquired specialist knowledge becomes at least partly based on scientific evidence. New knowledge-intensive jobs might develop in similar ways. At the same time, new ways for building shared knowledge bases and developing common standards are visible, such as hybrid forms of organisation and co-operative mastering of knowing and knowledge production. Contrary to individual and controlled professionalism and support received from strong institutions, expertise is produced here in multi-actor networks. One example of this kind of restructuring was seen during the recent financial crisis that decreased confidence in the competency of financial professionals. It indicated a need to redesign the learning systems that prepare professionals in the established professions, such as engineering, law, health care and management, and emerging professions, such as consultants, governance experts, EU experts and specialists in finance or law (Gijselaers et al. 2013). These working organisations are expected to adapt to the continuous and rapid change that comprises contemporary work practices and requirements. In a similar way, traditional forms of expertise such as medicine and law are based on scientific knowledge, professional agency and institutional traditions meeting the demands of rapid change, uncertainty and ambiguity of the societies (Karvinen-Niinikoski 2004). Meanwhile, we see more tendencies to bring professionals under public (i.e. politic, bureaucratic) control. These kinds of trends not only challenge professional autonomy but also threaten the further development of the occupation. The tendency towards de-professionalisation can be discerned in many ways. One example of this can be found in the field of medicine, where professional autonomy is increasingly being curbed by governments and health insurance companies. Certainly, Hargreaves's theories (Hargreaves 2000; Hargreaves and Fullan 2000) raise questions about whether the new professions and professionals follow the old pathways when establishing their education systems, institutes and practices, or if there are other, new ways to educate future experts for new jobs. As yet, it is not clear what kind of implications can be predicted on the basis of the historical developments of the 'old' professions. Likely, the development of a shared body of knowledge and its maintenance and improvement are presupposed, as well as integrating the common knowledge base to shared practices and jointly mastered codes and norms. This implies building professional standards for products and services. Also, new professional groups require a good balance between individual autonomy and group-level action and accountability for the quality of societally endorsed services provided. Altogether, it requires constant quality control and striving for improvement in professional actions.

As noted, various future reports (e.g. Talwar and Hancock 2010; Redecker et al. 2010; Davies et al. 2011) list various 'change drivers' that require coordinated, often global solutions, e.g. in the fields of environment, finance and security. The list includes various challenges, threats and possibilities, demographic changes, economic turbulence, politics that have become complicated due to the ever-growing demands for more services, norms and legislation, scientific and technology emphasis, crossroads of generations, redefinition of talent, education and training, global distribution of electronic media, transitions in societies and limits of natural resources. These change drivers can give birth to new jobs or hybridise existing jobs in complex ways. For instance, the growing pressure on natural resources creates major potential for clean fuels and alternative resources, including cradle-to-cradle production strategies and renewable energy systems (McDonough and Braungart 2002). This might lead to new jobs such as consumer energy consultant or scarce metal tracer. Similarly, global demographic changes and increasing lifespans will create a four- or even five-generation workforce that requires new formats for management, worker support and training. Talwar and Hancock (2010) analysed change drivers in terms of opportunities and implications for science and technology, and hence for associated jobs. Many job titles on their list may sound a bit futuristic (e.g. body part maker, nano-medic, farmer of genetically engineered crops and livestock, personal brander, social 'networking' analyst), but others, including the consumer energy consultant mentioned above or the old-age wellness manager, have already come into existence as private enterprises and can develop into new professions.

It is clear that globalisation, smart machines and electronic media have spread widely and continue to modify our daily lives. In contemporary times the overwhelming role of knowledge and information is an important change driver. New knowledge has already modified the nature of most jobs, and the wide availability of information influences clients and consumers' behaviours. This continuous change will restructure educational systems and the hierarchy of work and workplaces. Some occupational fields grow quickly and some exhaust, vanish and/or fade away. Even those old professions that seem to be stable and were established hundreds of years ago continually undergo reconstruction. This is not surprising given that they serve human needs, and these needs and how they are served constantly change. In general, the new jobs seem to be born at the edge of and in between various domains, such as the growing number of paraprofessions that service medicine (i.e. doctors and specialists). So, even the most prestigious of professions are not static entities. Some professions evolve and change, while others based on new technologies, unconventional philosophies or changing consumer interest merge into the mainstream. Overall, multi-scientific and multidisciplinary demands rise up; one example of this trend is sustainability science. It aims to address climate change and other sustainability challenges such as biodiversity loss, deforestation, depletion of marine fish stocks, global ill health, land degradation, land use change and water scarcity. It is, thus, an attempt to bridge the natural and social sciences to manage these complex challenges (Jerneck et al. 2011). In domains with the highest level of change, such as environmental sciences, energy efficiency or gene technology, there are often routines (e.g. legislation, manuals, recommendations and so on) to update experts' knowledge bases. However, in any field, a change can occur that radically transforms all practices and influences the cornerstones of the pre-existing system. An example regarding medical imaging technology shows how new technologies result in changing trajectories of professional development. The increasing importance of nuclear medicine has caused a situation where some practitioners, already specialists in radiology, are retrained to become positron emission tomography (PET) experts by building on rich prior experiences (in X-ray technology), while at the same time new experts are trained who have no experiences with older technologies (Gegenfurtner et al. 2009). This circumstance results in workplaces where old and new professional cultures coexist having implications for professional practices.

Given all of these changes, questions arise, such as: How is it possible to act professionally if the environment is constantly changing? How can educational institutes be helped to keep change and learning in their parallel traces, without losing either of them? The answers to these questions are complicated by the level of development of the new professions, and by diversity in prior training. A new domain of work might have a shared body of knowledge that is codified in best practices and embodied in people who have that knowledge. This kind of situation already provides a basis for teaching newcomers by 'traditional' means such as direct teaching and apprenticeship models and by participating in situations where the occupation is practised. If, however, commonly understood and jointly shared standards, best practices and norms are missing, traditional educational formats cannot provide an answer. Knowledge and practice construction should then become the first priority. Another complicating factor for training development is prior education. Many workers in new occupational fields were earlier trained in different fields, e.g. debt counsellors come from backgrounds as diverse as social work and law. Apart from the diversity that has to be accommodated in a training design, prior knowledge can have different effects on new learning. Often this prior knowledge facilitates new skills learning. Earlier training and enculturation in a different profession can also be an obstacle to acquiring the skills needed in the new occupation due to different underlying values and meaning systems.

Perhaps the easiest route for an educational programme is to trust self-directed learning, preferably integrated together in a system for recognising learning, as prior learning plays a central role in training (Fejes and Andersson 2009). Though, for all educational systems that are not standardised or tied to any pre-existing quality control, coupling with a recognition of prior learning (RPL) system is a step towards (new) standards. Evaluation criteria can form an orientation point towards which learning will be focussed in the future. A slightly more advanced model than leaning on loosely organised individual learning includes some support for transformational learning (a term borrowed from Mezirov 1991). This approach can include intentional trials to make sense of experiences found at work, engaging in deliberate and mindful efforts to learn and validating and expanding beliefs and understandings. Stahl's (2006) concept of group cognition captured the process during which personal meaning-making processes and understanding are coupled together as social knowledge building systems. Indeed, Stahl's model described transformative processes and their products, i.e. knowledge. Though the model was created in the context of computer-supported collaborative learning environments, it can be adapted for our purposes and linked to a consideration of emergent fields.

The analyses and partial solutions provided here show that each change is multifaceted and that education struggles with the question of how to provide training for new professions. Most analyses provided here regard further and post-initial lifelong training. But raising a question about one level of training immediately raises the question as to how that applies to the preceding stages. That is, what can institutions for initial education do to prepare people for new professions? Recently, Gijselaers et al. (2013) analysed the pedagogical requirements for training future 'new professionals' who must be able to deal with change in the environment they will work in and be responsive to the new challenges posed. These new challenges require educational formats that link the learner and the environment, connect content and context and teach practice near. There are some tried practices that are used in initial education that were developed, while universities sought for different ways to bridge the gap between theory and practice by incorporating practice into their curricula through cases and projects, or through learning methods that rely heavily on understanding practice (e.g. action learning, project-based learning and problem-based learning) (Gijselaers and Milter 2010). These methods might turn out to be the best choice for lifelong learning programmes for emerging professions.

8.2 Three Mechanisms for Emerging Fields

In the following section, we present three mechanisms for emerging professions. The first of them arises from bureaucracy and legislation (Cooper and Robson 2006). Recently, professional development is increasingly defined in global terms. In particular, some professions, such as business administration, are being transformed through complex transnational mechanisms, such as certificate systems (Gijselaers et al. 2013). Earlier professionalisation was understood as a local and geographically bound process in which the nation-state sets boundaries within which they emerge, structure themselves and interact with other professions. The trend has not been the same in all (European) countries. The literature usually differentiates between the state-regulated professions of continental Europe and the privately regulated professions of the Anglo-Saxon world. Present globalisation tendencies are complicated by these differences (Fourcade 2006; Beaverstock and Faulconbridge 2010). Within the European Union (EU), professions are increasingly transnational due to the free movement of workers and explicit political aim to increase mobility. At the moment, there is a licensing system for hundreds of professions in the EU. New transnational institutions provide sites, standards, knowledge and vocabularies of professional practice, and they increasingly represent national bodies in transnational debates about the professions and about standards for professional practice (Faulconbridge and Muzio 2012). Therefore, globalisation certainly has significant implications for the incumbent professions, with both the societies and the regulators around them changing and taking on new characteristics and forms. Also, at the national level, changes in legislation can result in new professional areas; one example of this is that new legislations about energy production and use have shaped the need to educate energy efficiency experts (Palonen et al. 2013).

The second mechanism is related to a multiplicity of the domains. Due to the complex and nontraditional nature of the problems to be solved, typical for many new areas of expertise, they are placed on the interface of traditional fields of expertise, infiltrating an entirely new area of research and knowledge production. Even if educational institutions are organised based on traditional disciplinary domains, this is not true for work organisations. Various problems are typically solved by multi-professional teams or by individuals who have expanded their expertise beyond traditional disciplines. The concept of 'hybrids' has been used to explain what is happening at work. The definition of 'hybrid' extends beyond organisational forms: hybrid practices, processes and expertise enable lateral information flows and cooperation across the boundaries of organisations, firms and groups of experts or professionals (Kurunmäki 2000; Miller et al. 2008).

The third mechanism for new jobs is based on technological development and new innovations. Technological and social innovations create opportunities for new kinds of marketable products and services. Examples are easy to find: the development of Facebook, chat services, outsourcing, smart houses, remote surveillance, crowd financing, nanotechnology, etc. For example, the fast increase of applications and business forms within social media has resulted in large numbers of new jobs, many of them requiring new expertise that did not exist earlier. Another route for new jobs originates from new needs arising, for example, as a result of these new services but also from demographic or other changes in societies. Job- and profession-wise we assume that the first group is inherently divergent as it is entrepreneurial in nature. Regardless of whether they are part of a business or self-employed, seeing and taking opportunities is in the first place an issue of the individual or small group who turns an idea into something real that is attractive to others. Their own skills and the market decide whether things become successful and can finally generate mainstream jobs. The latter case is inherently convergent, though. The needs arise when individuals, society or politics discover unwanted side effects of the new developments for certain groups in society that have to be remedied at the individual level and/or require new rules and regulations. New professionals pick up these problems. New practices have to be developed and professional standards need to be negotiated regarding the quality of work and conduct. These include the necessity of shared norms, values and procedures, i.e. a common understanding.

To conclude, when new jobs arise, they are, of necessity, based on informal and non-formal modes of learning rather than on the base of strong professional practices, traditional (educational) institutes and the always-cumulating stable knowledge base behind traditional actors. In the next section, we describe which features are essential when informal forums are wanted as a part of knowledge creation processes and structured learning procedures.

8.3   Informal Learning, Knowledge Creation and Adaptive Expert Practices

According to Marsick (2006), informal and incidental learning can be defined by their contrast with their formal learning counterparts. Formal learning is typically institutionally sponsored, classroom based and highly structured. Informal learning, instead, includes incidental learning that may occur in or out of institutions, but it is not typically classroom based or highly structured. Control of learning rests primarily in the hands of the learner. Incidental learning is a by-product of other activities. It can be deliberately encouraged by an organisation, but it is not necessarily so. Learning in informal and incidental modes 'just happens'; it is not designed or taught, and hence, it is not affected by pedagogical simplification. It is (1) integrated with work and daily routines, (2) triggered by an internal or external jolt, (3) not highly conscious, (4) often haphazard and influenced by chance, (5) an inductive process of reflection and action and (6) linked to the learning of others. Formal and explicit knowledge is a tool used by educated professionals to exchange and share knowledge in effective ways (Eraut 2000, 2004a, b; Lehtinen and Palonen 2011). Without explicit knowledge it is very laborious, if not impossible, to teach or learn complex domains. Educational practices in different domains are to a varying degree rooted in sound, agreed upon, formal knowledge bases. Due to a lack of such knowledge bases, educational practices aimed at preparing people for emerging fields face serious problems. Insufficiently explicated contextual and local 'craft' knowledge is not what organising formal education requires. Therefore, integration of formal and informal knowledge is needed when training for emerging professions is planned. Within educational institutes it is important to understand how a large part of an emerging field is built on pre-existing disciplinary knowledge and how much it relies on new, dynamically developing knowledge embedded in emerging practices. The advanced knowledge societies seem to require mastery of sophisticated knowledge and expertise. Therefore, creative human capabilities are becoming more important in an innovation-driven society or 'creative economy' in which people have to deliberately generate novelty, acquiring new competencies and breaking boundaries of earlier knowledge and competence. Instead of relying on once-acquired expertise, they have to move from one environment of professional activity to a new one and transit from one occupation and professional career to another, thereby breaking the boundaries of their earlier established capabilities (Hakkarainen 2009, 2010).

Traditionally, expertise has been defined as mastery of a well-organised body of usable knowledge (i.e. domain specific) that a participant can utilise to selectively focus on the critical aspects of a complex problem and thereby reach an exceptionally high level of performance (Chi 2006; Glaser and Chi 1988; Ericsson 2003, 2006). The knowledge and competencies in question do not, however, arise from the depth of the human mind but are embodied in social practices of expert communities and networks. Accordingly, sustained development of expertise is represented in evolving practices that significantly transform the participants' cognitive systems. Expertise, then, is a matter of a long-standing, effortful and deliberate process of socialisation and absorbing practices of an expert culture (Lave and Wenger 1991; Hakkarainen et al. 2004). Adaptive expertise appears to involve specific efforts to make the systematic pursuit of novelty and innovation a facet of one's established social practices. Even if individual experts' cognitive resources remain limited, collective activity allows specialisation, cognitive division of labour and sharing of intellectual efforts that provide qualitatively stronger creative resources than would otherwise be humanly possible. Across domains, significant human achievements appear to be correspondingly based on social distribution of cognitive efforts and collective merging and fusing of cognitions into higher-level systems (Hakkarainen 2009, 2010).

Knowledge practices, while sometimes just supporting routine learning (transmission), at their creative edge diverge from other routine social practices in that they take place in specific, purposefully dynamic and fluid settings designed for the furtherance of innovation and knowledge (Knorr-Cetina 1999, 2001). It seems that adaptive expertise is most important regarding emergent fields. Experts need to have the ability to quickly master and adapt to rapidly changing environments and move flexibly from one area to the next. This kind of learning based on knowledge creation practices is mainly happening out of formal educational institutions but is, however, deeply dependant on the disciplinary knowledge bases mediated in formal education.

8.4 Professional Expertise: The Integration of Individual Cognition and Professional Practices in the Context of Change

Expertise is expressed in the context of professional practice, integrating several dimensions. It is a synthesis of a particular knowledge base and the cognitive processes and internal integrative processes of the practitioner, building on interpersonal relationships with other professionals and affected by different kinds of external influences. From this perspective, the actual *doing* of professional practice is the hallmark of expertise. Conceptual models of professional expertise development (e.g. Ericsson et al. 1993; Mieg 2009; Schmidt et al. 1990) often integrate theoretical and practical learning and describe the development from novice to expert. They fail to show how practice development and professional expertise development can drive each other. They also fail to include the dynamics in the fields that are served and that are affected by the change drivers. In the following paragraphs we present a dynamic model of the development of professional practices in emerging fields (see Fig. 8.1). We do this by further elaborating on the model presented by Yielder (2004) and connecting it to more traditional expertise development literature, placing it in the context of change.

In this model, individual experts are equipped with a well-integrated knowledge base and cognitive and internal integrative processes. They interact with other professionals in mono- or multidisciplinary practice settings where ways of working, tools, organisational formats, client types and common and rare problems constitute the practices they work in, improve and further develop. Other factors affecting these practices are the goals that the companies, professionals or professions want to attain, and the conditions under which they do that. These conditions may include an implicit or explicit business philosophy such as sustainability, common good or maximising profits. Therefore, they define the standards for the goods or services delivered. External and internal influences lead to new practices; some may be very revolutionary, requiring experts to move to very new unknown fields. Yet it should be noted that this does not make them intermediates or even novices. What is and what is not transferable will largely depend on the individual professional and the domain at hand.

Knowledge base: The expert knowledge base is comprised of different kinds of knowledge with different qualities than what intermediates and novices have. Some knowledge kinds can be learned from books and other explicit sources, while others have to be learned from observation, experience, working alongside others and doing and applying theoretical knowledge in practical settings (Dornan et al. 2007). Expert knowledge bases are heavily integrated structures, which, on the one hand, should maintain scientific qualities as systems of meaning (Maton and Moore 2010; Wheelahan 2010) and, on the other hand, have built-in links to the problems and application situations of the specific profession. This knowledge base may include the integration of several knowledge domains and the development of domain-specific macro-concepts called 'encapsulations' and 'mental models' (templates or abstract schemata or scripts). Furthermore, experts have an extensive repertoire of cases dealt with earlier that can help justify or explain actions or decisions and a fathomless base of tacit and implicit knowledge (Boshuizen and Schmidt 2008). Experts approaching new fields will have to perform a lot of knowledge actions before they can be considered experts in these new areas. They have to rebuild parts of their knowledge base, first extending it and then restructuring it to fit the new problems and requirements leading to new encapsulations and new mental models. A less self-evident but also important aspect of the new knowledge that has to be acquired is the associated meta-knowledge, i.e. awareness of the qualities of the new

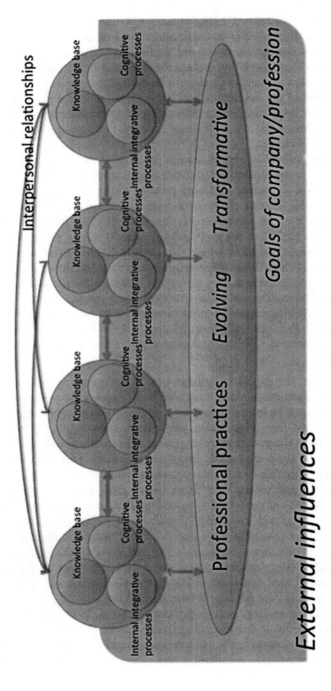

Fig. 8.1 The development of professional practices in emerging fields (Based on earlier work by Yielder 2004)

knowledge, such as its applicability and half-life. But more importantly, practical knowledge and practice-dependent knowledge structures will have to be attained during this stage of the development of a new profession, in cooperation with other new entrants who might be from very different domains.

Cognitive processes: Cognitive processes operating on these knowledge structures include information acquisition, reasoning processes, problem solving, perceptual ability and learning skills. Yielder (2004) also saw the metacognitive control of these processes as a cognitive process—an assumption we follow here. The quality of the knowledge base and the rigour with which these processes are executed define the quality of the outcomes. Yet, the quality is affected by the 'fit' between the knowledge base and the problems dealt with. These processes enable the integration and synthesis of information, taking a complex view of relationships and interactions. Depending on the familiarity of a task, context-based intuitive understanding and nonanalytical reasoning take place. These rapid, perceptual processes do not rely on independent analyses of separate cues but on encapsulations, integrated mental models and case-based reasoning based on experience, which allow for pattern matching along with rapid assessment, dynamic attention to critical cues, links, differentiations and invariants. Ill-defined, complex and changing situations, on the other hand, are novel and therefore difficult. These processes require the application of advanced knowledge for interpretation, reinterpretation, evaluation and justification in terms of meaningful relations among concepts. Experts' problem-solving processes include formulation of multiple alternative interpretations or representations of problems and rapid decisions based on cue recognition and detection of significance. Further, experts can generate, monitor and modify plans and strategies to meet the needs of changing situations. Task novelty requires an increased ability to explain and correct faulty reasoning, question assumptions and develop and use self-regulating metacognitive strategies.

Internal integrative processes: The processes that Yielder (2004) called 'internal integrative processes' relate to professional identity and responsibility towards science and profession (Mieg 2009), as well as towards the goals the company or profession wants to reach, observing the boundary conditions that are defined by their mission and raison d'être. They require an inherent interest and enthusiasm for professional practice. Internal integrative processes are tied to self-knowledge, awareness, assurance, esteem and confidence and make it possible to monitor, challenge and take responsibility for professionals' own and shared practices. Such processes require critical control of knowledge (Eraut 1994). They furthermore bear similarities to professional identity processes (Beijaard et al. 2004) and abilities at the highest levels of expertise required for professional or company goal awareness and the ability to make decisions in situations with ill-structured problems and time stresses, when routine action or thinking cannot be relied on. Recently, Boshuizen and Van de Wiel (2014) pointed out that performance improvement strategies of high-performing companies include key elements such as the development and discussion of standards, needs assessment, goal setting, describing job-relevant strengths and weaknesses based on assessment and feedback and coaching. For emerging professions the same strategies may be essential to improve internal integrative processes. Monitoring the process and outcomes could provide input for evaluation of the knowledge base. Finally, though the individual expert is responsible for his or her knowledge and cognitive and internal integrative processes, professional development in these respects must take place in cooperation with colleagues and professionals from other domains.

Professional interpersonal relationships: These establish a level of involvement, connection and engagement with clients and colleagues, in order to communicate expertise and teach others. Hakkarainen et al. (2004) developed a framework of 'networked expertise', a term that means:

> Higher-level cognitive competencies that arise, in appropriate environments, from sustained collaborative efforts to solve problems and build knowledge together. Networked expertise is relational in nature; it emerges from the tailoring and fine-tuning of individual competencies to specific conditions of the environment of the activity, and it is represented as a joint or shared competence of communities and organised groups of experts and professionals. ... heterogeneous networks involve – in addition to human actors – collectively developed knowledge artifacts and knowledge embedded in tools and practices. Networked expertise coevolves with the transformation of social communities, a process ...that may be facilitated by encouraging the participants to reflect on their current social and cognitive practices. (p. 9)

Professional practice: this practice requires the smooth and flexible application of knowledge and skills in situations that have known and unknown elements. Expert performances and practices are characterised by prediction and prevention, rather than by problem solving. Experts know much better than novices which conditions can cause problems and can take preventive measures long in advance or correct deviations at a much earlier stage. This ability is largely a consequence of the way experts' knowledge is represented (see Boshuizen and Schmidt 2008; Eraut 2008). Furthermore, expert practices are characterised by the integrated and coordinated execution of tasks with different time frames: fulfilment of short-term goals should not interfere with the fulfilment of long-term goals. Eraut (1994, 2008) has pointed out that the cognitive processes associated with these tasks also differ. Reading the situation in speedy tasks requires instant recognition, instant response and routinised unreflective action. Actions that occur at a somewhat slower pace may still require rapid interpretation and rapid decisions but can be monitored by reflection and hence altered in the process. Hakkarainen (2009) also talked about 'knowledge practices', with which he refers to personal and social practices related to working with knowledge. He includes explicitly or officially stated discourse as well as implicitly expressed habits in expert work. Knowledge practices sometimes just support routine learning (transmission) but at their creative edge also take place in dynamic and fluid settings designed for the furtherance of innovation and knowledge, rather than relying only on mundane habits or repetitive routines. Such newly established practices are aimed at solving emergent problems. It may be argued that the communities that follow such practices are themselves transformed to shared social practices through the cultivation of corresponding personal and collective competencies and patterns of shared activity (Knorr-Cetina 1999, 2001). An important aspect of professional practice is shared 'standards'. Professions, especially in care and aviation where clients' lives can be at risk, have set practice rules, codes of conduct, strategies, protocols, checklists or step-by-step plans that have to be followed. Such standards should be based on empirical evidence and regulate a lot of elements and aspects in practice. They define the actions that have to be performed, the priorities to be observed and the quality of the expected outcomes, and they regulate the interactions between the professionals involved. Standards should, however, leave room for professional judgment. Variations depend on factors such as the urgency of the situation, the amount of resources available and the litigation context (Farand et al. 1995).

A final view on the interaction between professional learning and practice development in situations of change comes from Mezirov (1991), who maintained that transformation and radical change require that we learn to negotiate meanings, purposes and values critically and reflectively, for it is through reflection that meaning schemes (specific knowledge, value judgments, feelings and beliefs that constitute interpretations of experience) and meaning perspectives (rule systems governing perception and cognition) can change and transform. However, much learning happens non-reflectively. According to Mezirov, we need to reflect *intentionally* for transformation to occur. While his emphasis on critical reflectivity assumes a retrospective analysis, the same process can be applied to reflection in action, using a shortened time scale (Eraut 1994, 2008). The importance of reflection *before* action is minimally addressed in the literature. Reflection-before-action practices might help to change those routinised and paced practices that are hardly permeable, whereas lack of reflection and hence lack of awareness of potential mistakes and mismatches may result in poor practice and the potential for mistakes.

As a concluding statement we want to emphasise that the analysis presented in this chapter provides a framework to examine at the interplay between change and novelty, practice development, expertise (re)development and educational measures for initial and lifelong learning. At the same time, it is apparent that each combination of factors provides new challenges and requires solutions that are tailor made to that unique combination. It is impossible, at least at this stage of our knowledge, to provide templates or guidelines for educational design that go beyond general advice of content and context coupling and practice-near methods. Yet, despite this vacuum many training courses have been developed that try to fill the gap between the present level of knowledge and the skill of professionals who take on new tasks and the required performance that might be expected in the case of the products and services delivered. As a final step we describe our experiences with a Finnish model of academic apprenticeship post-experience programmes.

8.5   Discussion and Experiences from Finnish Post-experience Programmes for New Jobs

In Finland, new educational courses have been developed in several fields in the frames of a newly established model of academic apprenticeship post-experience programmes (AAT) at a higher education level, to be organised together with working-life organisations. Since 2009 there have been approximately 1,200 participants yearly. RPL is expected to have an important role in the AAT model. From the beginning it was obvious that many of the programmes were aimed at expanding participants' skills and competencies in new and emerging fields. In many cases the participants' earlier training corresponds with another higher education degree, but the way it is acquired is working life based. In entrepreneurship and business education, for example, the contents correspond to a higher education degree level, but the execution and approach are tailored to the needs of businesses, e.g. turning knowledge into business in the fields of biotechnology. In general, the idea has been to create a framework for post-experience education with a significant amount of learning in authentic working-life environments. The name of the educational model (Academic Apprenticeship Training) may be somewhat misleading, as the pathway is not designed for newcomers or young students, but instead it is a way to educate experts for specialised and new tasks.

Ideally, the higher education institutions or networks that provide these programmes have research-based knowledge that can take the skills learned at workplaces to a new level. The general and established model includes theoretical studies that are organised around 6–10 contact teaching days, which can include workshops and group work. This is complemented with online studies and online tutoring and discussions. The most basic premise of AAT is learning by doing in the workplace, which takes up about 70–80 % of the time allocated for learning, though it is difficult to estimate how real the work organisations' input truly is. For a participant, a project assignment functions often as a skills demonstration during which a new product or service is developed and new skills are learned. In some cases there are extra measures to ensure learning outcomes through work arrangements (e.g. job circulation). The biggest problem with the AAT model has been in creating, controlling and recognising sufficient preconditions for learning at work (Korkeakoulutettujen oppisopimustyyppiset täydennyskoulutukset 2010). This is mainly related to the problem of controlling the quality of workplace environments or workplace tutors. Based on the findings of expertise research, a long working experience does not necessarily guarantee the development of expertise. Instead, there are indications that a long work career can even lead to incompetence in many individuals (Ericsson 2006). On the other hand, expertise research does not give evidence that the length of formal education correlates with increasing skills at work. New models to mediate knowing and maintaining expertise at work are needed. One of the most important concerns is whether specific workplaces are good environments to develop the new skills.

The question of how to recognise or assess expert performance is important because it will later indicate which skills and criteria need to be focused on in educational practices (Ericsson 2006). The assessment criteria have an important role here. There are problems in understanding how expert skills should be assessed. The traditional practices have been based on certificates, degrees and positions in professional bodies (Shanteau et al. 2002). Empirical results, however, indicate that these do not always show real expert performance (Ericsson 2006; Weiss and Schanteau 2003). One explanation for this has been that, for example, reaching a good position within a professional community can be based on many kinds of properties—some of the kind that are not related to professional skills (Ericsson 2004). Yet, it is obvious that when assessment is tied to direct action in real working environments, it is more reliable than creating assessment situations outside of it. In most cases it is not hard to distinguish a novice from an expert (Isaacs and Clark 1987). In addition, in knowledge-rich areas with long histories, it is quite easy to agree upon so-called golden standards that represent rather objective measures of professional performance (Weiss and Schanteau 2003; Ericsson 2006). The problems are much bigger when there are no standards that tasks can be based on. It is hard to make evaluations if there is no shared understanding of the right or optimal answers or solutions (Gigerenzer et al. 1999). In emerging fields these standards are under construction. What is especially needed is a guarantee that the theoretical part of knowing, i.e. knowing explicitly, fits together with the workplace part, i.e. knowing implicitly. This has been shown to be true in stable, traditional knowledge-rich domains. Yet, we may expect that in emerging fields, the control and quality problems will be met more often than in traditional fields. Emerging fields suffer from being fragmented, often being based on various and maybe competing knowledge paradigms. They do not form a coherent field and are under continuous change. Policy alignments, bureaucratic processes, European harmonisation procedures and decision-making structure the field and take precedence over professional practice building or local communities. Where shared practices and professional performance and product standards are lacking, practitioners' intentional networks and informal knowledge exchanges become increasingly important.

The newest knowledge needs to be integrated as a part of individual professionals' prior knowledge and skill repertoires and as a part of the professional body. It needs to be embedded as a part of the artefacts, tools, methods and routines, and therefore educational models that integrate professional training and practice development should be pushed forward along many frontiers, in flexible ways. One of the biggest problems is the lack of shared and certified knowledge and recognised experts, or maybe even a proper institution to do this. In the Finnish AAT model, the variation and diversity of the courses has been one of the big issues that have been discussed. The quality has been too closely tied to the person in charge, whereas the consolidated practices related to workplace learning have been lacking (Korkeakoulujen oppisopimustyyppiset täydennyskoulutukset 2010). Then, how can one organise a trusted educational model with relevant contents and control for quality? Following previous similar efforts (i.e. Dower et al. 2001) we want to set some important questions to be answered for when education is organised in the context of emerging fields:

1. Standards: Are educational opportunities standardised across the field? If they are, then how were the curricula standardised and who oversees maintenance of standards?
2. Apprenticeship models: Which components, competency assessments and supervision and mentoring elements are involved?
3. Recognising educational processes: Does the target group seek to recognise, through some sort of verification process, the credibility of education and training programmes? If it does, then in what way? Which of the education opportunities are accredited and by whom? If accreditation mechanisms are not used, are there other means to verify the competence of an individual entering into the profession?

4. Tests and examinations: Does the context involved have standardised tests individuals can take to demonstrate their knowledge, skills and judgment in the profession?
5. Work experience: Do the certifying mechanisms give credit for work experience? In what way? How is the training and assessment model matched to the professional practice? How is competence determined?
6. Ownership of the emerging field knowledge: Where is the new expertise located? How is practice-based knowledge (e.g. located inside companies) coupled with scientific knowledge? Are the actors that cultivate this knowledge willing to allow free access to it?

To sum up, expert performance is built on theoretical and practical knowing, self-regulation and metacognition that are integrated as a part of the sociocultural entity. Expertise includes both pre-existing prior knowledge and information of best practices and innovative adaptive elements. Deliberate practice and continuous development are a central feature of the expert lifespan that can be cultivated in rich and relevant contexts. Criteria for professionals' work are defined by the expert communities. New mechanisms are needed that support long-lasting, meaningful and functional practices. Many important problems related to emerging fields remain and there are questions that are not easy to answer. One of the most essential ones is how to bring practice-based knowledge and scientific knowledge production together, and should this even be done? What is the role of scientific knowledge in developing the content and quality assurance criteria for the emerging expertise fields? Project-based action and temporary plans, i.e. so-called *ad hocratia*, do not always make efforts in educational projects easy. It is difficult to reach or maintain sufficient standards for education, or to get the best experts to take part in the projects that are realised (only) occasionally. One should pay attention to educating whole units or communities or networks or clusters, instead of developing one course at a time. Education needs to be tied to larger entities instead of fragmented pieces of information, facts and random case-based thinking. This all takes time. When implementing new approaches and tools, one needs to be prepared for delays, problems and failures.

Acknowledgments Research has been funded by FUTUREX project that is part of European Social Fund programme; Finnish Ministry of Education and Culture (Asko-project), and Academy of Finland grant 263787. The article was written during professor Boshuizen's research period, funded by the Open Universiteit in the Netherlands.

References

Beaverstock, J. V., & Faulconbridge, J. R. (2010). Professionalization, legitimization and the creation of executive search markets in Europe. *Journal of Economic Geography, 10*(6), 825–843.
Beijaard, D., Meijer, P. C., & Verloop, N. (2004). Reconsidering research on teachers' professional identity. *Teaching and Teacher Education, 20*(2), 107–128.

Billett, S., & Somerville, M. (2004). Transformations at work: Identity and learning. *Studies in Continuing Education, 26*(2), 309–326.

Boshuizen, H. P. A., & Schmidt, H. G. (2008). The development of clinical reasoning expertise: Implications for teaching. In J. Higgs, M. Jones, S. Loftus, & N. Christensen (Eds.), *Clinical reasoning in the health professions* (3rd comp. rev. ed., pp. 113–121). Oxford, UK: Butterworth-Heinemann/Elsevier.

Boshuizen, H. P. A., & Van de Wiel, M. W. J. (2014). Expertise development through schooling and work. In A. Littlejohn & A. Margaryan (Eds.), *Technology-enhanced professional learning: Processes, practices, and tools* (pp. 71–84). London: Routledge.

Chi, M. T. H. (2006). Two approaches to the study of experts' characteristics. In K. A. Ericsson, N. Charness, P. Feltovich, & R. Hoffman (Eds.), *The Cambridge handbook of expertise and expert performance* (pp. 21–30). Cambridge, MA: Cambridge University Press.

Cooper, D., & Robson, K. (2006). Accounting, professions and regulation: Locating the sites of professionalization. *Accounting, Organizations and Society, 31*(4–5), 415–444.

Davies, A., Fidler, D., & Gorbis, M. (2011). *Future work skills 2020*. Phoenix: Institute for the Future for University of Phoenix Research Institute.

Dornan, T., Boshuizen, H. P. A., King, N., & Scherpbier, A. J. J. A. (2007). Experience-based learning: A model linking the processes and outcomes of medical students' workplace learning. *Medical Education, 41*(1), 84–91.

Dower, C., O'Neil, E., & Hough, H. J. (2001). *Profiling the professions: A model for evaluating emerging health professions*. San Francisco: Center for the Health Professions, University of California.

Englund, T. (1996). Are professional teachers a good thing? In I. Goodson & A. Hargreaves (Eds.), *Teachers' professional lives*. London/Philadelphia: Falmer Press.

Eraut, M. (1994). *Developing professional knowledge and competence*. Abingdon: RoutlegdeFalmer.

Eraut, M. (2000). Non-formal learning and tacit knowledge in professional work. *British Journal of Educational Psychology, 70*, 113–136.

Eraut, M. (2004a). Informal learning in the workplace. *Studies in Continuing Education, 26*(2), 247–273.

Eraut, M. (2004b). Transfer of knowledge between education and workplace settings. In H. Rainbird, A. Fuller, & A. Munro (Eds.), *Workplace learning in context* (pp. 201–221). London: Routledge.

Eraut, M. (2008). Learning from other people in workplaces. In K. Hall, P. Murphy, & J. Soler (Eds.), *Pedagogy and practice: Culture and identities* (pp. 40–57). London: Sage.

Ericsson, K. A. (2003). The acquisition of expert performance as problem solving: Construction and modification of mediating mechanisms through deliberate practice. In J. A. Davidson & R. Sternberg (Eds.), *The psychology of problem solving* (pp. 31–83). Cambridge: Cambridge University Press.

Ericsson, K. A. (2004). Deliberate practice and the acquisition and maintenance of expert performance in medicine and related domains. *Academic Medicine, 19*, 70–81.

Ericsson, K. A. (2006). The influence of experience and deliberate practice on the development of superior expert performance. In K. A. Ericsson, N. Charness, P. Feltovich, & R. Hoffman (Eds.), *The Cambridge handbook of expertise and expert performance* (pp. 683–704). Cambridge, MA: Cambridge University Press.

Ericsson, K. A., Krampe, R. T., & Tesch-Römer, C. (1993). The role of deliberate practice in the acquisition of expert performance. *Psychological Review, 100*(3), 363–406.

Farand, L., Leprohon, J., Kalina, M., Champagne, F., Contandriopoulos, A. P., & Preker, A. (1995). The role of protocols and professional judgement in emergency medical dispatching. *European Journal of Emergency Medicine, 2*(3), 136–148.

Faulconbridge, J. R., & Muzio, D. (2012). Professions in a globalizing world: Towards a transnational sociology of the professions. *International Sociology, 27*(1), 136–152.

Fejes, A., & Andersson, P. (2009). Recognising prior learning: Understanding the relations among experience, learning and recognition from a constructivist perspective. *Vocations and Learning, 2*(1), 37–55.

Fourcade, M. (2006). The construction of a global profession: The transnationalization of economics. *American Journal of Sociology, 112*(1), 145–194.

Gegenfurtner, A., Nivala, M., Säljö, R., & Lehtinen, E. (2009). Capturing individual and institutional change: Exploring horizontal versus vertical transitions in technology-rich environments. In U. Cress, V. Dimitrova, & M. Specht (Eds.), *Learning in the synergy of multiple disciplines: Lecture notes in computer science* (pp. 676–681). Berlin: Springer.

Gigerenzer, G., Todd, P., & The ABC Group. (1999). *Simple heuristics that make us smart.* London: Oxford University Press.

Gijselaers, W. H., & Milter, R. G. (2010). Issues in accounting/business education. In P. Peterson, E. Baker, & B. McGaw (Eds.), *International encyclopedia of education* (Vol. 3, pp. 39–44). Oxford: Elsevier.

Gijselaers, W. H., Dailey-Hebert, A., & Niculescu, A. C. (2013). Shaping the new professional for the new professions. In S. Baroncelli, R. Farneti, I. Horga, & S. Vanhoonacker (Eds.), *Teaching and learning the European Union: Traditional and innovative methods* (pp. 15–40). Dordrecht/Boston/London: Springer.

Glaser, R., & Chi, M. T. H. (1988). Overview. In H. T. M. Chi, R. Glaser, & M. Farr (Eds.), *The nature of expertise* (pp. xv–xxviii). Hillsdale: Erlbaum.

Hakkarainen, K. (2009). Knowledge-practice perspective on technology-mediated learning. *Computer-Supported Collaborative Learning, 4,* 213–231. doi:10.1007/s11412-009-9064-x.

Hakkarainen, K. (2010, May). *Expertise, collective creativity and shared knowledge practices.* Keynote address presented at the Fourth Finnish Conference of Cultural and Activity Research, Aalto University, Helsinki.

Hakkarainen, K., Palonen, T., Paavola, S., & Lehtinen, E. (2004). *Communities of networked expertise: Educational and professional perspectives.* Amsterdam: Elsevier.

Hargreaves, A. (2000). Four ages of professionalism and professional learning. *Teachers and Teaching: History and Practice, 6*(2), 151–182.

Hargreaves, A., & Fullan, M. (2000). Mentoring in the new millennium. *Theory into Practice, 39*(1), 50–56.

Isaacs, E. A., & Clark, H. H. (1987). References in conversation between experts and novices. *Journal of Experimental Psychology: General, 116*(1), 26–37. doi:10.1037/0096-3445.116.1.26.

Jerneck, A., Olsson, L., Barry, N., Anderberg, S., Baier, M., Clark, E., Hickler, T., Hornborg, A., Kronsell, A., Övbrand, E., & Persson, J. (2011). Structuring sustainability science. *Sustainability Science, 6,* 69–82.

Karvinen-Niinikoski, S. (2004). Social work supervision: Contributing to innovative knowledge production and open expertise. In N. Gould & M. Baldwin (Eds.), *Social work, critical reflection and learning organisation.* Aldershot: Ashgate.

Knorr-Cetina, K. (1999). *Epistemic cultures: How the sciences make knowledge.* Cambridge, MA: Harvard University Press.

Knorr-Cetina, K. (2001). Objectual practices. In T. Schatzki, K. Knorr-Cetina, & E. Von Savigny (Eds.), *The practice turn in contemporary theory* (pp. 175–188). London: Routledge.

Korkeakoulutettujen oppisopimustyyppiset täydennyskoulutukset. (2010). Kyselyn tiivistelmä. Futurex–hanke. Retrieved from http://futurex.utu.fi/julkaisut.php

Kurunmäki, L. (2000). *A hybrid profession: The appropriation of management accounting expertise by medical professions* (Discussion Paper 18). London: LSE Health, London School of Economics & Political Science.

Lave, J., & Wenger, E. (1991). *Situated learning: Legitimate peripheral participation.* Cambridge, MA: Cambridge University Press.

Lehtinen, E., & Palonen, T. (2011). Asiantuntijuuden luonne ja osaamisen tunnistamisen haasteet. *Ammattikasvatuksenaikakauskirja, 13*(4), 24–42.

Marsick, V. (2006). Informal strategic learning in the workplace. In J. S. Streumer (Ed.), *Work-related learning* (pp. 51–69). Dordrecht: Springer.

Maton, K., & Moore, R. (Eds.). (2010). *Social realism, knowledge and the sociology of education: Coalitions of the mind.* London: Continuum.

McDonough, W., & Braungart, M. (2002). Design for the triple top line: New tools for sustainable commerce. *Corporate Environmental Strategy, 9*(3), 251–258.

Mezirow, J. (1991). *Transformative dimensions of adult learning*. San Francisco: Jossey-Bass.

Mieg, H. A. (2009). Two factors of expertise? Excellence and professionalism of environmental experts. *High Ability Studies, 20*(1), 91–115.

Miller, P., Kurunmäki, L., & O'Leary, T. (2008). Accounting, hybrids and the management of risk. *Accounting, Organizations and Society, 33*(7–8), 942–967.

Palonen, T., Boshuizen, H. P., Hytönen, K., Hakkarainen, K., & Lehtinen, E. (2013). Nousevat ja nopeasti muuttuvat asiantuntijuuskäytännöt ja niihin kouluttautuminen. In A. Rouhelo & H. Trapp (Eds.), *Tulevaisuuden asiantuntijuutta rakentamassa*. Turun yliopiston koulutus- ja kehittämiskeskus Brahean julkaisuja B:1. Turun yliopiston koulutus- ja kehittämiskeskus Brahea.

Redecker, C., Leis, M., Leendertse, M., Punie, Y., Gijsbers, G., Kirschner, P., Stoyanov, S., & Hoogveld, B. (2010). *The future of learning: New ways to learn. New skills for future jobs. Results from an online expert consultation*. Luxembourg: Publications Office of the European Union. European Communities, 2010.

Schmidt, H. G., Norman, G. R., & Boshuizen, H. P. A. (1990). A cognitive perspective on medical expertise: Theory and implications. *Academic Medicine, 65*, 611–621.

Shanteau, J., Weiss, J. A., Thomas, R. P., & Pounds, J. C. (2002). Performance-based assessment of expertise. How to decide if someone is an expert or not. *European Journal of Operational Research, 136*, 253–263.

Stahl, G. (2006). *Group cognition: Computer support for building collaborative knowledge*. Cambridge, MA: MIT Press.

Talwar, R., & Hancock, T. (2010, January). *The shape of jobs to come: Possible new careers emerging from advances in science and technology (2010–2030)*. Final Report. Fast Future Research.

Weiss, D. J., & Schanteau, J. (2003). Empirical assessment of expertise. *Human Factors, 45*, 104–114.

Wheelahan, L. (2010). *Why knowledge matters in curriculum: A social realist argument*. Abingdon: Routledge.

Yielder, J. (2004). An integrated model of professional expertise and its implications for higher education. *International Journal of Lifelong Education, 23*, 60–80.

Chapter 9
Continuing Education and Training at Work

Sarojni Choy, Raymond Smith, and Ann Kelly

9.1 Case for Continuing Education and Training

Participation in education and training and in ongoing learning experiences at work has long been a means of accessing and securing the kinds of cultural, social and economic capital (Bourdieu 1986; Fevre 2000) foundational to personal wellbeing, organisational success and social and economic prosperity. In advanced industrial economies, the need to invest in continuing education and training (CET) and other forms of lifelong learning that strengthen the interdependent relationships between work, workers and workplaces has become central economic and political priorities (OECD 2010, 2013; Szreter 2000; Field 2005). For individual workers, such investment addresses their capacities to secure, sustain and advance employability within and across a range of work environments and labour markets that are constantly changing. For employing organisations, such investment addresses issues of competitive advantage and staff retention in increasingly global and mobile markets. For governments and regulatory bodies, it addresses broad issues of civic participation, political stability and economic growth as well as more immediate concerns of unemployment, skills training and workforce development. Within this context, this chapter discusses the nature of CET provision and enactment and advances suggestions for its enhancement within the Australian workplace learning context. These suggestions emerge from research that examined workers' and managers' perceptions of the quality and capacities of their CET learning experiences to support employability while addressing their needs in responding to the changing requirements of their work.

S. Choy (✉) • R. Smith • A. Kelly
Adult and Vocational Education, School of Education and Professional Studies,
Griffith University, Brisbane, QLD, Australia
e-mail: s.choy@griffith.edu.au; raymond.smith@griffith.edu.au; ann.kelly@griffith.edu.au

T. Halttunen et al. (eds.), *Promoting, Assessing, Recognizing and Certifying Lifelong Learning: International Perspectives and Practices*, Lifelong Learning Book Series 20, DOI 10.1007/978-94-017-8694-2_9, © Springer Science+Business Media Dordrecht 2014

The research identified a range of potential models and learning practices that bring CET training and its enactment closer, both proximally and conceptually, to the personal and contextual needs of work and workers increasingly impacted by forces of change (e.g. econo-structural, organisational, occupational and techno-logical). The models and practices advanced here require stronger integration of stakeholder resources, that is, greater collaboration among workers, enterprises, education providers and regulators who can collaboratively construct the learning frameworks and strategies that enact effective CET provision and practice. Importantly, indications of what and how such frameworks and strategies can be accomplished emerge from the considerations and experiences, first, of worker-learners, who participated in the research reported in this chapter and actively engage in the increasingly frequent and rigorous learning necessities of their work. These 136 working people, many with substantial work experiences and nationally accredited vocational qualifications, provided evidence that the prolif-eration of training in and for work is now a standard practice. Similarly, the 60 managers who were interviewed claimed that their role had expanded to one which required facilitating training on a regular basis to meet the changing demands that are both global and industry specific. Both groups reported on and explained the strengths and weaknesses of current CET provisions within their specific work situations and indicated what they required and would prefer in terms of learning provisions to better meet their needs and the changes that are currently impacting on their work.

In overview, the chapter argues that a national CET provision that simultane-ously addresses the learning requirements of workers and their enterprises and, ultimately, the socio-economic bases to support broader national goals needs to be based more on the individual circumstances of workers and their work environ-ments. A set of three complementary practice-based learning approaches that could form the foundation of CET models and associated learning practices is elabo-rated. The three approaches are: (1) individual practice, (2) expert guidance and (3) educational intervention. Together, these approaches offer an opportunity to achieve flexibility in integration of ongoing individual work-related learning within the broadening contexts of organisational, occupational and national frameworks within which CET is situated.

In advancing the case for these three approaches as potential bases for a national CET provision, and following from this introduction, the chapter progresses through the following four sections. The first offers an outline of the conceptual underpin-nings for CET models and practices. The second summarises the research design, methodology and participant details. The third section presents some of the findings that emerged, and the fourth and final section discusses key implications that arise from basing a national CET provision in the specific circumstances of individual workers. Importantly here, the focus on the circumstances of individual workers does not represent the promotion of learning alone. Rather, it heightens a focus on learner-centred learning for work as a socio-personal accomplishment that needs to be acknowledged and supported.

9.2   Conceptual Context for Continuing Education and Training

Continuing education and training pertains to ongoing requirements and provisions of learning in and for work for existing workers to advance initial entry level training. In the broad sense, CET entails the provision of work-related learning opportunity and experience that accords with immediate needs and future prognoses, be they planned and necessary or incidental and aspirational. At the individual level, its focus is on work-life learning to sustain employability. At a more macro level, its focus is on increased organisational capacity and workforce development (EQAVET 2013; CEDEFOP 2009) and, ultimately, social cohesion and economic prosperity. Essentially, CET is the facilitation of targeted work-related learning practices that address known goals and intentions for skill development and performance improvement. At micro and macro levels, its focus is equipping and enabling workers and their organisations to meet current and expected industry workforce requirements (COAG 2012). In both the general and specific senses, CET is change oriented and can be viewed as a vehicle for and safeguard against the kinds of econo-social changes that characterise contemporary work.

Workers and their enterprises are increasingly required to both generate and respond to the pace and extent of changes in occupational and work requirements and changing work practices and concepts. These requirements necessitate participation and engagement in CET to develop capacities for the ensuing challenges such changes bring, be they technical, cultural or structural. Intrinsically, these changes influence the kinds of work available to be undertaken, how that work is organised and practised, the occupation-specific requirements of that work and with whom workers need to interact to understand and successfully complete their work (Billett 2006a). Ellström et al. (2004) contend that 'occupational learning occurring in the context of work is influenced by local rules, values, attitudes, expectations etc… and shaped and transformed by material, social, discursive and historical conditions and relations' (p. 479). Because changes impact distinctively in different occupations and workplaces, workers need to constantly reinvent themselves by developing and creating new and actionable knowledge and skills as well as dispositions, personal qualities and 'ways of being' (Eraut 2004) that are appropriate for particular types of work (Barnett 2006). Further, learning for and in response to these various changes and influences require workers to interact with others to make meanings with different people, through different work tasks in disparate situations. Such interactions and socialisation with others in the workplace, for purposes of occupational learning, become imperative. These commentaries imply that learning through work is relational, a shared accomplishment mediated by the vast array of contextual and situational factors shaping its enactment. Kemmis (2005) supports this view, adding that collaboration with fellow workers and clients extends the scope of learning. So, relations between workers and all the other human resources that constitute their work (e.g. colleagues, clients, managers and trainers) shape learning in personally and situationally distinct ways, thereby enriching its utility (Billett 2006b).

However, some argue that much of the learning at and through work tends to be mostly about acquiring 'job knowledge' (e.g. Howell et al. 2001), that is, to meet workplace-specific requirements. The implication here is that such learning is too situational and, therefore, insufficient to meet the broader demands of sustaining employability within industrial and economy-wide changes. Fuller and Unwin (2003) caution that workplaces can restrict effective work-related learning and potentially limit workers and organisations to domains of practice, forms of participation and task orientations that are singular, repetitive and non-collaborative. In such environments there can be little chance of the kinds of experimentation, reflection and boundary crossing known to support rich learning experiences. Additionally, work-related learning may be different and even opposed to what is prescribed in tertiary education and training curricula. Nevertheless, tertiary socialisation in the workplace is likely to assist workers learn and engage in critical dialogue and performances that will improve work outputs, quality of life and economic success. Evans and Rainbird (2001) describe tertiary socialisation as the new archetype for CET, giving a new meaning to what counts as learning and knowledge in and through work, and this way extending traditional dualisms of tertiary and work-based learning provisions. It exacts new roles and responsibilities for a range of stakeholders (e.g. workers, employers, tertiary education and training institutions and governments) and a rebranding of CET that will actively engage and commit all stakeholders to achieve more productive outcomes. Therefore, the development of curricula, and contexts that facilitate and support effective situated learning, demands careful consideration. Significant within such considerations is the point that Lave and Wenger (1991) illuminate through their concept of communities of practice. That is, learning is not some isolated activity simply situated within a given work context, rather an activity of that context and, as such, constitutes that context. Learning cannot be understood apart from the community of practice by which it emerges in the form of description and explanation of the kinds of changes that characterise any specific community of practice. According to Lave and Wenger (1991), 'Learning, transformation and change are always implicated in one another' (p. 57).

What is apparent within accounts of the social and situated nature of workers' learning in and for work is that learning, in order to respond to workplace changes and influences, needs to extend beyond the traditional curricula of tertiary education and training provisions and to include richer contributions of situated and inter-relational aspects of learning in and through work. Significantly, two key factors characterise the 'traditional' system. First, it is primarily focused on preparatory and entry level training such as apprenticeships, traineeships and lower levels of certification. Second, it is highly institutionalised and operates very much along the lines of a 'schooling' model where students are taught in large groups in classroom situations facilitated by a single teacher or trainer at prescribed times.

So how can busy workers, that is, those who are already in employment and now subject to the many and varied demands their changing work requires, access, participate and be better supported to engage in CET? What curriculum and pedagogical practices are best suited to meet their learning and contextual circumstances? How can their learning be recognised and accredited within the qualification frameworks that govern the ways that current provisions are institutionalised? Such questions call for an examination, of current work-related learning provisions for those workers who have advanced beyond initial and entry level training, in order to propose the types of CET models and approaches that can appropriately develop the necessary occupational capacities of individuals and their organisations.

The research study appraisal reported in this chapter began with identifying, reviewing and assessing the utility of a set of models and strategies for CET (see Billett et al. 2012). The review of literature related to these is outlined in the following section.

9.3 Appraisal of Current Models and Approaches

Typically, variations of three main models of CET provisions serve the needs of workers: (i) wholly education institution based, (ii) wholly practice-based experiences and (iii) a combination of practice-based experiences with educational interventions. These are briefly summarised below:

(i) *Wholly education institution-based models*

This type of learning is attractive to workers who have little choice when learning needs to be accredited by tertiary education and training providers against qualifications. Provisions in this mode offer formal training and, in some cases, workplace experiences to gain both canonical and practical knowledge and skills to enable learners become occupationally competent. These kinds of experiences allow individuals to engage in structured learning for the purpose of developing their capabilities to effectively manage new or emerging aspects of work tasks (e.g. using specialised technologies or upgrading for registration and licensing purposes), and for personal and professional advancement (e.g. to become front line managers, or qualified VET trainers). There is a danger in adopting this mode, though, that knowledge and skills gained through traditional classroom arrangements may only include limited or no practical experiences, and engender a passive 'acquisition' orientation to engagement in learning activities. Indeed, it is widely acknowledged that wholly institution-based educational experiences are not sufficient for developing the kinds of capacities required for active and productive occupational practice (Griffiths and Guile 2003; OECD 2009, 2010). While the acquisition of theoretical knowledge through wholly educational institution-based provisions may support the development of canonical occupational capacities (i.e. those required and expected of practitioners), it is the applied nature of occupational knowledge and skills that necessitates experiences in authentic settings.

(ii) *Wholly practice-based models*

Ideally, wholly practice-based experiences contribute to occupational competence as well as occupational (career-related) development. Through the development of legitimised dispositions, knowledge and skills, such experiences contribute to three key areas of competence, namely, performing specific job and occupational tasks, being a 'member' of the work community and being proficient and effective in using the situational discourses and assessing one's work and ways of working and acting (Paloniemi 2006, pp. 443–444). Learning is realised through on-the-job experiences when individuals engage in everyday activities and interactions and extend their knowledge and skills, both directly or indirectly, through access to more experienced co-workers. It is through the interactions with others during work that workers acquire 'job knowledge' such as the types of interpersonal skills required for specific occupations, the ability for 'deep acting' (Handy 1995) and an understanding of the distinct social, cultural, political and economic contexts that shape work and can then appropriately engage with and respond to these. The concept of deep acting relates to dealing with different situations by broadening one's dispositional abilities. Learning for deep acting exposes workers to different uses they can make of what they know and have learnt, thereby stretching beyond 'routines invented by others, servicing aspirations invented by others, realizing goals invented by others, and giving expression to values advocated by others' (Kemmis and McTaggart 2000, p. 570).

Further, three forms of practice-based experiences are common. The first is practice-based structured experiences which are intentionally rich, often novel to participants and extend the scope of work roles and experiences. The second form is practice-based experiences with direct guidance such as shadowing, mentoring and coaching by more experienced colleagues. Learning is organised purposefully to enrich the capacities of workers through joint problem-solving and engagement in a range of routine and nonroutine activities. The third form of practice is opportunity-based experiences as part of routine work roles. An example of such experiences is seen in the handover practices that characterise occupations such as nursing. These types of experiences could be further enriched by critical reflection during and after the handovers. However, because workplaces focus more on productive work performances as opposed to learning per se, worker-learners need to have a genuine and mindful interest in learning, actively access opportunities and be self-directed in their work and learning. Furthermore, effective occupational outcomes are achieved if the curriculum is enacted in ways that invite individuals to develop competencies that are valued for and by key others at work (Billett and Choy 2011). Hence, workplace affordances play a critical part in inviting workers to negotiate opportunities to support different forms of learning.

(iii) *Practice-based experiences with educational interventions models*

Practice-based experiences with educational interventions allow workers to engage in action learning or action research projects, work improvement projects, quality enhancement projects, training and development programmes or projects organised by the employer, where these lead to formal credits towards a qualification. There are two variations to this model (Choy et al. 2008): an *extension model of entry level preparation* intended for experienced workers or those who are changing careers and using past experiences as a basis for entry into a new occupation (e.g. child care centre directors) and an *extension model for further development*, which is better suited for workers who already have completed their initial occupational development and have some experience to draw from. Here employment-based experiences are supported by educational provisions outside of work time and augmented with additional provisions in the evening, at weekends or by distance services.

From the elaboration of the three models listed above, the conceptual basis for CET could comprise a range of learning experiences in tertiary education and training institutions as well as workplaces that Australian workers can engage in. Of these, it is the third models that allows the development of conceptual as well as practical capacities of workers and meets the requirements for qualifications and, where necessary, registration and licensing. These considerations were an important aspect in the development of the interview schedules of the study that is reported in some detail below and in the analysis of the findings that resulted.

9.4   Examining Workers' and Managers' Perceptions of Learning Provision and Preference for CET

A total of 136 workers and 60 managers from five industries (Health and Community Services (mainly aged care), Transport and Logistics, Mining, Financial Services and Hospitality Services) participated in the research reported here.

9.4.1   Worker Sample

The locations, gender and age groups of worker participants are presented in Table 9.1.

As shown in this table, almost equal proportions of the worker sample came from metropolitan and regional areas (45 % and 47 %, respectively). There were more female (61 %), a majority from the aged care industry, and most of the male workers came from the Transport and Logistics and Mining industries. Almost half the participants (52 %) belonged to the 30–39 and 50–59 age brackets. Very few were aged below 20 years or over 60 years (4 and 10, respectively). A majority of the participants (63 %) had work experiences ranging between 1 and 5 years, with another 23 % with 6–10 years, 7 % with 11–15 years, 5 % with 16–20 years and about 3 % with over 20 years of work experience in their current jobs. (15 cases were missing.) These figures suggest that the participants in the study had different levels of knowledge and expertise in their work and experiences in learning about their work to provide valuable insights about their participation and engagement in CET.

Table 9.1 Workers' region, gender, age and mode of employment

		Sector					
		H&CS (aged care)	Transport and logistics	Mining	Financial services	Services/ hospitality	Total
Region	Brisbane	19	14	0	9	8	42 (23 %)
	Qld regional	10	7	7	0	0	24 (18 %)
	Perth	18	0	9	0	0	27 (20 %)
	WA regional	4	0	22	0	0	26 (19 %)
	Melbourne	0	0	0	3	0	3 (2 %)
	Vic regional	0	0	0	0	6	6 (4 %)
	NSW regional	0	0	0	0	8	8 (6 %)
	Total	51 (38 %)	21 (15 %)	38 (28 %)	12 (9 %)	22 (16 %)	136 (100 %)
Gender	Male	9	17	24	0	3	53 (39 %)
	Female	42	4	14	4	19	83 (67 %)
	Total	51	21	38	4	22	136
Age	15–19	0	0	3	0	1	4 (3 %)
	20–29	7	2	13	2	3	27 (20 %)
	30–39	10	3	12	1	9	35 (27 %)
	40–49	14	3	5	0	1	23 (17 %)
	50–59	12	9	4	1	7	33 (25 %)
	60–69	4	4	1	0	1	10 (8 %)
	Total	47	21	38	4	22	132

9.4.2 Manager Sample

The locations, gender and age groups of manager participants are presented in Table 9.2.

Over half (61 %) of the manager sample came from metropolitan areas. There were slightly more female managers (53 %) than male (47 %). Most of them (70 %) were aged between 40 and 59 years. A majority of the participants (78 %) had work experiences ranging between 1 and 5 years. Of the remaining managers, 15 % had 6–10 years, 2 % had 11–15 years, 4 % had 16–20 years and about 2 % had over 20 years of work experience in their current jobs. (5 cases were missing.) These figures indicate the managers' possible experiences in learning and arranging or supporting learning for CET as a basis for providing data for this project.

9.4.3 Data Collection and Analysis

Semi-structured interviews lasting 30–40 min were conducted with the workers and managers individually at their worksites. In a few instances, and in order to meet workplace conveniences, some workers were interviewed in small groups. During

Table 9.2 Managers' industries, regions, gender, and age groups ($n = 60$)

		Sector					
		H&CS (aged care)	Transport and logistics	Mining	Financial services	Services/ hospitality	Total
Region	Brisbane	7	9	0	0	4	20 (33 %)
	Qld regional	4	6	1	0	0	11 (18 %)
	Perth	10	0	2	0	0	12 (20 %)
	WA regional	0	0	4	0	0	4 (7 %)
	Melbourne	0	0	0	5	0	5 (8 %)
	NSW regional	0	0	0	1	7	8 (13 %)
	Total	21 (35 %)	15 (25 %)	7 (12 %)	6 (10 %)	11 (18 %)	60 (100 %)
Gender	Male	1	11	5	3	8	28 (47 %)
	Female	20	4	2	3	3	32 (53 %)
	Total	21	15	7	6	11	60
Age	20–29	1	2	0	1	1	5 (8 %)
	30–39	1	2	3	3	1	10 (17 %)
	40–49	8	6	1	1	2	18 (30 %)
	50–59	10	4	3	1	6	24 (40 %)
	60–69	1	1	0	0	1	3 (5 %)
	Total	21	15	7	6	11	60

the interviews participants also completed a short survey containing tick boxes. Workers were asked to indicate how they were currently learning, how they preferred to learn, how they were currently supported with learning in the workplace and their preferences for support for future learning. Similarly, managers were asked to indicate their perceptions of workers' learning and their contributions to supporting and facilitating this learning.

All interviews were audio-recorded with consent from participants. The recordings were transcribed and de-identified by allocating pseudonyms. The research team analysed the transcripts, individually and then collectively, to identify and categorise factors that assisted and inhibited workers' learning, including their preferences for how such learning should be organised and supported. The findings are presented in the ensuing sections.

9.5   Indications of Improved CET Provision

The findings here highlight two important observations: first, that workers want to learn *at* and during work rather than attend courses outside the work premises and, second, they prefer their learning to be guided and supported by more experienced others who could be supervisors, co-workers or, alternatively, experts/ trainers from outside their workplaces. Two reasons for learning at work were expressed regularly. The first was that learning while working allowed workers to immediately practise what was learnt, be guided when doing this to ensure they have appropriately applied the new knowledge and skills and accomplish types of outcomes to meet distinct workplace needs. The second reason was that workers were able to continue working without disruptions to the daily routines and goals of their workplaces. For some workers, going away from the worksite meant loss of pay because not all employers afforded learning off-site, or having to make time after working hours, which was difficult to manage. For drivers in the Transport and Logistics industry, whose schedules for long distance driving meant being away from work depots and home for days, attending training off the job was not easy to organise. They relied on learning while on route from one location to another. '... if you going to have a trainer, they've got to be in the truck with you...' said Geoff, one of the drivers.

Overwhelmingly, the knowledge and skills of co-workers was much valued, hence the preference to learn from them while at work. The following account from Ivy (Aged Care), an administration worker, explains why workers like her prefer learning from others at work:

> ... my colleagues who are most knowledgeable about what I do, not outside people ... and I most relish being with my experienced buddies who were doing my job, who were deeply familiar with what I was doing, who could give me insights into my job. People from the outside, their advice was often ... less relevant because they didn't have intimate details of my job ... I learn individually from other workers; I'm doing that almost always, asking questions, observing this and discussing that, frequently, yes. And, likewise an experienced person within the group. In-house, they know. They know the system. Outside people don't.
> ... outside people are essential for teaching us new stuff that we just don't know. Having said that, it's the people that I'm working with who I'm learning from more, much more.

Similarly, Jack from the Mining sector expressed views similar to those from other workers:

> ... probably my most effective way of learning is actually just doing it with other people, watching, asking them questions and even just seeing them, observing them when they work and how they even talk to other people, how they look at things that I look at ... It's easier to talk to someone ... It's good to be able to ask stupid questions and not feel stupid.

Both these workers show awareness of workplace pedagogies such as questioning, observing and listening, discussing and modelling (Billett 2004). For learning from others outside their workplace to be most effective, workers expected them to understand the context of the workplace and its performance requirements. They also expected high quality instructional strategies for learning. Guided learning strategies such as demonstrations, use of the most relevant examples and case studies were quoted as examples that assisted workers' learning.

Like the workers, managers also preferred workers to learn and be trained at work. Their reluctance to release workers to attend training off-site was mainly due to the implications of replacement costs that not many employers in small- and medium-sized enterprises could afford. Large enterprises with regional and metropolitan sites had their own training and development arrangements where groups of staff met once or twice a year at a common location to spend a few days together. For example, an aged care organisation with facilities in rural and regional areas organised training at a city location. All expenses were paid for by the employer. Workers in this organisation looked forward to these sessions because it allowed them to share examples of practices in different settings. However, these types of sponsored training were very enterprise specific and great importance was placed on its relevance to work tasks and immediate application. This suited the workers who were able to practice and apply their new skills immediately, and thereby reinforce what they had just learned.

Similar to the statements from workers, and not surprisingly, managers also wanted external CET providers such as VET teachers, industry suppliers and experts to make their learning content effective by contextualising it for purposes of work performances at the worksite. Nathan, a manager from the Mining sector, explained that his organisation has 'built a training and assessment department that sits within the field because that way we can bring a level of professionalism to what is required'. Robert from the Services industry said his organisation used a holistic approach to training that involved learning in circumstances of work:

> We train in every aspect of the club. He's done payroll, accounts, cellars, stores. He's now into gaming. He's done point of sale, rostering … It cements him into the club and gets him thinking about how to do things differently … We pay and keep it going that way.

Job rotation as a way of learning and systems thinking is a common induction practice but can also contribute to continuing education and training. Interestingly, managers often referred to structured training and guided learning. They valued highly skills-based training facilitated by experts from within their organisation or external providers. However, this training needed to be aligned with specific workplace goals. This is not surprising because employers expect immediate returns on investment in training, for example, in the forms of increased efficiencies and productivity, or reduced losses through accidents. However, managers did not discount the efficacy of learning from co-workers and recognised that workers' learning can be better assisted if they show interest and are willing to learn, have previous experience and qualifications and are able to establish positive relationships with those they work and train. Their views highlight the importance of informal learning with co-workers, and learner agency. Above all, managers in the sample were committed to building the capacity of workers through CET as reflected in the following statements from Peter, manager from a mining company:

> … If a guy's prepared to stick around we'll invest in him … If they're prepared to have a go, especially in a crew and they fit in … We invest and you have to invest … It's our responsibility to make sure that our people are trained properly …

Both, workers and managers indicated a preference for CET provisions to be situated in and through work. Workers emphasised the immediacy of such provision and the benefits of its relevance and direct application. They qualified this with the need of expert guidance and support during and following specific instructional experiences, and the value of shared learning experiences. Managers emphasised efficiencies, the need to balance training provision with production requirements, and to ensure targeted resources secured appropriate outcomes in terms of skills development. Unanimously, workers and managers from all the industry groups noted and accepted that work entails and requires ongoing learning and training.

9.6 Indications of How CET Is Best Enacted

The workers expressed preferences to learn through three complementary approaches in practice settings: (i) individually, (ii) with direct guidance from more knowledgeable and experienced workers and (iii) with 'educational' interventions by in-house or external trainers, where possible in groups. These three preferences are now elaborated:

(i) Learning individually

Individuals constantly learn during work activities although not always deliberately and often that learning is not acknowledged as learning per se, because learning and work are intricately integrated (Nijhof and Nieuwenhuis 2008). However, learning and appropriation of what is learnt within the context of work are likely to be more potent when individuals actively engage in personally effortful ways (Billett 2008) and collaborate with other workers (e.g. buddies and supervisors) and external agents (e.g. clients, vendors, suppliers) (Bound and Lin 2013). Regardless, it is the individuals who form the nexus for such appropriation, with learning not necessarily confined to situations of social isolation. For the workers interviewed in this project, individual learning is about 'getting on with work tasks' in the absence of direct guidance and support, and practising to cultivate self-reliance and self-accountability. Hence, it relies on individual ability and motivation, intention, agency and action and on the learning skills acquired in previous experiences, both at work and in school or tertiary education settings. Additional to interest, confidence, self-directedness and commitment, individual learning also requires some prior knowledge of what is required of the work task in terms of performance outcomes. Therefore, some initial instructions or opportunities to observe examples of the tasks to be learnt by more experienced others are necessary and helpful before individuals engage in learning on their own. The data from our project showed that individuals valued what they learnt by 'just doing it'. Brenda (Mining) explained why learning individually was valuable: 'I like to do it individually because to me it seems to sink in better.' Individual learning also allows workers to reinforce good practices, as explained by Anne (Finance), '… good to take a step back and just reflect on what you actually have learnt – it just helps to reinforce'. This type of self-reflection is advocated by Eraut and Hirsh (2007). The sample variously reported individual learning to be challenging, but rewarding and motivating, and a way to build self-confidence. For instance, David (Services) said:

> Well the one good thing about it, when you do a trial and error thing like that, you don't just learn it goes here, that goes there, you know why it goes there because you had to work through the process to understand it.

What the workers and managers said is consistent with other research (e.g. Paloniemi 2006) showing that learning individually allows workers to practise, reinforce and hone what is known, but when supplemented with engagement in novel activities that are not automated, it may result in cognitive dissonance. When such learning is followed by debriefing (Paloniemi 2006) though, often new learning is generated. So there are extended benefits in encouraging and supporting individual learning in the workplace. However, learning individually is premised on the efforts and capacities of individuals as observers, imitators and initiators engaged in practice. In these ways mimesis becomes a major approach to learning, which Marchand (2008) claims is one of the most common forms of learning through work. However, such personal efforts may be insufficient to access knowledge that is opaque and hidden from view and sensation. It needs to be supplemented with active engagement in explicit procedural and conceptual knowledge from within the workplace, and from other sources that are not necessarily made explicit or are structured. Furthermore, boundaries set by others (e.g. owners, managers, unions), more experienced workers or regulations governing the conduct of the particular occupation may constrain the processes of learning. So individuals need to exercise agency within boundaries created by others and also transcend and extend those boundaries (Evans 2007) with help from other workers who can guide them.

(ii) Individually with direct guidance

Workers reported that learning with co-workers gave opportunities to share, interpret and test new ideas, techniques and procedures that build understanding and capacities to act effectively. These interactions grant spaces to discuss issues, consider different perspectives and solve problems as a team. However, where shared and guided learning arises from a need to solve a problem, it relies on genuine and mindful interests of individuals to initiate and actively access opportunities available in and through the workplace, and be self-directed in work and learning (Doos and Wilhelmson 2011). Learning from others is further reinforced if workers are given opportunities to practise what they learn through direct guidance. Such practices are most useful when done almost immediately after the learning episode and when directly related to addressing authentic work task problems (Smith 2006).

The participants explained that learning with others could be on a one-on-one basis between those who work in close proximity or as a member of a group brought together to undertake a specific task or training, guided by an internal experienced worker or an external expert. In these ways, mutually receiving and providing assistance was a common and welcomed practice as observed in a study by Ellström et al. (2004). In some cases, though, workers reported their learning was formal and structured as well as informal to serve 'just in time' and 'just what I need' instances. Although the workers and managers did not always give details of pedagogical strategies used during guided learning episodes, there were strong indications that modelling and coaching were familiar and frequent practices. Further, workers indicated that personal guided learning support was considered to be most effective when it was 'on-site and hands-on' and conducted by experts and when supervisors work individually with workers. Other forms of direct guidance were also available through work teams and these presented opportunities to gain understandings about goals and processes at a whole of business perspective (i.e. seeing the 'big picture'). Importantly, it was emphasised that co-workers who constitute guided learning support need to be knowledgeable and experienced persons who are familiar with the requirements of expected effective performance, be willing to provide support and engage in constructive interactions, be available for immediate and relevant interactions and have the skills to provide quality instructions.

The interview data illustrated numerous examples of learning from and being guided by other workers. Whether they are supervisors, mentors or buddies, peers or experienced workers, co-workers can provide effective learning assistance for developing competence and confidence required for work. However, guided learning may not necessarily take on an instructional approach (where the focus is on 'teaching' a worker) and be in the form of advice in a problem situation. Bruce's (Transport and Logistics, a diesel mechanic) example of guided learning from his supervisor illustrates this point:

> Well I would go as far as I can and really challenge myself before I had to ask. Then if I came to something that I couldn't get past I'd ask someone older like the supervisor and he would come out and not ... not actually tell me how to fix it but show me the right way so I can learn it myself. I think that's a good way of training instead of just coming out and saying, 'well there's the problem there...' I learned how to do it through my supervisor. Very tricky bit of work. One on one, it was something that no-one else has done in the workshop.

This worker also gave an example where an external expert was brought in to guide a worker:

> Well one of the guys on day shift wanted to know how to do the basic head repair on one of the engines and no-one in the workshop actually knew, so they got one of the guys to come in to work and spent three days on our engine showing one of the other guys how to do it, stuff like that.

Regardless of where the experts came from, particular importance was placed on the need for their guidance and support both during initial instruction and subsequent follow-up if needed.

The accounts here present evidence of shared cognition, mediated learning, distributed everyday cognitions, cognitive apprenticeship and situated learning and everyday cognition (Resnick et al. 1991). The agency of individuals as well as communities of learners in both creating and utilising learning spaces to optimise capacity building was apparent. However, according to Bryson et al. (2006), it is the interplay between workplace affordances (organisational factors) and the individual's agentic roles that influence learning and capacity building within workplaces.

Although there were frequent references to guided learning from more experienced others, examples of learning from those who may not be as experienced were also mentioned. For instance, buddies in Aged Care facilities and truck drivers in the Transport and Logistics industry sometimes relied on whoever was available, and these could be new workers who had engaged in recent learning.

The data repeatedly shows that co-workers play an important role in guided learning in the workplace, but this mode requires colleagues to be accessible and approachable. According to the worker and manager samples, the outcomes of learning from this source include 'effective and efficient performance, acquisition of different perspectives, ways of understanding and acting, collaborative problem-solving and development of competence and confidence'. Seeing these benefits, it becomes necessary to consider ways in which co-workers can assist each other with learning. However, Clarke (2010) cautions that guided learning from others in the workplace relies on a climate of mutual trust so that knowledge can be shared and discussed openly.

(iii) Individually with educational interventions

Education interventions refer to formal courses delivered by registered training organisations. These courses are mostly delivered in tertiary education and training institutions and some components may be delivered within the worksite. Where it is delivered at work, it is funded by the employer, typically completed during working hours, and customised for the enterprise concerned and with options for accreditation. Workers preferred such training to be organised for groups so that, following the training, members of these groups could discuss and reflect on what they learnt and how this learning could be applied in different ways in the context of their work. Engagement in group learning shapes how one experiences and values learning in ways that are meaningful within the work context (Weighartd 2009). It is the socio-cultural context of workplaces that allow learners to construct their understandings to a level of sophistication that is influenced by and linked to the circumstances of practice (Gheradhi 2009).

The research found cases where individuals engaged in tertiary education and training courses outside work, and these were mostly funded individually and completed after work. These workers invested in such studies to advance their careers either within or outside their current industry.

Especially in regional and remote areas, access to educational interventions through training programmes was often problematic because lengthy travel to learning sites and inconvenience to workers and trainers usually added to the cost of training. However, this was not always the case. For instance, readily available training provisions were on local mining leases and provided by on-site trainers, although access to learning support and resources at remote worksites was problematic for 'fly-in' and 'fly-out' mining workers. For some workers, being rostered off the worksite when training was conducted on site generated anxiety about 'keeping up to speed with skills'. The lack of opportunities to interact with co-worker-learners because of physical or geographical isolation, and apparent increased workload in regional locations where training was not seen as a high priority, added to these concerns.

While learning individually and through guidance from other more knowledgeable and experienced workers or experts, wholly in the workplace, assists learning for goal-directed activities at work, these approaches may not offer opportunity to engage in the types of theoretical knowledge and canonical occupational capacity development required and expected of workers. Such experiences may be better enacted through tertiary education and training provisions. Hence educational interventions to supplement what is learnt in the workplace are necessary for learning that leads to a qualification within the Australian Qualification Framework. However, on-site real-time assessment needs to consider currency and validity of assessment for any qualifications.

Trainers from tertiary education and training institutions were welcomed because they were seen to bring new ideas and were able to share unique and tested examples from other sites and sources. For example, Colin (Mining) described a training course with an external trainer:

> We were all sitting down here, a lot of us. It was the first time we'd been exposed to this course, we learned a hell of a lot and we were able to discuss a lot of things and get things clear that we've always wondered about.

Benefits of training on employer premises have been reported by Newton et al. (2006) who found such training to be more relevant to participants' work tasks.

In the Mining sector, workers reported that access to expertise was restricted by the size of groups being trained, claiming that if the groups were 'too big' (Xavier, Mining), then close guidance from the trainer was limited. In circumstances where expert training and guidance were not available, workers needed to find alternative sources of support for their learning and/or problem-solving. They noted that these sources were not always effective and reliable. Nonetheless, workers and managers preferred educational interventions to become an integral part of workers' development in the workplace when and as needed. Such 'just in time' training is widely known to be more effective (Eraut et al. 2000). The findings show that there is interest from workers, managers and enterprises in educational interventions from tertiary education and training organisations. This suggests demands for a curriculum for CET that harnesses the strengths of practice-based learning to supplement provisions of tertiary education and training institutions.

The responses from workers and managers were consistent across the four industries, in regional and metropolitan areas and by gender and age groups. The findings from workers' and managers' data convincingly favour new approaches and strategies to be considered as a basis for national CET provisions. Notably, much of the learning through the three approaches discussed above, while significant for mastery of jobs and work roles, do not always or necessarily fall within the scope of qualifications – which is the main premise of tertiary education and training provisions.

9.7   Bases for National Continuing Education and Training Provisions

What the workers and managers prefer and suggest about CET challenge many of the current practices and provisions by tertiary education and training institutions. Equally, they challenge understandings about the capacities of workplaces as sites of planned learning opportunities and the intents of policymakers and regulators who seek efficiencies for both known current and unknown future CET provisions. Further, they challenge understandings of the purposes of CET and the range and intensity of interests, goals and priorities such learning incorporates. The key challenge for enhanced CET provision lies in how best to integrate stakeholder requirements and preferences for learning yet supports workforce skill development, meets individuals' developmental needs and career aspirations and addresses requirements of the national qualification framework as well as legislative requirements of individual industries, doing so within the circumstances of urgency that increasingly characterise the nature of socio-economic change.

In meeting the challenges, two broad bases are strongly endorsed by the data from workers and managers. First, there is a need for greater utilisation of workplaces as sources and sites of learning because there is an appeal for workplaces to become more central venues for learning, and to increasingly utilise their many resources, learning spaces and affordances for purposes of CET. However, this does not imply that the kinds of 'school'-oriented practices of trainers and instructors should be withdrawn from familiar training institutions and transplanted into workplaces. Rather, the relationships between tertiary education and training institutions and workplaces need to transform from that of a client-contractor to accommodate partnership for mutual futures that are robust enough to include the necessary and equally partner-oriented contributions of industry and professional organisations. The nature of CET models and partnership arrangements they both require and generate needs to be focussed on *learning* rather than 'teaching'.

In pursuing more integrated forms of CET provision, considerations of what resources can effectively be brought together are paramount. Tynjälä's (2008) research shows that work-based learning opportunities will not necessarily be organised in educationally optimal ways because the key imperatives for workplaces are on the services they provide and/or goods they produce. Similarly, others (e.g. Säljö 2003; Fuller and Unwin 2003; Howell et al. 2001) caution against an uncritical acceptance of workplaces as sites of learning. Nonetheless, Jordan (2011) advocates conversion of worksites where the enactment of occupational activities and the learning co-occur because these result in highly productive outcomes for individuals and their workplaces. Similarly, Nijhof and Nieuwenhuis (2008) advance perspectives of how and why the workplace needs to be considered and accepted as the potential site of the kinds of learning experiences that are foundational for effective CET. Important within these considerations is better understanding of how workers are engaged in what Eraut and Hirsh (2007) describe as implicit learning even when workers are not aware that they are learning. Essentially, the greater utility of workplaces lies in developing integrated cultures of learning where the immediacy of work and the enactment of and planning for change can be simultaneously experienced as an acknowledged and accepted requirement of work and not an additional impost on workers and enterprises.

The second base relates to the facilitation of curriculum and pedagogic provision and support (across all sites of work-based learning) that enacts a developmental pathway for learning individually in the first instance, then with direct guidance and finally including educational interventions – not necessarily in a linear progression but within the personal preferences of individual workers. Such provision accounts for 'beyond entry level training' that CET addresses. Mature and existing workers bring experience and an extensive range of work and learning competencies that can be deployed in generating and responding to the kinds of changes contemporary work necessitates. Hence, their pathways need to reflect person dependence within familiar contexts and be quite different from initial entrants and yet support a range of perspectives on the nature and value of the changes taking place. Change may be ubiquitous and accelerating in contemporary work, but it cannot be accepted as homogenous and accommodated through concepts of 'one-size-fits-all' CET provisions. Hall (2006) identified major forces and sources of workplace change and development as growth in knowledge work, the changing nature of labour supply and demand, changes to product and service markets, the changing role of governments and of the community sector, organisational restructuring and technological change. He went on to explain that "The complex interplay of these forces will continue to result in different outcomes for different kinds of workers, in different industries, markets, occupations, professions and organisations" (p. 22). Hall further claimed that CET provisions that can address such changes will need to support person-dependent developmental pathways that reflect the choices and priorities of workers if it is to be more than simply reproductive and responsive.

The implications for accommodating these two bases of CET provision extend not only to individuals and tertiary education and training providers, but also employers who need to consider new ways of contributing to and benefiting from CET provisions. So, both the intents and outcomes of CET become important considerations. Above all, those participating in CET (worker-learners) must remain the central clients who need access to appropriate learning experiences to meet individual and workplace-specific requirements (and accreditation if possible). What the research data indicate is the importance of learning spaces afforded to them in busy workplaces to 'get on with the tasks' and at the same time offer opportunities to consolidate, test, reinforce and reflect on their individual performance. Learning individually also extends the ability to apply knowledge and skills in new situations, take on challenges and extend self-confidence. Thus, time and opportunities to practise are essential affordances to achieve these types of outcomes. Nevertheless, affordances can be subject to contestation. Unless workers have access to learning opportunities and autonomy for self-direction, only the select few will benefit. Given that it is the individual who makes decisions about how much of themselves they will invest in learning, workers' agentic participation depends on two reflexive factors: opportunities to participate and the extent of personal engagement and participation (Billett 2004).

There is potential for all CET stakeholders (workers, employers, TET institutions and policymakers) to leverage on the richness of learning opportunities and support within workplaces. Essentially, carefully conceptualised and practical models of CET are necessary. Workplaces need to realise their capacities and contributions to learning and set out expectations and performance standards. For their part, curriculum designers and facilitators need to include work-related tasks that accommodate the scope of the job roles, yet offer challenges to advance to more complex learning tasks that are worthwhile and valued by the learners. Learners need to take responsibility for an agentic role in learning and developing the competencies that address performance levels and expectations in their workplaces and favourably orient them for sustained employability. Regardless of the nature of CET models, the focus needs to be on *learning* through practice that serves the needs of individuals, enterprises, industry and wider Australian social goals, rather than *teaching* through the intentions of those who are removed from practice. In summary a national CET system needs appropriate combinations of learning settings, availability of suitable learning resources and willing workers who have the capacity to learn, seek and access opportunities available and so can be appropriately supported.

Acknowledgement This work has been produced under the National Vocational Education and Training Research (NVETR) Program, which is coordinated and managed by NCVER on behalf of the Australian Government and state and territory governments.

References

Barnett, R. (2006). Graduate attributes in an age of uncertainty. In P. Hager & S. Holland (Eds.), *Graduate attributes, earning and employability*. Dordrecht: Springer.

Billett, S. (2004). Learning through work: Workplace participatory practices. In H. Rainbird, A. Fuller, & A. Munro (Eds.), *Workplace learning in context*. London: Routledge.

Billett, S. (2006a). Constituting the workplace curriculum. *Journal of Curriculum Studies, 38*(1), 31–48.

Billett, S. (2006b). Relational interdependence between social and individual agency in work and working life. *Mind, Culture, and Activity, 13*(1), 53–69.

Billett, S. (2008). Learning throughout working life: A relational interdependence between social and individual agency. *British Journal of Education Studies, 55*(1), 39–58.

Billett, S., & Choy, S. (2011). Cooperative and work-integrated learning as a pedagogy for lifelong learning. In R. K. Coll & K. E. Zeegward (Eds.), *International handbook for cooperative and work-integrated education: International perspectives of theory, research and practice* (2nd ed., pp. 25–31). Lowell: World Association for Cooperative Education Inc.

Billett, S., Henderson, A., Choy, S., Dymock, D., Beven, F., Kelly, A., James, I., Lewis, J., & Smith, R. (2012). *Continuing education and training models and strategies: An initial appraisal*. Adelaide: NCVER.

Bound, H., & Lin, M. (2013). Developing competence at work. *Vocations and Learning*. doi:10.1007/s 12186-013-9102-8.

Bourdieu, P. (1986). The forms of capital. In J. G. Richardson (Ed.), *Handbook of theory and research for the sociology of education* (pp. 241–258). New York: Greenwood Press.

Bryson, J., Pajo, K., Ward, R., & Mallon, M. (2006). Learning at work: Organisational affordances and individual engagement. *Journal of Workplace Learning, 18*(5), 279–297.

CEDEFOP. (2009). European Centre for the Development of Vocational Training. http://www.cedefop.europa.eu/EN/publications/13125.aspx. Accessed July 2013.

Choy, S., Bowman, K., Billett, S., Wignall, L., & Haukka, S. (2008). *Effective models of employment-based training*. Adelaide: National Centre for Vocational Education Research.

Clarke, N. (2010). Emotional intelligence and learning in teams. *Journal of Workplace Learning, 22*(3), 125–145.

COAG. (2012). Council of Australian Governments. National agreement for skills and workforce development. http://www.federalfinancialrelations.gov.au/content/npa/skills/skills-reform/national_agreement.pdf. Accessed July 2013.

Doos, M., & Wilhelmson, L. (2011). Collective learning: Interaction and a shared action arena. *Journal of Workplace Learning, 23*(8), 487–500.

Ellström, P., Svensson, L., & Åberg, C. (2004). Integrating formal and informal learning at work. *Journal of Workplace Learning, 16*(8), 479–491.

EQAVET. (2013). European Union Quality Assurance in Vocational Education and Training. http://www.eqavet.eu/qa/gns/glossary/c/continuing-education-and-training-cvet.aspx. Accessed July 2013.

Eraut, M. (2004). Transfer of learning between education and workplace settings. In A. F. Rainbird & H. Munro (Eds.), *Workplace learning in context* (pp. 201–221). London: Routledge.

Eraut, M., & Hirsh, W. (2007). *The significance of workplace learning for individuals, groups and organisations*. London: ESRC Centre on Skills, Knowledge and Organisational Performance.

Eraut, M., Alderton, J., Cole, G., & Senker, P. (2000). Development of knowledge and skills at work. In F. Coffield (Ed.), *Differing visions of a learning society* (Vol. 1, pp. 231–262). Bristol: The Policy Press.

Evans, K. (2007). Concepts of bounded agency in education, work and the personal lives of young adults. *International Journal of Psychology, 42*(2), 85–93.

Evans, K., & Rainbird, H. (2001). The significance of workplace learning for a 'Learning Society'. In L. Unwin, P. Hodkinson, & K. Evans (Eds.), *Working to learn: Transforming learning in the workplace* (pp. 7–28). London: Kogan Page.

Fevre, R. (2000). Socialising social capital: Identity, the transition to work and economic development. In S. Baron, J. Field, & T. Schuller (Eds.), *Social capital: Critical perspectives* (pp. 94–110). Oxford: Oxford University Press.

Field, J. (2005). *Social capital and lifelong learning*. Bristol: The Policy Press.

Fuller, A., & Unwin, L. (2003). Learning as apprentices in the contemporary UK workplace: Creating and managing expansive and restrictive learning environments. *Journal of Education and Work, 16*(4), 406–427.

Gheradhi, S. (2009). Community of practice or practices of a community? In S. Armstrong & C. Fukami (Eds.), *The Sage handbook of management learning, education, and development* (pp. 514–530). London: Sage.

Griffiths, T., & Guile, D. (2003). A connective model of learning: The implications for work process knowledge. *European Educational Research Journal, 2*(1), 56–73.

Hall, R. (2006). *Workplace changes: Change and continuity in workplaces of the future* (Voices, pp. 22–31). Sydney: TAFE NSW International Centre for VET Teaching and Learning.

Handy, J. (1995). Rethinking stress: Seeing the collective. In R. Newton (Ed.), *Managing stress: Emotion and power at work* (pp. 85–96). London: Sage.

Howell, S. L., Carter, V. K., & Schied, F. M. (2001). Making workers visible: Unmasking learning in a work team. *Journal of Workplace Learning, 13*(7), 326–333.

Jordan, B. (2011). *The double helix of learning: Knowledge transfer in traditional and technocentric communities*. Unpublished manuscript.

Kemmis, S. (2005). Knowing practice: Searching for saliences. *Pedagogies, Culture and Society, 13*(3), 391–426.

Kemmis, S., & McTaggart, R. (2000). Participatory action research. In N. K. Denzin & Y. S. Lincoln (Eds.), *Handbook of qualitative research* (pp. 567–605). Thousand Oaks: Sage.

Lave, W., & Wenger, E. (1991). *Situated learning: Legitimate peripheral participation*. Cambridge: Cambridge University Press.

Marchand, T. H. J. (2008). Muscles, morals and mind: Craft apprenticeship and the formation of person. *British Journal of Education Studies, 56*(3), 245–271.

Newton, B., Miller, L., & Braddell, A. (2006). *Learning through work: Literacy, language, numeracy and IT skills development in low-paid, low skilled workplaces* (IES Report 434). Brighton: Institute of Employment Studies.

Nijhof, W., & Nieuwenhuis, L. (Eds.). (2008). *The learning potential of the workplace*. Rotterdam: Sense.

Organisation for Economic Co-operation and Development. (2009). *Jobs for all: Initial report*. Paris: OECD.

Organisation for Economic Co-operation and Development. (2010). *Reviews of vocational education and training: Learning for jobs*. Paris: OECD.

Organisation for Economic Co-operation and Development. (2013). *Economic policy reforms: Going for growth 2013*. Paris: OECD.

Paloniemi, S. (2006). Experience, competence and workplace learning. *Journal of Workplace Learning, 18*(7/8), 439–450.

Resnick, L. B., Levine, J. M., & Teasley, S. (Eds.). (1991). *Perspectives on socially shared cognition*. Washington, DC: American Psychological Association.

Säljö, R. (2003). From transfer to boundary-crossing. In T. Tuomi-Gröhn & Y. Engeström (Eds.), *Between school and work: New perspectives on transfer and boundary-crossing* (pp. 311–321). Amsterdam: Pergamon/Elsevier Science.

Smith, R. (2006). Epistemological agency in the workplace. *Journal of Workplace Learning, 18*(3), 157–170.

Szreter, S. (2000). Social capital, the economy, and education in historical perspective. In S. Baron, J. Field, & T. Schuller (Eds.), *Social capital: Critical perspectives* (pp. 56–77). Oxford: Oxford University Press.

Tynjälä, P. (2008). Perspectives into learning at the workplace. *Educational Research Review, 3*(2), 130–154.

Weighartd, S. (2009). *Learning from experience. A resource book by and for co-op/internship professionals*. Brookline: Mosaic Eye Publishing.

Chapter 10
Lifelong Learning Policies and Practices in Singapore: Tensions and Challenges

Helen Bound, Magdalene Lin, and Peter Rushbrook

10.1 Introduction

At a 1998 Singapore May Day rally, a speech by the then Prime Minister Goh Chok Tong outlined a vision for lifelong learning that both cemented the hard-won lessons of the small and young nation's recent past and offered a hard but realisable road to the future:

> Looking beyond the immediate future we must focus on lifelong learning and employability in the long term. Our future prosperity will be built on a knowledge-based economy… The future economy will be driven by information technology, knowledge and global competition. The types of jobs change, and change rapidly. This means that workers must have broad basic skills and the capacity to learn new skills. Only then will they have employable skills throughout their working lives. So we must have Thinking workers and a Learning Workforce
>
> In fact, the whole country must become a Learning Nation. We must make learning a national culture. We will have to evolve a comprehensive national lifelong learning system that continually retrains our workforce, and encourages every individual to learn all the time as a matter of necessity. (Goh, in Kumar 2006, p. 501)

PM Goh's appeal to collective commitment in the face of potential external threats, whether to national security or the national economy, forms part of what has been referred to by founding Prime Minister Lee Kwan Yew as 'the Singapore Story' (Lee 1998). Part reality, part myth, the Singapore Story is a pragmatic representation of Singapore's 'can do' reputation embedded deep in the national psyche, though not without a degree of contestation (Tan 2011). Drawing freely from global discourses privileging human capital investment and institutional managerialist solutions to complex social and economic challenges, the Singapore Story flows widely and deeply through all levels of national education policy.

H. Bound (✉) • M. Lin • P. Rushbrook
Institute for Adult Learning, Research and Innovation Division, Singapore, Singapore
e-mail: helen_bound@ial.edu.sg; magdalene_lin@ial.edu.sg; peter_rushbrook@ial.edu.sg

T. Halttunen et al. (eds.), *Promoting, Assessing, Recognizing and Certifying Lifelong Learning: International Perspectives and Practices*, Lifelong Learning Book Series 20, DOI 10.1007/978-94-017-8694-2_10, © Springer Science+Business Media Dordrecht 2014

This chapter seeks to untangle some of the connections between contemporary lifelong learning policy and practice within Singapore's adult or vocational Continuing Education and Training (CET) sector. This account is not simple and is heavily nuanced by individual and collective cultural ways of being, including the relationship between agency and structure (Giddens 1979). Through these lenses we offer a view of CET practice that challenges one-dimensional economic readings of lifelong learning applications, whether through policy framing or programme implementation. We achieve this through five connected and cascading approaches. First, we briefly outline the international origins of lifelong learning policy and its contemporary bifurcation into humanist and human capital representations. Second, we locate the tensions within these representations in an account of how lifelong learning has been constructed in Singapore. Third, we outline a conceptual framework to account for how lifelong learning plays out in practice-based adult learning environments. Fourth and drawing on two adult learning research projects undertaken by the authors, we contextualise the policy and conceptual frameworks outlined. Fifth and finally, we discuss how cultural ways of being differentially mediate policy through practice in ways that both reinforce and challenge the status quo.

10.2 Contextualising Lifelong Learning in Singapore

The examination of lifelong learning policy and practice within the Singaporean context has value both at the local and international level when viewed through the lens of post-colonial and globalisation theory, which situates collectives within Appadurai and Taylor's notion of a 'social imaginary', or set of 'common understandings that make every day practices possible' (Rizvi 2006, p. 196). Rizvi argues further that social imaginaries now have global reach and possess a capacity to both incorporate and 'normalise' theory within commonsense and institutional understandings of everyday practice, including education systems within nation states. He and others suggest that two such theories – neo-liberalism and the new public management – are examples receiving global acceptance as the rationale for widespread national government institutional and bureaucratic reform, including Singapore (Rizvi 2006, p. 197; Fusarelli and Johnson 2004). Neo-liberal and new public management have theoretical rationales that incorporate assumptions relating to improving public sector management and structures, including practices consistent with those of private enterprise, presuming increased effectiveness and efficiency (Hewitt de Alcantara 1998). The international neo-liberal imaginary has been informed largely by the requirements of global funding bodies such as the World Bank (WB) and the International Monetary Fund (IMF), which are mandated not to interfere in national political systems but can suggest 'once-removed' bureaucratic reforms to facilitate the enactment of neo-liberal free-market economic systems.

Nested within this global rationale for local economic development is a particular Singaporean 'human capital' reading of lifelong learning that accords closely with that promoted by the WB and IMF. This is largely informed by the Singapore Story's rhetoric – its own social imaginary – that as a country lacking abundant land and natural resources, its only true resource is its workforce and the knowledge and skills it generates, which must remain globally competitive in the country's open market (Lee 2009; Amaldas 2009). As such lifelong learning must be targeted to learning specific skill sets through nationally sanctioned education and training programmes (Kumar 2006; Ng 2012; Amaldas 2009; Law 2006). This perspective contrasts with a broader 'humanist' view of lifelong learning proffered by such international bodies as UNESCO and their commissioned Faure (1972) and Delors (1996) reports which offer a view of lifelong learning inclusive of learning to know, learning to do, learning to live together/learning to live with others and learning to be (Kearns 1999, p. 5). Billett (2010) equates the human capital approach to lifelong *education* through legitimated formal programmes (an 'institutional fact') and the humanist approach to lifelong *learning* through largely informal socio-personal processes (a 'personal fact'), but he does admit that in practice these overlap.

Certainly, Singapore has implemented globalisation selectively, producing a 'Singapore paradox' (Amaldas 2009, p. 985) of economic radicalism more or less in line with globalising imperatives and a local social moral conservatism within a totalising governmental framework. Though eschewing the idea of a welfare state, the government's essentially Confucian collective ethos (Xiong 2011; Lee 2009; Kam and Gopinathan 1999, p. 112) nevertheless offers a range of education and training programmes that both encourage and subsidise preemployment and post-employment learning for the workforce (Kam and Gopinathan 1999; Tan and Gopinathan 2000; Kong 2011). For several decades the connection between participation in education and the economy has been promoted as 'lifelong learning'. Though referred to generally as 'adult education', in global parlance Singapore's CET sector more closely approximates those national sectors offering vocational education and training programmes. It could be suggested, too, that this consensus, firmly located within the Singapore social imaginary, was largely in place well before the winds of globalisation blew across the island, often referred to as 'efficiency through pragmatism' (Kam and Gopinathan 1999, p. 116; Tan 2011), It is an approach, then, informed by human capital rather than humanist assumptions, which within Billett's schema is more an institutional fact of lifelong 'education' than it is a personal fact of lifelong 'learning'. We will, however, for reasons of consistency, continue to refer to Singapore's policies and practices as 'lifelong learning' and 'adult education'.

Though lifelong learning was first mooted in 1986 within the Ministry of Education (Kam and Gopinathan 1999, p. 105) and also practised since this time within Singapore's extensive community centre network, lifelong learning is publicly identified through CET policy and practice. Prior to the creation of the CET sector in 2000, lifelong learning enjoyed a modern history dating from 1960 while still under British influence. After this time a legislated funding source was established (1979), along with training for non-professional and lower-skilled workers (1983), and a National Skills Recognition System (2000), which modelled closely those emerging around the world at the same time. Prompted by an economic downturn in 2001–2004, which also included the SARS outbreak, the Singapore government in 2003 established the Workforce Development Agency (WDA) to consolidate and rapidly expand the initiatives of previous decades (Willmott and Karmel 2011, pp. 6–20). The effects of globalisation, including the freeing-up of international markets, the rise of 'knowledge-based' or 'intellectual capital' (Ng 2012, p. 3) industries and the dominance of transnational free markets and neo-liberal and new managerialist discourses, profoundly influenced the shape of the new bureaucracy, in concert with internationally comparable systems (Lassnigg 2012; Rizvi 2006, p. 200). This impact was no more evident than in the regimes of educational governance instituted to align the WDA's new system of Workforce Skills Qualifications (WSQs) with the skill requirements of industry and the nation's demand for increased international competitiveness through qualitative and continuous improvement of its human capital base. A competency-based training framework derived largely from Australia and the United Kingdom (Clemans and Rushbrook 2011; Anderson et al. 2004) was utilised to develop WSQ standards within a complex regulatory framework of programme design, delivery and management. A high compliance regime was considered essential because of the inexperience of mostly private-for-profit providers (Approved Training Organisations or ATOs) of CET programmes and the perceived need for steerage, quality assurance and surveillance. The policy frameworks outlining the WDA vision and practice imperatives are expressed through a series of binding 'Masterplans'. Recent iterations of the Masterplans demonstrate an easing of compliance regimes over time as the sector matures and assumes greater self-management responsibilities (Willmott and Karmel 2011, pp. 20–22; pp. 52–55).

Singapore, therefore, has a lifelong learning strategy and policy environment that links the circumstances of its history with the contingencies of a willing engagement with contemporary globalisation. These links have at once a compatibility of interests through nationally shared social imaginaries emphasising the pragmatism of economic purpose through free markets and their attendant infrastructures as well as a trickle-down effect of linking positive economic outcomes with formal and institutionalised lifelong workplace skilling. It is, however, through the implementation of CET lifelong learning policy and how it plays out at the local level that its assumed seamlessness has the potential to be challenged and reinterpreted. It is to the explanation of how this process may occur that we now turn.

10.3   Conceptual Framework

As we have suggested, Singapore's adult education system focuses not so much on the need and development of individuals but on the capacity of the system to produce workers with knowledge, skills and attitudes for increasing productivity within the knowledge economy. Such a view of education assumes that it is both a public and private good: public as it contributes to the well being and social development of a community; private as it serves individual economic interests within a competitive labour market. This view of education systems, geared towards fulfilling the needs of the market, has become globally ubiquitous (Rizvi et al. 2006). However, despite the commonality of these policies and their accompanying social imaginaries (Rizvi et al. 2006), we know that they are often contested, value-laden and dynamic (Ball 1994). Like any social imaginary or set of common understandings, therefore, Singapore's ecocentric and pragmatic (Rizvi et al. 2005; Tan 2011) approach to lifelong learning is far from homogenous in its acceptance and enactment.

For our purposes, then, the question is: How are policies and their contested social imaginaries actually enacted in practice? Gaonkar (2002) explains that

> [social imaginaries] are first-person subjectivities that build upon implicit understandings that underlie and make possible common practices. They are embedded in the habitus of a population or are carried in modes of address, stories, symbols, and the like. (Gaonkar 2002, p. 4)

Given that policies and their social imaginaries are deeply embedded (Bound 2007) in practice and not external to practice, one way we can unpick the diversity of enacted lifelong learning policies is through the lens of mediated action. Through this construct we can begin to understand the diverse ways in which agential thinking is able to mine the weak points and cracks, or liminal spaces, embedded within CET policy and practice (Billett 2010). Mediated action regulates our interactions with the world through the use of signs and symbols (Vygotsky in Engeström 1999). We include policies, social imaginaries and cultural ways of being as part of these signs and symbols, first referred to in the work of Vygotsky and which a range of authors (e.g. Engeström 1999; Wertsch 1998) refer to as 'cultural tools' or ways of thinking within areas that include academic learning or the study of particular disciplines. Such tools may but not necessarily 'afford or enable effective or more expert means of doing that discipline' (Polman 2006, p. 222). This is not to say that tools *determine* our actions, rather that they *influence* our actions and in turn our actions asymmetrically influence practice. As such, we 'do not react to the environment but instead enact it' (Jennings 2010, p. 229). We both reproduce our environment *and* act on it; we are not powerless. However, our degree of influence and power depend on where we are differentially positioned in our social world (O'Connor 2001) and if we are acting alone or with others.

Pertinent to our discussion also is the sociocultural work of Wertsch (1998) who argues further that action is mediated through the goals we aim to achieve, the embeddedness of historical practices in the cultural tools and mental models we use. These tools are distributed asymmetrically as power and influence are embedded within tools and actions. Of particular interest to us within this framing of mediated action are Wertsch's concepts of 'mastery' and 'appropriation'. 'Mastery' is described as knowing and following the rules and uses of cultural tools without necessarily valuing or believing in them. In a sense, mastery is then an action-based rendition of agency. It may involve full knowledge of a prescribed area of knowledge that is enacted through artefacts such as policy, regulations, curricula, texts and embedded practices, but not internalised as part of self or professional identity. As such, mastery may leave liminal spaces for the actor either to resist silently or openly criticise and act. On the other hand, 'appropriation' is considered a similar action-based process of internalising historical, cultural and institutional patterns embedded in tools and actions, including disciplinary knowledge, but because of its internalisation as a constituent part of identity, including professional identity and practice, it may limit the actor's capacity to resist or act through the 'taken-for-granted' nature of the appropriated knowledge. Disciplinary assumptions and practices, then, including the systems that constitute, reproduce and legitimate them, tend to remain tacit as structured silences eluding self-interrogation. Within these systems, including education and training, mediated action may take the form of mastery or appropriation with one a source of potential agential activity or silent resistance and the other a source of potential compliant activity and system and knowledge reproduction (O'Connor 2001; Polman 2006, pp. 223–224).

We are positing here, then, a range of possible responses to the implementation of policy and its suggested regulatory practices at the local level. We claim from the literature that policy imposition is rarely total and may always be contested through the subjectivities of agency (Giddens 1979; Ball 1994). Contestation, however, may vary according to the degree to which critical cultural tools and their variants are appropriated, internalised and practised by individuals and collectives. We consider 'mastery' and 'appropriation' useful heuristic devices to capture these nuances of agency, not only for their capacity to account for the range of subjectivities employed in implementing and critiquing lifelong learning programmes but also as a means of exploring their agential relationship with collective and subjective social imaginaries. We commence this exploration through consideration of the stories of four adult educators interviewed within the context of two case studies investigating the implementation and outcomes of curriculum practice within Singapore's adult education sector.

10.4   Two Case Studies: Finding and Acting in Liminal Spaces

From our early research work, it was of little surprise that our interview cohorts' reading of policy and its practice looked different on the ground from that which was intended by those who instigated and prepared them. Consequences were played out and rules and procedures were interpreted in multiple ways. Through the lenses of mastery and appropriation, we explore four actor-vignettes that represent some of the possibilities and outcomes of mediated practice within potentially restrictive CET policy and regulatory spaces. As will be seen, the examples are heavily nuanced by the messiness of reality and as such do not fit neatly within any simple explanation of mastery and appropriation but nevertheless point to their value as interpretive cultural tools.

10.4.1   The Diploma of Adult and Continuing Education (DACE)

The Diploma of Adult and Continuing Education (DACE) is a course that further develops the educational capacities of those working in the CET sector. The project referred to here consists of two sequential subprojects examining the efficacy of the course. The first examined the issue of adult educator perceptions of what was meant by 'quality curriculum' (Bound et al. 2013) and the second the 'novice to expert' journey of curriculum writers and learning facilitators (Rushbrook et al. 2013). Both subprojects used as subjects a range of adult educators and participants in the CET sector's DACE programme, which is considered an advanced teacher-educator and curriculum writing course. DACE programme managers and course designers were also interviewed. The subprojects aimed to elicit information that indicated the degree to which a programme learner, in the argot of this chapter, 'mastered' or 'appropriated' over time the desired knowledge and practices promoted by the DACE programme outcomes. While mastery or critical interpretation of DACE programme content was the desired outcome of course participation, the initial research demonstrated a tendency for learners to appropriate or comply in practice-based environments (Bound et al. 2013). This tendency tended to shift, however, in later cohorts, towards interpretive or 'mastery' practice (Rushbrook et al. 2013). A senior manager within the CET sector expressed a hope that the DACE programme would over time foster the development of

> somebody who is a reflective practitioner, a person who has a broader educational background, an educational set of understandings, and somebody who is adjusted...[T]he idea was to create more of an educator, somebody who could have a discussion about the different approaches to assessment, who, if wanted, could talk curriculum...The idea is not to have a conformist but people who will have critical perspectives. (April, 2012)

However, as suggested, this outcome was not always the one manifested in practice. From the subprojects, we have selected two examples of programme 'mastery' and 'appropriation', the one leading to adopting of 'critical perspectives' as suggested and the other of acceptance and integration within the existing social imaginary of implied system-based curriculum and facilitation compliance. The examples are considered 'typical' of the responses gathered during the life of the project.

We have selected first, Sydney, a highly experienced adult educator who first completed and now teaches within the DACE and related programmes. Ever mindful of the potential restrictions of WDA and WSQ regulations in programme design and delivery, he was nevertheless able to practice a 'mastery' discourse within carefully mined liminal spaces (i.e. the limited opportunities afforded to break away from the tightly prescribed curriculum) of his own making. He achieved this through his consummate skills as an educator, combined with expert knowledge of relevant content areas. He acknowledged that while some modules within his teaching programme appear to provide limited creative or innovative opportunities for the experienced educator, they nevertheless could be reworked imaginatively within the stated competencies and content. His flexible and dynamic approach was reflected in his assumptions about how to utilise a learning space:

> It's a space so the teacher can be a student, the student can be a teacher. So whoever comes and interacts in that space...results in learning happening. [It can be] designed that way. [And he believed the skilled educator can] make 'it happen anywhere.

He used the example of tea breaks, a liminal learning space that can potentially provide powerful educational opportunities, if managed correctly:

> The tea break can be forty-five minutes and it is designed with a specific learning objective in mind. That's what I mean. There's formal learning and there's informal learning but even informal learning can be designed.

Sydney acknowledged that there is a degree of risk in stepping outside the suggested module instructional guidelines. However, he holds that this kind of learning space should be recognised within the design process: 'there must be a caveat in it that says that this is just recommended, please feel free to amend accordingly'. He is also critical of a perception among other WSQ facilitators and Accredited Training Organisations (ATOs) that such innovatory practices are frowned upon by quality assurers and CET providers:

> I mean, I listen to all the trainers in a WSQ setting, they said they can't even take out one slide, I can't even do this, do that. I must send my amended slides to whoever, ATO to approve first then I can use. So they feel very hampered and I think that is never a good thing because there are trainers, there are facilitators, you got to trust their professional judgement of what is the best route to get them, get the learners to the outcome.

Sydney's position as an experienced educator also influenced heavily his conception of what was meant by quality curriculum; he considered it at the point of the sharing of module content with the facilitator and the learner in a learning space. As such, he explained, when discussing the 'features of good curriculum, the engagement must intrinsically be very high. That means in the hands of any facilitator this curriculum will fly because the curriculum in itself has been designed so that it is engaging already. In whosever hands, the curriculum will be very engaging'. He explained that this moment is the point at which facilitators should be systemically encouraged to take risks in their practice to maximise the learners' educational experience. Therefore, he suggested, if the facilitator is able to interpret further the curriculum to fit the needs of his or her learners, then the experience will be even richer: 'I'm very mindful that it is not a one size fits all kind of cookie-cutter curriculum. I cannot assume that the people who come through this all start from zero because that's never true'.

Second, we have selected Kenneth, a WSQ curriculum designer. He considers good curriculum a means of achieving a desired outcome measured as a return for money on training investment, in the manner of the Singapore Story imaginary:

> Good curriculum is to get the design outcome...If you have a good training programme, especially for employers who spent money to train the employees, you must get the desired outcome, so in a good curriculum the elements would be the whole process, the development process will actually [make obvious] all the necessary gaps that need to be aware of, will actually address.

On the other hand, bad curriculum 'can be due to different gap at different places, different possible points, so if you don't identify the right needs...of course it's poor curriculum. So if similarly you cannot translate that into standards and all the standards cannot be understood by the person who writes the curriculum, then of course the outcome will not lead to the desired kind of objective'. And, unlike Sydney, Kenneth believes that the trainer or facilitator must be held to account or 'really conform' when delivering the prescribed programme: 'if the trainers cannot really deliver to the expectation of this then also it will affect the outcome'. His system-aligned and detailed, but uncritical, approach to extant CET sector curriculum design and facilitation practice suggests a stance of compliance or appropriation, though not without a degree of skilled self and system referenced reflection and application. As such, like Sydney, he also acts within a liminal space, but its location within an appropriated framework permits only a form of compliant agency.

What we have here are two readings of agency, one carrying possibilities for change and the other embedding, refining and reinforcing existing practice. Sydney is a change agent who through mastery has developed an acute and critical but distanced understanding of the practicalities of curriculum implementation. He 'knows his stuff' but is also able to transcend his understanding through innovative, imaginative teaching strategies. Kenneth, too, knows his materials but through appropriation rather than mastery works for change within extant materials and processes to make them work more effectively. The cultural tools employed, therefore, lead to different outcomes, one challenging and the other accepting the status quo.

10.4.2 Tools for Learning Design (TLD)

The Tools for Learning Design (TLD) project (Stack and Bound 2012) examined how introducing meta-tools, meta-thinking processes and practitioner-based research can assist individuals who work within the Workforce Skills Qualifications (WSQ) framework. It aimed to do this by deepening pedagogical understandings and thus engage in and encourage innovative practices within their own contexts. The project involved three 2-day workshops over 15 weeks with nine participants with managerial responsibilities in WSQ training centres. Each participant also carried out an individual research and innovation project that addressed an area of their work they were interested in exploring further. As part of their projects, most participants tried making small changes in their practices undertaken with ongoing support from the researchers who took on the roles of critical friends, mentors and project facilitators. Typically, their context had not changed; rather, they had perceived possibilities for alternatives and with support were able to innovate outside their normal practices, finding liminal spaces and soft boundaries within a system some had described as rigid.

Data was collected through initial interviews with participants, video footage of the workshops that captured the interactions, collected workshop artefacts and workshop and other conversations that took place between the researchers and participants.

In the first and second workshops, the researchers introduced resources and activities that facilitated reflection and discussion on system-wide constraints, orientations and assumptions to teaching and learning, and practitioner research. The use of resources such as the dialogical inquiry model (Bound 2010; Stack 2007) that permits a consideration of multiple perspectives and teaching metaphors and their philosophic origins (Davis et al. 2008) helped participants to surface and critique existing practices. The researchers also created an 'ecology room', a managed learning space, with nine interconnected activity-based stations and invited the participants to navigate through them as they wished. This approach offered an entirely different modelling of teaching and learning for participants, giving them as learners greater control and trusting that they would make meaning and sense of their experiences, particularly with the following debriefing session. For most of these participants, this was the first time they were part of a process where they experienced for themselves the power of alternatives outside standard curriculum design and facilitation techniques. Before starting on their research projects, the participants considered how their research questions could be addressed from the different quadrants in the integral theory (i.e. I, IT, WE, ITS) (Wilber 2000) and determined their own preferred outcomes. The latter ranged from achieving a particular task, improving their students' learning, deepening their own understandings and opening doors to new ways of seeing things. The researchers gave the participants ownership and asked them what support they needed. Here, they were modelling a student-centred approach to learning which is quite novel in the local training context.

After 12 weeks, at the third and last workshop, the group came together, shared their experiences and gave each other feedback from different perspectives. This final workshop located each participant's work within the larger Continuing Education and Training (CET) system and gave them the opportunity to reflect on the qualities of a facilitator they valued and wanted to emulate. With their research projects, there was a sense of closure for some but continuing relationship with different goals for others.

We now examine the practices of two of the TLD participants, Michelle and Philip, and the ways in which they worked with a range of meta-tools and meta-thinking processes within their selected research projects. It is important to acknowledge within this framing the power of context and agency and how they can potentially play out as mastery. While the researchers intentionally selected individuals with managerial responsibilities, one's level of agency also depends on factors such as external barriers and inner attitudes. The examples further illustrate the ways in which agentic action (Billett and Pavlova 2005) is mediated by our positions in the social world (O'Connor 2001).

Michelle was moving from being a manager in charge of the development, delivery and review of WSQ training programmes to being a manager in charge of the professional development of adult educators, including those who work outside the WSQ system. As such, she explored 'the being and becoming of a teacher' for her research project. She reflected and shared that she 'started as a teacher and became an adult educator. And it was an up and down journey. There were various impulses and situations that led me to this point'. She bravely re-created an ecology room for her own training team with the intention of 'help[ing] people express the different issues with and aspirations of being a teacher'. Having heard their stories, she was more determined to help people find their way and become trainers. This resolve was driven by her awareness of her position within the organisation and the larger CET system as a whole; she described herself as 'a kind of catalyst, a kind of connector, a bit of a mover and a shaker... also kind of a guide'. At the final debriefing workshop, she underscored the importance of her research project within 'self, team, organisation, system, nation', all of which she has access to, and the magnitude of her project, 'that is what I am there for, that is why I need a long time to do what I need'.

In contrast to Michelle, Philip was relatively new to CET work and was differently positioned within the CET system, having far less power and access to resources and influence. He found the workshops valuable as he was given the space to explore various aspects of teaching and learning:

> I have the opportunity to discuss with people coming from diverse experiences and perspectives of the system. There are some very experienced and knowledgeable people here, who are deeply questioning their assumptions about teaching and learning as part of the workshops. I want to understand more about pedagogy and learning. Sometimes I am lost but other times I have clarity. I am having different sorts of conversations here than in my workplace, and it is helping me to see things in new ways. I am being asked to think about what I really value as an educator.

As part of his critical thought process, Philip began to question the notion of academic grading and, through conversations with researchers, decided to look at assessment, specifically peer assessment, for his research project. As he trialled a peer assessment pro forma with his students, he realised that he needed to address a more fundamental teaching and learning question. He teaches his module on programming by giving his students small components that are manageable, but by doing this, 'I have actually taken away important problem-solving skills they need'. Other attributes of a programmer that he noted as being important include persistence, trying new things, using online networks to find answers and framing questions to ask such networks. He went back and started posing reflective questions regarding learning strategies and thinking as part of his students' assessment reports and found this process useful as he was able to better understand how they learn and change his approach towards teaching. More importantly, he observed changes in his students, 'it helps them to see things together, to be able to see other points of view and to start realising their own mistakes'. However, he also added that implementing this change across his organisation would be a challenge:

> Time is a big issue for me, but others coming from traditional approaches to teaching also pose a problem. It would involve a considerable change in mindsets about programming and about learning.

Here, we observe how participants do not receive the same supportive reactions when they try to implement changes because making such changes involve both individual practices in the classroom and cultural and structural changes.

Whereas Sydney and Kenneth demonstrate the enactment of the concepts of 'mastery' and 'appropriation' within adult education practice as variants of agency, Michelle and Philip add the dimension of power and its possibilities to further influence or hinder change. Sydney and Kenneth more or less enjoy the same potential influence over the power to offer change directing curriculum strategies. Sydney, however, chose to exercise it through mastery and critical distance and Kenneth through the acceptance of appropriation. Michelle, on the other hand, is able to use her powerful managerial position to advance her cause to implement an ecology room. Philip, on the other hand, is far more tentative because of his relatively junior teaching experience and, as a consequence, in spite of his agential potential as a team leader, is not confident that his views will prevail. From this it may be suggested that simple mastery or even appropriation as cultural tools for agential change at a range of levels is not enough unless there is also access to institutional regimes of power. Sydney, Kenneth and Michelle enjoy this to various degrees; Philip does not, though may in the future. We now conclude by exploring the implications of how mastery and appropriation work as cultural tools within the Singaporean lifelong learning context.

10.5 Discussion

Our description and analysis of lifelong learning and how it plays out in practice from the nuanced perspectives of actor-agents working within the CET sector have taken place within an assumed and cascading context of international and largely derivative national policy frameworks. We have, though, emphasised that these frameworks have been mediated through a unique Singaporean social imaginary equally informed by global capitalism and its structural imperatives and a sympathetic home-grown cultural system underwritten by conservative values and the subjugation of individual and social needs before national economic survival and continued growth objectives. Within this framework, however, we have demonstrated that liminal spaces – creative and agential learning moments – exist in the messiness of practice that holds possibilities for educational resistance, action and innovation. Equally, these spaces may also produce further degrees of compliance and limited change. We have used the lenses of mastery and appropriation as tools to capture these cultural ways of being.

So, heeding PM Goh's 1998 vision, we have represented here examples of thinking workers, a learning workforce and an imputed Learning Nation. However, this enacted vision may also putatively extend the promoted economic and workplace vision of lifelong learning to include the broader humanist lifelong learning goals of inclusivity and active citizenship promoted by Delors and Faure. That this has taken place within an economically sanctioned and legitimised lifelong *education* environment rather than more traditionally humanist and informal lifelong *learning* spaces (Billett 2010) demonstrates that at some ends of the policy chain, what we have called 'liminal spaces' are opened for agential exploration by educational actors, but in a variety of nuanced ways, for example, Sydney's use of the morning and afternoon tea breaks to explore the implications of his shared class material and Michelle's position of power to brave the workplace introduction of an ecology room learning space. To implement these apparently small learning gestures required a large break from the assumptions informing CET learning delivery, hence their agential qualities.

From the four vignettes, we have seen how these ways play out in practice. Both Sydney and Kenneth are experienced practitioners but read their educational world in differing ways. Sydney's mastery of his environment has led to a deep understanding of his workplace practice space and a capacity to rework and interpret his conceptual tools and skills for the benefit of his learners. He is in this sense a true interpretivist. Kenneth, too, has a capacity to innovate but only within the proscribed regulatory criteria. As such, his is an appropriated stance but consciously worked through to incorporate a more limited form of mastery. Michelle is comfortable with the approaches, perspectives and tools she was introduced to. She has been a teacher for many years, so it was not an issue for her to appropriate these as she had the 'space' for it. She was able to readily make the link between her own 'space' and creating similar spaces for others, using her social positioning and mastery skills. Philip, however, cannot be said to occupy the same powerbases or experience levels enjoyed by Sydney, Kenneth and Michelle. He is in the process of mastering and gradually appropriating new perspectives and the use of different tools. The suggestion is that perhaps he needs to do this before he feels comfortable enough to innovate and challenge the system.

The vignettes are illustrative, then, of how cultural ways of being and differential placement within an ostensibly rigid system play out in ways that vary from officially sanctioned outcomes. Potential spaces, therefore, exist within the somewhat rigid CET system for agential reflection and action. So, in spite of itself, Singapore may be exposing its workers, citizens and other learners to a broader range of lifelong learning possibilities than it promotes. This exposure, though accidental, is inevitable because of the distance between the higher echelons of policy promulgation and its implementation in practice. While social imaginaries reach from historical precedent, international economic strategies and contemporary policies to the local level, including embeddedness in the subjectivities of adult educators, such penetration can never be totalising of those subjectivities. Perhaps this is because agency, though constitutive of the contexts within which it is practised, including social imaginaries, also includes equally nuanced practices shaped by biography, peer interaction, collective learning and reflection to produce novel readings of learning environments. In other words, the cultural tools of mastery and appropriation are able to play out to produce a range of responses to the policy environment, all of which have implications for practice and change in unanticipated ways. Lifelong learning and its trajectories, then, though officially proscribed as a course of collective action, remain at least in part within the ambit of socially mediated individual choice, which many would argue is desirable for the long-term health and growth of lifelong learning societies.

References

Amaldas, M. (2009). The management of globalisation in Singapore: Twentieth century lessons for the early decades of the new century. *Journal of Alternative Perspectives in the Social Sciences, 1*(3), 982–1002.

Anderson, D., Brown, M., & Rushbrook, P. (2004). Vocational education and training. In G. Foley (Ed.), *Dimensions of adult learning: Adult education and training in a global era* (pp. 234–250). Sydney: Allen & Unwin.

Ball, S. (1994). *Education reform: A critical and post-structural approach.* Philadelphia: Open University Press.

Billett, S. (2010). The perils of confusing lifelong learning with lifelong education. *International Journal of Lifelong Education, 29*(4), 401–413.

Billett, S., & Pavlova, M. (2005). Learning through working life: Self and individuals' agentic action. *International Journal of Lifelong Education, 24*(3), 195–211.

Bound, H. (2007). *Institutional collaboration, learning and context: A case study of Tasmanian information technology institutions.* Doctoral thesis, Faculty of Education, University of Tasmania.

Bound, H. (2010). Developing quality online dialogue: Dialogical inquiry. *International Journal of Teaching and Learning in Higher Education, 22,* 2.

Bound, H., Rushbrook, P., & Silvalingam, M. (2013). *What is quality curriculum? Programme design, delivery and management in Singapore's Diploma of Continuing and Adult Education.* Singapore: Institute for Adult Learning.

Clemans, A., & Rushbrook, P. (2011). Competency-based training and its impact on workplace learning in Australia. In M. Malloch, L. Cairns, K. Evans, & B. N. O'Connor (Eds.), *The SAGE handbook of workplace learning* (pp. 279–292). London: SAGE.

Davis, B., Sumara, D., & Luce-Kapler, R. (2008). *Engaging minds: Changing teaching in complex times.* New York: Routledge.

Delors, J. (1996). *Learning: The treasure within.* Paris: UNESCO.

Engeström, Y. (1999). *Expansive learning at work: Toward an activity-theoretical reconceptualization.* Paper presented at the Changing Practice Through Research: Changing Research Through Practice, Surfers Paradise.

Faure, E. (Chair). (1972). *Learning to be: The world of education today and tomorrow.* Paris: UNESCO.

Fusarelli, L. D., & Johnson, B. (2004). Educational governance and the new public management. *Public Administration and Management: An Interactive Journal, 9*(2), 118–127.

Gaonkar, D. (2002). Toward new imaginaries: An introduction. *Public Culture, 14*(1), 1–19.

Giddens, A. (1979). *Central problems in social theory: Action, structure and contradictions in social analysis.* London: Macmillan.

Hewitt De Alcantara, C. (1998). Use and abuses of the concept of governance. *International Social Science Journal, 50*(155), 105–113.

Jennings, J. (2010). School choice or schools' choice? Managing an era of accountability. *Sociology of Education, 83*(3), 227–247.

Kam, H. W., & Gopinathan, S. (1999). Recent developments in education in Singapore. *School Effectiveness and School Improvement, 10*(1), 99–117.

Kearns, P. (1999). *Lifelong learning: Implications for VET.* Leabrook: NCVER.

Kong, L. (2011). From precarious labor to precarious economy? Planning for precarity in Singapore's creativity economy. *Culture, City and Society, 2*(2011), 55–64.

Kumar, P. (2006). Lifelong learning in Singapore: Where are we now? *International Journal of Lifelong Education, 23*(6), 559–568.

Lassnigg, L. (2012). 'Lost in translation': Learning outcomes and the governance of education. *Journal of Education and Work, 25*(3), 299–330.

Law, S. S. (2006). *Vocational technical education and economic development – The Singapore experience* (ITE Paper No. 9). Singapore: Institute of Technical Education.

Lee, L. K. (1998). *The Singapore story: Memoirs of Lee Kuan Yew.* Singapore: Marshall Cavendish.

Lee, L. K. (2009). *From Third World to First: The Singapore Story: 1965–2000*. Singapore: Marshall Cavendish.

Ng, P. T. (2012). An examination of lifelong learning policy rhetoric and practice in Singapore. *International Journal of Lifelong Education, 32*(3), 318–334.

O'Connor, C. (2001). Making sense of complexity if social identity in relation to achievement: A sociological challenge in the new millennium. Sociology of Education at the dawn of the 21st Century. Vol. 74, 59–168.

Polman, J. (2006). Mastery and appropriation as means to understand the interplay of history learning and identity trajectories. *The Journal of the Learning Sciences, 15*(2), 221–258.

Rizvi, F. (2006). Imagination and the globalisation of international policy research. *Globalisation, Societies and Education, 4*(2), 193–205.

Rizvi, F., Engel, L., Nandyala, A., Rutkowski, D., & Sparks, J. (2005). *Globalization and recent shifts in educational policy in the Asia Pacific: An overview of some critical issues* (APEID/UNESCO Bangkok Occasional Paper Series No. 4, pp. 1–59). Bangkok: APEID/UNESCO.

Rizvi, F., Lingard, B., & Lavia, J. (2006). Postcolonialism and education: Negotiating a contested terrain. *Pedagogy, Culture & Society, 14*(3), 249–262.

Rushbrook, P., Bound, H., & Sivalingham, M. (2013). *The journey from novice to expert: Curriculum design and learning facilitation in Singapore's Continuing Education and Training (CET) sector*. Singapore: Institute for Adult Learning.

Stack, S. (2007). *Integrating science and soul in education: The lived experience of a science educator bringing holistic and integral perspectives to the transformation of science teaching*. Unpublished dissertation, Curtin University of Technology.

Stack, S., & Bound, H. (2012). *Tools for learning design research project*. Singapore: Institute for Adult Learning.

Tan, K. P. (2011). The ideology of pragmatism: Neo-liberal globalisation and political authoritarianism in Singapore. *Journal of Contemporary Asia, 42*(1), 67–92.

Tan, J., & Gopinathan, S. (2000). Education reform in Singapore: Towards greater creativity and innovation? *NIRA Review, 7*(3), 5–10.

Wertsch, J. (1998). *Mind as action*. New York: Oxford University Press.

Wilber, K. (2000). *Integral psychology: Consciousness, spirit, psychology, therapy*. Boston: Shambhala.

Willmott, G., & Karmel, A. (2011). *CET systems update developments in policy, systems and delivery: United Kingdom, Australia and New Zealand* (Research report). Singapore: Institute for Adult Learning.

Xiong, J. (2011). Understanding higher vocational education in China: Vocationalism vs Confucianism. *Frontiers of Education in China, 6*(4), 495–520.

Part III
Recognising and Certifying Lifelong Learning: Policies and Practices

Chapter 11
Professionalisation of Supervisors and RPL

Timo Halttunen and Mari Koivisto

11.1 Guiding and Supporting the Recognition of Prior Learning

The process of recognising and certifying learning arising from experiences outside of educational programmes is now well established and exercised in a range of countries. Yet, in different ways, it has been found that merely having a process for the recognition of prior learning (RPL) is insufficient. Instead, there is a need for processes to guide individuals through these processes and to support their progression and also to optimise the recognition and certification of what they know and can do. The need for guidance is required before participants enter educational programmes as learners may be unaware of the possibility for the recognition of their prior learning, and thus, it is crucial to share information of institutional policies and practices. In most cases, the resources available for supporting the RPL process are reserved for students enrolling in programmes. Entering into the RPL process is left to the interest of the student, and not every student will take the opportunity of making a case for accreditation. It is also fair to say that, in many countries, the recognition of prior learning does not cover the entire higher education system, but the more professionally oriented sector of it. Some universities often declare that they are occupied with other demands of educational development, such as creating opportunities for world-class research and innovation. The recognition of learning from work or leisure activities is said to fit better those institutions focused on developing professional practices, such as universities of applied sciences (i.e. polytechnics), because the nature of the education is more practically oriented. The same argument supposes that learning from experience is too practical for the theoretical studies in the research-intensive universities. However, there are cases

T. Halttunen (✉) • M. Koivisto
Brahea Centre, University of Turku, Turku, Finland
e-mail: timo.halttunen@utu.fi; mari.koivisto@utu.fi

T. Halttunen et al. (eds.), *Promoting, Assessing, Recognizing and Certifying Lifelong Learning: International Perspectives and Practices*, Lifelong Learning Book Series 20, DOI 10.1007/978-94-017-8694-2_11, © Springer Science+Business Media Dordrecht 2014

where interest about RPL has spread also beyond these higher education institutions. Yet, supervision becomes ever more important when learning from experience is compared to educational programmes provided by research-intensive universities.

Finland provides an interesting case for the recognition of prior learning (RPL) as both the universities of applied sciences and the research-intensive universities are involved in developing their policies and practices. In Finland, RPL is embedded in creating Personal Study Plans (PSP), which is a key process used in higher education and constitutes the main counselling measure for students entering university education. The PSP is usually introduced and completed during the first semester of the students' studies and implemented through a form of a structured or semi-structured interview. During this interview, the students and the supervisors tailor the kinds of courses the students will take to match their personal interests thereby creating a learning or, more precisely, an educational plan. The plan is a written document, usually signed by the two parties. As the studies proceed, each student and the supervisor are expected to review and revise the plan on a periodical basis. The follow-up and update of the PSP have benefited from the use of information technology as the documentation process becomes easier to manage. Recently, there has been a move to augment this process with the use of the recognition of prior learning. The introduction of RPL in the PSP process generated the need for staff training to secure for students a transparent and equal process of recognition and accreditation. According to an initial needs analysis at the Finnish higher education institutions, staff training on personal study planning was more frequently offered to the staff in the universities of applied sciences (i.e. polytechnics) than in the research-intensive universities. Because of the novelty of RPL in the educational process, only a few supervisors at the universities where this is being trialled had preparation in linking prior learning to the PSP process. As the needs for professional development unfolded for these supervisors, it was found that in many institutions the supervisors had not collectively discussed their roles and responsibilities. There were neither support mechanisms for the supervisors' work nor a clear picture of how the overall counselling is organised in the university level. Therefore, the RPL training programmes for supervisors had to embrace also the development of general competences of the supervisors, such as the abilities to understand student-centred learning and to engage in dialogue with students. Yet another challenge for supervisors' professionalisation comes from the fact that in the Finnish higher education system, there are professionals giving supervision for personal planning. They include, e.g. teacher tutors, study counsellors, senior students acting as peer tutors and study administrators. The roles and tasks of the supervisors may differ greatly across the higher education institutions. Compared to many other countries, these roles may also involve the assessment of learning. In comparison, the Dutch system separates the tutor and the assessor (see Chap. 12), and in the French system there are specialist staff who conduct this work (see Chap. 15). The variety of institutions involved as well as the heterogeneity of the professional backgrounds provides an interesting case on studying how the supervisors are able to embrace a novel task in their work role.

In making its case, this chapter, firstly, describes the challenges involved in the recognition of learning outside educational programmes in higher education.

Secondly, it addresses the issue of students reflecting their prior learning as a process of constructing professional identities. Thirdly, it explores the need for supervisors' professional development drawing on the case study from Finland. Finally, there is an analysis of the development of supervision practices as a transformation of a professional identity and a practice of agency.

11.2 Learning Outside of Academia

The recognition of prior learning can enable learners to make visible and get formal certification for the competences acquired in education, at work and during leisure time. Learning from experience may occur during a course of action at a specific time and place or during the daily routines. Individuals engaged in this learning may not be able to give a rationale or an explanation about the way that learning arises, not to mention being able to exercise introspection that would align this learning to the prescribed learning outcomes for the particular programme. In comparison, formal education – such as studies in higher education – emphasises the importance of theory, concepts and critical thinking. A teacher is usually involved in the process and is able to clarify and give meanings to the different aspects of the learning process. In learning outside educational programmes, the experience is the 'teacher', and the learning is triggered by individuals' active engagement with the learning affordances present in the various circumstances they encounter in everyday life. Reflection on learning from the experience is quite a demanding task, even for the teachers and tutors themselves. Without proper supervision it is likely that RPL will not be used in its full potential, and students are directed to attend education on knowledge, skills and competences they have already acquired elsewhere. To make that prior learning visible, it is important that students are able to describe their learning in terms used in educational programmes. For novices, it may be difficult to master the language and discourses used in a specific discipline, and the description and analysis of the learning from the experience may be seen as 'too practical' to be accredited by an academic institution. Therefore, it is vital that the teachers, tutors and assessors of these learners are competent to guide the *development of expertise* in the process of recognising prior learning and give value to learning outside of auditoriums, classrooms and laboratories. This recognition is regulated to some extent by the policies and practices at the national and institutional level.

Based on educational policies, educational institutions have become aware of the need to recognise prior learning. Depending on the country, the different sectors of education have adopted this approach more or less willingly. For example, in Estonia, RPL has first been practised in higher education and recently extended to vocational education and training. In Finland, the VET sector has a long tradition on RPL, and there has been some hesitance to adopt the practices in higher education. In Scotland, an RPL articulation network between the sectors has been established to increase mobility inside the education system. However, RPL is not limited to education providers but involves also other stakeholders within the educational policies.

Denmark has been developing the social recognition of learning from experience without comparing this learning to a specific educational programme. The aim of the social recognition is to build an interest in lifelong learning and increase motivation for education attainment amongst those with bad experiences on comprehensive school. In Iceland, the RPL system is very much driven by the businesses and the focus is on upskilling the workforce. As indicated in chapters within this volume, in Ireland and in the Netherlands, the recognition of prior learning is also used as a labour market initiative.

To effectively practise RPL in higher education, a few structural elements need to be available. A competency-based curriculum is sometimes considered as a requisite for successfully transferring the knowledge, skills and competencies acquired through learning from experience into learning outcomes provided by an educational programme. In a learner-centred approach, the outcomes of the curricula are described in terms of student learning thus increasing flexibility to broaden the assessment of learning to outcomes achieved outside the academia. That is, it focuses on outcomes to be achieved, rather than processes to be followed. The institutional policies, procedures and resources may or may not open to students the possibility to receive exemptions from studies or get an advance standing in the programme. Despite the general acceptance of RPL in the national and institutional level, the recognition of prior learning has not been able to increase the attainment to higher education on a large scale. Only a few candidates from the large number of potential learners actually achieve a full diploma or even a substantial part of a diploma through RPL. The policies and practices of institutions have been criticised by a heavy burden of documentation required from applicants. However, little interest has been shown on the actual process of how the recognition of prior learning is related to a novice member entering the community of practice in the academia.

Depending on the national and institutional policies being enacted, learners may be asked to identify the elements that identify, e.g. the development of professional practice, customer service or management. By doing so, the learners engage in a process of constructing their professional identity by using discursive elements from their own past and elements that are considered significant to the academic community. It follows then that the next section discusses the reflective process of the learners in the recognition of prior learning from the perspective of identity work and socially constructed self-identities.

11.3   New Social Identities in the Making

Identity work and socially constructed self-identities have been of interest to many researchers. Watson (2008) discusses these by elaborating the concept of sociological imagination by Mills (1959, 1970) together with more recent contributors such as Giddens (1991), Dachler and Hosking (1995), Alvesson and Willmott (2002) and Sveningsson and Alvesson (2003). In his research on managerial identities, Watson (2008) describes how individuals negotiate their work identities with discursive elements from various internal personal and external social identities. Some of these work identities are more static, some more loosely carried by professionals. Watson defines self-identity as 'the individual's own of who and what they are' and social identity as 'cultural, discursive or institutional notions of who or what any individual might be' (2008, 131). Eteläpelto and Vähäsantanen (2008) suggest that questions on personal or professional identity are usually brought into discussion in a situation of change or transition. They also claim that awareness of the professional identity and ability to rewrite one's expertise has become compulsory for lifelong learners (Ibid.). Social identity is of interest to the recognition of prior learning as experienced members of the academia provide novices an opportunity to position themselves favourably in the academic community of practice and present their self-identity in relation to the professional identities defined by the educational institutions.

Wenger (2007, 1998) argues that there is a profound connection between identity and practice. Developing a practice needs the formation of a community where members engage with each other and construct a learning trajectory. Practice entails the negotiation of ways of being a person in a professional context, and therefore, a community of practice is also a negotiation of identities (Ibid.). In this negotiation, social identity can be seen as the missing link between the individual and the social structure. In a community of practice, the professional identities are constructed in an interaction between the individual and the social environment, e.g. colleagues, managers, clients, professional bodies and educational institutions. In terms of the recognition of prior learning, the transition from novice to expert in a (research) community differs according to the culture and routines adopted by some experienced members of academy. The interest to become a researcher may be developed during a study programme or at a later stage of life. For those with prior experience, the construction of a researcher or other academic identity can be seen as a negotiation between the old and new professional identity. While members are engaged in the practice, the professional identity is transforming constantly in relation to the social structure as the individual is in interaction with other members in the community and the discourses they construct (Eteläpelto 2007; Saarinen 2007).

In the process of the recognition of prior learning, students are asked to show evidence of the relevance of their learning from experience at a given professional context and reflect this in comparison to the learning outcomes described in the educational programme. In this process, the learner is supposed to decontextualise the prior learning and align it to the theories and methodology used in the discipline from which they are seeking recognition. In practice, middle managers from small to medium enterprises may be given an assignment to reflect on their prior learning in comparison to the theories of leadership and management. A successful presentation of the case may result in an exemption of a course, an advancement in the programme or even an access to vacancies in research programmes. As the manifestations of newcomers' social identity are compared to the reflective practices of the expert members of the community, the positioning of participation in those communities depends on the students' ability to construct presentations of themselves as professionals. Using concepts and theories to link the learning from experience to the learning provided by the institution, the novices negotiate their position closer or further away from the core of the community of practice.

Watson (2008) argues that there are several kinds of social identities the professionals use when they construct their professional identities. When recognising learning from experience, the supervisors may need to practise sensitivity in their work to bring out the voice of learners despite their social category or formal-role social identities. Learners with an immigrant background may be labelled according to their social status. A male nurse may be suggested to hold more potential for technical or managerial skills than his female colleagues. Social workers without formal qualification at a specific educational level may be treated as a coherent group despite the variety of the professional activities they have undertaken. Other potentially troublesome forms of identities are the culturally stereotyped social identities, often rising from the agenda of widening participation to higher education. These forms may include mothers who have stayed an extensive period at home and taking care of their children or entrepreneurs who have gradually mastered their trade without any formal qualification. Supervisors have to be aware of these cultural assumptions in their judgments as some of these social identities may or may not give implications of a self-directed learner who has engaged in the offered learning opportunities.

To continue on the path paved by Watson, learners with local-organisational social identities have the greatest scope for professionals to position inwardly to themselves or outwardly to others (see Watson 2008, p. 131). These presentations of the self-identity may bring out the deliberate practice of the professional, such as a middle manager of a small- or medium-sized company involved practically in all dimensions of the work from accounting to marketing and from strategy planning to customer relations. The supervisors may also encounter learners with strong local-personal social identities, individuals with characterisations by others in the context of specific situations or events. Learners who have participated actively in student unions or political parties may present themselves with ease compared to learners who have spent their working career as freelance artists, for instance.

A closer examination of students reflecting their professional identities suggest that there is quite a demand for guidance and counselling during the various stages of the process of the recognition of prior learning, and the needs for this might differ widely across countries. The following section explores a case study from the Finnish higher education to describe an attempt to identify the needs for professional development and the key competences of personal study planning supervisors in order to enhance the effectiveness of RPL.

11.4 Professional Development of Personal Study Planning Supervisors

As stated before, the introduction of the recognition of prior learning into the process of personal study planning has generated the need for supervisor professionalisation. The work practices in personal study planning are governed by socially, culturally and historically defined local contexts. This situation has created a need to meaningfully construct and display the professional identity of the PSP supervisors. In the following section, the notion of professional agency is discussed, and a case study on a professional development course tailored for the PSP supervisors in the Finnish higher education system is presented.

The meaning of professional agency in the professional identity negotiations has been of interest to many researchers. Hökkä et al. (2012, p. 84) describe the professional as an agent renegotiating professional identities by participation in the practices and discourses of the work organisations. In the practices the professionals are interdependent by professional identity and perceived agency (Billett and Smith 2006; Eteläpelto 2008; Watson 2008; Ybema et al. 2009). In their article on teacher educators' negotiation of professional identities, Hökkä et al. (2012) bring about the discursive emphasis to the theoretical understanding of identity, agency and power. They suggest that teacher educators' agency is constrained and constructed within different discourses. Thus, the negotiation of professionals' agency is practised by utilising these different discourses as a process of identity negotiations. In short, teacher educators' agency is about a 'capacity to negotiate and renegotiate professional identities within their local work practices' (Hökkä et al. 2012, p. 86).

For instance, the University of Turku has been coordinating a national development project on RPL in higher education. Within this project, staff training has been a crucial element. Therefore, a training programme for the personal study planning supervisors was designed. The aim was to give an introduction to the recognition of prior learning and an opportunity to develop the knowledge, skills and attitudes needed for tailoring prior experiential learning to the university curricula. Based on the initial needs analysis and interviews with the guidance and counselling experts from the universities in Finland, the following learning outcomes were established for the training programme:

1. To know the context and basic principles of RPL (Bologna process, EQF, NQF, learning outcomes)
2. To explain the guidance and quality processes in higher education
3. To guide, plan and develop the RPL process as part of the PSP process
4. To apply the main methods for recognising prior learning
5. To guide students to manage their study paths and to develop their expertise
6. To cooperate with and give guidance to other staff involved in the RPL process

The training programme was focussed on university staff involved in student counselling and guidance. The programme attracted participants from 10 universities and 19 universities of applied sciences (i.e. polytechnics) in Finland. The majority of the Finnish universities were included and there were over a 100 participants. The programme was implemented using the methods of multiform learning (i.e. expert lectures, written assignments, group work, online discussions and peer reviewing) which included 3 seminar days with lectures from RPL experts and two workshops with guided group work. The seminars and workshops were complemented by online learning and peer reviewing tasks. The participants worked with an RPL-related development project throughout the training, either individually or in groups. The participants were divided into eight subgroups consisting of 9–16 members.

The size of the subgroups was kept low to create a safe environment for the exchange of experiences. The subgroups were also formed so that they included a good balance amongst the participating universities. The participants were engaged in the recognition of prior learning through presentations and discussions with national and international experts during the seminar. The trainers called the subgroups together for two workshops with their tutor. The first workshop focused on the challenges involved in the supervision of the recognition of prior learning. Each participant defined an individual project to structure the development needs in their own work and at the broader institutional level. The second workshop focused on the competencies the supervisors in higher education should hold for the good quality provision of the personal study planning and the recognition of prior learning.

The data from the workshops were collected and grouped to explain the current situation and to form competence descriptions.

11.5   Key Competences of a Supervisor Tailoring Prior Learning

During the RPL training programme, the participants were encouraged to reflect their own experiences of supervising RPL cases and to link their final assignments to existing work-related development issues. In their final assignments, the following subjects emerged as the main interests for development:

– RPL and guidance processes
– Roles and responsibilities of RPL staff
– Tools and methods for recognising prior learning
– Networking in RPL counselling
– A module for master-level students in recognising professional expertise

The participants were also asked to list the key competencies of a supervisor involved in the personal planning and the recognition of prior learning. The subgroups of the training programme listed the competences individually, and the following competences were most frequently mentioned in the lists of all subgroups:

– Knowledge of learning support
– Interaction skills
– Knowledge of the working life
– Command of the curricula
– Knowledge of the RPL policies and practices in the institution
– Content knowledge of the studies
– Supervisor's own motivation and commitment

Other competences mentioned in the subgroups were organisational skills, networking skills, creativity, sense of equality and ability to make decisions. These competences describe the general knowledge, skills and attitudes of the supervisor work as well as more topical questions related to the RPL function in the supervisors'

Table 11.1 The suggested key competences of a supervisor and their frequency in the case study

Competence	Frequency of suggested competencies (eight lists and 118 respondents in total)
Knowledge of learning support	8 (8)
Interaction skills	8 (8)
Knowledge of working life	6 (8)
Command of curricula	6 (8)
Knowledge of the RPL policies and practices in the institution	5 (8)
Content knowledge of studies	5 (8)
Supervisor's own motivation and commitment	5 (8)
Organisational skills	4 (8)
Networking skills	4 (8)
Creativity	3 (8)
Sense of equality	3 (8)
Ability to make decisions	2 (8)

role. Knowledge of the working life relates to the working life relevance often discussed in educational policies. Matching the learning from experience to the learning outcomes of the studies most probably forms the two most demanding factors in terms of supervisor professionalisation.

The following table presents the competences and their number of frequency in the competency description lists made by the subgroups of the RPL training programme. The highest frequency competencies, the knowledge of learning support and interaction skills, fall into the category of more general supervisor competences. This ranking is probably due to the fact that the supervisors had not been attaining any specific training programme for the preparation to their role. The following, knowledge of working life and command of curricula, refers to the task at hand, to understand learning at work (and leisure time) and to have the ability to make links between the learning outcomes in the education. The novelty of RPL in the PSP process brought up the need to discuss and share practices. The less mentioned competences may describe the variation between the institutions and local preferences. In some universities, the RPL policies and practices were unclear and in the making. Surprisingly, sense of equality is less frequently mentioned in the listings, yet it has been one of the core values listed in the national recommendations for RPL systems in higher education. Equality, transparent policies and practices as well as trustworthiness have been seen amongst the main factors driving the development in the national level (Table 11.1).

The following table explains and explores the characteristics of the supervisor competences most mentioned by the training groups. When examining these competencies, we can see that the meanings supervisors give to these competencies reflect both organisational policies and practices and the discretion in the supervisor role. In terms of guidance and counselling, the role of the learner may vary from novice to intermediate practitioner in the field, and addressing these diverse needs requires competences from supervisors that should enable professionalisation and growth of expertise in learners. To enhance the effectiveness of RPL in higher education, the competences of the supervisor should be geared towards bringing the advanced learners closer to the core of expertise in the academia and not positioning them in the margins of the community of practice. In the following these competences are described in detail (Table 11.2).

What these data suggest is that supervisors need organisational skills in mediating between the learning affordances available in the work context (e.g. study programme, faculty or administration), networking skills in engaging in negotiations with co-workers (i.e. other supervisors, teachers, study coordinators) and ability to make decisions when processing the proposed case between individual offerings and the institutional demands in learning. Furthermore, the organisational policies and practices should have a clear statement on the core values of the RPL function, such as equality, transparency and diversity. These values should then be taken into the level of practice, e.g. sense of equality can be seen as practising prior learning recognition in a transparent way, giving an unbiased and equal opportunity for all learners.

The following sections align the personal experiences of the personal study planning supervisors with the academic contributions on transforming professional identities and practices of professional agency. There are also some citations from the participants of the RPL training programme stating their views on the organisational and collegial support needed in the RPL work.

11.6 Tailoring Individual Learning Histories to Higher Education Curricula

One of the prominent topics the recognition of prior learning in higher education relates to is how learners have been able to make use of the various learning affordances in these contexts. Added to that is whether the learning achieved is meaningful in relation to the intended learning outcomes of the higher education curricula. Learners are required to provide evidence of making use of their capabilities as learners and to reflect on this learning from the experience. Evidence is often collected in a portfolio, accompanied with a critical reflection on how the outcomes of the achieved functions at work or during leisure time are aligned to the outcomes of the course, module or degree.

Given the importance of the factors governing the reflective process of learners with prior experiential learning, they are discussed in this section through an examination of how learners are capable of engaging with the learning affordances at work and leisure time, construct a professional identity and practice professional agency.

In her theoretical survey on the capability approach, Robeyns (2005) suggests capabilities may be seen as a framework of thought that can be used for a wide range of evaluative purposes beyond interest to an individual well-being and social development. Robeyns elaborates the theories presented by Sen (e.g. 1990) and Nussbaum (e.g. 2000, 2003) and insists that we need to scrutinise the economic production and social interactions taking place. Furthermore, she suggests that there are cases

Table 11.2 The suggested key competences of a supervisor and their justifications

Element	Justification
The knowledge of learning support	Is the most common, yet the most demanding set of skills for the supervisor. Reflection and critical commentary on prior learning involves understanding the learning affordances in different contexts, the roles and responsibilities of the learner, the agency, the timely sense of the learning and the level of learning. The student should bring all this together in order to produce a well-argued RPL case for the supervisor and the staff with content expertise
Interaction skills	Involve the aptitude needed to create a dialogue between the student and the supervisor. The supervisor needs to be able to listen and pay attention to the learner and to give value to the prior learning. The face-to-face interaction includes knowledge on conversational features such as using open and closed questions, reading 'between the lines' and structuring the discourse for a profound interpretation of the learning. A good performance in dialogue requires sensitivity to the situation, when to interrupt and ask for details and when to give room for the voice of the learner. Interactional skills also include the ability to bring the student cases to the experts or administrators and to argue the cases using the appropriate professional context and language
The knowledge of working life	Is distinctively different between the more professionally oriented universities of applied sciences (i.e. polytechnics) and the research-intensive universities. Although traditional universities educate distinct professions such as teachers, doctors and lawyers, these occupations are regulated by legislation which restricts the flexibility of the studies. The knowledge of work practices is also different in disciplines leading to the profession-specific labour market and especially strictly regulated professions in contrast to the generalist degrees of the universities. The supervisor should be able to detect the degree of learning and the management skills at the occupational level based on the student's work certificates and other material which often lack the detailed descriptions of gained competences
A good command of the curricula	Entails an overall understanding of the degree structure and the competences gained in the course, module and degree level. This includes awareness of the flexibility in the curricula, when and how to recognise prior learning to best support a holistic learning process. The content knowledge refers to the intended learning outcomes of the studies. The supervisor has to be able to transfer prior learning to the curricula
The knowledge of the RPL process	Refers to policies, practices, roles and tasks of the institution. The supervisor carries out agency by using his or her knowledge and understanding to negotiate the optimal correspondence between the intended learning outcomes of the institution and the prior learning of the individual. A good supervisor knows when his or her knowledge of the content is not enough and when to seek assistance from teachers or other personnel. As prior learning may have taken a different shape and size than the courses and modules, the supervisor may need to negotiate the student assignments and the methods of assessment with several stakeholders. The supervisor works in line with the policies and practices of the institution and tries to ensure a transparent and equal treatment for all learners
Supervisor's own motivation and commitment	Refers to expanding the work role of a teacher or tutor to tackle the recognition of prior learning as part of the personal study planning process. The supervisor has to build interest in and to explore the special characteristics of this new task. It is most likely that the participants of the professional development course were amongst the more development-oriented teachers and tutors in higher education

and situations where it makes more sense to investigate the people's achieved functions over their capabilities. Individuals may or may not use their capacities for learning and engaging with the learning affordances available in their daily life (Robeyns 2005).

In the supervisor and assessor role, academics are positioned to screen the case for RPL and identify evidence of individuals' role and responsibilities during learning as well as of the authentic and timely features of that learning in order to define whether they equal to the higher education standards. In short, in the recognition process the supervisors should screen whether the individuals have used their capabilities in learning in a specific level and bring about these learning achievements for assessment. These assessments have shown that, like educational institutions, not every workplace is an ideal learning environment, nor do all managers or co-workers fulfil their roles as the tutors of practical learning. Nevertheless, like what occurs in educational institutions, the learning that arises through workplace activities and interactions is not wholly premised on the affordances of the physical and social setting. Instead, it is premised on the individuals' effort, participation and intentions. Sometimes, it is also unclear whether the learning has taken place to the extent the student suggests. Focus on evidence and critical reflection on prior learning may help supervisors make judgements on learners' achievements outside classroom, combining the learning potential of the individual with the affordances and constraints of the specific context at work or during leisure time. Ybema et al. (2009) describe the articulation of self and the social structure as a 'permanent dialectic'. The individual takes a position within existing discourses in their identity work, whether it is a cultural script, professional rhetoric or management discourse. They regard the notion of 'identity' as a concept helpful in understanding how individuals define and redefine themselves in their social contexts.

The interplay between the self and the corporate identity is seen as discursive articulation. Filliettaz (2010) refers to the workplace affordances and individual engagement pointed out by Billett (2008) and describes how the actual interaction between workplace supervisors and learners may or may not support learning at work. Filliettaz (2010) argues that the efficiency of practice-based learning supervision relies on several aspects and that the availability of expert supervision and the willingness of these experts to tutor the novice for the development of professional identity are of great importance. He reports that guidance comprises a dynamic process, sequentially and collectively constructed by a range of social participants. Guidance in authentic workplace situations may include various interactional patterns, each bearing a specific meaning in the context, such as speech, gaze, gesture, body orientation or use of material objects. The use of these above mentioned elements may enable or disable the professional development, as e.g. the possibility to ask questions may first be welcomed as part of the work practices, but later be unwelcomed if repeated too many times (Ibid.). Billett and Smith (2006) illustrate Filliettaz' arguments on the supervision of early-career professional development by revealing how, e.g. the adjustment of their own behaviour and attitude may help the employees to negotiate the conditions of the work more favourable for knowledge acquisition, supervision or rewards. Such practice of agency may also be used through observing the more experienced co-workers to engage in constructing meaning to the experiences they face during the initial phase of their career in the trade. By doing so, individuals' scope of agency is regulated by the social practices prevalent in their workplaces. Intentionality, such as the focus and direction of engagement, and the degree of intensity, in the form of priority and potency, describes the epistemological agency of the individual (Ibid.).

Students are not the only actors facing challenges in understanding the process of recognition of prior learning in the university. In terms of learning support, the question is not that much of the willingness of the supervisors to provide the student with guidance and counselling upon their prior learning but more likely the difficulty of negotiating between the individual claim on prior learning and the institutional demands. Therefore, students' capability in constructing professional identities and coherent descriptions of their agency as learners are determined by the supervisors' capability to master their work role and influence the culture and structures in the institution.

11.7 Institutional Demands in PSP Supervision Practices

Based on the supervisor professional development programme, we can state that for supervisors as agents it is vital to construct a coherent picture of a professional identity in relation to the expanding work role. This is important not only in the personal level as identity work but also in the intrapersonal level as a sense of belonging to a group of practitioners willing to master the supervision of learners interested in the recognition of prior learning. At the organisational level, the supervisors negotiate between the affordances and constraints of the social structure of their work, such as the quality management system of their institution. In terms of supervisor professionalisation, the referral to discursive analysis of identity as 'situated practices of talking and writing' (Grant et al. 2004; Ybema et al. 2009, p. 303) is fruitful in explaining how supervisors position themselves in relation to the current discourses of educational policies and those of the institution. In the following, consideration is given to the negotiation between institutional demands and supervisor practices by interview extracts from supervisors participating in a professional development programme:

> As this RPL business is not yet established in our university of applied sciences, the colleagues are not often convinced of their own expertise. It helps me to orientate if I discuss with other "RPL colleagues" and explore the RPL guidelines of our organisation. Thus it is not enough just to have the knowledge and the competences. I believe that the meeting of the "RPL colleagues" resembles a meeting between "religious" people. *Senior Lecturer, University of Applied Sciences*

> In my opinion general and administrative RPL guidelines create just the surface for the RPL system. It is essential to bring RPL to the core of the various fields of study and to train supervisors for the RPL procedure. The national guidelines appear to be too general for the solution of specific problems. *Senior Lecturer, University of Applied Sciences*

> A good supervisor has knowledge of the RPL process, its stakeholders and his or her own role in it. *Planning Officer and Student Counsellor, University of Applied Sciences*

The situated practices in these cases are still in the making. The supervisors should integrate RPL to the PSP process at a time when the national guidelines are not yet translated into organisational policies and practices. In reference to Ybema et al. (2009), the professional development programme offers supervisors an opportunity for a co-constructed or dialogical articulation of their professional identity. The conversations related to the autonomy of the supervisor's work describe a metanarrative, a set of more general discourses where the practice of professional identity work and agency is compared to. These conversations include discursive elements mentioned before such as comparing the work role between supervision, research and teaching, or comparing the work of academics to administrative staff members. The description of key competences for effective supervisors may, therefore, be considered not only as an effort to give meaning to the new task but also as an attempt to redefine the professional identity of supervisors in relation to the metanarratives constructing their work. The outcome of the comparison between the different roles of the staff members provided a rather positive view on managing the novel work role of prior learning recognition in a network. The interviewed supervisors sought peer support for their professional development beyond their own organisational context, thus supporting the exercise of the competencies mentioned earlier like 'knowledge of the RPL process' and 'supervisors own motivation and commitment'. Here are two quotes by higher education supervisors stating the importance of a professional network:

> A supervisor needs a good supportive network that can provide help in challenging situations. A supervisor needs to know the staff of the study programme to be able to seek help in problematic cases. *Programme Manager, University of Applied Sciences*

> It is very important for the supervisor to get involved with the network of similar experts and to share good practices with them. *Nurse Educator, Faculty of Medicine, University*

The reflective processes of the supervisors created also an interesting comparison between the different educational tasks of the higher education institutions, namely, between the universities and the universities of applied sciences. In spite of their differences, the supervisor role was seen more or less the same. The conversations related to the tutoring of the future graduates towards the expectations of the working life were equalled to the supervision for becoming an expert or to the supervision for professional growth. To clarify the differences between the Finnish higher education institutions, the universities provide research-intensive education catering more general educational outcomes, and the universities of applied sciences provide education leading to more practical occupations in the working life. The commitment to the role of a supervisor is based on motivational factors and on an engagement to the guidance processes of the institution. Motivation is rooted in the interest towards the professional development of the student. That is, the supervisor is willing to work with the student and overcome the obstacles. Effective supervisors are interested in developing the work practices and inviting other members of their network to support students. These claims are illustrated by the interview excerpt below:

> I consider it important to have peer support. It is not always found inside our own university. In these cases it is great to be able to contact RPL supervisors in other universities. I've had

the pleasure of joining an email list that includes persons from my field of study. This has given me support especially when I started my job as I don't have a colleague with similar tasks in my unit. *Departmental Coordinator, Language Centre, University*

Guidance and counselling are part of the workload for many supervisors. The working hours are divided between research, teaching, guidance and administrative work. The development of guidance and counselling seems to fall low in the priorities, as illustrated below:

The students are not informed of RPL in a large scale. This is partly due to the fact that there is not a proper procedure for RPL. We are clearly lacking this in our university. *Educational Coordinator, Faculty of Natural Sciences, University*

Evidencing RPL should not be harder to do than the course the exemption is sought for. One of the fears in developing the RPL process is that the process will be much more arduous for students and teachers than a "routine tuition". This is definitely one reason why we have not developed many methods for the non-formal recognition of prior learning in our department. *Coordinator, Faculty of Social Sciences, University*

It has been shown that the RPL supervision in the universities is dependent on many factors related to the culture and structure of the institution. The strategies and policies describe the outline of the function, but the interaction between the stakeholders in practising recognition may encourage or discourage their agency. When activities at the practitioner level are examined, yet another dimension emerges as an influencing factor, namely, the discipline-specific views on professionalism. The subcultures of various disciplines may hold different levels of flexibility regarding their views on the construction of professional identity and the mechanisms related to the process of the novices becoming experts in their professions. Another potential contrasting viewpoint is the divide between the professionally oriented and more research-oriented sectors of higher education. In the recognition of prior learning, these may create challenges, especially when a student is changing from one discipline to another, between institutions in the same sector or between institutions in different sectors.

11.8 PSP Supervision as a Transformative Professional Practice

Research on the professional development in the higher education teaching underpins the understanding of the supervisors' situation. Archer (2000, 2007) ties structure and agency together, exposing the importance of the social complexities of power and inequality in taking action. Leibowitz et al. (2012) apply Archer's theory to explain how academics enhance their teaching in research-intensive universities. Interviews with South African teachers demonstrated that being a good lecturer involves interplay between structure and agency. The researchers noted that biographical and immediate contextual features constrain or enable the lecturer to exercise agency. According to Leibowitz et al., students may have a positive role in enhancing the lecturer's sense of agency. Teachers' good performance is tied over by a 'sense of fit' between the aspirations and interests of the student and the lecturer (2012, p. 360). Kahn et al. (2006, 2008a, b, 2012) approach the interplay between personal and sociocultural factors by reflection on academic practice amongst early-career academics. Based on a critical realistic theory on learning, Kahn et al. (2012) also stress the meaning of personal powers in professional learning. In their article on structure and agency in learning, these researchers argue that learning is dependent on social structures and personal powers, and this dependency is mediated through the exercise of powers of reflexive deliberation and the occurrence of social interaction. Taken into the level of this chapter, these two interpretations of Archer's theory of interplay between structure and agency suggest to paying attention to both the sociocultural and individual aspects of professional learning of the supervisors.

In their review on the literature of reflective practice, Kahn et al. (2006) point out observations by Kember et al. (2000) and Schön (1987) on the actual problems the professionals face in their daily work. According to them, the tasks of the professionals are not clearly identified; they are multifaceted and do not necessarily lead to an ideal solution. These researchers augment Schön's argument on the need for professional education to equip students to become reflective practitioners by referring to various aspects of a directed reflective process. Kahn et al. (2006) list constraints such as research dominance over teaching, availability of time and the scope to introduce change and thus refer to the limited possibility for engaging in a reflective process at work. As stated below by two higher education supervisors, the reflection on RPL in the personal study planning process has brought into discussion the interplay between the social structures and the supervisor work role:

> In (Finnish) universities it will still take some time to introduce RPL and change the mind-set for it and to take away certain "fears" of it. But most of all it will require an increase in knowledge and training of RPL to accept the fact that a part of the degree studies can be and could have been learnt through other means and methods than those of the university scholars. *Chief of Academic Officer, Faculty of Science, University*

> I feel that there is not much appreciation for guidance expertise in (Finnish) universities. A good example is RPL. It has been discussed for many years but it seems to be difficult to apply it beyond the formal recognition of education/learning. It is difficult for a single person to advance RPL if it is approached by the university community in a belittling and doubtful manner. Or it will just take some time to get the approval of it. *Training Coordinator, Open University, University*

The quotes describe the social complexities of power and inequality in taking action, more precisely working effectively in the supervisor role for prior learning recognition. The personal study planning supervisors have to negotiate between contrasting opinions on the importance of RPL in higher education. In order to enhance the RPL process, they have to practise agency and negotiate their way in introducing RPL to their academic community. In Finland, the voice of student unions has been considered as a powerful companion to those seeking allies in educational development. Kahn et al. (2012) bring into the discussion of student learning in higher education the debate between sociocultural and psychological considerations. They contribute to the discussion by offering a theory combining the two discourses. In reference to Marton et al. (1997), the perception of the context for learning, the tutors' conceptions, the culture of the discipline and the similar issues influence student learning. However, the interplay between the sociocultural and individual factors is of interest to Kahn et al. (2012). According to them, capacity to engage in reflection on academic practice is valuable for the professional development of the supervisors as well.

By embracing the learning experiences outside of educational programmes, the supervisors extend the dialogue of professional learning in the academia beyond educational settings. As suggested by the researchers upon their review on Archer (2000) and Cranton and Carusetta (2002) as well as McIntyre and Cole (2001), the supervisors were called to participate in a collaborative learning intervention on their current practices, offering a time and place for dialogue with peers and a request to extend their interaction with other practitioners on the faculty level as well. In our study, the personal study planning supervisors found a professional development programme to be a venue for negotiating between the contrasting aims of the work. In a network, they constructed key competences of the RPL supervisor in order to create a work practice that can negotiate the individual learning histories and the institutional demands of the university. This can be seen as an example of a collaborative practice (Kahn et al. 2006) within the reflective process of the supervisors. To succeed in this creation, a crucial aspect is made by the researches. The practitioner needs to have ownership and ability to engage in a reflective process based on personal qualities and personal or professional identities. The critical realist theory suggested by Kahn et al. (2012) calls for reflection on professional practice in order to see the political and social environment of higher education. Brännlund et al. (2012) approach professional learning by drawing attention to the nonmarket outcomes of education. The researchers argue that outcomes of higher education should indeed go further than future revenues or career choices of the graduates. By introducing the capability approach elaborated by, e.g. Robeyns (2005) and Sen (2009), Brännlund et al. (2012, p. 820) suggest that capability of agency is closely connected to individual's capacity to act as a full citizen. However, agency and voice as two vital nonmarket capabilities are affected by level of education and field of study.

According to their research on the Swedish educational system, Brännlund et al. (2012) stress the importance of university education as the central factor contributing to voice and agency, but suggest that a field of study affects agency significantly. A degree from a 'soft' field of study, such as social sciences, may result in lower market-based rewards such as lower earnings and career opportunities, but result in higher nonmarket rewards. In comparison, a degree from humanities and education, natural sciences as well as health and service indicates lower capabilities of agency compared to social sciences and business. Brännlund et al. (2012) found health sciences as an exceptional field of study showing significantly lower probabilities in voice in comparison to social sciences and business.

In our case of supervisor professionalisation, the question of capability to critical reflection had some field-specific importance. Disciplines such as humanities, education and social sciences were seen more in favour with reflective writing compared to natural sciences. This was the case both with learners and their teachers and tutors. In the professional development programme, the supervisors brought into discussion the need for a variety of assessment methods for prior learning recognition. The culture of the discipline may favour, e.g. rooting the learning into the specific social context and to the different elements of the past time or to a universal theory of physics and chemistry, thus calling the need for different methods.

11.9   Concluding Remarks and Implications for Further Study

In the Finnish higher education system, the personal study planning is a procedure every student needs to accomplish in the beginning of the studies. The idea of the personalised learning pathways has been rooted in the younger generation already during the early childhood. The personal study planning is also familiar to the teachers, counsellors and learners in the pre-school and general education. Despite the study skills developed in the general or vocational education prior to university studies, learners often find academic studies very demanding. New students ought to make course choices and selections in the initial phase of the studies without the needed information. Therefore, it is essential that a tutor can fill in the gaps when needed. When the recognition of prior learning is introduced to the higher education, the role of a professional supervisor is even more important. As a novel practice, the RPL brings changes to the construction of professional identities and practice of professional agency both in students and supervisors alike. However, if the practical transformations of student and teacher roles are aligned to the theories of professional development as proposed in this chapter, this process of identifying and seeking recognition of students' learning may lead to increased capability in voice and agency amongst the graduates.

As RPL is considered a student-oriented process, learners are supposed to make a claim for their prior learning based on a comparison to the intended learning outcomes of the courses, modules or the degree in question. However, RPL is not only making a comparison between learning from the experience and the intended learning outcomes of the curricula. The students in higher education are also constructing a professional identity, based on prior experiences and practices. These identities combine both personal life histories and social identities. The recognition of prior learning is therefore not only about making tacit knowledge visible, but it is also negotiating a favourable position of newcomers amongst the more experienced members of the academia. Students are granted a legitimate peripheral position in the community of practice in the academia, and prior learning assessment may draw them closer to the core of practitioners if these individuals are able to construct a professional identity matching to the culturally and socially defined rules of the institution. It is fair to say that recognition of prior learning questions the traditional roles and concepts of learning and in tailoring a high quality learning process. In practising the recognition of prior learning, supervisors are often the initial source of the policies and practices of the institution. The management and administration makes these legitimate by giving orders at the institutional or departmental level. The novelty of the recognition of prior learning pushes the institutions to develop practices on the go. While developing the recognition procedures, the supervisors face both lack of understanding and willingness amongst their peers. The negotiation between the individuals' learning histories and institutional demands can be seen as a practice of professional agency from the part of the supervisors. As the supervisors engage in this reflective process, they are also constructing a new professional identity amid the constructing demands of their work. However, the question is whether they want this identity. Higher education institutions and disciplines differ in their professional cultures. Social studies and humanities embrace more easily a reflective process of the student. It is likely, that the institutions and professions differ also in the supervisor and teacher conception of a professional identity. In relation to the findings of Brännlund et al. (2012) reported earlier, this chapter brings out the need for a further study to explore the interplay between agency and voice contributed by more research-intensive, traditional universities and the more professionally oriented universities of applied sciences. Of further interest is also the potential difference between the nonmarket learning outcomes of disciplines leading to the profession-specific labour market and the so called generalist disciplines. Finally, it can be stated that the potential of RPL lies in the activity of students supported by engaged and capable teachers and supervisors.

Acknowledgements This chapter has been produced in the framework of the European Social Fund-financed project Recognition of Prior Learning in Higher Education (Finland).

References

Alvesson, M., & Willmott, H. (2002). Identity regulation as organizational control: Producing the appropriate individual. *Journal of Management Studies, 39*(5), 619–644.

Archer, M. S. (2000). *Being human: The problem of agency.* Cambridge: Cambridge University Press.

Archer, M. (2007). *Making our way through the world: Human reflexivity and social mobility.* Cambridge: Cambridge University Press.

Billett, S. (2008). Emergent perspectives on workplace learning. In S. Billett, C. Harteis, & A. Eteläpelto (Eds.), *Emerging perspectives of workplace learning* (pp. 1–15). Rotterdam: Sense.

Billett, S., & Smith, R. (2006). Personal agency and epistemology at work. In S. Billett, T. Fenwick, & M. Somerville (Eds.), *Work, subjectivity and learning* (pp. 141–156). Dordrecht: Springer.

Brännlund, A., Nordlander, E., & Strandh, M. (2012). Higher education and self-governance: The effects of higher education and field of study on voice and agency in Sweden. *International Journal of Lifelong Education, 31*(6), 817–834.

Cranton, P., & Carusetta, E. (2002). Reflecting on teaching: The influence of context. *International Journal for Academic Development, 7*(2), 167–177.

Dachler, H. P., & Hosking, D. M. (1995). The primacy of relations in socially constructing organizational realities. In D. M. Hosking, H. P. Dachler, & K. J. Gergen (Eds.), *Management and organisation: Relational alternatives to individualism* (pp. 1–28). Aldershot: Ashgate/Avebury.

Eteläpelto, A. (2007). Työidentiteetti ja subjektius rakenteiden ja toimijuuden ristiaallokossa [Work identity and subjectivity in the cross-current of structures and agency]. In A. Eteläpelto, K. Collin, & J. Saarinen (Eds.), *Työ, identiteetti ja oppiminen* [Work, identity and learning] (pp. 90–142). Helsinki/Porvoo: WSOY.

Eteläpelto, A. (2008). Perspectives, prospects and progress in work-related learning. In S. Billett, C. Harteis, & A. Eteläpelto (Eds.), *Emerging perspectives of workplace learning* (pp. 233–247). Rotterdam: Sense.

Eteläpelto, A., & Vähäsantanen, K. (2008). Ammatillinen identiteetti persoonallisena ja sosiaalisena konstruktiona. In A. Eteläpelto & J. Onnismaa (Eds.), *Ammatillisuus ja ammatillinen kasvu* [Promoting professional growth] (pp. 26–49). Aikuiskasvatuksen 46. vuosikirja. Kansanvalistusseura ja Aikuiskasvatuksen Tutkimusseura. Vantaa: Hansaprint.

Filliettaz, L. (2010). Guidance as an interactional accomplishment. Practice-based learning within the Swiss VET system. In S. Billett (Ed.), *Learning through practice. Professional and practice-based learning* (pp. 156–179). Dordrecht: Springer.

Giddens, A. (1991). *Modernity and self-identity: Self and society in the late modern age*. Stanford/Cambridge: Stanford University Press/Polity Press.

Grant, D., Hardy, C., Oswick, C., & Putnam, L. (2004). Introduction: Organizational discourse: Exploring the field. In D. Grant, T. Keenoy, & C. Oswick (Eds.), *Handbook of organizational discourse* (pp. 1–36). London: Sage.

Hökkä, P., Eteläpelto, A., & Rasku-Puttonen, H. (2012). The professional agency of teacher educators amid academic discourses. *Journal of Education for Teaching: International Research and Pedagogy, 38*(1), 83–102.

Kahn, P. E., Wareham, T., Young, R., Willis, I., & Pilkington, R. (2006). *The role and effectiveness of reflective practices in programmes for new academic staff: A grounded practitioner review of the research literature*. York: Higher Education Academy.

Kahn, P. E., Wareham, T., Young, R., Willis, I., & Pilkington, R. (2008a). Exploring a practitioner-based interpretive approach to reviewing research literature. *International Journal of Research and Method in Education, 31*(2), 169–180.

Kahn, P. E., Young, R., Grace, S., Pilkington, R., Rush, L., Tomkinson, C. B., & Willis, I. (2008b). A practitioner review of reflective practice within programmes for new academic staff: Theory and legitimacy in professional education. *International Journal for Academic Development, 13*(3), 199–211.

Kahn, P., Qualter, A., & Young, R. (2012). Structure and agency in learning: A critical realist theory of the development of capacity to reflect on academic practice. *Higher Education Research & Development, 31*(6), 859–871.

Kember, D., Leung, D., Jones, A., & Loke, A. Y. (2000). Development of a questionnaire to measure the level of reflective thinking. *Assessment and Evaluation in Higher Education, 25*(4), 381–395.

Leibowitz, B., van Schalkwyk, S., Ruiters, J., Farmer, J., & Adendorff, H. (2012). "It's been a wonderful life": Accounts of the interplay between structure and agency in "good" university teachers. *Higher Education, 63*(3), 353–365.

Marton, F., Hounsell, D., & Entwistle, N (Eds.). (1997). *The experience of learning: Implications for teaching and studying in higher education*. Edinburgh: University of Edinburgh Press. http://www.tla.ed.ac.uk/resources/EoL.html. Accessed 25 Apr 2013.

McIntyre, M., & Cole, A. L. (2001). Conversations in relation: The research relationship in/as artful self-study. *Reflective Practice, 2*(1), 5–25.

Mills, C. W. (1970, originally 1959). *The sociological imagination*. Harmondsworth: Penguin.

Nussbaum, M. (2000). *Women and human development: The capabilities approach*. Cambridge: Cambridge University Press.

Nussbaum, M. (2003). Capabilities as fundamental entitlements: Sen and social justice. *Feminist Economics, 9*(2/3), 33–59.

Robeyns, I. (2005). The capability approach: A theoretical survey. *Journal of Human Development, 6*(1), 93–114.

Saarinen, J. (2007). Subjektius ja sukupuoli tutkimustyössä. In A. Eteläpelto, K. Collin, & J. Saarinen (Eds.), *Työ, identiteetti ja oppiminen. [Work, identity and learning]* (pp. 143–155). Helsinki/Porvoo: WSOY.

Schön, D. (1987). *Educating the reflective practitioner*. San Francisco: Jossey-Bass.

Sen, A. (1990). Justice: Means versus freedoms. *Philosophy and Public Affairs, 19*, 111–121.

Sen, A. (2009). *The idea of justice*. Cambridge, MA: Belknap of Harvard University Press.

Sveningsson, S., & Alvesson, M. (2003). Managing managerial identities: Organizational fragmentation, discourse and identity struggle. *Human Relations, 56*(10), 1163–1193.

Watson, T. J. (2008). Managing identity: Identity work, personal predicaments and structural circumstances. *Organization Articles, 15*(1), 121–143.

Wenger, E. (2007, originally 1998). *Communities of practice: Learning, meaning, and identity*. Cambridge: Cambridge University Press.

Ybema, S., Keenoy, T., Oswick, C., Beverungen, A., Ellis, N., & Sabelis, I. (2009). Articulating identities. *Human Relations, 62*, 299–322.

Chapter 12
Securing Assessors' Professionalism: Meeting Assessor Requirements for the Purpose of Performing High-Quality (RPL) Assessments

Antoinette van Berkel

The idea that excellence at performing a complex task requires a critical minimum level of practice surfaces again and again in studies of expertise. In fact, researchers have settled on what they believe is the magic number for true expertise: ten thousand hours. (…) Practice isn't the thing you do once you're good. It's the thing you do that makes you good. (Gladwell 2009, pp. 43, 46)

12.1 Introduction

Practice definitely plays an important role in improving assessor skills, although less than the often quoted ten thousand hours are required to become a qualified and proficient assessor. This chapter addresses the question of how assessor professionalism can be secured feasibly and efficiently. In advancing the answer to this question, a three-step programme for assessor professionalisation and certification is described as developed through a programme offered by the Amsterdam University of Applied Sciences/Hogeschool van Amsterdam (AUAS/HvA) RPL Centre. In providing this description, first, a brief overview of RPL in the Netherlands and at the AUAS/HvA is given to outline the context and necessity of securing assessor professionalism. Next, the notion of assessor competence is explored and reasons are advanced for introducing assessor certification. Following this discussion, the three-step programme is examined sequentially. Additionally, for those interested in implementing assessor certification, two tried and tested certification programmes are compared to make a more informed decision as to how this can be done. Special attention is paid to lessons learnt in developing and enacting these programmes. They are presented as essential preconditions that have to be met for securing

A. van Berkel (✉)
Amsterdam University of Applied Sciences/Hogeschool van Amsterdam,
Amsterdam, The Netherlands
e-mail: a.van.berkel@hva.nl

T. Halttunen et al. (eds.), *Promoting, Assessing, Recognizing and Certifying Lifelong Learning: International Perspectives and Practices*, Lifelong Learning Book Series 20, DOI 10.1007/978-94-017-8694-2_12, © Springer Science+Business Media Dordrecht 2014

high-quality RPL assessments, leaving aside the availability of qualified and professional assessors.

In all, the subject discussed here offers an insight for those who are concerned with the quality of assessments in general and with assessor professionalism in particular, such as assessors' trainers, RPL or assessment developers and advisers and quality assurance (policy) advisers and agencies. Similarly, the professionalisation programmes described apply to both RPL assessors and assessors who perform assessments in competence-based educational programmes. From such a point of view, this contribution is also potentially applicable to managers, examination boards and advisers in (higher) professional education.

For the readability of this chapter the grammatical masculine form is used to refer to both male and female persons.

12.2 Recognition of Prior Learning in the Netherlands

Over the past 10 years, the recognition and accreditation of prior learning (RPL/APL[1]) has gained increasing attention in the Netherlands. The history of RPL in the Netherlands started in the 1990s, when the Dutch government and social partners realised that employees could no longer count on lifetime employment with one employer. The government and social partners, therefore, encouraged the broader concept of recognition and accreditation of prior learning. The concept was defined as 'the process of recognising the competences an individual has gained through formal, informal or non-formal learning in various settings. This definition implies that competences acquired by learning on-the-job, in society or in voluntary work are in principle comparable to the competences acquired in formal education' (Dutch Knowledge Centre for APL 2009, p. 1). Thus, individuals' work experience translated into learning outcomes may provide the basis for formal recognition or even directly result in a certificate or diploma. The ultimate objective was that RPL reports as such, by valuing acquired knowledge and skills through any form of learning, would in the long run be equivalent to diplomas and certificates issued by the formal education system.

In 2001 the Dutch Knowledge Centre for APL was established to collect and share knowledge and exemplary practices on the accreditation of prior learning in the Netherlands. To bring all practices together and to assure a basic quality of RPL procedures, a national quality assurance programme, the so-called RPL quality code, was introduced in 2006. The code is used to assess procedures, create more transparency and set a minimum standard for RPL procedures. It consists of five subcodes, one of which includes assessor quality. Providers that meet the requirements in the code are recorded in a national register for accredited APL procedures, and their assessees gain tax benefits. In addition, between 2007 and 2012, the Dutch government funded national projects on RPL and lifelong learning for educational institutions to encourage the development and implementation of RPL and flexible educational degree programmes.

---

[1] Both RPL and APL are used for the Dutch equivalent EVC: Erkennen van Verworven Competenties.

After all these years of RPL developments and the introduction of regulations and codes, RPL has definitely gained a position in Dutch lifelong learning policy. Generally speaking, RPL is conducted on the basis of two different kinds of assessment standards. One comprises using professional standards accredited by a particular professional domain in the labour market. When these standards are applied, RPL primarily becomes a tool for sustained employability. The aim here is for an RPL report, with valued knowledge and skills on the basis of such standard, to create opportunities for employees to change jobs during their longer working lives both within their own organisations and on the labour market. The second type of RPL standard comprises assessment against the learning outcomes of a particular formal degree programme. In this case, RPL is basically considered as a tool in lifelong learning for the reason that the acknowledged competences can be translated into exemptions for parts of the particular educational programme. In this way, degree programmes may be shortened and, ideally, customised, which makes (higher) professional education more accessible for working adults. Educational institutions in the Netherlands that perform RPL on this basis usually refer to it as intake assessment. This specific use of assessment aligns with the present government policy that aims at 50 % of the working population to be highly educated in order for the Netherlands to remain one of Europe's top 5 knowledge economies (Ministry of Economic Affairs 2013).

12.2.1 RPL at the Amsterdam University of Applied Sciences

The Amsterdam University of Applied Sciences/Hogeschool van Amsterdam (AUAS/HvA) offers a total of 80 bachelor's and master's degree programmes divided over seven so-called schools for approximately 46,000 students with 3,500 employees. Since 2002 AUAS/HvA has had its own RPL Centre that carries out procedures for part-time bachelor's degree programmes for adult learners. Between 2006 and 2011, the centre was registered and accredited as an RPL provider. Over the years, the centre has extended its range of activities to developing and implementing assessments and enhancing assessor professionalism in bachelor's degree programmes. In this role, it was the first one to obtain the Hobéon[2] quality label for assessment centres in 2012. To meet the required quality standards, a number of criteria have to be met, one of which is the availability of excellent assessors. For that reason, over the years, the RPL Centre has trained, supervised and certified large numbers of assessors both from bachelor's degree programmes and from the professional field[3] to improve their performance. Besides, a successful professionalisation and certification programme was developed on the basis of required assessors' competence as outlined in the next section.

---

[2] Hobéon is a national quality assurance agency with a wide expertise in the field of (higher) professional education.

[3] Per assessee, two assessors, one from the professional field and one from the bachelor's degree programme related to the particular standard in question, co-operate in performing an RPL procedure.

Although the training and professionalisation programme was primarily developed for RPL assessors performing RPL procedures at the RPL Centre, it is now widely used to train and support assessors carrying out competence-based assessments in bachelor's degree programmes both at the AUAS/HvA and at other institutions for higher professional education.

12.3   Assessors' Competence

In RPL procedures, portfolio assessment is the most commonly used. This form of assessment is 'generally accepted as a method for presenting evidence of the achieved level of knowledge, skills or competence in general (Barret 2003) and in evaluating competences acquired in informal or non-formal contexts in particular' (Firssova and Joosten-ten Brinke 2007, p. 1). It, therefore, fits well the RPL approach (Joosten-ten Brinke et al. 2008). Assessor tasks accompanying portfolio assessment include evaluating a portfolio (both individually and with a peer assessor), conducting a criterion-focused interview, determining an assessee's competence level, reaching a substantiated judgement, giving feedback and writing a report.

Performing these tasks requires specific abilities. In quality assurance programmes, criteria for assessor quality generally refer to independence and expertise. In this context, independence means that assessors do not have any other relationship with assessees than that of being their assessor at a particular moment in time. Furthermore, an independent assessor does not have any personal interest, whatsoever, in the outcome of the assessment. This criterion can fairly easily be met. However, when it comes to assessors' expertise, it is not so straightforward because assessors are often considered a weak link in assessment procedures (Van der Vleuten et al. 2010; Schoonman 2005; Hofstee 1999; Kane and Bernardin 1982). Expertise in relation to assessor quality refers to three different aspects, namely, basic qualifications, personal characteristics and assessor skills. Basic qualifications, first and foremost, relate to relevant degrees in formal education such as a bachelor's degree in the specific field of the assessment standard. In addition, wide and varied professional experience in and expertise on the domain of the assessment standard is necessary to have a good view of what an assessee may come across in day-to-day practice and what potential strategies there are for handling different practical situations (Straetmans et al. 2011). Moreover, assessors should be well aware of the latest developments in the professional field, and they should be able to look beyond the scope of their own work situation. In short, assessors should be acknowledged as professionals in their field of practice. When it comes to personal characteristics, assessors are required to be at least honest, sensitive, communicative and accurate. Besides, they are expected to be curious and sincerely interested in the development of others. It stands to reason that assessors are also assumed to have self-knowledge and are prepared to invest in their own professional development. The third category of qualifications can be referred to as assessor skills. Examples of these skills include being able to inspire trust and to create a proper atmosphere for assessees, being familiar with different questioning, interviewing and assessing techniques and being committed to providing feedback on

Table 12.1 Example of an assessor competence profile

Assessor competence profile
A. *Basic assessor qualifications*
Has relevant and wide expertise in the domain of the assessment standard
Works for a specific degree programme (in accordance with the assessment standard) and/or has experience with professional practice
Has obtained a bachelor's or master's degree in higher professional education
Communicates in an accessible and convincing manner, both verbally and in writing
B. *Personal characteristics*
Is sensitive and empathises with the assessee
Is aware of one's own frame of reference and knows how to handle it appropriately when carrying out tasks
Is client oriented and genuinely interested in the professional development of others
Works efficiently and accurately and fulfils agreements
Is learning oriented and prepared to invest in oneself
C. *Assessor skills and behavioural indicators*
The assessor has the ability to assess substantively and professionally whether the assessee fulfils the required competences. Since the development and assessment of competence may be based on a wide range of practical situations, it is particularly important for assessors to show that they understand the 'world behind the indicators'. This requires the ability to relate a competence to various practical situations and behaviour
D. *Behavioural indicators*
Creating an atmosphere which will fully do justice to the assessee
Structuring the assessment interview
Applying different questioning and interviewing techniques at the right time aimed at
Purposefully gauging the assessee's competence level
Maintaining control during the interview
Relating experiences, method of work and proof the assessee presents to the relevant competence criteria
Recognising products as usable proof
Reaching a substantiated final judgement and conveying this in a convincing and constructive manner
Recording the judgement in an accessible manner on the appropriate forms or in a report
Giving development-focused feedback
Handling objections to the final judgement adequately and in a customer-oriented manner

Source: Adapted from RPL Centre, Van Berkel (2011)

the match between learning outcomes and the assessment standard. For assessors to develop and apply these skills adequately and in a similar way, training is required (Van der Vleuten et al. 2010; Straetmans 2006).

Based on these assessor qualities, an assessor profile has been drawn up and presented in Table 12.1. The profile is in accordance with the European guidelines for validation of non-formal and informal learning (Cedefop 2009, pp. 67–68). It comprises the basic principles for selecting assessors on the basis of qualifications and personal characteristics, for designing tailor-made training programmes on the basis of skills and behavioural criteria and for assessor certification. In the next sections, it will also be shown that the profile includes the guidelines for assessor professionalisation.

12.4 Professionalisation and Certification Programme for Assessors

The professionalisation and certification programme for assessors as designed by the RPL Centre of the Amsterdam University of Applied Sciences was first introduced in 2002 and has been used in its present form since 2006. The following three steps can be distinguished in the programme: professional development, performance assessment and maintenance of the certificate. In the next three sections, each step will be described in more detail. Firstly, a few words need to be said on the necessity of certification as such. That professional development of assessors cannot be dispensed with is widely acknowledged in view of the complicated task of assessing competences (Straetmans 2006; Sluijsmans 2013). However, assessor certification, implying proven assessor competence as described in Sect. 12.4.2, is quite a different matter. Hence, a few reasons for having certification are now provided here. The first reason is that, even though they meet the basic qualifications and personal characteristics of the assessor profile, not all junior assessors have the ability to meet the behavioural indicators (Table 12.1). This conclusion implies that the validity and reliability of assessments may be at risk, which jeopardises assessees' abilities for their (prior) learning to be captured. An assessment for certification in which junior assessors must show the required skills and behaviour makes these deficiencies visible. In the Netherlands, further support for assessor certification is gained from the Dutch national quality code for RPL. This code includes six subcodes, one of which refers to expert and transparent assessor quality. Ever since its introduction, providers have been required to assure and prove this quality. Together with the other subcodes, this quality aims to assure more reliable and valid RPL assessments. Another motive for certification lies in recent Dutch educational history. In 2012, the Dutch Inspectorate of Education (2012) raised critical questions about exemptions on the basis of RPL outcomes in degree programmes in higher professional education. This has led to a much stricter quality assurance regime with regard to both higher professional education and RPL procedures in which transparency is a key criterion. Assessor quality is a crucial factor in assessing learning outcomes in both professional education and RPL, which is why this quality must be beyond doubt. Certification by means of an assessment on the basis of clear and uniform criteria with the assessor in the assessee's role is an instrument for realising this transparency.

12.4.1 Professional Development

Professional development appears in various forms. A basic training for the purpose of applying the assessment standard uniformly, carrying out the procedure in a uniform way and applying questioning, interviewing and assessing techniques adequately, has proved very useful as a start. An outline of such a programme of training is given in Sect. 12.4.1.1. Once assessors have completed the training successfully, they are given the opportunity to further develop their skills and knowledge along the lines described in Sect. 12.4.1.2.

12.4.1.1 Basic Training

For assessors the first step in developing assessor skills is participating in a basic training (Straetmans 2006) which focuses on gaining these skills as per the behavioural indicators of the assessor competence profile (Table 12.1). At the start of such preparation, novice assessors tend to ask questions like 'How do we fully do justice to assessees in the limited time of an assessment?' and 'Can we actually assess competences objectively?' These are legitimate questions in view of the assessor tasks described in Sect. 12.3. A closer examination of the definition of competence assessment further clarifies this. A commonly used definition is this: competence assessment is meant to assess whether an assessee is able to adequately perform particular professional tasks in a wide variety of contexts and situations (Van Berkel 2012). This definition covers indeterminate elements such as 'adequately', 'certain professional tasks' and 'a wide variety of contexts and situations', revealing the complexity of the assessor's task and signifying the need of a solid assessment standard in which these elements are transparently specified. Such a standard provides assessors with a uniform framework while it still leaves room for the wide variety of situations and contexts in which assessees acquire competences.

As standards are generally derived from competence profiles of educational programmes or from job or professional profiles (Sect. 12.2), it stands to reason that there are as many standards as there are profiles. Therefore, each training programme is tailor-made in that one specific assessment standard and an authentic portfolio in accordance with that standard are the central elements on which the training is designed. This explains why only those assessors who are acknowledged as professionals in the field of this specific standard can participate in the training. Moreover, the training includes three areas of skill development involving the ability to apply the assessment standard, the evaluation of a portfolio and the acquisition of assessor skills.

Refining and Applying the Assessment Standard

Mastering the assessment standard is one of the basic assessor skills, which makes it a very important element of the training programme. The variety with which standards themselves are elaborated is quite wide, and in many cases they do not prove to be workable in that they are either too detailed or too vague (Van Berkel 2012). As this lack of clarity represents a serious problem with competence assessments, the training programme pays special attention to making standards feasible by defining three elements that make them appropriate for use:

1. Typical professional tasks the assessee should be able to perform. These are defined as key tasks, activities, critical situations and problems or dilemmas.
2. Criteria that describe what competent performance entails, i.e. what adequate behaviour is expected.
3. Examples of proof that assessees may submit to demonstrate competent performance (Van Berkel and te Lintelo 2007).

Table 12.2 Competence assessment playing field

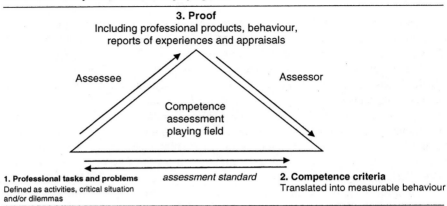

Source: Van Berkel and Te Lintelo (2007)

These elements must be defined in a transparent way so as to prevent too detailed information or overlap (Baartman 2008, p. 36). When the elements are connected in a triangle, the competence assessment playing field – also called the assessor playing field – appears as shown in Table 12.2. For each element of the assessment standard, the skill is to systematically link up the three aspects with each other. It is important for assessors to stay within the assessment triangle, focusing on professional tasks, proof and criteria.

In order to apply the standard adequately, assessors should have a comprehensive understanding of these elements. Competence criteria, however, are generally open and generic as is shown in Table 12.3. They leave room for variation and complexity within the context, which is why they require professional interpretation. The same goes for the professional tasks, which can be developed in various situations and with different degrees of complexity, which makes the outcomes of competence development hard to compare. For these reasons, during the training, there emerge questions such as: 'What activities are missing or redundant in a particular professional task?', 'How do we interpret "competence criterion x"?' and 'What behavioural indicators belong to it?' In addressing these questions, assessors complement each other, based on their own professional expertise and experience. They also gain insight into each other's professional field and the way in which competences are handled in this context. In this manner, the refined standard should become a joint 'product' and a mutual reference and assessment framework.

Evaluating a Portfolio

By focusing on an authentic portfolio during the training, assessors have the opportunity to determine collectively what they will accept as proof of a competence or

Table 12.3 Examples of competence criteria

Consider the professional task: conducting a consultation meeting
Examples of competence criteria for assessing competent behaviour when performing this task in day-to-day practice are: being inquisitive, being sensitive and being convincing

not and what additional information they would like to obtain in order to make a judgement (Van Berkel and te Lintelo 2007). Again, the assessment standard plays an important role in determining what information is missing. For discussing these issues in a structured way and for recording notes and findings at this stage in the assessment process, an evaluation form is available. Apart from providing structure, it also makes the final judgement more transparent.

Acquiring Assessor Skills

Instead of practising parts of an assessment interview and asking questions on parts of the portfolio, it has proven to be more effective to conduct an entire assessment interview and collect all the necessary information in the available time. This process comprises a simulation of an authentic assessment. After having studied the contents of the portfolio, an actor with experience of professional practice assumes the assessee's role. One pair of assessors at a time asks questions to obtain information on all competences in the portfolio. Meanwhile, the remaining assessors observe the interviews and give feedback using the behavioural indicators of the assessor competence profile. The actor will portray different types of assessees to assist in dealing with undesirable behaviour while maintaining control. After the interview, the pairs of assessors reach their final judgement about the assessee. All judgements are subsequently compared with each other and discussed with all assessors present. Where judgements differ, assessors explain what has led them to reach a certain judgement. In this way, they collectively add more content to the standard and make it more workable for their specific situation. It is interesting to note that in many cases assessors were surprised to find out that they had reached the same judgement independently of one another (Van Berkel and te Lintelo 2007). Assessors value the use of the assessment standard and an authentic portfolio during their training. This underlines the fact that practising interviewing and assessment techniques without knowing what exactly should be assessed is a rather meaningless exercise.

An overview of the elements in the training programme and the corresponding learning outcomes is shown in Table 12.4. Obviously, the training method described allows assessors to learn a great deal about applying the standard as well as practising interviewing and assessment skills. It also offers assessors the opportunity to experience that an entire interview can be conducted within the time set. However, as noted, when it comes to developing assessor skills, training only appears to be a first step.

Table 12.4 Elements of basic assessor training summarised with learning outcomes and indication of time investment

Activity	Explanation	Learning outcomes
1. Applying the assessment standard and clarifying the assessor's role	Attention is paid to ✓ Necessary elements for assessing competences ✓ Studying and refining the assessment standard at issue ✓ Explaining the assessor's competence profile	Assessors have a clear picture of their role and know how to apply the available assessment standard
Materials include – A model for competence assessment (the assessment triangle) comprising the competence assessment playing field – The assessment standard and instruments at issue – The assessor's competence profile consisting of basic qualifications, personal characteristics and assessor skills for quality assessor performance Time investment: 4 h		
2. Evaluating a portfolio	Attention is paid to ✓ Relating professional products in the portfolio to professional activities and competence criteria in the assessment standard ✓ A critical review of a portfolio with regard to its structure, contents and size	Assessors have a clear picture of – What they need to find in a portfolio – Which information they additionally need to gather in the criterion-focused interview
Materials include – An authentic portfolio – A standardised report for assessing the portfolio and preparing the interview Time investment: 4 h		

3. Acquiring assessor skills by performing a complete assessment

Attention is paid to

✓ The skills required and defined in the behavioural indicators (assessor profile)

✓ Preparing the assessment interview by discussing the portfolio in pairs

✓ Carrying out the assessment interview

✓ Giving feedback to colleague assessors

✓ Constructing a well-founded judgement on the basis of competence criteria in the assessment standard

✓ Giving feedback to the assessee

✓ Handling undesirable assessee behaviour

Materials include

– An authentic portfolio

– A standardised report for recording the assessment findings and judgement

– An actor performing the role of assessee

Time investment: 8 h

Assessors have a range of techniques at their disposal to perform assessments and know how and when to use them properly to get the best out of the assessee

12.4.1.2 Continuing Professional Development

Continuing professional development (CPD) aims at ensuring that the skills and knowledge assessors have acquired in the basic training remain current and are constantly updated. For the systematic maintenance, improvement and broadening of assessor skills, the CPD part of the programme facilitates assessors in at least four ways. First of all they are offered the opportunity to gain experience by performing authentic assessments in practice according to the behavioural indicators in the profile (Table 12.1). Preferably, they do so in pairs of novice and certified assessors. This enables novice assessors to copy the art of assessing by learning 'by example and good observation' in the real-world context (Ruijters et al. 2004, p. 16). This approach has appeared to be very effective, which can be explained by the theory that 70 % of learning is experiential and 20 % comes from working with others (Cross 2007). Simons and Ruijters (2004, p. 209) add that 'a learning professional is elaborating on his or her work-competencies by learning from and in practice'. It is also argued that such learning meets the competence development of staff better than learning on courses (Illeris 2011).

Another substantial part of assessor development consists of frequently sharing assessment experiences and discussing critical situations and dilemmas with peer assessors in order to refine the collective interpretation of the standard. Evaluation meetings and peer reviews are a means to support assessors in finding a balance between the open criteria in the assessment standard and their personal judgements while aiming at intersubjectivity.

Thirdly, a learning context of 'experimentation' (Ruijters et al. 2004) is created by organising workshops and role plays on specific questioning and interviewing techniques periodically. Here, assessors have the freedom to experiment, ask questions, receive feedback and reflect on their performance under the supervision of an expert assessor or trainer. Common assessor errors are also subject of the workshops. These errors include failing to apply interviewing techniques fully and adequately by not using a technique appropriately and not applying the right technique at the right moment and failing to construct an underpinned judgement. Assessors also find it hard to give constructive and development-focused feedback (Van Berkel 2011).

A fourth effective approach to enhancing assessor skills is feedback on the job, i.e. while performing an assessment. This method, which is increasingly acknowledged as assessment *for* learning (Earl 2003; Dochy et al. 2007), is particularly useful for assessors to get a clear picture of their personal qualities, skills and pitfalls or learning points. Feedback is given on the behavioural indicators in the assessor competence profile (Table 12.1). An independent and expert assessor observes an individual assessor and provides feedback, which shows the level the assessor has reached regarding the indicators in the profile and at the same time makes it clear which of these indicators need further development.

12.4.2 Performance Assessment for Certification

After having developed sufficient proficiency in performing assessments as per the behavioural criteria in the assessor profile, assessors move on to the next step in the certification programme, which is a performance assessment. An independent and expert assessor (and trainer) observes and assesses an assessor on the job while conducting an authentic assessment interview. The expert writes a report in which he relates his observations and findings to the standard as described in the behavioural indicators in Table 12.1. Only if the assessee meets all these indicators to a satisfying degree, will he be granted a certificate and thus become a certified assessor. Expert assessors must be authorities in the field of assessment and development (Straetmans 2006). Their qualifications need some closer examination here. It will be obvious that the two basic criteria of independence and expertise, as explained in Sect. 12.3, apply to expert assessors as well. When it comes to expertise, these experts at the very least meet the behavioural indicators of the assessor standard themselves. Moreover, basic qualifications for experts include a wide and varied experience either with training assessors or in the professional practice of assessment and development. In addition, the personal characteristics listed in the assessor profile also apply to expert assessors. Naturally, certified assessors can develop into expert assessors.

It should be noted that the performance assessment is carried out with only one expert assessor, which makes the final judgement rather vulnerable as the behavioural indicators are open and hence multi-interpretable. Therefore, the standard has been more refined in that the criteria of behaviour have been added to the indicators. For example, Table 12.5 shows how the indicator of 'applying different questioning and interviewing techniques at the right time' has been broken down into criteria. These criteria give focus to both the assessors when developing their assessor skills and the experts when assessing them during a performance assessment. However, they are in no way meant to be used as a checklist to make assessors' behaviour tangible.

Expert assessors are expected to apply their professional expertise effectively to reach a holistic judgement, i.e. one in which the significance of the parts can only be understood in terms of their contribution to the significance as a whole. The bottom line question is 'Do they consider the assessor capable of performing high-quality assessments?' Apart from refining the standard for certification as shown in Table 12.5, meetings are arranged for expert assessors to compare their judgements, exchange experiences and discuss critical situations in order to collectively determine what assessor behaviour is indispensable within the framework of the standard for certification. These meetings, which are held twice yearly, further contribute to intersubjective judgements. In spite of these measures, assessors may still object to the final judgement and ask for a second opinion. For this reason, a sound recording of each assessment interview is available and can be used for this purpose.

Finally, a few points should not go unmentioned about this programme. The assessors are continuously working on their assessor skills and expertise and do so

Table 12.5 A behavioural indicator broken down into criteria for the purpose of assessing the assessor

Behavioural indicator: applying different questioning and interviewing techniques at the right time	
Criteria of behaviour	An assessor
	Listens actively
	Applies appropriate interviewing techniques such as STAR(R)T[a] to generate information as regards displayed professional behaviour and underlying thought and decision-making processes
	Explores the scope of competences through transfer questions and questions about the opposite
	Maintains control during the interview by applying the technique of 'listening – summarising – probing'
	Applies the technique of meta-communication at the level of contents and relationship, if necessary
	Communicates effectively by adapting one's use of language to the assessee's level
Result: An in-depth interview in which the required information for competence assessment is collected	

[a]The letters in STAR(R)T represent the words situation, task, activities and approach, result, reflection and transfer

mainly through performing assessments in RPL processes and in degree programmes. This requires no extra time investment, which makes improving assessor skills cost-effective. Also, when an assessor is assessed for certification, this happens as a random assessment process. This demonstrates that assessors are expected to deal with all different types of assessees and get the best out of each assessment and for every assessee, which is what assessor professionalism is all about.

12.4.3 Maintenance of the Certificate

Assessor certification is based on assessor skills and proficiency, which makes it necessary to maintain the certificate. It is assessors' responsibility to prove the maintenance of their skills. Although there are various possibilities for maintenance, having one's hands tied by too many tests and regulations is not one of them. Gaining more experience with performing assessments appears to be a far more practical and efficient way. In the certification programme discussed here, additional guidelines for maintenance are given as suggestions for continuing and enhancing professional development. Examples of these guidelines are listed in Table 12.6 (Van Berkel et al. 2008). They leave certified assessors with room for their own choices, learning preferences and method of working when fulfilling the maintenance requirements.

A closer examination of the sample guidelines shows that the activities include basic elements of a professional learning community (Birenbaum et al. 2011;

Table 12.6 Examples of guidelines for maintenance (*Source*: Van Berkel et al. 2008)

Working as a professional in the field of assessment and development or as an assessor
  in degree programmes
Performing a minimum number of assessments on a yearly basis
Asking feedback on the assessor standard from peer assessors (on the job)
Providing feedback on the assessment standard to junior assessors (on the job)
Organising assessor meetings for sharing experiences and discussing critical situations
Practising interviewing techniques with junior assessors (in workshops)
Contributing to the improvement of assessment instruments and standards
Attending expert meetings, conferences and seminars on assessment-related topics

Sluijsmans 2013) where certified assessors reflect on their practice. There is also an interesting role for them in enhancing the professional development of novice and less experienced assessors by giving them feedback on their assessment performance. Besides, the expertise of certified assessors is priceless as regards the fine-tuning of assessment policy, including standards and instruments. In brief, a wide variety of assessor activities related to the improvement of competence assessments is relevant for the purpose of maintenance.

For assessors to report on and prove their maintenance activities over a period of time, a standardised form is available. Naturally, a portfolio is an effective instrument for collecting items of proof such as reports of feedback given to novice assessors, programmes of workshops, meetings or seminars one has participated in, etc. In practice, however, a list of accomplished activities suffices, and additional information and proof will only be requested if the list fails to convince. Of course, such a procedure is built on a certain degree of trust, which may be abused. However, it saves the monitoring authority from examining an increasing number of portfolios over the years, which is a very time-consuming and expensive activity. It should be noticed here that so far there is neither a register of certified assessors nor a set of formalised guidelines for continuing education and training in the Netherlands. Therefore, the guidelines as mentioned above suffice for the time being. However, a national register with accompanying rules for certification and continuing education is expected to be in use before long, due to stricter governmental policies in view of assessments in general and RPL assessments in particular in response to the call for a more transparent assessment quality as outlined in Sect. 12.4.

Finally, two minor issues related to the maintenance of certification need pointing out. The first concerns the question who fulfils the role of the monitoring authority. In the current programme, this is the RPL Centre. Monitoring maintenance is complementary to its tasks of providing a basic training for assessors and organising and supervising the further development of assessor skills, and, for that reason, it fits in logically. In this context, the RPL Centre has set itself the task of arranging special assessor meetings for the maintenance of the certificate, which are similar to the activities for assessors' CPD as outlined in Sect. 12.4.1.2. The second issue involves the validity of the certificate. In the present programme, the certificate is valid for an indefinite period of time provided that assessors meet the maintenance requirements as described above.

12.5   Certification and Quality Assurance

Having discussed the three-step professionalisation and certification programme in the previous sections, it is now time to go into the role of the authority that provides the certificates and assures the quality of the certification programme. The AUAS/ HvA RPL Centre has found a reliable partner in the Amsterdam Centre for Continuing Education.[4] The centre is regionally known for its programmes and activities for teachers at all levels of education. For this reason, it adds value to the assessor certificate (external validation). A closer examination of the tasks that are assigned to this authority will make apparent the qualifications for selection. Three quality assurance tasks can be distinguished:

1. Assuring that the experts who assess the performance assessment meet the expert criteria as outlined in Sect. 12.4.2
2. Visiting performance assessments at random to find out whether they are carried out in accordance with the procedure agreed on
3. Checking experts' assessment reports regarding completeness and the underpinning of the judgement.

A fourth task, different in its kind, is providing the certificate.

These tasks show that a quality assurance authority must meet the requirements of independence and expertise in the field of competence assessments to perform them adequately. Independence in this case may well be interpreted as 'at some distance from the assessee'. As to the expertise of this quality assurance authority, an excellent reputation is to be recommended in the field of continuing education for a specific target group, such as teachers. Being a qualified assessor can after all be considered a specific teacher role.

12.6   Certification Programmes Compared

In this section, the professionalisation and certification programme described above will be compared to other certification programmes that have been developed in the Netherlands recently. The Amsterdam assessor professionalisation and certification programme was set up in 2002 and achieved its present form in 2006. The programme was the first of its kind, and it is still unique in that it includes a performance assessment. Choosing this type of assessment seemed obvious, as it fits the purpose of the programme, namely, assessing assessors' behaviour. It is, therefore, in accordance with the so-called principle of congruence. Over the last six years, educational institutions and quality assurance agencies in the Netherlands have developed additional certification programmes, which, without exception, include portfolio assessments. In these programmes, assessors collect proof of their assessor

---

[4] The centre is called 'Centrum voor Nascholing Amsterdam (CNA)'.

qualities in a portfolio. This proof consists of sample assessment reports, a self-evaluation of the assessor standard, feedback obtained from and given to peer assessors, etc. Having accomplished all this, assessors conduct a criterion-focused interview with two expert assessors. In these programmes, the principle of congruence is met by having assessors perform a portfolio assessment from the point of view of the assessee.

All certification programmes require a basic training and CPD (Sects. 12.4.1.1 and 12.4.1.2) in order to prepare for the assessment that leads to certification. The main difference between the programmes is the type of assessment, which is either a performance assessment or a portfolio assessment. In Table 12.7, these assessments for certification are compared together with related aspects such as the number of expert assessors involved, time investment and validity of the certificate. Additionally, (dis)advantages of both types of assessment for certification are discussed. The comparison may help those considering introducing such a programme to make an appropriate and deliberate choice. Also, there might be a need to develop a new programme by combining elements of the programmes compared here.

A few conclusions can be drawn from this comparison in terms of (dis)advantages. When it comes to advantages of performance assessments, it is obvious that no extra efforts or preparation is needed from assessors. For this reason, these assessments are far less time-consuming than portfolio assessments for which proof must be collected and portfolios composed. In addition, only one expert assessor is involved in performance assessments as opposed to two in portfolio assessments, which limits costs for performance assessments. Furthermore, it is important to note that performance assessments require assessors to get the best out of any assessee, as they are 'real-life' assessments. Portfolio assessments, however, offer assessors the opportunity to show their best practices in a portfolio and criterion-focused interview.

An advantage of portfolio assessments over performance assessments is that assessors get a clear picture of themselves as professionals. Part of the proof in their portfolios includes feedback obtained from peer assessors and a reflection on the assessor's role in relation to the assessor's profile (Table 12.1). In the criterion-focused interview, this process serves as input for expert assessors to discuss the assessor's professional qualities and points of development in depth. Nevertheless, one specific disadvantage of portfolio assessments must also be mentioned here. It has to do with proof such as films and recordings of assessment interviews in assessors' portfolios. This kind of proof often appears to be inadequate for evaluation purposes in that, for instance, only part of an assessment interview is recorded or problems with sound or picture quality and appliances arise. It goes without saying that this complicates the expert assessors' task considerably.

To sum up, performance assessments are less time-consuming and more cost-effective than portfolio assessments. Moreover, they mirror the purpose of assessing assessors' behaviour in accordance with the principle of congruence. Portfolio assessments, however, are an excellent tool to make assessors aware of their own professionalism. And as assessors need to be learning oriented and prepared to invest in themselves (Table 12.1), this is a perfect start of their continuing development.

Table 12.7 Two assessor certification programmes compared

Assessment for certification	Performance assessments	Portfolio assessment
Subject of assessment	Assessor behaviour in one specific context which is selected at random	Examples of and reflection on assessor behaviour in various contexts
Form of assessment	On-the-job observation	Portfolio evaluation with a criterion-focused interview
Necessary documents supplied by assessor	Assessor's file including – A curriculum vitae – Feedback report by expert assessor – Assessor's points of development derived from assessor standard – Evaluation form completed by assessor – Manager's letter of permission for doing the performance assessment	Assessor's portfolio including – A survey of assessments performed – A curriculum vitae – A self-evaluation on the assessor st-andard – Recordings of criterion-focused interviews – Feedback report by peer assessor – Feedback report to peer assessor – Assessment reports – Assessor's points of develop-ment derived from assessor standard
Number of expert assessors involved	1[a] Please note: a sound recording is available for second opinion, if applicable	2
Time investment expert assessors	3 h (one expert involved)	8 h, i.e. 4 h for two experts each
Time investment assessor	Participating in professional development activities as described in Sects. 12.4.1.1 and 12.4.1.2	– Participating in professional development activities described in Sects. 12.4.1.1 and 12.4.1.2 – Compiling a portfolio (about 20 h) – Conducting a criterion-focused interview (1 h)
Validity certificate	For an indefinite period of time, provided that the guidelines for maintenance are yearly met	Usually for a period of 3 years, followed by another portfolio assessment

[a]It stands to reason that a performance assessment can also be performed by two expert assessors. However, this implies an increase in costs

12.7 Lessons Learnt: Preconditions

As argued earlier in this chapter, performing competence assessments is far from easy. That is why the assessor professionalisation and certification programme was set up in the first place. Although assessor quality is a critical element in high-quality assessments, it does not guarantee the demanded assessment quality level as such. Additional factors affect assessors' performances. They include preconditions for quality assessments (Van Berkel 2012). Together these preconditions represent the lessons learnt from improving and enhancing assessor professionalism for over a decade, and they will be briefly touched upon in this Section.

A workable and transparent assessment standard is by far the most essential precondition for high-quality assessments. The triangle as outlined in Sect. 12.4.1.1 provides assessors with a reference and interpretation framework. Assessors consider it an indispensable instrument for evaluating portfolios and for preparing and conducting criterion-focused interviews. Deviating from the standard or departing from the assessor's playing field is a very common pitfall assessors need to be aware of as it results in information that is irrelevant for the judgement. Another precondition for assessors to perform their task appropriately involves well-structured portfolios that are limited in size. Assessors might become irritated by an information overload that they cannot ignore. A certain degree of frustration is also caused when the relation between particular proof and the required competences is not clear. The lack of structure causes assessors to bypass the contents of the portfolio. It is therefore highly recommended to provide a clear framework for portfolios including requirements for structure, to set a limit to the items of proof for each competence and to give some examples of acceptable proof as pointers. A third precondition refers to a uniform and workable assessment procedure. For this purpose, a transparent and complete manual is required in which the tasks and responsibilities of all those involved are clearly described. Terminology should be consistent and instructions unambiguous. Assessment instruments such as forms for evaluating a portfolio, preparing the interview and recording the judgement should be available. Moreover, there is the factor of time. Frequently, assessors find themselves faced with the dilemma of performing assessments in far too little time. In order to grant them sufficient time and to have an indication of the time required, it is worthwhile to calculate the average time investment for an assessment on the basis of the tasks assessors perform. A task overview is given at the top of Sect. 12.3.

Carrying out a professionalisation and certification programme as described in this chapter would be meaningless if the preconditions outlined above are not fully met. Furthermore, it should be kept in mind that even if novice assessors meet the basic qualifications and personal characteristics required to take part in the programme, it will be no guarantee for all of them to become certified assessors. Some of them prove to be better at supervising than at assessing. Others are not prepared to really invest in improving their assessor skills. For certification to become feasible, the individual assessor's ambition and determination must prevail.

12.8   Conclusion

In this chapter, the importance of qualified assessors for carrying out high-quality (RPL) assessments has been emphasised along the lines of a professionalisation and certification programme developed by the RPL Centre of the Amsterdam University of Applied Sciences/Hogeschool van Amsterdam. In this programme, much emphasis is placed on basic qualifications and personal characteristics for assessor selection purposes. However, experience has shown that not all novice assessors will develop into certified assessors. The three-step programme discussed appears to contribute to securing enhanced assessor quality. In this programme, special attention is paid to basic training, continuing professional development and a performance assessment for assessor certification. Another important success factor is the presence of an independent, well-qualified and reputable authority for providing the certificate and assuring quality as it validates not only the procedure but also the certificate. Those who consider introducing a professionalisation and certification programme may benefit from the comparison made between the various aspects of existing programmes. In addition, the lessons learnt from performing and refining the Amsterdam programme over the past decade show that, apart from assessor quality, a number of preconditions must be met to assure high-quality assessments. These preconditions include a workable standard, well-structured portfolios that are limited in size, clear and transparent information on the assessment procedure and instruments and also sufficient time for assessors to carry out assessments. It is important to bear these lessons in mind, before embarking on a programme to enhance assessor professionalism.

12.9   Further Study

Once the practices of assessors' professional development programmes are more commonly used and more advanced, practitioners and scholars may critically compare the existing programmes in more detail. Some suggestions for further study are put forward here.

Ruijters et al. (2004), Ruijters (2006) studied the learning behaviour of professionals in the workplace and found that adults have different learning preferences dependent on professional tasks and contexts. She developed a 'language of learning' in which she distinguishes five learning preferences: copying the art, participation, acquisition, experimentation and discovery (Ruijters et al. 2004, pp. 16–18; Ruijters 2006, pp. 185–268). It may be assumed that professionalisation programmes will be more effective if individual assessors' learning preferences are taken into account. Developing such a programme is a challenge in itself. A critical analysis of the outcomes of such a programme in terms of assessors' learning, development and performance may contribute to refine the currently available programmes.

Positive effects of assessment *for* learning have been proved in studies related to classroom assessments and educational contexts (Shepard 2000; Earl 2003; Dochy et al. 2007). An issue for further research involves the extent to which these benefits of assessment *for* learning translate into the CPD activities of adult learners such as assessors in professional practice.

A number of studies on professional development programmes have been carried out in the educational context in view of teachers' performance. They have 'indicated that teachers' beliefs about their own level of competence and their sense of self-efficacy[5] affect their practice and students' performance' (Hendriks et al. 2010, p. 28). It may be worthwhile to explore if these findings apply to teachers in the assessor's role as well. In other words, does assessors' sense of self-efficacy influence assessment practices and enhance assessees' motivation and performance?

References

Baartman, L. K. J. (2008). Assessing the assessment. Development and use of quality criteria for Competence Assessment Programmes. http://igitur-archive.library.uu.nl/dissertations/2008-0423-200627/baartman.pdf. Accessed 4 Mar 2013.

Bandura, A. (1997). *Self-efficacy: The exercise of control*. New York: Freeman.

Barret, H. C. (2003). Electronic portfolios. In A. Kovalchick & K. Dawson (Eds.), *Educational technology: An encyclopedia*. Santa Barbara: ABC-Clio.

Birenbaum, M., Kimron, H., & Shilton, H. (2011). Nested contexts that shape assessment for learning: School-based professional learning community and classroom culture. *Studies in Educational Evaluation, 37*(1), 35–48.

Cedefop. (2009). *European guidelines for validation non-formal and informal learning*. Luxembourg: Office for Official Publications of the European Communities.

Cross, J. (2007). *Informal learning. Rediscovering the natural pathways that inspire innovation and performance*. San Francisco: Pfeiffer.

Dochy, F., Segers, M., Gijbels, D., & Struyven, K. (2007). Breaking down barriers between teaching, learning and assessment: Assessment Engineering (Chapter 7). In D. Boud & N. Falchikov (Eds.), *Rethinking assessment in higher education: Learning for the longer term* (pp. 83–100). London: Virgin Publishing.

Dutch Knowledge Centre for APL. (2009). Information APL in the Netherlands. http://www.kenniscentrumevc.nl/index.php/mt-apl-intro. Accessed 4 Mar 2013.

Earl, L. M. (2003). Assessment *of* learning, *for* learning, and *as* learning. In L. Earl (Ed.), *Assessment as learning: Using classroom assessment to maximize student learning* (pp. 21–28). Thousand Oaks: Corwin Press.

Firssova, O., & Joosten-ten Brinke, D. (2007). *Portfolio for assessment of prior learning: Design issues*. Paper presented at the ePortfolio conference 2007, Maastricht, The Netherlands.

Gladwell, M. (2009). *Outliers. The story of success*. London: Penguin.

Hendriks, M., Luyten, H., Scheerens, J., Sleegers, P., & Steen, R. (2010). Conceptualizing teacher professional development as a means to enhancing educational effectiveness. In *Teachers' professional development. Europe in international comparison. An analysis of teachers'*

---

[5] Self-efficacy is defined here as 'a future-oriented belief about the level of competence a person expects he or she will display in a given situation' (Bandura 1997).

professional development based on the OECD's Teaching and Learning International Survey (TALIS) (pp. 19–41). Twente: University of Twente.

Hofstee, W. K. B. (1999). *Principes van beoordeling. Methodiek en ethiek van selectie, examinering en evaluatie.* Amsterdam: Harcourt Assessment B.V.

Illeris, K. (2011). *The fundamentals of workplace learning. Understanding how people learn in working life.* London/New York: Routledge.

Inspectie van het onderwijs. Ministerie van Onderwijs, Cultuur en Wetenschap. (2012). *Goed verkort? Over de programmering en verantwoording van (ver)korte opleidingen in het hoger beroepsonderwijs (2012).* Utrecht: Inspectie van het Onderwijs.

Joosten-ten Brinke, D., Sluijsmans, D. M. A., Brand-Gruwel, S., & Jochems, W. M. G. (2008). The quality of procedures to assess and credit prior learning: Implications for design. *Educational Research Review, 3,* 51–65.

Kane, J. S., & Bernardin, H. (1982). Behavioral observation scales and the evaluation of performance appraisal effectiveness. *Personnel Psychology, 35*(3), 635–641.

Ministerie van Economische Zaken (2013). Uitwerking regeerakkoord voor versterking kenniseconomie. http://www.rijksoverheid.nl/documenten-en-publicaties/kamerstukken/2013/02/11/uitwerking-regeerakkoord-voor-versterking-kenniseconomie.html. Accessed 7 Mar 2013.

Ruijters, M. C. P. (2006). *Liefde voor leren. Over diversiteit van leren en ontwikkelen in en van organisaties.* Ph.D. thesis. Deventer: Kluwer.

Ruijters, M. C. P., Noorman, S., Rockwell, B. J., & Simons, P. R. J. (2004). *Creating strategic value through the language of learning: Building a transparent learning architecture.* Conference of the Academy for Human Resources, Development International (AHRDI), Limerick (Ireland).

Schoonman, W. (2005). De zwakste schakels. Over assessment door assessoren. *Onderzoek van Onderwijs, 34,* 10–14.

Shepard, L. (2000). The role of assessment in a learning culture. *Educational Researcher, 29*(7), 4–14.

Simons, P. R. J., & Ruijters, M. C. P. (2004). Learning professionals: Towards an integrated model. In H. P. A. Boshuizen, R. Bromme, & H. Gruber (Eds.), *Professional learning: Gaps and transitions on the way from novice to expert* (pp. 207–299). Dordrecht: Kluwer Academic Publishers.

Sluijsmans, D. (2013). *Verankerd in leren. Vijf bouwstenen voor professioneel beoordelen in het hoger beroepsonderwijs. Lectorale rede.* Zuyd Onderzoek: Heerlen.

Straetmans, G. J. J. M. (2006). Assessment van competentie: definitie, knelpunten, ontwerpbeslissingen. In E. Roelofs & G. Straetmans (Eds.), *Assessment in Actie* (pp. 13–40). Arnhem: Cito B.V.

Straetmans, G. J. J. M., Roelofs, E., & Peters, M. (2011). Vaststellen van didactische bekwaamheid tijdens de LIO-stage. *Tijdschrift voor lerarenopleiders (VELON/VELOV), 32*(1), 4–11.

Van Berkel, A. (2011). *Handleiding assessorvaardigheden.* Amsterdam: EVC Centrum, Hogeschool van Amsterdam (internal document).

Van Berkel, A. (2012). Kritische reflectie op competentietoetsen in het hbo. *OnderwijsInnovatie, 2*(14), 17–26.

Van Berkel, A., & te Lintelo, L. (2007). Recht doen aan de kandidaat bij EVC. De rol van de assessor. *Develop 3*(4), 28–37. Voorburg: Anne Westerhof.

Van Berkel, A., Van Dinther, M., Oudkerk Pool, I., & Speetjes, J. (2008). Certificeren van assessoren in het hbo. Waarom en hoe? *OnderwijsInnovatie, 2*(10), 17–25.

Van der Vleuten, C. P. M., Schuwirth, L. W. T., Scheele, F., Driessen, E. W., & Hodges, B. (2010). The assessment of professional competence: Building blocks for theory development. *Best Practice & Research Clinical Obstetrics and Gynaecology, 24,* 703–719.

Chapter 13
Problems and Possibilities in Recognition of Prior Learning: A Critical Social Theory Perspective

Fredrik Sandberg

13.1 Introduction

This chapter focuses on how recognition of prior learning (RPL) can both be critically scrutinised and give suggestions for development using critical social theories. Insights from a research project exploring RPL for the accreditation of prior experiential learning to qualify for course credits in the healthcare sector are used to develop the analysis (Sandberg 2010, 2012a, b, 2013; Sandberg and Kubiak 2013). RPL for accreditation has for long been criticised for its instrumentalism and technical character. However, there is a need for a more balanced view and informed analysis with emphasis on developing RPL as a fair and valid process (Sandberg 2012b). It is proposed that Habermas' theory of communicative action and Honneth's recognition theory can be used to analyse the benefits as well as elucidate ways forward. Habermas' and Honneth's theories encourage mutual understanding and recognition between assessors and students, between students and tutors and between students to enhance social integration, solidarity, recognition and the possibility of enhancing self-realisation through work. As such, they position and consider an RPL process that is something more than a strategic and goal-oriented process with the means-end goal of assessing and reordering prior experiential, often tacit, learning against the educational system. This form of RPL process can also promote processes of mutual recognition, learning and development through critical scrutiny of prior learning.

RPL is commonly understood as the practice of recognising, assessing and acknowledging skills and knowledge adults gain through experiential learning and formal education (Thomas 2000). In Sweden, RPL is described as a process of structured assessment and evaluation of knowledge and competencies gained within as well as outside of formal education. Sweden does not yet have a National

F. Sandberg (✉)
Department of Behavioural Sciences and Learning,
Division of Education and Adult Learning, Linköping University, Linköping, Sweden
e-mail: Fredrik.sandberg@liu.se

T. Halttunen et al. (eds.), *Promoting, Assessing, Recognizing and Certifying Lifelong Learning: International Perspectives and Practices*, Lifelong Learning Book Series 20, DOI 10.1007/978-94-017-8694-2_13, © Springer Science+Business Media Dordrecht 2014

Vocational Qualification framework (NVQ), as other countries, such as the UK, do. RPL was introduced through the concept of *validation* in 1996 and was linked to processes that sought to develop adult education and learning through a major reconstruction of adult education in Sweden during the years 1997 and 2002 (Andersson 2008). General definitions of RPL do not apply to all contexts in which RPL is used in Sweden as there is no NVQ system. This chapter specifically explores an RPL process focusing on assessing individuals' prior experiential learning to receive course credits. This form of RPL has been a concern among several researchers (Howard 1993; Murray 1994; Houston et al. 1997; Michelson 1996; Taylor 1996; Briton et al. 1998; Heath 2001; Spencer 2005; Wheelahan 2006; Scott 2007, 2010). RPL for accreditation is often characterised as quite instrumental processes and, therefore, promotes a technical view of education in its focus on grades and assessment.

As a worldwide assessment or perhaps educational movement (Spencer 2005), RPL has been implemented in countries around the globe. While RPL is increasingly introduced in both policy and practice, research is needed to inform both its design and implementation (Harris and Wihak 2011). Likewise, research on the impact of RPL on practitioners and workplace practice has received little attention. As pointed out above, RPL for accreditation has been criticised for its technical, bureaucratic and instrumental objectification of individuals' prior learning, but research into the personal benefits of the experience is lacking in nuance in the ongoing debate.

This chapter draws on a study of RPL in an in-service training programme at the upper secondary level in Sweden. It was attended by 14 female healthcare assistants. The purpose of this programme is to deliver an opportunity for healthcare assistants to become licensed practical nurses through RPL and further education. Most of the assistants work in the elderly care sector. The in-service training programme is at the upper secondary level and lasts for approximately 1½ years. The participants continue to work 80 % of the time and invest 20 % of their time in coursework. In this context, many of the procedures involved in the RPL process included various forms of assessment. For instance, the teachers evaluate the students in assessment interviews and through group discussions. The participants' prior learning is also assessed in practice by tutors during a 6-week RPL placement.

Even though the primary focus of RPL often is certification or accreditation, this chapter argues that such processes could support enhanced self-confidence, self-awareness and self-esteem when it is founded within worthwhile learning experiences (as been suggested by Brown 2001, 2002; Lamoureux 2005; Stevens et al. 2010; Whittaker et al. 2006). However, apart from a few exceptions (e.g. Somerville 2006), changes in self-concept and identity have received little attention in the research literature. There is also a deficiency of theoretically informed research into RPL at large (Andersson and Harris 2006; Harris et al. 2011). Honneth and Habermas' work with its concerns with the relationship among recognition, self-esteem, self-realisation, communication and mutual understanding offers instructive ways forward to make these assessment and learning processes more effective and just.

13.2   Communicative Action and Recognition Theory

Honneth (1995, 2007) and Habermas (1984, 1987) develop normative critical social theories focusing on the concept of recognition and communicative action. Educational research drawing on the work of Habermas can be traced back to the beginning of the 1970s (Ewert 1991), and educational academics are still instigated by the issues he advances both in general (Murphy and Fleming 2010; Moran and Murphy 2012; Fleming 2011) and in relation to adult education (Mezirow 1981; Brookfield 2005; Welton 1995). Despite RPL's connection to adult education, little attention has so far been paid to his theorisations with the exceptions of some recent developments (Houlbrook 2012; Sandberg 2010, 2012a, b; Sandberg and Andersson 2011). Honneth's work was only recently introduced to education (Huttunen and Heikkinen 2004; Huttunen 2007), and only a small range of publications draw on his recognition theory to explore RPL (Hamer 2010, 2012; Sandberg and Kubiak 2013). In the following, these theories are discussed, beginning with the theory of communicative action.

The theory of communicative action (Habermas 1984, 1987) is a heterogeneous theory developed chiefly with reference to philosophy and sociology. On the macro-level, Habermas identifies the problems facing contemporary societies by dividing society into 'system' and 'lifeworld'. The system is developed with reference to bureaucracy, where the steering media of power reproduce the system and money takes on similar reproductive functions in the economy. Systems can be traced to contexts where social integration is not necessary for legitimate reproduction. In distinction, the lifeworlds are located in social contexts where language and social integration are necessary for legitimate reproduction. Habermas specifically refer to education and the family as milieus where the lifeworld is established. Lifeworld as concept is not easy to comprehend (Brookfield 2005). It refers, in a more abstract matter, to a horizon from which we constantly move within when we communicate. More specifically, culture, society and personality structure the lifeworld. Thus, the reproduction of the lifeworld is essential to sustain culturally valid knowledge and solidarity and to contour individual identities. Habermas' concern is that systems in modernity move into the lifeworld and colonise it through power and/or money, thus ignoring the fact that lifeworlds such as the family and education are social contexts. With reference to education, the system could engulf social integration through an emphasis on grades and tests. Students may consequently become obliged to act egocentrically to achieve their goals, and mutual understanding would in such a scenario become superfluous. This kind of action threatens opportunities for students to advance culturally legitimate knowledge and to commit to acts of solidarity while distracting from the development of individual personalities. As discussed above, these issues become significant in RPL for accreditation, because such procedures focus on assessment and grades as the means-end goal often overlooking the necessity of incorporating mutual learning processes in such procedures. Practices of RPL might thus influence the education system to emphasise a synchronisation of RPL by means of grades and administration to ensure eminence.

Although the macro-level concepts of the system and lifeworld, discussed above, are useful for a more general analysis of RPL, the micro-level of communicative action contributes with further theoretical tools. In communication Habermas maintains that individuals can refer to exactly three worlds. First, when people raise a truth claim, they address something in the objective world. Second, when individuals raise a claim to normative rightness, they are saying something about the social world. Third, when individuals claim to be truthful or sincere, they are referring to something in the subjective world. In communicative action, actors try to harmonise their individual goals through consensus (Habermas 1984). By raising truth claims and claims to normative rightness and truthfulness – thus referring to the objective, social and subjective worlds – individuals can engage in dialogue and harmonise plans for action (Habermas 1987). They attempt to reach a mutual understanding of the goals of the process, determine how to act in a manner that is normatively correct and describe their subjective thoughts through dramaturgical action. Two of the more important features of communicative action are its teleological and communicative aspects. The goals of the individual are connected with those of other individuals, and these persons can pursue goals cooperatively based on communication and a shared definition of the situation. If we consider these propositions by Habermas, we can more clearly come to terms with the norm of communicative action. Communicative action encompasses at least two actors that focus on reaching mutual understanding. These actors first try to define the situation: they attempt to speak the truth following the legitimate rules of conduct and to act truthfully. Aberrations from these norms, such as lying, manipulating and acting egocentric or in normative dishonest ways, are hence deviations from the norm of communicative action.

If we now turn to Honneth, he argues that the reproduction of social life is driven by the need for mutual recognition. As humans, we can only develop a positive and practical relation to self as an independent and individualised being when we have learned to view ourselves from the position of other persons. This, as Honneth calls it, intersubjective recognition occurs in three stages: (a) self-confidence is developed through love in the relationships we have within the family and among close friends; (b) the public recognition as a person with legal rights develops self-respect and (c) self-esteem arise out of recognition of an individual's achievements, aspirations and capabilities, and hers or his contribution to the realisation of goals in the workplace or, as argued here, further education. Although the English translation of Honneth's work (e.g. Honneth 1995) defines the mutually sustaining social environments in which people are supportive of each other's individual aspirations as a form of 'solidarity', the term 'mutuality' may be a more correct descriptor because solidarity is rather built from the outcome of such processes of mutuality.

Individuals are also at risk of misrecognition, disrespect or nonrecognition. In its most basic form, love is substituted by violence, rights are violated and processes of mutuality are broken. Insults, humiliation and denial of recognition could destroy the individual's sense of self. Moreover, structural exclusion from the possession of certain rights within society also risks damaging subjects' self-respect. Finally, when mutuality and group solidarity are destroyed and subjects are deprived of social approval and recognition from others, for instance, in the workplace, there is a risk of damaging subjects' self-esteem. For instance, if your colleagues or boss does not recognise your traits, a worst-case scenario would be being bullied or ignored.

In Honneth's normative view, contemporary pluralistic societies should provide unrestricted recognition for its citizens. He proposes that in answering the question of how a framework of recognition is constituted, empirical analysis of these three patterns is needed. First, this would require studies on practices of socialisation, familial forms and relations of friendship; secondly, on the content and application of positive law; and finally, on actual patterns of social esteem. With regard to this last dimension of recognition, and considering related research, we can claim with relative certainty that people's social esteem is measured largely according to what contributions they make to the society in the form of formally organised labour (Honneth 2007).

As such, the project discussed in this chapter drew on these two theories. However, these theories are not totally compatible and they are used separately in the analysis. Honneth has also been critical of Habermas but still suggests the need to integrate his thoughts into a recognition theory. Honneth argues that the problems of pluralistic societies cannot be explained fully in Habermasian terms as colonisations of the lifeworld – a process where money and power force their way into social lifeworld contexts. For Honneth, the focus should not be on this conflict between system and lifeworld but on the social reasons underpinning the systematic violation of conditions for recognition. In the next part, these theories are discussed in terms of their relationship to RPL.

13.3 Communicative Action, Recognition Theory and RPL

Research drawing on Habermas to analyse RPL is developing. Concepts drawn from Habermas have been proposed occasionally (Harris 1997), but scholarly more direct connections to RPL are infrequent. Houlbrook's (2012) recent paper is one of the few examples. He draws especially on the concepts of lifeworld and system to analyse the experiences of students in social science and community services at the graduate level. RPL for accreditation has three important aspects that are relevant for a discussion of RPL in the context of the community sector: (1) formal knowledge is favoured over informal; (2) access risks have normalising results and (3) there are main discourses that decide what is credentialed learning. He concludes that alternative RPL framings could enable resistance to a lifeworld colonisation. This alternative would be a critical RPL model that can be viewed as an implicit act of solidarity with the lifeworld in which learners exist. In a lifeworld-sustaining RPL model, Houlbrook (2012) argues for the need of being critical by engaging in mutual discussions. This raises issues about the engagements on behalf of the assessor in RPL. The assessor must thus understand the meaning and validity of the lifeworld that is captured in assessment. There is hence potential for RPL to maintain lifeworld meanings and resist hegemonic influences that reproduce power relationships. Based on such a model, there is a possibility for individuals unfamiliar with formal education to benefit from RPL.

If communicative action raises important issues in RPL about the tension between system and lifeworld, the possibility for communicative action or the risk of assimilation and colonisation, Honneth's theory is concerned with the recognition, self-realisation and the threats of misrecognition or nonrecognition. For Honneth, work is a place for self-realisation, where the rank of the tasks performed through labour and how skills and traits are recognised is important. RPL could here possibly have an impact on lowly socially esteemed paraprofessional occupations, including healthcare work, by acknowledging the skills that those workers possess.

As in Habermas' theory of communicative action, there are few examples of using Honneth's recognition theory to analyse RPL. Hamer (2012) has recently used Honneth to analyse RPL. Writing in an Australian context and focusing on the assessor–candidate relationship, she argues that Honneth's theory of recognition highlights the ethical and moral perspectives on RPL relevant for social inclusion. Hamer identifies five potential ways of using Honneth to analyse this matter: (1) mutual recognition is needed in enabling self-actualisation; (2) self-actualisation for all members of society is needed to secure social justice; (3) recognition must be intersubjective, i.e. both parties (in the assessor–candidate relationship) must recognise each other; (4) recognition is a relational process rather than a one-way acknowledgment by the assessor; and (5) recognition can be attained both through institutions and personal relationships. Of particular importance is that RPL assessment processes recognise the 'who' of both the assessor and assessed, as it is necessary to take the normative perspective of the other to understand the other's particularity. Hamer (2010), thus, argues that we need to move from a one-way normative judgement, where the assessor's normative view dominates to overcome ontological insecurity (Giddens 1991) on behalf of the assessed and epistemological authority (Michelson 1996) on part of the assessor. This recognition must be intersubjective (i.e. leading to mutual recognition and understanding). The assessor must know who the assessed is and recognise and understand the ontological context (i.e. practice of work and family) with which he or she is familiar. The assessor and assessed must therefore develop mutual understanding in the RPL assessment to be able to reach beyond processes where the assessor forces epistemological authority upon the assessed (Hamer 2012; Also see Sandberg 2010; Sandberg and Andersson 2011).

Thus, there has been some focus on RPL in relation to the theories developed by Habermas and Honneth, but these efforts are quite recent. The discussions have focused on how to assess prior learning properly and with focus on an understanding of the assessed and the contexts in which prior learning developed.

13.4   From a Caring Ideology and Power, to the Possibilities of Communicative Action and Recognition in RPL

In the following section, four cases of the RPL process described above are developed. In the first two cases, the focus was to critically scrutinise the power issues. In the third and fourth cases, the focus was to enhance an understanding of the potentials of the process, i.e. analyse the possibilities for critical learning, change and what consequences the 'recognition' in RPL could have for the individual.

13.4.1 A Caring Ideology, Power and the Consequences of Lack of Mutual Understanding in RPL

In the first analysis in the study described above, Habermas' theory of communicative action was used to progress the idea of a caring ideology. Observations and interview data from the field study were used for the analysis.

The three essential qualities distinguished in the relationship between the teachers and healthcare assistants in the RPL process are (1) teachers' strategic actions of always acknowledging the participants, (2) teachers' adoption of a caring attitude and (3) how these two aspects built a trusting relationship with participants. The teachers acknowledge participants through personal and affective comments. This caring strategy has some consequences. Firstly, it allowed the teachers to obtain power over truth claims; secondly, it made mutual understanding superfluous; and thirdly, it confused several participants. Though participants felt confused, they put their faith in the teachers' authority. It is further held that this authority developed from the teachers' adoption of a caring ideology. The last theme of the findings addressed further consequences, especially the personal recognition the teachers provided for the participants. This form of recognition seems to confirm the participants' personality and identity as healthcare assistants, i.e. who they are. The main outcome is that this caring ideology adopted by the teachers risks reproducing a normative view of care work uncritically. What is true is not critically discussed; it is instead determined by the system. Because caring is seen in essentialist ways, complex skills thus seem to go unnoticed in the RPL process. The participants are acknowledged as doing healthcare work correctly, but what this means more in depth is never manifested or critically scrutinised. An important question here is thus whether RPL should only reproduce existing normative discourses. Should RPL only retool the workforce or could it also have other more emancipatory goals?

Using Habermas' theory of communicative action and viewing RPL as a social practice, this case concludes that the RPL process develops through a caring ideology. This ideology is constructed through strategic actions, and such actions are characterised as acknowledgements and performed with a caring attitude, aspects that become vital for building a trusting relationship with the participants. Through this ideology, the system strategically controls the RPL process by building the participant's faith in the teachers' authority. The teachers possess the validity claim of truth. This validity enables a strategic assimilation of experiences that fit into the curriculum as well as informal and uncritical acknowledgements of the participants' caring identity as care workers. It is important to gauge this caring ideology that unreflectively reproduces a normative discourse in a highly gender segregated job, performed by women with a low socioeconomic background. The RPL process also seems to neglect the complexity of caring, when caring is viewed as something connected to the personality of the healthcare assistants.

The second study also drew on communicative action, albeit focusing in more detail on the students' understanding of the assessment interview. The teachers performed this interview taking on different roles. One of the teachers asked questions to the participant and another took minutes. The focus in this study was also to evaluate the results of the analysis against ideals in adult educational research. The data drew primarily on interviews but also to some extent observations. Drawing from the theory of communicative action, the following questions were used to analyse the process: What consequences do certain actions have and how do these actions shape the RPL process and its outcome? How can the validity claims inform the process? How can the rationalities inform the process? Is the communicative process rational? Methodologically, the analysis was inspired by Habermas' method of rational reconstruction.

Through a reconstructive analysis of the observations of the assessment interview, it was suggested that the assessment interview was based on the teacher's goal-oriented and strategic actions, pushing the participants to act dramaturgically by excavating into their subjective world. This process was then explored through the participant's perspective. The main results suggested that the process followed an instrumental rather than communicative rationality. Using Habermas' concept of rationality, the following is proposed. Firstly, the students did not know by which means the assessment was conducted or what its goal was. Secondly, they did not know how to orient their actions towards the normatively prescribed values in the process (e.g. 'being a student', 'how to reflect in the right way so their prior learning can be made visible'). Thirdly, they did not know how to present themselves truthfully, i.e. it was difficult for the students to describe their subjective experiences. By reconstructing the process as a communicative action, the following set of factors was suggested. Students and teachers, firstly, must agree on a mutual definition of the assessment process prior to its implementation, and the teachers should be clear about what it is they want the participants to accomplish. It raises the questions: How are the students supposed to act? What is the goal of the process? However, the assessment interview process must also in general be more oriented towards mutual understanding. The question–response focus, secondly, must be changed towards a more conversation-focused interview. Teachers in the RPL process must then more clearly inform students that anything may be said, questioned or discussed in the process. A mutual conversation at the end of the process, thirdly, could include a thorough discussion of how the student's prior learning is transformed into course credits. What prior experiences did the students have? How were these experiences assessed in terms of the curriculum? A more communicative action-oriented process could promote the students' understanding of the process, and they could build on that as they move on to new learning contexts.

13.4.2 Critical Learning, Change, Self-Realisation and Identity in RPL

In the third analysis, the RPL placement process in which the participants were assessed in practice was focused. The aim of the analysis was to examine the potential for critical learning and change in the RPL placement process, also drawing on Habermas' theory of communicative action. The analysis drew on interview data. The all-embracing question was: What are the impediments and possibilities for critical learning and change in the context of the RPL placement? Interviews with participants were used for the analysis. Analytical questions drawn from theory included the following: Is the RPL placement based on mutual understanding between tutor and participant? How do the participants' and tutors' actions allow this process to progress? What does focusing on validity claims in the communication processes between tutor and participant uncover? Is the process rationally communicative? Have the involved tutors and participants reached an agreement about their goals and action norms and are they open to trying to understand each other's subjective perspective?

The findings were structured into three main themes (the two first themes also included subthemes): (1) the potential for mutual understanding in RPL placements and the challenges of mutual understanding; (2) critical discussions and learning and (3) RPL placements as a potential context advancing action and change.

Within the first theme, one core feature of the RPL placement was the collegial interpersonal relationships that many students developed with their tutors. Such dynamics were especially apparent among participants that were able to orient their actions towards mutual understanding. However, the students' and tutors' experiences were not always compatible, which hindered satisfying engagement in the RPL process and in some cases restricted mutual understanding.

Within the second theme, many participants made positive comments about the time spent at their placements and their collaboration and dialogue with their tutors. However, the data also suggested that the placement experience became a process of critical review of several aspects of caring practice. From a Habermasian perspective, this process could be observed as occurring primarily within the normative dimension of care work, where the prescribed norms of caring practice are considered critically through discussions.

The findings also raised the question of the potential for action and change through RPL (theme 3). Three important factors facilitate change: (1) most participants and tutors essentially share the same social lifeworld because of their involvement in caring practice, which makes it easier for them to orient their actions towards mutual understanding; (2) most processes focus on such mutual understanding, and thus mutual cooperation is made possible; and (3) if these two conditions are fulfilled, i.e. mutual understanding and cooperation, many tutors and participants can enter into critical discussions about caring practice.

The results indicate the importance of a mutual understanding of RPL among educational institutions, teachers and students. Instead of merely rejecting this form of RPL, as has been argued previously, we should strive to create equilibrium between the lifeworld of work and the education system. The results presented here suggest that an RPL process could be developed that would focus on mutual understanding and critical discussion. RPL could thus legitimately encourage critical learning and promote change, instead of merely assimilating prior workplace-oriented learning by assigning grades based on that work within the education system. Though this type of RPL model does appear to have potential, it must be further developed in the future.

The fourth and last analysis focused on illuminating the significance of Honneth's theory of recognition for understanding RPL by analysing six case studies of the RPL experiences of paraprofessional workers in health and social care in England and Sweden. As such, this analysis also drew on data from another project in England. A model of varying conditions of identification and recognition was created for and used in the analysis. This model included four identificatory positions: (1) self-realisation, (2) resistance, (3) marginalisation and (4) rejection. These positions were discussed in three themes: (1) varied conditions of recognition, self-realisation and marginalisation; (2) varied conditions of identification, experiences of resistance and rejection; and (3) the fluidity and ambivalence of identificatory positions.

The first theme argued that the identificatory position of self-realisation involves a co-occurrence of recognition and identification. The workplace is an important place for recognition because it is a context where the social esteem of individual achievements and abilities develops. It is also a site within which people construct and sustain their identities. RPL appeared to play a role in self-realisation. Possessing the qualification or successfully completing aspects of it was a matter of personal identification, not least because years of experience and skills were made visible and recognised. For Honneth, solidarity can be understood as an interactive relationship in which subjects empathise with different ways of life because, among themselves, they have shared esteem for each other. Practices withholding recognition of individuals' unique characteristics and contributions limit their opportunity for self-realisation.

In the second theme, the discussion was concerned with identification and recognition and how they could create conditions for self-realisation. A lack of identification with the affordances opened by recognition placed people in a position of resistance. Identification at work was intertwined with additional financial reward.

The third theme held that nonrecognition could marginalise or confine individuals to the periphery of practice, limiting their opportunities to develop. According to Honneth, the quest for recognition lies at the heart of social conflict. The potential for resolving a conflict in favour of a particular party creates the possibility that the individual's identificatory position can change from resistance to self-realisation. Identificatory positions are thus dynamic and fluid rather than set and immutable. The nature of the participants' experience revealed that identificatory positions could be somewhat ambivalent. The community of practice may recognise some aspects of the individual; similarly, the individual may identify with particular facets of its practice. Recognition and identification are thus often ambivalent and contradictory, further underscoring the potential for individuals to shift between the different identificatory positions depending on how they interpret their experience.

It is difficult to consider recognition in absolute terms. Participants received recognition from multiple sources, such as colleagues and family. The three levels of recognition thus cannot be viewed as discrete but as mutually influencing.

RPL can here be a potential way of raising the value of the tasks performed by workers within these professions and allow self-realisation through work. To be able to progress and develop in work, other individuals such as colleagues, managers and, in the RPL process, tutors and other students must recognise the individual's skills and unique contributions. When one is not recognised, one's freedom to participate in work practices as an autonomous subject and learn thus becomes limited. Individuals must also identify with the practices of the community. Intersubjective recognition, for instance, in work, forms the basis of identity and self-esteem, because for Honneth we as humans develop through being recognised (as well as recognise others) as significant persons. While Honneth argues that intersubjective recognition enables self-realisation and self-esteem, this depends on the extent to which the individual identifies with the associated participatory opportunity. A question arises about what the educational process and conferring of the qualification represent. RPL is a potential source of validation in recognising an individual's competencies gained through work. It can open up further participatory opportunities and sources of solidarity. If RPL allows participants to transcend nonrecognition in the workplace, it represents a widening of the cultural values available to participants when appraising their qualities. With government targets and expectations for qualifications, RPL legitimises individuals beyond what may be available through workplace practice. However, these benefits are only possibilities that depend on the individual's identification with the associated practices and the particular currents and crosscurrents of recognition and nonrecognition in each particular practice. RPL and recognition appeared to raise the participants' self-awareness: they had a deeper appreciation of the skills and knowledge they possess. Arguably, RPL enables the participant to forge an enhanced identification with the self that can increase the positive relationship with oneself, when the traits and abilities learnt through practice are recognised. Framing this in Honneth's work, the result of enhanced self-esteem could have a positive effect on the individual's work communities. Solidarity is not possible if individuals do not have this positive and practical relationship to themselves; low esteem and confidence threatens to destroy the prospect of solidarity at work. RPL can, based on these results, play a positive role in esteeming workers.

13.5 Critical Social Theory, RPL Research and Practice: What Is the Way Forward?

In RPL research, 'Kolbianism', that is, Kolb's (1984) theory, has for long been rather dominating. Such a perspective has been necessary to understand RPL, but there is also a need to problematise RPL more in depth, to enable an instigation of the power issues in RPL practices. When such issues can be scrutinised, the possibility to progress discussions on developing RPL becomes feasible. RPL research has for

long halted behind up-to-date advancements in social and educational theory
(Andersson and Harris 2006). Even though, prior research on RPL for accreditation
is critical, arguments are seldom underpinned by theories. There is a need for
theoretical analyses that disturb and question RPL and do so by forming strong and
solid arguments based on theory, but such scrutiny is not worthwhile if there is not
at the same time a constructive discussion of the potentials for development. It is
certain that prior experiences and learning cannot always be seen as helpful. Such a
naïve romantic view of adult's prior learning can hide power issues in RPL practices
(Brookfield 1998). Such a view impends reproducing work practices in normatively
illegitimate ways, and a simple view of prior learning does not create suitable and
critical adult learning environments and thus jeopardises to lessen RPL to a process
of instrumental assessment.

RPL practices can hopefully learn, at least something, from research that focuses
on advising such practices in informed and constructive ways. This chapter built on
such research and, for instance, demonstrates the importance of mutual understanding
and recognition, between teacher and participant, tutor and participant and among
participants in RPL. It is as such not helpful to ignore the potential of RPL for
accreditation. Instead, instrumental and formal assessments should focus on mutual
understanding integrated with critical discussions of prior learning. RPL for
accreditation could, by reflecting the results of communicative action, thus be a
process that strengthens social integration and solidarity and develops personal
identity among its participants. RPL would then encourage critical learning in
the lifeworld of education through reflections on prior learning, experiences and
knowledge gained in the lifeworld of work. Communicative action could then
inform and enhance a teacher's work with RPL. It is also important that the results
of the RPL process and assessment are clearly communicated. This would enable
these experiences to be mobilised when students move on and use these learning
experiences in new contexts. As the fourth study discussed, Honneth's recognition
theory can help RPL teachers understand what impact the recognition in RPL could
have for an individual's self-esteem development and how RPL processes can
support self-realisation. Such processes thus require mutual recognition. Teachers
should understand that participants must identify with the recognition offered
in RPL and as such teachers must be more focused on understanding the views of
those individuals that participate in such processes.

References

Andersson, P. (2008). National policy and the implementation of recognition of prior learning in a
    Swedish municipality. *Journal of Education Policy, 23*(5), 515–531.
Andersson, P., & Harris, J. (Eds.). (2006). *Re-theorising the recognition of prior learning.*
    Leicester: NIACE.
Briton, D., Gereluk, W., & Spencer, B. (1998). *Prior learning assessment and recognition: Issues
    for adult educators.* Paper presented at the CASAE conference proceedings, University of
    Ottawa Ontario, Canada.

Brookfield, S. (1998). Against naive romanticism: From celebration to the critical analysis of experience. *Studies in Continuing Education, 20*(2), 127–142.

Brookfield, S. (2005). Learning democratic reason: The adult education project of Jürgen Habermas. *Teachers College Record, 107*(6), 1127–1168.

Brown, J. O. (2001). The portfolio: A reflective bridge connecting the learner, higher education and the workplace. *The Journal of Continuing Higher Education, 49*(2), 1–13.

Brown, J. O. (2002). Know thyself: The impact of portfolio development on adult learning. *Adult Education Quarterly, 52*(3), 228–245.

Ewert, G. D. (1991). Habermas and education: A comprehensive overview of the influence of Habermas in educational literature. *Review of Educational Research, 61*(3), 345–378.

Fleming, T. (2011). Fromm and Habermas: Allies for adult education and democracy. *Studies in Philosophy and Education, 31*(2), 123–136.

Giddens, A. (1991). *Modernity and self-identity: Self and society in the late modern age.* Cambridge: Polity Press.

Habermas, J. (1984). *The theory of communicative action: Vol. 1. Reason and the rationalization of society.* Cambridge: Polity Press.

Habermas, J. (1987). *The theory of communicative action: Vol. 2. Lifeworld and system: A critique of functionalist reason.* Cambridge: Polity Press.

Hamer, J. (2010). Recognition of prior learning – Normative assessment or co-construction of preferred identities? *Australian Journal of Adult Learning, 50*(1), 100–115.

Hamer, J. (2012). An ontology of RPL: Improving non-traditional learners' access to the recognition of prior learning through a philosophy of recognition. *Studies in Continuing Education, 34*(2), 113–127.

Harris, J. (1997). *The recognition of prior learning (RPL) in South Africa: Drifts and shifts in international perspectives: Understanding the changing discursive terrain.* Paper presented at the international conference on experiential learning, The University of Cape Town, Cape Town.

Harris, J., & Wihak, C. (2011). Introduction and overview of chapters. In J. Harris, M. Breier, & C. Wihak (Eds.), *Researching the recognition of prior learning: International perspectives.* Leicester: NIACE.

Harris, J., Breier, M., & Wihak, C. (Eds.). (2011). *Researching the recognition of prior learning: International perspectives.* Leicester: NIACE.

Heath, V. (2001). Accreditation of prior (experiential) learning: Making the difference. *Nurse Education Today, 21,* 496–500.

Honneth, A. (1995). *The struggle for recognition: The moral grammar of social conflicts.* Cambridge: The MIT Press.

Honneth, A. (2007). *Disrespect: The normative foundations of critical theory.* Cambridge: Polity Press.

Houlbrook, M. C. (2012). RPL practice and student disposition – Insights from the lifeworld. *Journal of Education and Work, 25*(5), 555–570.

Houston, Y. L., Hoover, J., & Beer, E. (1997). Accreditation of prior learning: Is it worth it? An evaluation of a pilot scheme. *Nurse Education Today, 17,* 184–191.

Howard, S. (1993). Accreditation of prior learning: Andragogy in action or a 'cut price' approach to education? *Journal of Advanced Nursing, 18,* 1817–1824.

Huttunen, R. (2007). Critical adult education and the political-philosophical debate between Nancy Fraser and Axel Honneth. *Educational Theory, 57*(4), 423–433.

Huttunen, R., & Heikkinen, L. T. H. (2004). Teaching and the dialectic of recognition. *Pedagogy, Culture and Society, 12*(2), 163–174.

Kolb, D. (1984). *Experiential learning: Experience as the source of learning and development.* Englewood Cliffs: Prentice-Hall.

Lamoureux, A. (2005). *Adult learners' experience of change related to prior learning assessment.* Doctoral dissertation, Walden University, Minnesota.

Mezirow, J. (1981). A critical theory of adult learning and education. *Adult Education Quarterly, 32*(1), 3–27.

Michelson, E. (1996). Beyond Galileo's telescope: Situated knowledge and the assessment of experiential learning. *Adult Education Quarterly, 46*(4), 185–196.

Moran, P., & Murphy, M. (2012). Habermas, pupil voice, rationalism and their meeting with Lacan's objet petit A. *Studies in Philosophy and Education, 31*(2), 171–181.

Murphy, M., & Fleming, T. (Eds.). (2010). *Habermas, critical theory and education.* New York: Routledge.

Murray, J. P. (1994). Portfolios and accreditation of prior experiential learning (APEL) make credits … or problems? *Nurse Education Today, 14*, 232–237.

Sandberg, F. (2010). Recognising health care assistants' prior learning through a caring ideology. *Vocations and Learning: Studies in Vocational and Professional Education, 3*(2), 99–115.

Sandberg, F. (2012a). A Habermasian analysis of a process of recognition of prior learning for health care assistants. *Adult Education Quarterly, 62*(4), 351–370.

Sandberg, F. (2012b). *Recognition of prior learning in health care: From a caring ideology and power, to communicative action and recognition.* Linköping: Linköping University.

Sandberg, F. (2013). A reconstructive analysis of the potential for critical learning and change in recognition of prior learning: A Habermasian analysis. *British Educational Research Journal.* doi:10.1002/berj.3113.

Sandberg, F., & Andersson, P. (2011). RPL for accreditation in higher education: As a process of mutual understanding or merely lifeworld colonisation? *Assessment & Evaluation in Higher Education, 36*(7), 767–780.

Sandberg, F., & Kubiak, C. (2013). Recognition of prior learning, self-realisation and identity within Axel Honneth's theory of recognition. *Studies in Continuing Education, 35*(3), 351–365.

Scott, I. (2007). Accreditation of prior learning in preregistration nursing programmes: Throwing out the baby with the bath water? *Nurse Education Today, 27*, 348–356.

Scott, I. (2010). Accreditation of prior learning in preregistration nursing programmes 2: The influence of prior qualifications on perceived learning during the foundation year. *Nurse Education Today, 30*, 438–442.

Somerville, M. (2006). Becoming-worker: Vocational training for workers in aged care. *Journal of Vocational Education and Training, 54*(4), 471–481.

Spencer, B. (2005). Defining prior learning assessment and recognition. In L. English (Ed.), *Encyclopaedia of adult education.* Basingstoke: Palgrave Macmillan.

Stevens, K., Gerber, D., & Hendra, R. (2010). Transformational learning through prior learning assessment. *Adult Education Quarterly, 60*(4), 377–404.

Thomas, A. (2000). Prior learning assessment: The quiet revolution. In A. Wilson & E. Hayes (Eds.), *Handbook of adult and continuing education.* San Francisco: Jossey-Bass.

Taylor, T. (1996). Learning from experience: Recognition of prior learning (RPL) and professional development for teachers. *Asia-Pacific Journal of Teacher Education, 24*(3), 281–292.

Welton, M. R. (1995). In defense of the lifeworld: A Habermasian approach to adult learning. In M. Welton (Ed.), *In defense of the lifeworld: Critical perspectives on adult learning* (pp. 127–156). Albany: State University of New York Press.

Wheelahan, L. (2006). Vocations, 'graduateness' and the recognition of prior learning. In P. Andersson & J. Harris (Eds.), *Re-theorising the recognition of prior learning* (pp. 241–260). Leicester: NIACE.

Whittaker, S., Whittaker, R., & Cleary, P. (2006). Understanding the transformative dimension of RPL. In P. Andersson & J. Harris (Eds.), *Re-theorising the recognition of prior learning* (pp. 301–320). Leicester: NIACE.

Chapter 14
Changing RPL and HRD Discourses:
Practitioner Perspectives

Anne Murphy, Oran Doherty, and Kate Collins

14.1 Introduction

This chapter takes changing discourses in political, social and economic contexts of recognition of prior learning (RPL) within human resources development (HRD) at the time of writing – mid-2013 – as its point of departure. The perspectives and analytical comments are those of the authors who are variously involved in work-based and work-related learning and in recognition of experiential learning, as practitioners, researchers and policy influencers in Irish higher education. The authors contend that instances of RPL practice are invariably temporally and spatially bounded regardless of meta-trends in policy and generic tools in practice and that this has consistently been the case. It also argues that RPL thrives only where there is really useful interface between an immediate need for it – a 'problem' – *and* a scalable solution with a developmental core.

The term 'discourse' in this chapter refers to the reasoning processes and lines of thinking formally expressed in spoken and written form in discussions, debates, documents and publications. The authors readily acknowledge the limitation of using only materials available in the English language in this regard. The meaning-in-use also includes discourse as an institutional style of expression and preference for particular codified language which of itself identifies particular positionalities and

A. Murphy (✉)
Higher Education Policy Research Unit (HEPRU), Dublin Institute of Technology,
143-149 Rathmines Road, Dublin 6, Ireland
e-mail: anne.murphy@dit.ie

O. Doherty
RPL & WBL Office, Letterkenny Institute of Technology,
Port Road, Letterkenny, Co Donegal, Ireland
e-mail: oran.doherty@lkit.ie

K. Collins
Career Development Centre, University College Dublin, Belfield, Dublin 4, Ireland
e-mail: katecol@gmail.com

T. Halttunen et al. (eds.), *Promoting, Assessing, Recognizing and Certifying Lifelong Learning: International Perspectives and Practices*, Lifelong Learning Book Series 20, DOI 10.1007/978-94-017-8694-2_14, © Springer Science+Business Media Dordrecht 2014

suggests particular interpretation, thereby setting boundaries around *what* can be said and done about a particular topic and about *how* it is said and done.

The broad meaning of human resource development as used here refers to provision of learning and training opportunities both within companies and organisations *and* at the level of the state. In the former, the focus is primarily on capacity building of employees towards organisational goals. In the latter, the focus can include mass accreditation and subsequent upskilling of workers in particular sectors, reskilling of workers in vulnerable sectors of employment and reskilling of recently unemployed workers from vulnerable and unsustainable sectors into sectors with growth potential.

Human resource management in this context is defined more narrowly as the efficient organisation of staff within the objectives of the organisation, though it does not preclude a focus on the developmental.

RPL in the chapter is an inclusive term for practices which articulate an individual's formal and non-formal learning at a particular point in time for the purpose of assessment and accreditation or as a mechanism to identify current and future education and training needs.

The chapter is structured into four additional sections. The first and second sections discuss discourses related to recognition of prior learning within meta-human resource development policies and within qualifications framework contexts at the global level. In Sects. 14.3 and 14.4, a brief narrative and analysis of RPL in Ireland is offered with three examples of RPL for human resource development in enterprises and in labour market activation initiatives. The final section returns to the issue of competing RPL and HRM discourses and their implications for RPL practitioners who operate within them.

14.2   The Global Reach of Learning Recognition Systems

A search of extant narrative, policy and analytical literature about APEL/RPL and their variants available in the English language generally locates the genesis of scaled-up RPL in post-Korean war United States strategies to manage the future careers of returning veterans. It was a pragmatic and efficient approach to both recognition of prior and current competences and to future training needs analysis. A state-supported scheme such as that invariably drew in providers of training and education in a new relationship with citizens and the world of work. The subsequent work of CAEL (1999) was significant in providing a catalyst for other nations to apply both the theory and practices of APEL to their own immediate human resource development needs. Additionally it contributed to a scholarly curiosity about the nature of experiential learning in relation to occupational qualifications and academic awards, leading to a range of pedagogical and curriculum design mod in both work-related learning and in community-based adult education for marginal sectors of the population. This dual human capital-social justice discourse has permeated RPL policies and practices to varying degrees since the 1980s (Anderson and Harris 2006; Breier 2009; Cooper and Walters 2009; Fenwick 2004; Harris et al. 2011).

14.2.1 Meta-discourses

It is useful in a chapter such as this to broadly sketch the meta-developments around recognition of qualifications and recognition of learning through qualifications frameworks since our argument revolves around the requirement for RPL practices to operate within the ideological and policy space of micro, local developments mindful of the facilitatory potential of the meta and macro. With this in mind, a selective summary of the global reach of RPL is offered now followed by reflections on dominant discourses, tensions and contradictions.

14.2.1.1 UNESCO and the Council of Europe

Legal agreements between countries and regions to allow for the international mobility of students and of skilled labour came about in 1976 in the form of UNESCO conventions for promoting the recognition of academic qualifications. Currently the conventions include recognition conventions in African States (1981), Arab States (1978), Asia and the Pacific (1983), Latin America and the Caribbean (1974), European Region (1979), Arab and European States bordering on the Mediterranean (1976) (Collins 2011a). In addition to these conventions, there are also UNESCO recommendations that relate to the recognition of qualifications including Recognition of Studies and Qualifications in Higher Education (1993), Status of Higher Education Teaching Personnel (1997), Criteria and Procedures for the Assessment of Foreign Qualifications (2001) and Code of Practice for the Provision of Transnational Education in 2001 (ibid).

The 2012 UNESCO guidelines for recognition, validation and accreditations of the outcomes of non-formal and informal learning (RVA) following from the Belêm Framework (2009) clearly link recognition systems to a knowledge-based, global economy in each national context for optimum use of human talent and resources and increased options for individuals in the labour market, indicating a shift in emphasis from the humanitarian to the economic (UNESCO 2012).

With regard to data-bases for mutual recognition, key developments were the Council of Europe/UNESCO Convention of 1997 which established the NARIC (National Academic Recognition Information Centres) and the European Commission development of the ENIC (European National Information Centres) network. Their aim was to improve the recognition of academic qualifications and study periods in European member states and in the European Economic Area and Central and Eastern European countries, focused on providing information about education systems, recognition of foreign academic and professional qualifications as well as mobility for academic and professional purposes. ENIC was subsequently linked to systems in the United States in 2000 as well as to recognition of qualifications from the Russian Federation (Collins 2011a, c).

The Bologna Process from 1999 onwards led the move to create a European Higher Education Area (EHEA), while the Bergen Communiqué in 2005 set in motion a move towards greater transparency of qualifications, mobility of learners and flexibility in, and access to, education and training, in which the recognition of qualifications plays a central part. For the most part, the type of recognition involved was formal, codified and accredited.

14.2.1.2   The OECD and Cedefop

The OECD consistently takes a socioeconomic or human capital perspective on lifelong learning, on the demands of knowledge-based economies and on the uneven distribution of learning opportunities (OECD 2007). They see the role of RPL in HRD as opportunities for individuals to constantly update skills and to achieve higher earnings, opportunities for enterprises in relation to skill and competence of workforces, for economies in terms of positive relationship between educational attainment and economic growth and for society in terms of social cohesion (Ibid). The OECD RNFIL (recognition of non-formal and informal learning) country background notes and subsequent summary report focused on operational matters, on auditing and on return on investment (OECD 2011). Likewise Cedefop takes a mechanistic approach to the link between learning outcomes and labour markets with a consistent technicist discourse at operational level (Cedefop 2008).

14.2.1.3   Global Interregional Initiatives for Mutual Recognition

The Bologna Framework appears to have triggered other interregional higher educational reforms, inter alia, in North Africa and the Mediterranean region, the Community of Portuguese Speaking Communities (CPLP) and the Association of Southeast Asian Nations-European Union (ASEAN-EU), the Asia-Pacific region. The influence of Bologna can now be felt beyond the 46 participating countries that have signed up to it, and geographically the EHEA covers an area from Iceland to Russia, almost the entire continent of Europe except for Belarus, Monaco, Northern Cyprus and San Marino (Collins 2011a, b, c). A number of regions remain outside of the EHEA. Some have taken the Bologna model as a template: others have not. But all have entered into the spirit of international collaboration that appears to be growing in a more globalised higher education system with common discourses, strategies and systems centred around formal university level programmes and awards for the most part (ILO 2013; World Bank 2002).

14.2.2   National Qualifications Frameworks

The OECD suggests that there is a link between the development of lifelong learning in any country and the development of qualifications systems, with common mechanisms such as credit transfer, recognising non-formal and informal learning, creating new routes to qualifications, optimising stakeholder involvement in the qualifications system, expressing qualifications as learning outcomes and establishing qualifications frameworks (OECD 2007). This policy discourse argues that frameworks of qualifications have emerged to facilitate making qualifications visible (Murphy et al. 2011, 2012). It is suggested that not providing a range of means for the recognition of experience and/or qualifications leads to considerable misallocation or underuse of resources which could otherwise, with the proper support, address certain skill shortages. Furthermore, learning inputs, the question of when, where and how learning takes place, have traditionally decided the nature, significance and level of qualifications. The emphasis is now moving away from learning inputs to learning outputs or outcomes, namely, what a learner knows, understands or is able to do. This shift to a learning outcomes discourse is part of a multiagency lifelong learning agenda where they act as a common reference point for qualifications. Learning outcomes facilitate the formal assessment of learning against specified learning outcomes or specific standards. Collins et al. (2009) concluded that the Irish National Framework of Qualifications, with its focus on learning outcomes, has considerable potential for use in recruitment, developing career pathways, planning work-based learning and recognising transferable skills – the core values of a human capital HRD discourse (Fenwick 2004). Furthermore learning outcomes contribute to the recognition process by acting as descriptors relevant for academic or professional practice and can therefore accommodate competencies and qualifications acquired in non-formal, nontraditional and non-tertiary settings, albeit in relation only to learning specified in those learning outcomes.

14.2.3 Being Qualified or Holding a Qualification?

Disputed definitions of qualifications as distinct from definitions of 'being qualified' and the resulting focus on credentialism are emerging criticisms of the move towards qualifications frameworks. What remains unproblematised in meta-literature is precisely what the various discourses of qualifications actually mean for RPL and WBL practitioners. Bowen-Clewley et al. (2005) suggest that a qualification varies according to the internal agenda behind it, so that it can affirm a person's ability to do a particular job, act as a means of access to a job, recognise knowledge and skills gained informally and provide a means for the comparability of qualifications and credentials. Furthermore, being qualified appears to be more to do with being competent, while a qualification does not necessarily imply the same. From an organisational point of view, qualifications can be of benefit as a way of ensuring legal compliance, managing risk, acknowledging the value of employees, motivating employees, providing for succession planning and building organisational skills and knowledge. Formalising workplace learning by way of assessment and accreditation can structure learning in a way that is meaningful to an organisation, but probably not beyond it, thereby reducing transferability and mobility potential. Recognising qualifications can also imply a narrowing of curricula in that only that which can be assessed really matters. This so-called neoliberal ideology is much critiqued in scholarly literature and likely to be continuously critiqued (Fisher 2005; Tynjälä et al. 2006; Fleming 2008; Kenny 2009; Teichler 2009).

Despite this critique, information on the value of a qualification is a necessity now for professionals as well as for employers since professionals need to be able to comply with the requirements of the professional and/or regulatory body in another country. The WTO's (World Trade Organisation) recognition agreement, GATS (General Agreement on Trade and Services) since 1995, is a means of setting standards and criteria to meet the regulatory standards of certain professions. The European Certificate of Experience is another initiative for workers which act as evidence of their experience, training and qualifications in craftwork areas. There are legitimate questions to be asked in this regard. In the move towards comparable and compatible degree structures in higher education which attract professional, harmonised recognition, are they leaving the trade and craft sectors to devise parallel mechanisms for mutual recognition and qualifications progression?

14.2.4   Positive Aspects of Qualifications Frameworks

Some of the many value-adding characteristics attributed to NQFs include an increased consistency of qualifications, better transparency for citizens and increased currency with explicit level and value. Ideally they are a reference point for qualification standards, clarification of learning pathways and progression, portability of qualifications and a platform for strengthening co-operation between stakeholders. However, an NQF alone cannot do any of the above: it is the stakeholders – social partners, learning providers, qualification agencies – who make these benefits available with the NQF as a means to promote dialogue and co-ordination between them (Murphy 2009, 2010, 2013). Responding to a broader range of learners in the lifelong learning agenda means that qualifications are becoming more complex and diverse, as are work practices. Therefore, the labour market at the sectoral level is also demanding more diverse types of qualifications. This calls for greater levels of transparency, consistency and coherence of qualifications, and description of qualifications, and quality assurance mechanisms. These demands are fueling an RPL industry as a service for in-employment capacity building, for recently unemployed and displaced workers and for migrant workers. The jury is still out regarding whether for-profit RPL services are a good thing or not.

14.2.5   The EQF as Honest Broker

The EQF-LLL (European Qualifications Framework for Lifelong Learning) came into operation in 2008 as a translation device to compare qualifications and as a reference point and system for classifying qualifications levels beyond the Bologna higher education framework. The EQF-LLL aims at facilitating transnational mobility and lifelong learning, particularly for occupational sectors. Countries must find a way to refer their own national qualifications to levels on the EQF. If each country has its own qualifications framework based on learning outcomes, it is reasonably feasible to compare and contrast these to the EQF level descriptors in a general way. A number of international organisations such as the ILO and the OECD are also looking to NQFs as systems for reform in Russia, Ukraine, Sri Lanka, Malaysia, Thailand, Namibia and Botswana (Collins 2011c). It could be argued that there are excessive expectations that NQFs can be sufficiently inclusive to meet the expectations of diverse meta-stakeholders (Murphy et al. 2012).

14.2.6   Sectors and Professions

The EQF-LLL is very much tied to the discourses of the Lisbon Process in promoting lifelong learning and professional mobility using the language of learning outcomes. Critical questions are emerging, however, about the nature and the sustainability of qualifications among professional groups which somehow float above national and meta-frameworks in relation to professional practice. The Irish National Framework of Qualifications, for instance, has made efforts to include the awards of regulatory, professional and international bodies to ensure the wide use of the framework on the labour market. Sectoral and professional systems of recognition of qualifications are extending such as in engineering with the European Network for Accreditation of Engineering Education (ENAEE), FEANI (Fédération Européene d'Associations Nationales d'Ingénieurs), the International Register of Professional Engineers, the Washington Accord (1989) and subsequent agreements (ibid). The nursing, medical and architectural professions have taken steps to facilitate recognition for practitioners across countries and to recognise experiential learning (Collins 2011a, c). Within these professional and regulatory bodies, RPL and learning through work practice have a discrete internal epistemology and operational discourse which is largely unproblematic to them pedagogically or politically, supporting our argument that recognition systems work well in contexts where they are tailored to specific HRD contexts.

14.2.7   Dominant RPL Discourses and Agendas
for Particular Sociopolitical Purposes

In a nutshell, this chapter argues that RPL practices largely reflect political and ideological discourses appropriate to the context. For instance, the development of RPL in post-apartheid South Africa had a dual human capital-social justice/redress agenda around public recognition of the competences of the majority population and their access to qualifications valued by the labour market. The RPL movement in South Africa added significantly to both the political and epistemological dimensions of RPL practice identifying the links between paradigms of RPL and particular views of human capital (Breier 2009). The genesis of RPL/PLAR in Canada was likewise linked to labour markets and worker interests in a context of worker mobility and diversity (Van Kleef 2011). RPL development in Australia also reflected a work-related focus with emphasis on occupational standards and mobility of qualifications and with perhaps lesser emphasis on the justice issues surrounding recognition of indigenous knowledges (Wheelahan et al. 2002).

In Europe RPL models tend to reflect the dominant ideologies of society at the local level with varying emphasises on human and economic capital or on social and cultural capital. It could be argued that the individualistic and legally based validation des acquis de l'experience system in France differs in intent from the work-related RPL paradigm in Scotland but that the impact is broadly similar. Likewise it could be argued that the highly complex RPL systems in England are as effective as the RPL service centre model in the Netherlands in terms of access and accreditation opportunities for individuals but that neither is totally strategic at the state level in relation to human resource development needs. It could also be argued that Malta has customised its RPL approach to its own specific needs and capacities as has Malaysia, Mauritius, Slovenia, and so forth.

From the perspective of this chapter, the common thread among countries where there is state-supported RPL is that in each case, there is a greater emphasis on the needs of labour markets than on satisfying individual desires or addressing inequalities in society. What is also noteworthy is that RPL scholarship and the intellectual energy allocated to it in each geographic region show much ideas-borrowing and localised application.

It is reasonable to argue that the development of national and meta-qualifications frameworks has provided useful, common tools for RPL practitioners such as level descriptors, learning outcome models and credits systems. It is also reasonable to argue that sectoral frameworks and zones of mutual recognition may be even more powerful. It could be further argued that there is a degree of weariness with the almost-forensic application of the technologies of qualifications frameworks in a naive search for homogeneity and standardisation (Zaharia et al. 2008). There is a danger that RPL could get itself caught in this trap and lose sight of the local and immediate.

14.3   RPL for HRD in Ireland

In this section, the development of RPL in Ireland is summarised as a backdrop for the examples of practice in Sect. 14.4 subsequently.

The first instances of RPL in Ireland followed hard upon the heels of the early APEL movement in the United States, particularly in relation to the accreditation of experiential learning in regulated occupation and professions such as engineering, nursing, early childhood education, social care, literacy training and training of the disability sector (Murphy 2011a, b). At a systems level, the early practices of APEL in the institute of technology lead by the National Council for Education Awards (NCEA) were overhauled by the sudden massification of participation in higher education due to population growth, the abolition of university fees and the arrival of private providers. Economic growth and high employment rates from the mid-1990s diverted education attention towards new qualifications and higher levels of awards as manifest in the design of arrangements for access, transfer and progression in the national qualifications framework in the early 2000s. During those years, RPL was used on a scaled-up basis towards regulation of professional occupations and in the voluntary sector in the manner of HRD, while individualised RPL continued as a minority practice, principally within vocational training and within adult and community education (ibid).

14.3.1 RPL in Companies and Organisations

The indigenous enterprise sector in Ireland traditionally sought training and development through the Industrial Training Authority and later the more inclusive National Training Authority (FAS), generally within traditional model of occupational, technical and craft standards. When regional development disparities and attendant social disadvantage became evident in the mid- to late 1990s, a series of state-supported initiatives were tried, among which was the Líonra upskilling initiative for small enterprises in the border-midland-west geographic area. Central to Líonra was the belief that RPL would be the starting point for relevant, regional labour force development to stimulate economic growth and to attract new enterprises, using a model of partnership between existing enterprises and the regional technical colleges to recognise and accredit skills and competences acquired in the workplace. Two hundred companies and seven higher education and training providers contributed to Líonra using RPL as a training need analysis tool for continuing professional development (Collins 2011b, c). Capacity in the pedagogic aspects of RPL was built, and cross-sectoral discourses reflected a shared understanding of non-formal and informal learning as manifest in the real-world practices of SMEs (Collins 2011c). Whether the Líonra initiative was predominantly instrumentally top-down, organically bottom-up or a hybrid of both is debatable. Its legacy is that it provided a HRD and academic space to play with RPL in a serious way, to build relationships for work-related learning and to extend capacity across companies and education providers. The Líonra model was undone for two main reasons. First was the sudden economic downturn after 2006 which impacted significantly on SMEs in peripheral regions. Second was the availability of recent graduates and migrant workers who rarely required additional capacity building (ibid). Local capacity was not lost however as evidenced in the examples of practice in Sect. 14.4 of this chapter.

14.3.2   National Principles and Operational Guidelines for RPL But No Policy or Strategy?

RPL in Ireland is generally described as a self-organising and context-specific activity (EGFSN 2011) relying in equal measure on academic enthusiasm for pedagogic innovation and on sectoral HRD needs, as reflected in the first APEL Higher Education Network of the late 1990s. National principles and operational guidelines for RPL were agreed by stakeholders in 2005 through a consensus process facilitated by the Qualifications Authority reflecting the diversity of practices and significant indigenous competence. Institutional RPL policies likewise grew from local practice experiences and local research scholarship (Murphy 2011a, b). The direction of RPL in Ireland was supported significantly by the particular national qualifications framework model with its range of major, minor, special purpose and supplemental award types and overarching level descriptors for access, transfer and progression (Murphy 2012). It is reasonable to argue that RPL extended its reach and public awareness through the technologies of the NQF itself, through sectoral progression pathways already established and through the ENIC-NARIC systems. At the height of the economic boom of the *Celtic Tiger years*, enthusiasm for RPL centred on its potential for responsive upskilling of the existing labour force in pursuit of a knowledge-intensive economy with employers organisations, trade unions, enterprises and voluntary organisations sharing a common discourse (Murphy 2012). Interestingly, no national policy or strategy emerged for RPL: there was no demand for a state-provided or private service, possibly because the further and higher education providers were sufficiently responsive and flexible to maintain public trust and confidence, and possibly because the qualifications frameworks were based on awards and not on learning per se (EGFSN 2011; Scattergood 2012).

In 2013 however the model of the Qualifications Authority was radically changed by the government, and new discourses were evident in the series of Green Papers related to the future shape of the authority and its operational functions (QQI 2013). What is worthy of note for the perspective of this chapter is the radical change of discourse evident in the Green Paper on RPL which takes an enigmatic, narrow, technicist and operational perspective regarding the purposes of RPL, seeming to ignore two decades of research and scholarly activity *and* ignoring the self-initiating *and* government-funded initiatives in occupation sectors, professional regulatory bodies and in the voluntary sector. How this will play out in the future is unclear at the time of writing, but it exposes the precarious nature of education development in volatile administrative reform contexts and the risks for innovative practitioners within such contexts.

14.4   RPL Responding to the Immediate and Local: Three Examples

An argument in this chapter is that RPL practices for HRD are sustainable only when there is an immediate, contextual problem to be addressed. In this section, brief descriptions of three cases of current practice in Ireland are offered in this regard: a regional service for industry, a strategy for upskilling in occupational sectors, and a strategy for activation and reskilling of recently unemployed workers. The descriptions are followed by critical commentary on their significance for RPL practice.

14.4.1   Example 1: RPL Regional Services for Industry

The local area concerned here is County Donegal in the northwest of Ireland. The local economy is based on a mix of agriculture, tourism, fishing, service industries and manufacturing industry. The strategy for local economic development includes support for indigenous small to medium enterprises (SMEs) and for multinational companies which locate in the region. One of the main human resource development (HRD) support providers is the regional third-level college: Letterkenny Institute of Technology (LKIT) which has a tradition of working closely with local industry in work-based learning (WBL) and in recognition of prior learning (RPL) (Doherty 2012).

14.4.1.1   Origin and Operation of RPL Through WBL

In 2006 LYIT participated in the government-funded RPL networking Líonra project aimed at recognising learning in the workplace, as described earlier. To achieve certification, individuals completed a portfolio to match the learning outcomes in information technology (IT), communications, sales, marketing, HRM, office administration, managing people and customer care. Awareness of this certification opportunity was built through open information session, press releases and targeted literature. Of the first 300 employees who prepared portfolios, a significant number had no prior higher education experience but later enrolled on part-time courses. Employers reported improved morale and easier recruitment with the positive partnership experience for RPL leading to the development of Work-Based Learning (WBL) programmes. Partners included individual companies, consortia of companies, employers' organisations and sectoral networks.

Since 2007, over 800 learners have enrolled on WBL programmes, and over 60 college staff have completed training programmes on the design and management of Work-Based Learning (WBL) and RPL, representing a self-motivating HRD wave which has been a catalyst for sectoral training networks at a national level through the Skillnets structure, described later below.

14.4.1.2   Critical Success Factor for Combined RPL
and WBL in Programme Design for Industry

Evaluation exercises from industry programmes identified key prerequisites for successful partnerships between higher education providers and industry in the development and delivery. The main success factors are listed below and are largely self-evident (ibid).

Success Factors

1: The WBL programme should be jointly developed by the education provider and the employer.

2: There needs to be continuous communications between the partners.

3: Cultural barriers need to be overcome.

4: Higher education staff involved with companies should have relevant industrial experience.

5: The work-based learner requires support from both the education provider and the employer.

6: The programme requires flexibility in terms of delivery and assessment.

7: Assessment should be negotiated with companies and related to work practices.

8: A system for recognition of both prior and concurrent learning from work through RPL is essential.

9: The employer must feel there is a good return on investment.

14.4.2   Example 2: *Skillnets: Regional and Sectoral Training Networks*

Skillnets is a unique Irish model of sectoral and regional training networks established in 1999 by the government and the social partners: employers, trade unions, agriculture, community and voluntary sector. Its remit is to provide immediate and tailored training responses to the HRD needs of companies, organisations and sectors. Each Skillnet is enterprise-led and funded by the Department of Education and Skills through the National Training Fund. Over 50,000 enterprises are members of over 300 Skillnets at the time of writing such as Skillnets for digital media; design, print and packaging; aviation funding; polymers; retail; manufacturing and engineering, languages and international trade. Training through a Skillnet enables economies of scale, efficiency, lower costs and opportunities for networking and knowledge sharing. The training programmes developed are owned by the Skillnet and negotiated with education and training providers, ranging from vocational level through to masters (Skillnets 2012).

Skillnets actively encouraged RPL as a training needs analysis device and designed its own RPL mentor training programme in 2010 to standardise the approach across networks (ibid).

Since the economic downturn, Skillnets have become involved in training redundant workers for growth sectors, taking the model from a HRD function to management of unemployment. The provenance of Skillnets in a social partnership model made this transition easy, and the attendant discourses reflect a seamless convergence of HRD ideology with social justice intent towards the regions and towards unemployment in those regions, supported by additional state funding.

14.4.3 Example 3: *RPL and Labour Market Activation (LMA) Initiatives*

As a blunt definition, activation strategies aim to encourage jobseekers to be more active in their efforts to find work and/or increase their employability (OECD 2007). The key attributes of an activation strategy include:

- Registration for placement and assessment of availability for work in order to receive benefit payment
- Regular interventions by the public employment services for the duration of unemployment
- Regulations regarding job search requirements
- Referrals to vacant jobs
- Referrals to ALMPs (active labour market policies) including education, training and employment programmes (Kelly et al. 2011)

14.4.3.1 Policy Context of LMA

A key policy influence on Irish labour activation models was the National Skills Strategy report: *Tomorrow's Skills: Towards a National Skills Strategy*, produced by the Expert Group on Future Skill Needs (EGFSN) in 2007. The strategy focused on upskilling individuals in the labour market by at least one level on the National Framework of Qualifications (NFQ) with the logic that such qualifications enhancement would lead to a more skilled workforce and *ipso facto* lead to economic growth (EGFSN 2007). The current and future skill needs, as identified in the EGFSN Annual Skills Bulletins, determined the types of upskilling programmes that were funded through labour market activation funding between 2008 and 2013 in ICT, biopharma and pharmachem, food and beverages, international financial services, medical devices, wholesale and retail (HEA 2012).

14.4.3.2 RPL as an Element of Labour Market Activation

In 2011 the EGFSN published a report on how RPL could contribute to the upskilling objectives of the National Skills Strategy including labour market activation (EGFSN 2011). RPL was specifically prioritised for its relevance to initiatives designed to reduce unemployment, to utilise education and training resources more efficiently and to provide individuals and enterprises with access to flexible and relevant education and training systems (EGFSN 2012).

So, the question then arose about how precisely RPL was to be used within labour market activation schemes: RPL of itself does not upskill, reskill or cross-skill individuals, only new learning can do so. The strategy which emerged was that all tenders for delivery of LMA programmes would include specific details of how

RPL would apply and how it would be operationalised. This brought RPL into a centre-stage practice position for curriculum and pedagogical design in a real-world context of immediate application (Murphy 2008).

14.4.4 Significance of the Three Examples

From the perspective of this chapter, the three examples above nicely sit at the interstices of RPL pedagogic practices, work-based learning and the principles of sustainable development of the labour force. RPL practitioners intimately involved in the examples are cognizant of the need for well-conceived, negotiated and achievable design of HRD interventions in employment and in unemployment, mindful of mega-trends and dominant political ideologies Murphy 2008.

The examples confirm the need for organically developed RPL solutions supported by state resources where the stability of society and equity of access to normative life expectations are central. There are, of course, instances where economic and human capital imperatives will be elided with social capital desires and where partnership models are essential for sustainability of impact.

14.5   Changing Discourses of RPL and HRD

RPL practitioners with long track records in formal education, such as the authors of this chapter, will invariably be RPL researchers and scholars involved in influencing policy and inventing practices. Most will be members of practitioner networks and have contributed to working groups and international conferences. In many ways, practitioners lead discourses in their communities of practice, change discourses as developments unfold and comment critically on the discourses of other practitioners and policy makers. Most are acutely aware of the gaps between meta-policies and their local experiences and aware of the need to play the meta-policy game to achieve national and/or international support. Most practitioners are aware of how existing discourses become colonised by more powerful discourses or by denying the legitimacy of existing practices. Practitioners appreciate that discourses are dynamic and imbued with nuances of power and powerlessness and that innovatory RPL practices range in ideology from the redemptive practices of adult education to the neo-liberalism of human capital models.

From the perspective of this chapter, RPL practitioners need to be tightrope walkers, avoiding tipping points into undesired directions and continuously seeking a space of ideological equilibrium where real-world practices can actually benefit individuals to achieve sustainable lives of their choosing *and* serve regional and national interest.

References

Anderson, P., & Harris, J. (Eds.). (2006). *Re-theorising the recognition of prior learning.* Leicester: NIACE.

Bowen-Clewley, L. (2005). *So what does 'being qualified' really mean? A critical perspective on a growing trend of 'credentialism' and its relevance in workplaces of the 21st century.* Sydney: International Conference of Work and Learning.

Breier, M. (2009). *The RPL conundrum.* Cape Town: HRSC.

CAEL. (1999). *Prior learning assessment. A guidebook to American institutional practices.* Chicago: Hunt Printing Co.

Cedefop. (2008). *The shift to learning outcomes: Conceptual, political and practical development in Europe.* Luxembourg: European Union.

Collins, T., Kelly, F., Murdock, H., Raffe, D., & Murphy, A. (2009). *Framework implementation and impact study: Report of study team.* Dublin: NQAI.

Collins, K. (2011a, May). Recent trends on the compatibility and recognition of qualifications. *European Journal of Qualifications, 2.*

Collins, K. (2011b, June). Higher education in the economic crisis: RPL as a tool for the recognition of qualifications, student mobility, up-skilling and re-skilling. *Level3, Issue 9.* http://level3.dit.ie/html/issue9_list.html. Accessed 4 Oct 2013.

Collins, K. (2011c). *An exploration for RPL (Recognition of Prior Learning) in companies and organisations in Ireland: Valorisation, return on investment and emerging trends.* Unpublished doctoral thesis, Dublin Institute of Technology.

Cooper, L., & Walters, S. (Eds.). (2009). *Learning/work: Turning work and lifelong learning inside out.* Cape Town: HRSC.

Doherty, O. (2012, November). *Institutional perspectives on RPL.* In NIACE RPL seminar Flexible ties with higher education, Prague.

EGFSN. (2007). *Tomorrow's skills: Towards a national skills strategy.* Dublin: Forfás.

EGFSN. (2011). *Developing recognition of prior learning: The role of RPL in the context of the national skills up-skilling objectives.* Dublin: Forfás.

EGFSN. (2012). *Guidance of higher education providers on current and future skills needs of enterprises: Springboard 2012.* Dublin: Forfás.

Fenwick, T. (2004). Towards a critical HRD in training and practice. *Adult Education Quarterly, 54*(3 May), 193–209.

Fisher, S. (2005, June). Is there a need to debate the role of higher education as a public good? *Level3, Issue 3.* http://level3.dit.ie/html/issue3_list.html. Accessed 4 Oct 2013.

Fleming, T. (2008, June). We are condemned to learn: towards higher education as a learning society. *Level3, Issue 6.* http://level3.dit.ie/html/issue6_list.html. Accessed 4 Oct 2013.

Harris, J., Breier, M., & Wihak, C. (Eds.). (2011). *Researching the recognition of prior learning: International perspectives.* Leicester: NIACE.

HEA. (2012). *Springboard 2011 first stage evaluation, February 2012.* Dublin: Higher Education Authority.

ILO. (2013). *World of work report 2013: Repairing the economic and social fabric.* Geneva: International Labour Organisation.

Kelly, E., McGuinness, S., & O'Connell, P. J. (2011, November). *What can active labour market policies do?* (Renewal Series Paper 1). Dublin: Economic and, Social Research institute (ESRI).

Kenny, A. (2009, June). The dynamics of human capital and the world of work: Towards a common market in contemporary tertiary education. *Level3, Issue 7.* http://level3.dit.ie/html/issue7_list.html. Accessed 4 Oct 2013.

Murphy, A. (2007). *APEL matters in higher education.* Kilkenny: Red Lion Press.

Murphy, A. (2008, June). The interface between academic knowledge and working knowledge: Implications for curriculum design and pedagogic practice. *Level3, Issue 6.* http://level3.dit.ie/html/issue6_list.html. Accessed 4 Oct 2013.

Murphy, A. (2009, July). *University-industry partnerships: Love affairs or marriages of convenience?* UNISO (University in Society) conference, Amiens.

Murphy, A. (2010). *Negotiating partnerships with small and medium sized enterprises: Options for the university.* 9th UNISO (university in Society) conference, Timisoara, Romania, July 2009.

Murphy, A. (2011a, July). *Why minor awards in the Bologna framework first cycle are important for the labour market.* 11th UNISO (University in Society) conference, Paris.

Murphy, A. (2011b). Policy development and implementation procedures for recognition of prior learning: A case study of practice in higher education. *European Journal of Qualifications, Number 2.*

Murphy, A. (2012, July). *Labour market activation initiatives from the perspective of higher education: A case study from Ireland.* UNISO (University in Society) conference, Sigisoara, Romania.

Murphy, A. (2013, September). *University-industry partnerships: Learning to live in sectoral harmony?* 3E (Environment, Energy, Efficiency) conference, Galati, Romania.

Murphy A., Duff, T., & Collins, K. (2011, July). *Comparative assessment of terminology and qualifications framework design.* Bucharest: HEQ-bridges Project and in *European Journal of Qualifications, Number 4.*

Murphy, A., Nicholas, A., & Zaharia, S. (2012). *Case studies in sectoral qualifications: Qualifications provision, job descriptions, learning outcomes and framework placement.* Bucharest: HEQ-Bridges Project.

OECD. (2007). *Qualifications systems: Bridges to lifelong learning.* Paris: OECD.

OECD. (2011). *Education at a Glance 2011: OECD Indicators.* Paris: OECD.

QQI. (2013). *Green papers for consultation.* Dublin: Qualifications and Quality Ireland (QQI).

Scattergood, J. (2012). *RPL in the university sector: Policies, case studies and issues arising.* Dublin: University Framework Implementation Network (FIN).

Skillnets. (2012). *Skillnets annual report 2012.* Dublin: Skillnets.

Teichler, U. (2009). *Higher education and the world of work: Conceptual frameworks, comparative perspectives, empirical findings.* Rotterdam: Sense Publications.

Tynjälä, P., Välimaa, J., & Boulton-Lew, G. (2006). *Higher education and working life: Collaborations, confrontations and challenges.* Amsterdam: Earli and Elsevier.

UNESCO. (2012). *Guidelines for recognition validation and accreditation of the outcomes of non-formal and informal learning.* Geneva: UNESCO.

Van Kleef, J. (2011). Canada: A typology of prior learning assessment and recognition (PLAR) research in context. In J. Harris, M. Breier, & C. Wihak (Eds.), *Researching the recognition of prior learning: International perspectives.* Leicester: NIACE.

Wheelahan, L., Dennis, N., Firth, J., Miller, P., Newton, D., Pascoe, S., Veemker, P., & Brightman, R. (2002). *Recognition of prior learning: Policy and practice in Australia.* Report commissioned by the Australian Qualifications Framework, October 25, Lismore, Southern Cross University.

World Bank. (2002). *Constructing knowledge societies: New challenges for tertiary education.* Washington, DC: The World Bank.

Zaharia, S., Mivonor, C. M., & Borzea, A. E. (2008, June). The competences issue in the entrepreneurial university. *Level3, Issue 6.* http://level3.dit.ie/html/issue6_list.html. Accessed 4 Oct 2013.

Chapter 15
French Approaches to Accreditation of Prior Learning: Practices and Research

Vanessa Rémery and Vincent Merle

The French experience of validating the knowledge, skills and competences acquired through informal and non-formal learning is unique in the world. In 2002, the French Parliament passed a law recognising the right of all working individuals to earn a diploma or professional qualification through the Accreditation of Prior Learning (APL). This means that since the law was passed, all vocational certifications[1] are potentially accessible through traditional schooling, continuing education or APL.

---

[1] In France, the term certification is used to refer to all documents that attest to the acquisition of knowledge, skills or competences, from a qualification to operate construction site equipment to certifications established by the social partners within a professional sector or university diplomas. The term diploma traditionally refers to the certifications issued by the Ministry of National Education and other educational institutions like business schools. Some ministries, excluding National Education, customarily refer to their certifications as 'titres' (e.g. the Ministry of Labour). But the word 'titre' also sometimes refers to certain categories of diplomas, as, for example, the diplomas issued by some engineering schools (selected by a special committee), which grant the 'title of engineer'. The law specifies that all certifications are eligible for accreditation of prior learning once they are recorded in the National Registry of Vocational Certifications (NRVC), as will be discussed later in this text. The only certifications that are excluded are those that attest to the learning of certain job-required skills but that does not constitute preparation for a job or a job function exercised in the private or public sector. Examples would be certifications that are part of a quality approach or that are obtained to comply with safety regulations. For convenience, we denote all the certifications available through APL by the words 'diplomas' or 'certifications' in the rest of this article.

V. Rémery (✉)
Equipe Interaction et Formation, Laboratoire RIFT, Université de Genève, Genève, Suisse

Centre de Recherche sur la Formation, Conservatoire National des
Arts et Métiers, Paris, France
e-mail: vanessa.remery@unige.ch

V. Merle
Centre de Recherche sur la Formation, Conservatoire National des
Arts et Métiers, Paris, France

T. Halttunen et al. (eds.), *Promoting, Assessing, Recognizing and Certifying Lifelong Learning: International Perspectives and Practices*, Lifelong Learning Book Series 20, DOI 10.1007/978-94-017-8694-2_15, © Springer Science+Business Media Dordrecht 2014

This chapter argues for the singularity of this experience in France. We first review the beginnings of APL movement, from the early experiments until its current modes of functioning. We show, in particular, how the implementation of APL introduced a significant break in the French educational model that attaches great importance to diplomas obtained within the school system. In this way, APL radically transformed the landscape of classic means of certification. It established a strong distinction between diplomas and pathways to gain certification, by recognising the formative dimension of work experience. The issue which then arises is not so much the recognition of knowledge, skills and competences that have been acquired at work, but the means by which the recognition can be operationalised. Indeed, APL requires intense preparation from candidates to match their acquired experience with the knowledge, skills and competences described in the diploma standards.

In this chapter, we focus, therefore, on the methodological resources provided to support candidates and to assist the complex process by which they are expected to put into words their work experience. To do so, we discuss recent research conducted in France in the field of psychology and educational sciences that investigate the counsellors' activities. This research, we argue, opens up interesting perspectives in terms of training and professionalisation in the field of APL.

15.1 The Beginnings of APL and Its Modes of Functioning

This first part of the chapter traces the history of APL and discusses its current modes of functioning. Characterised by an education system grounded on the model of 'republican elitism' (Merle 2007), the French context seems a priori reluctant space for considering alternative ways of gaining certification. Yet a change in attitudes occurred in the 1990s to respond to socioeconomic developments, which gives a way to new forms of certification (Sect. 15.1.1). The implementation of APL can be seen as a 'small revolution' in France. A distinction now exists between qualifications and pathways to obtain it, which caused important institutional changes (Sect. 15.1.2). Finally, after showing how the APL is an approach inspired by earlier programmes, we will draw up a balance sheet of the device after a decade of decline (Sect. 15.1.3).

15.1.1 A Weakness in the French Model of Equal Opportunity

The French APL movement is quite surprisingly strong, given the importance attributed to the diploma obtained at the end of traditional education with regard to a future career. The French educational system operates to a great extent on a model that can best be termed 'republican elitism'. Students are essentially evaluated on the basis of academic criteria and future job orientation at all levels as determined by academic results. This selectivity based on school performance (Verdier 2008) is particularly striking because, in addition, the possibility of returning to school later in life is quite low. The type of diploma and its prestige value have key roles in the entry-level position and, more generally, in the entire career trajectory. Far more than the knowledge, skills and competences acquired in the school system, the prestige of the diploma is very important for students, their families and future employers. As Dubet (2010) observed, only one type of competition matters in France: academic, after which everything else is pretty much determined. The obvious downside of this system is that the stronger the belief that school alone defines the professional worth and effectiveness of individuals, the more likely we are to believe it is fair to let a diploma determine professional status.

It seems fairly evident that such a system is not likely to develop programmes to encourage the recognition and validation of informally acquired learning experience. Informal and non-formal learning would have little value when measured against formal learning in such a system, and APL might even appear to be a threat to the very principles of an academic meritocracy. This suggests an intriguing question: How did France end up with a vibrant APL movement? Several factors entered into France's decision to pursue this route.

Toward the end of the 1990s, a general awareness of the limits of the republican elitism system reached a critical point. Two phenomena particularly contributed to this change: a persistent high rate of school dropouts (from 10 to 14 % of any given student generation, depending on the report) and the disenfranchisement of underemployed youth who, despite years of university study, found themselves locked out of worthwhile employment and careers because they lacked the 'right' prestigious diplomas. In addition, the stalled careers of many adults whose professional skills could not compensate for the lack of the 'right' diploma obtained at the 'right' time became more marked. Yet, more generally, the principle of equal opportunity, which supposedly legitimated the system, conflicted with a persistent social reproduction in the schools. As Dubet (2009) notes, when diplomas establish social position and income in the name of meritocracy, the reproduction of social inequalities is high. In France, where diplomas continue to have a powerful influence, 40 % of a child's future income is determined by the parents' current income, whereas in Sweden the percentage is 20 % because diplomas have a less decisive role in determining one's future.

The ongoing debates about job security also helped to create a climate conducive to developing procedures to validate knowledge acquired outside of educational programmes. Precarious employment, disruptions in career paths due to layoffs or retrenchments, the growing number of workers called on to change jobs or job skills in order to adapt to technological and organisational changes – all these factors encouraged employees to insist that their skills be recognised. A diploma or vocational certificate granted during the course of job performance came to be seen as a 'passport' to a more secure future.

15.1.2 A Dissociation Between the Diploma and the Path Taken to Obtain It

In this context, the Secretary of State for Vocational Training made APL a central element in the continuing education reforms undertaken by Lionel Jospin's government (1997–2002). The White Paper on vocational training published in 1999 by Secretary of State Nicole Péry was the starting point for a vast and concerted effort that led to the Social Modernisation Law of January 2002, which was unanimously approved by the Parliament.

Several options were presented as possible ways forward. For example, one such option was to create specific certifications for working adults. This type of system would have adapted certifications to an adult population, notably by developing standards focused on skills rather than formal knowledge. This proposal was first made in 1996 by Michel de Virville in a report to the Minister in charge of vocational training at that time. The report suggested that a 'National Registry of Vocational Certifications' be created in consultation with all social partners, parallel to the diplomas granted after traditional education. These certifications would be awarded by assessment centres. The second option was to facilitate access to the traditional diplomas through APL, and this option was chosen. In addition to the technical difficulties of creating an alternative system for vocational qualification, there was the risk that the standards for qualification would be lower than those for the traditional path. Given the weight accorded to diplomas in France, this risk was high. Yet, by granting diplomas through the Accreditation of Prior Learning, the implicit message was that different learning paths have the same value. Indeed, the law stipulated that a diploma obtained through APL would 'produce the same effects' as that obtained by following the traditional path (tests of knowledge at the end of the educational programme).

This second option implicitly recognised a diploma as primarily an indicator of knowledge, skills and competences matching a job description. Although the diploma continues to confer a certain distinction, this function has become secondary to the function of sending a 'signal' to the labour market. The law of 2002 was based on the assumption that the ultimate value of a diploma is independent of the path taken to obtain it. In a system that has given such importance to the prestige of academic study, this was nothing less than a 'small revolution'.

Once this option was chosen, the work of defining which diplomas could be conferred through APL was undertaken. The law introduced a new mechanism for regulating the vocational certification system through the creation of the National Registry of Vocational Certifications (NRVC) managed by a national commission (the National Commission on Vocational Certification, NCVC, composed of the representatives of the ministries awarding diplomas, various social partners, professional organisations and regional government councils). The diplomas awarded by ministries (e.g. National Education) are recorded by law in the NRVC as soon as they have been agreed upon by the social partners (advisory committees now found in almost all ministries). All others must first obtain the approval of the NRVC ('recorded on demand' procedure), which assesses their relevance with regard to current business needs (one of the criteria is the type of job held after obtaining the diploma). The NCVC can also register vocational certifications jointly established within certain professions (and more recently among several professional sectors). According to the 2002 law, all certifications registered with the NRVC are accessible by APL. Qualifications of a general nature (e.g. a degree in comparative literature or an MA in art history) might have been excluded from the registry, but it was finally decided that all diplomas issued by the Ministry of National Education (with the exception of the general baccalaureate) would be recorded.

This choice has had far-reaching consequences. In particular, all diploma-granting institutions are required to define their framework in terms of the knowledge, skills and competences related to job descriptions. The NRVC is not interested in the curriculum, courses or programme content. It is focused on the 'learning outcomes', to borrow an expression in common use within the European Union. Most institutions, therefore, have had to rewrite their guidelines and standards for diplomas, which has not always been simple, especially in higher education. Procedures for accreditation have also had to be put into place, including how candidates should demonstrate acquired skill and knowledge, how they should be counselled and guided in building a solid candidature and how juries should be chosen. In practice, not all diplomas are accessible through APL, in part because many teachers continue to view the principle of APL with reluctance. However, of the 7,500 vocational certifications currently registered in the NRVC (when all certifications are recorded, the NRVC should include about 15,000 certifications, with most being Bachelor and Master's degrees), most have been gradually made accessible by APL. These include diplomas from engineering and business schools that recruit their students through an entrance examination.

It should be noted that with the 2002 law, the term 'certification' emerged to describe both diplomas – a term without a strict legal definition – and certificates of qualification established jointly in specific professional sectors. Other types of certification do not, strictly speaking, refer to job 'qualifications', as the term is commonly used in France. This is the case, for example, of certifications to operate certain machines or within the framework of a quality procedure. Since the law was passed, the NRVC has been used to distinguish those certifications that are registered from those that are not. For example, some public funding is reserved only for training that leads to NRVC certification. This decision breaks, in part, with French tradition. Historically, the diplomas awarded by the Ministry of National Education and the Ministry of Higher Education were the 'gold standard', with all other qualifications consigned to a supplementary role. In 1940, a law even granted the Ministry of National Education the monopoly for issuing diplomas. The change brought about by APL has, therefore, not always been well-received by those who remain strongly attached to the principle of academic merit. This change again demonstrates that adopting the principle of validating informal learning is in many ways inseparable from changing the certification system itself. The NRVC is not a mere appendix to the 2002 law; in the words of the current NRVC President, they are two sides of the same coin.

15.1.3 An Approach Inspired by the Past, Gradually Formalised and Developed

France did not undertake this ambitious project in a vacuum. The country had launched similar projects in the past, on a smaller scale but always inspired by the same principle. In 1934, the so-called government-granted engineering diploma was created to allow engineers coming up through the ranks to reach the formal status of engineer based on their work experience. This occurred at a time when the state Engineering Commission (EC) was establishing regulations for engineering education with only those schools accredited by the EC can confer the title of engineer. Yet, the government-granted engineering diploma still exists and, every year, it allows about a hundred people to become engineers. Also, in 1985, legislation was passed to allow people with significant work experience to enter a higher education programme without possessing the diploma generally required for admission; one example is entering a Master programme without possessing the Bachelor degree. This programme, called 'Validation of Acquired Work Experience' (VAWE), was not abolished by the 2002 law on APL. It continues under the title 'VAWE 85' in admission procedures and is particularly useful for workers who want to return to full-time study.

Finally, in 1992, a law addressing VAWE stated that adults with work experience could be exempted from the exams leading to National Education diplomas (teaching in secondary and higher education). This was presented as an exemption from conforming to the standard diploma qualifications. Furthermore, the candidates had to present for at least one of the exams from the traditional diploma path. As we have seen, the law of 2002 is based on the assumption of separation between the actual diploma and the path that leads to it. A diploma granted through APL confers the same standing/prestige as a diploma acquired through the traditional path (at least on paper). The APL programme is much more developed than the VAWE programme, which, in any case, had attracted very few candidates (about 1,000 per year when the 2002 law was passed).

Specifically, the law laid down the general rules for obtaining certification through APL and left each organisation the choice on how to organise the process according to its own constraints.

– To obtain a diploma through APL, candidates must first demonstrate that they have worked in a relevant paid or volunteer setting for at least 3 years (or longer, if required by the organisation issuing the certification).
– After this first phase of 'admissibility', candidates must then provide evidence to a jury that they have acquired the knowledge, skills and competences described in the diploma standards. This evidence usually takes the form of a written personal and professional history showing evidence of all opportunities to develop the required knowledge, skills and competences. In some cases (e.g. for certifications issued by the Ministry of Labour), the jury may observe the candidate in real or simulated work situations.
– The jury members are appointed by the organisation issuing the certification (e.g. as represented by the President of the University). The jury systematically includes teachers and professionals (professor-researchers must make up the majority for higher education diplomas).
– The jury examines the applications and may interview candidates to obtain more information (in higher education, the interview is systematic).

- The jury may grant all or part of the certification. In case of partial delivery, candidates can complete their training or re-elaborate their application and present again before the jury within the 5 years that follow.
- Candidates may take a 24-h leave of absence to prepare the APL candidature. The law does not require that salary be paid in this case, but it is usually covered by public funding set aside for vocational training.
- The law does not require that candidates be assisted through formal counselling sessions. Most organisations delivering certification, however, provide paid advice and guidance. Again, this expense is often covered by funding set aside for vocational training.

With a decade of hindsight, we can now assess the effects of the 2002 law (Merle 2008). Since its enactment, APL has attracted considerable interest from employees, employers and continuing education professionals. This enthusiasm has never wavered, although the number of candidates has declined slightly over the past 1 or 2 years. In 2010, 66,000 candidatures were admissible, 53,000 candidates appeared before juries and 30,000 candidates obtained full certification. This was 7 % less than in 2009 but 3 % more than in 2008 and 2007. These figures include only those diplomas and certificates issued by ministries. Half of all candidates seek to validate a level V certificate[2] and 87 % present for certification at a level equal to or below the baccalaureate. About 800 of diplomas that were applied for through APL do not concern higher education. Moreover, almost half of these focus on a dozen certifications, mainly in the health and social services (home-health aid, childcare, etc.). Three quarters of the candidates are women, and seven out of ten applicants are employed.

In addition to these quantitative factors, a significant movement has emerged among businesses to make APL an effective tool for recognising skills and encouraging career progression. In the companies involved in this movement, the number of employees who actually commit to APL with their employer's support is relatively low. Moreover, this is often confined to a particular sector, like the employees in a distribution company who validate their skills and abilities to become assistant store managers or department managers or hospital workers who receive certification as nurse's aides. Yet, the effects are usually judged to be very positive, with reports of gains in self-confidence, greater company loyalty, the desire to obtain more advanced certification, pride in one's job, the discovery of unsuspected skills and so on. The fears sometimes expressed about APL in a collective context have proved to be unfounded; in most cases, there have been few requests for automatic salary increases or departures to other companies. In contrast, most people have seen their careers rebound after this step, which essentially has required them to take distance from their own experience in order to analyse it and put into words the knowledge that has been gained. In a country of 'glass ceilings' separating one qualification level from another, APL holds out hope of breaking through for many of these

---

[2] In France, this refers to the National Education diplomas called 'Certificat d'Aptitudes Générales' (CAP) or 'Brevet d'Études Professionnelles' (BEP), which are granted in secondary school.

employees. The gradual adoption of APL may also help businesses to develop a different perspective on the formative nature of work situations and the diversity of professional excellence. In a country that has long emphasised formal and academic knowledge above all, APL is a significant step in acknowledging the validity of other ways to learn and develop.

Such positive effects, for both employers and employees, would not be possible without the intense work of the candidates to match their acquired experience with the knowledge, skills and competences described in the certification standards. Often, they need help in doing this. The provision of advice and guidance has also been a focus for some very interesting thinking about each step in the APL process, the system of actors who support the candidates in their commitment to it and the process of actually formalising prior learning.

15.2 The Practices of Advising and Guiding APL Candidates

The second part of our contribution is more focused on support provided to candidates. We discuss the existing forms of support according to the stages of APL (Sect. 15.2.1). These forms of support, which are afforded to candidates during the application procedure, require participation from various actors and institutions working together to inform and guide candidates in the preparation of their applications. The APL programme is based on a formal assessment of the candidate's experience, objectified and made public through a booklet. The production of this booklet makes it possible for skills, knowledge and competences to be organised, represented and assessed. In this booklet, candidates have to describe and analyse experienced work situations in order to link up with formal knowledge described in the diploma standards. In this section, we identify how the formalisation of prior experience can be seen as a nodal element of the procedure (Sect. 15.2.2). Finally, we provide a brief overview of the main research streams in France which have focused on coaching practices in APL and have investigated their contribution to professional and personal development (Sect. 15.2.3).

15.2.1 Types of Guidance According to the Step in the Process

The implementation of VAWE then APL created a new job function and brought new members into the adult education field, i.e. advisers to assist candidates. Assistance to APL candidates has nevertheless not been mandated by legislation, and certifying organisations have been given the responsibility for defining the form of this guidance. From the many experiments in the field by the advisers themselves since VAWE was first launched in the mid-1980s, stable and effective practices have gradually emerged. We can now distinguish several types of assistance for the various steps in the process. Although assistance is officially set by legislation at the end of the step of 'admissibility', types of assistance have developed upstream of admissibility and for the outcome of the jury decision in cases of partial validation or rejection. Each type of assistance has its own characteristics, which we will describe briefly.

Before admissibility, certifying organisations increasingly offer assistance through a public service of information and advice. This service is not a mandatory step for APL candidates but it does give them direction for the upcoming steps. The assistance is offered in group meetings and/or individual interviews. The services are similar to those made by the Information/Counsel Points (ICP). Under the responsibility of the Regional Councils, these services are offered within the framework of France's many employment-oriented agencies, such as local employment or career development agencies. The assistants provide information on APL and help potential candidates to analyse the relevance of their experiences. In doing so, they can also reorient individuals toward other services, such as skills assessment. This type of assistance also allows potential candidates to situate themselves with regard to the range of certifications, to find the appropriate certifying organisation for the diploma they are seeking and to explore the private or public funding opportunities. At the end of this step, those wishing to pursue APL obtain an application package from the certifying organisation. The package contains 'booklet 1', which guides candidates, further ensuring that they meet all the conditions for requesting APL.

Once admissible, candidates then move on to the next step: preparing 'booklet 2', which is the documentation of the informal prior learning that will be presented to the jury for accreditation. Guidance at this point is officially recognised in the legislation on APL. Counsellors provide methodological help to the candidates as they match their experience to the diploma-qualifying standards and help in the actual writing of the booklet. They help the candidates to clearly put into words their work experience so that they can then identify the relevant work situations described and analysed in the booklet as proof of prior learning. Most of the assistants from certifying organisations use the same basic outline in accomplishing this work.

Step 1: Potential candidates become familiar with the standards for the diploma they are seeking through APL.

Step 2: Candidates explore and analyse their work history and their informally acquired knowledge and skills.

Step 3: Candidates select the most relevant work experiences related to the chosen diploma.

Step 4: Candidates are advised and guided in preparing a descriptive analysis of their work activities.

Step 5: Candidates formalise the application, with assistance in preparing the final document. Counsellors verify the inclusion of key skills needed for the diploma. They also intervene, if need be, by requesting that candidates supply more detail, for example.

Step 6: Candidates prepare to for the assessment by the jury through simulated interviews.

Candidates may apply for funding if they wish to have their supervision sponsored. Vocational funds usually cover this cost, and the length of the assistance varies with the status of the applicants. Between 8 and 24 h of assistance is usually given over a 6- to 9-month period. The objective is to help the candidates to validate their case by clearly identifying and describing their work activities and matching their skills to those required for certification, all with a clear understanding of the criteria for evaluation. This assistance is highly recommended because, statistically, it has been demonstrated to be a successful approach to APL. The assistance at this stage is most often offered by the APL counsellors of the certifying organisations, although private providers are now also offering these services. In fact, the APL counselling market now has so many types of guidance on offer that candidates sometimes find it difficult to identify the most relevant form of assistance.

Following the jury's decision, the certifying organisation ensures the follow-up assistance, with the primary goal of preventing abandonment after partial validation. This may take the form of an interview to guide the next step or help in finding an internship or training programme. The assistance depends on the jury's recommendations, ranging from a single interview to a regular follow-up until the candidate returns to the jury.

15.2.2   Formalising Prior Learning: The Nodal Point of the Approach

As we have seen, the APL procedure has several steps: candidates must choose the diploma best suited to their work experience and skills, make a formal request for accreditation from the appropriate certifying organisation ('booklet 1') and build a solid record of evidence ('booklet 2'). This written document must argue convincingly, through the description and analysis of work situations that the knowledge acquired during these work experiences is closely linked to the formalised knowledge required for the diploma. This document is the foundation on which the jury members will base their decision.

Although APL gives people access to a diploma on the basis of prior experiential learning acquired while working, it is not necessarily the professional skills that candidates have developed and mobilised in their work that are validated. The APL process puts a great emphasis on candidates' written and oral skills: the jury will assess their ability to analyse their work activities and communicate the knowledge underlying or driving these activities from their written or oral productions. As Barbier (2006) pointed out, in this type of programme, *skills in managing actions* and *skills in communicating about actions* are evaluated, rather than actual *skills in carrying out actions*.

In the general field of certification, it is relatively rare to evaluate applications on the candidates' ability to analyse and communicate about their acquired experience. APL is thus distinguished from 'traditional' diploma paths by the very nature of the knowledge that is communicated and then assessed. Whereas diploma candidates following traditional paths are still mainly oriented toward learning and reproducing the contents of legitimatised knowledge, APL candidates undertake a process that requires greater commitment. APL is not based on the communication of knowledge taught in an education and training space or without reference to learners' experiences. Instead, APL is based on candidates' production of knowledge *about* their own experiences. It must be underlined here that to produce knowledge about one's experience in a context of assessment, and to do so in a well-structured and well-argued manner, is a complex activity.

Although at first glance, the instructions suggest that the preparations for an APL application are a simple administrative formality, they nevertheless embark candidates on a far-reaching analysis of work situations. During sessions with the counsellor, all the work situations that the candidate will report are discussed and reflected upon. These sessions are, therefore, key moments when candidates can express themselves on their prior learning and refine their arguments. They provide the opportunity for candidates to learn how to convincingly demonstrate the links between work activities, the knowledge acquired during these activities and the theoretical knowledge detailed in the standards for the diploma.

This approach, therefore, amounts to a project of analysis and writing that goes well beyond an account of a job history. The expected narrative requires a high capacity for reflexivity and subjectivity by the candidates, who must structure their career paths retrospectively, evaluate them to identify the significant experiences and finally show the knowledge that has been acquired. This exercise means that candidates must be able to put into words the meaning that past work activities have had for them. Work experience as a practice is thus taken as an object of reflection, analysis and learning (Magnier 2001). It is precisely this work that enables candidates to construct their experience with another meaning: the meaning attributed a posteriori to an experience as practice. Indeed, experience is both a practice and the knowledge that can be built from it (Astier 2001). Experience as knowledge is the memory of lessons one has learned from events (Vincens 2001). It is a conscious acquisition; it is not the obligatory result of the work, and, therefore, it is not a joint product of the activity, or is so only in part (p. 22). We can see here the extent to which confusion persists for candidates applying for APL between experience as an *activity* and experience as the *product of a constructed meaning of the activity*, even though APL is focused on the latter (Mayen 2008).

The work needed to formalise prior learning is not straightforward. The assistance and guidance offered in APL is mainly methodological and helps candidates to identify their assets. That is, to assist them in constructing the meaning of their experience of the activities they describe, as well as to help them verbalise and write this constructed meaning in a well-organised narrative. It is this expression of meaning – first constructed and then rendered socially accessible through interactions with the assistant – that provides the key information on the nature of prior experience. Acquired knowledge, thus, is revealed in the co-analysis of experience by the candidate and the counsellor.

15.2.3   A Field of Research in Full Expansion

We identified three main research streams focused on the practices of counselling and guidance in APL. The life history approach to adult education or lifelong learning was the first to focus on the formative effects of work experience. These studies provided a methodological framework for many APL counsellors by offering a structure and tools. Next, studies conducted with the clinic of activity approach in work psychology[3] and professional didactics in the educational sciences[4] sought to analyse the activity of assisting rather than to produce models of action. Although theoretically distinct, these two lines of research both used methodologies for analysing work activity and focused on the processes of personal and activity development in the course of APL.

15.2.3.1   Life Histories in Lifelong Learning

The life histories approach (Orofiamma et al. 2000) produced the first studies on the practices of guidance in APL. This research stream began very early on to explore the issues and problems of recognising workplace acquired knowledge. The first experiments in APL and skills assessment in the mid-1980s were notably inspired by the tools developed from the French-Canadian work on skills portfolios. Lainé (1998), whose research was rooted in the life history approach to lifelong learning, formalised a method for assisting candidates that he also implemented on behalf of the Ministry of Youth and Sports. His book 'When Experience Makes Itself Known: Assisting in the Validation of Informally Acquired Knowledge' (2005) served as an essential guide for APL assistants. In it, he described the journey of candidates from the initial information about the regulations to the jury's decision and showed how this approach is a process of self-directed learning during which candidates change the way they look at their own experience. In addition to giving numerous examples of assistance, Lainé himself deployed his method. In this regard, he noted how methods for analysing work activity like the 'explicitation interview' (Vermersch 1994) contribute to 'making experience speak', which prompted many to train in this technique to better assist candidates in describing their work activities.

---

[3] The clinic of activity is a French research stream that developed in the 1990s based on the work of Clot ('Le Travail sans l'homme? Pour une psychologie des milieux de travail et de vie', Paris, La Découverte, 1995). Clot's work dealt with the development of the power to act in one's work activity and the tasks and missions assigned in the context of work organisation. It also analysed the conditions for the processes of development using specific methodologies for intervention.

[4] Professional didactics is a French research stream that developed in the 1990s based on the works of Pastré ('La didactique professionnelle. Approche anthropologique du développement chez les adultes', Paris, Presses Universitaires de France, 2011). The objective is to analyse work activity with a view to training for professional skills development. It is situated at the confluence of a field of practices, adult education and three theoretical perspectives: developmental psychology, cognitive ergonomics and the didactics of school disciplines.

15.2.3.2 Professional Didactics

In the field of professional didactics, Mayen and his team (1999) undertook a series of studies on the work and training of workers involved in APL. Their objective was to better understand APL work to professionalise and create training programmes for it. They, thus, focused on the work of juries, assistants, counsellors at information points and candidates. As an extension of their earlier work on mentoring in the workplace, they sought to determine the conditions where a work situation becomes a circumstance in which and by which an individual can learn. Theoretically, they tried to articulate the models from the cultural-historical perspective of Vygotsky and Bruner with those of professional didactics (Mayen 1999, 2002) using a methodology for analysing mentor/apprentice interactions. The APL field gradually became a research focus because of the similarities between situations of counselling and situations of workplace mentoring (Mayen 2004). APL guidance was considered to be a form of joint activity carried out in and through the interactions between counsellors and candidates, and the APL sessions were notably analysed as the assistants' *mediation* of the candidates' conceptualisations of their work activity. The *processes of pragmatic development* proposed by Vergnaud[5] in the didactics of mathematics – and widely taken up in professional didactics – make up a relevant category for analysing transformations in the meaning of work activity, which occur during the APL process as candidates seek to match the knowledge acquired in work with the formalised knowledge for the diploma standards. Nevertheless, the studies conducted within this category have given no attention to the assistants' contributions to this process of transformation. The theories of Vygotsky and Bruner, and, particularly, the notion of scaffolding (Chakroun and Mayen 2009), have yielded interesting analyses on the role of language interactions in the processes of conceptualising and elaborating experience, and studies from this perspective have shown under what conditions a situation of assistance can become a *potential situation for development*.

15.2.3.3 The Clinic of Activity

About 15 years ago, several studies using the clinic of activity approach were conducted for the Ministry of National Education on the Accreditation of Prior Learning (Clot and Prot 2003). These studies also focused on naturally occurring practices in the validation process: by candidates, assistants and jury members. From the unique clinical and developmental perspective of this approach, researchers analysed activities of assisting candidates and assessing their applications using an approach based on 'crossed self-confrontation interviews', which was helpful for individuals working together to develop the meanings and practices of their profession. These studies also analysed the development of knowledge in action, its formalisation and its relation to the formalised knowledge required for diplomas

---

[5] Vergnaud, G. (1990). La théorie des champs conceptuels. *Recherches en didactique des mathématiques*, vol. 10, n° 2–3, p 133–170.

granted through the traditional path. Contrary to the approach taken in professional didactics, the work situations in APL were conceptualised using Vygotsky's distinction between *everyday concepts* and *scientific concepts* in the framework of a theory on the relationship between thought and language (1934/1997). In particular, the exchanges between candidates and validation juries were analysed (Kostulski and Prot 2004) to show how language and interactional activities could be used to develop a *potential concept* articulating scientific concepts and everyday concepts (Prot 2003). This perspective combined the clinic of activity and speech analysis to show the transformation in thinking that occurred in the conversational chaining and sequencing in sessions for the joint analysis of work activities. Language and interactional activities were assumed to be spaces for the realisation of thought – its construction and development – in order to articulate the development of both language and psychological processes. Within the APL framework, language interactions reveal an *activity genre* that is in itself a tool for development (Kostulski and Clot 2007).

The presentation of these works on APL from the perspectives of professional didactics and the clinic of activity shows how language and interactional activities in counselling and guidance situations underlie developmental processes. These works demonstrate that the assistance session is characterised by cooperation in the sense that prior experiential learning emerges from a joint discursive construction and is formalised during a process of scaffolding. The elaboration of work experience, thus, presents as a process of co-construction that is collectively carried out and negotiated in the assistant/candidate dialogue. Acquired experience can be expressed and reconfigured through the interposition of language and interactional work between the assistant and the candidate, which opens up new insights and opportunities for action. We recently investigated this process and showed how the assistance given to APL candidates is an opportunity for development (Remery 2012, 2013a, b, in press). Our analyses, which focused on the discursive and interactional dimensions of scaffolding, revealed a broad diversity in the forms of assistance given, as well. Sometimes, for example, assistants played the role of evaluators to prepare the candidates to argue their positions before the jury. This approach created certain tensions and provoked negotiations about identity during the sessions. Sometimes, these assistants took a supportive role by sharing their own interpretations of candidates' work activities. This sharing was often the case when assistants had once worked or were currently working in the same job as the candidate, in addition to their role of assistant. More particularly, we showed how these shared interpretations contributed to the transmission of an interpretative culture of work activities, which added to the professionalisation of the candidates.

15.3   Conclusions

Our contribution aimed at showing how the introduction of APL in France can be seen as a singular experience. France may well be unique in its decision to make nearly all diplomas and certifications accessible through the accreditation of prior learning. Yet, despite the political consensus regarding APL, it nevertheless remains somewhat incongruous in the French social landscape. French APL emerged from the same concerns expressed in many countries on how to recognise and accredit informal and non-formal knowledge, but France chose an ambitious response that has deeply shaken conceptions long rooted in its collective representations. Today, although APL is gradually finding its place in career development and is no longer perceived as an 'inferior' route to certification, it nevertheless continues to raise questions for those working in the field, albeit those in regional governments, professional sectors, companies or the certifying organisations in charge of organising assistance and juries.

Our contribution aimed at exploring how to operationalise the principles of recognition of knowledge and skills within the programme itself. We focused our discussion on the guidance practices aiming to help candidates to formalise their prior experience. Progress remains to be made, particularly in helping businesses to develop policies for job security and in implementing APL more broadly with an emphasis on further professionalising the juries and assistants of the certifying organisations. Research in recent years that we have reviewed above provides insight into the APL practices that have been progressively constructed by the actors in the field. The findings also open up interesting prospects for training and profes-sionalising the actors based on the analysis of their work activity, although certainly more research is required.

References

Astier, P. (2001). *La communication de l'expérience professionnelle: éléments d'analyse de l'activité du sujet.* Thèse de doctorat sous la direction de J.-M. Barbier. Paris: Cnam.

Barbier, J.-M. (2006). Le modèle francophone de la VAE. *Revue Sciences humaines, 175,* 10–11.

Chakroun, B., & Mayen, P. (2009). L'accompagnement en validation des acquis de l'expérience: une situation potentielle de développement de l'expérience. *Céreq, Relief, 28,* 69–86.

Clot, Y., & Prot, B. (2003). De l'analyse du travail à la validation des acquis. *L'orientation scolaire et professionnelle,* numéro spécial.

Dubet, F. (2009). Les pièges de l'égalité des chances. *Journal Le Monde, n° du 1° décembre.*

Dubet, F. (2010). *Les places et les chances – repenser la justice sociale.* Paris: Seuil.

Kostulski, K., & Clot, Y. (2007). Interaction et migration fonctionnelle: un développement en auto-confrontation croisée. *Psychologie de l'interaction, 23–24,* 73–108.

Kostulski, K., & Prot, B. (2004). L'activité conversationnelle d'un jury de validation des acquis: analyse interlocutoire de la formation d'un concept potentiel. *Psychologie Française, 49,* 425–441.

Lainé, A. (1998). *Faire de sa vie une histoire. Théorie et pratiques de l'histoire de vie en formation.* Paris: Desclée de Brouwer.

Lainé, A. (2005). *Quand l'expérience se fait savoir. L'accompagnement en validation des acquis.* Paris: Erès.

Magnier, J. (2001). Expérience, connaissance, une conquête des candidats à la validation des acquis professionnels. *Education Permanente, 146,* 143–150.

Mayen, P. (1999). Des situations potentielles de développement. *Education Permanente, 139,* 65–86.

Mayen, P. (2002). Le rôle des autres dans le développement de l'expérience. *Education Permanente, 151,* 87–107.

Mayen, P. (2004). Caractériser l'accompagnement en VAE. Une contribution de didactique professionnelle. *Education Permanente, 158,* 11–23.

Mayen, P. (2008). L'expérience dans les activités de Validation des acquis de l'expérience. *Travail et Apprentissage, 1*, 58–75.

Merle, V. (2007). Genèse de la loi de janvier 2002 sur la validation des acquis de l'expérience. *La revue de l'IRES, 55*, 3.

Merle, V. (2008). La VAE, la loi a-t-elle tenu ses promesses? *Actualité de la formation permanente, 212*, janvier-février.

Orofiamma, R., Dominice, P., & Laine, A. (2000). Les histoires de vie. Théories et pratiques. *Education Permanente, 142*, 45–61.

Prot, B. (2003). *Le concept potentiel, une voie de développement des concepts*. Thèse de doctorat sous la direction de Y. Clot. Paris: Cnam.

Rémery, V. (2012). Élaboration de l'expérience, tensions identitaires et transformation des représentations de soi. Expérience d'une candidate en accompagnement à la VAE. *Revue internationale francophone de Carriérologie, numéro consacré à "La reconnaissance des acquis entre expérimentation et institutionnalisation", coordonné par G. Pinte, 12*(3), 257–270.

Rémery, V. (2013a). Étayer la formalisation de l'expérience. Une analyse de l'activité d'accompagnement en VAE. *XIIIe Rencontres internationales du réseau de Recherche en Éducation et en Formation (REF)*. Université de Genève, 9–11 Sept.

Rémery, V. (2013b). Élaboration conjointe de l'expérience en accompagnement. L'exemple de la Validation des Acquis de l'Expérience. In J.-M. Barbier & J. Thievenaz (Coord.), *Le travail de l'expérience*. Paris: L'Harmattan.

Rémery, V. (in press). Tensions et négociations identitaires en entretiens d'accompagnement à la Validation des Acquis de l'Expérience. In F. Gutnik & M. Sorel (Eds.), *Pratiques sociales: enjeux de sens et d'identités?* Paris: L'Harmattan.

Verdier, E. (2008). L'éducation et la formation tout au long de la vie: une orientation européenne, des régimes d'action publique et des modèles nationaux en évolution. *Sociologie et sociétés, 40*(1), 195–225.

Vermersch, P. (1994). *L'entretien d'explicitation*. Paris: ESF.

Vincens, J. (2001). Définir l'expérience professionnelle. *Travail et emploi, 85*, 21–34.

Vygotski, L. S. (1934/1997). *Pensée et langage*. Paris: La Dispute.

Chapter 16
Recognising and Certifying Workers' Knowledge: Policies, Frameworks and Practices in Prospect: Perspectives from Two Countries

Stephen Billett, Helen Bound, and Magdalene Lin

16.1 The Recognition of Learning Outside of Educational Programmes

This chapter seeks to consider how factors and processes associated with the recognition and certification of learning outside of educational institutions are and should be enacted in particular national contexts and how the practicalities, barriers, imperatives and sensitivities associated with recognising and certifying workers' knowledge might be confronted and redressed.

The need for recognising learning outside of educational institutions arises from a requirement for workers of all kinds to demonstrate their workplace competence against regulated occupational requirements. Hence, before individuals are allowed to take up employment in a particular work situation, they are required to demonstrate the ability to work safely and within ways regulated for that occupation. In many instances, workers have learnt these capacities in their working lives and outside of educational programmes and the certification they offer. There is also a growing demand for the recognition of learning for equity purposes. There are solid justifications here as the acquisition of qualifications as well as their level and standing is strongly and positively correlated to levels of remuneration (Groot et al. 1994; Grubb 1996; Lengerman 1999; O'Connell 1999), associated with occupational identity (Noon and Blyton 1997; Pusey 2003), the standing of the work individuals are permitted to engage in (Darrah 1996) and increasingly now as a means of demonstrating current competency.

S. Billett (✉)
Education and Professional Studies, Griffith University, Brisbane, QLD, Australia
e-mail: s.billett@griffith.edu.au

H. Bound • M. Lin
Institute for Adult Learning, Workforce Development Agency,
1 Kay Siang Road, Singapore, Singapore
e-mail: Helen_bound@ial.edu.sg; Magdalene_lin@ial.edu.sg

T. Halttunen et al. (eds.), *Promoting, Assessing, Recognizing and Certifying Lifelong Learning: International Perspectives and Practices*, Lifelong Learning Book Series 20, DOI 10.1007/978-94-017-8694-2_16, © Springer Science+Business Media Dordrecht 2014

In addition, the certification of individuals' skills is becoming increasingly important for sustaining employability across working lives. From the work of cleaners who ensure the cleanliness and hygiene of the places they service through to the procedures carried out by highly paid professionals such as doctors and pilots, there is a growing requirement for the ongoing certification of the currency of what these workers competency. Central to this trend is recognising learning that arises outside of educational programmes (e.g. RPL), which as is argued throughout this book and is likely to be the case for the vast majority of workers throughout their working lives.

However, levels of participation in and outcomes of RPL processes have been far less than expected in some countries by policy makers and educational institutions, often because of procedural concerns (e.g. cost of assessment). Furthermore, the expectation that RPL would be accessed by those most disadvantaged through lack of certification has not been fulfilled. Rather, those who already have higher levels of education have accessed RPL (Dyson and Keating 2005). Nevertheless, RPL is considered important as a contribution to lifelong learning as it supports pathways for undertaking further (formal) education. RPL is also important because individuals should not be required to unnecessarily repeat and pay for experiences for knowledge they already possess. Similarly, governments and taxpayers should not have to pay for such learning experiences to be repeated, even in an era of rapid changes in technology and science. Indeed, much of learning associated with meeting those changes arises through addressing them in workplaces (Wheelahan et al. 2003). RPL also provides opportunities for enterprises to achieve efficiencies in ensuring their workforce meets quality system requirements (Blom et al. 2004) through assessment of skills processes.

Nevertheless, the assessment of occupational competence outside of educational institutions is often constrained by a range of practicalities, barriers, imperatives and sensitivities associated with recognising and certifying workers' knowledge. The particular country and institutional context is usually generative of many of these factors. These include the standing of the particular work or occupation, its affiliation with other kinds of work and the particular need for recognition and certification (i.e. licensing to practice). Then, there are the institutions that are authorised to award certification and the extent to which the frameworks for the assessment are recognised. For these institutions, there may be significant structural barriers. For instance, when individuals' skills have been learnt through work and outside of educational provisions, there may be a lack of documentary evidence for the largely administrative-based processes of assessing, certifying and recognising that knowledge. There may also be intolerance to learning arising outside of educational programmes, with it being seen less rigorous than what is learnt through educational programmes. Yet, in countries such as Australia and Singapore, many workers have learnt their skills through work and before courses existed, so there were no other options. So, whereas newcomers have access to courses and their certification, experienced workers who have learnt their skills through work activities have no equivalent certification. In some instances, even if workers wanted to gain recognition of their skills, there are no benchmarks such as course outlines and objectives against which their skills can be assessed. Hence, in these circumstances, the process of recognising of skills cannot progress because there are no courses, benchmarks or other means against which assessment and certification can progress.

There can be other kinds of barriers, such as societal sentiments associated with different kinds of work and views that such work is of low worth (e.g. security work in Singapore and domestic cleaning in Australia). That even if recognised and certified in some way, it would still remain largely unworthy and perhaps barely legitimate. In addition, often such workers find themselves in circumstances in which few, if any, organisations or agencies will promote their interests, let alone push for effective recognition and certification of their skills. Yet, it is these very workers who are in most need of such certification as, personally and occupationally, they stand to be restricted in their potential for sustaining employment and promoting their employability without certification that is seen as worthwhile and legitimate. At the same time, it is more difficult for these workers to engage with other kinds of employment and promote their advancement when they lack measures which certify their competence and recognise their capacities.

However, it is wrong to assume that all forms of work require certification and all workers are desirous of securing it. This is not the case. For instance, there can be forms of work that are quite enterprise-specific. Efforts to certify this knowledge may have very limited worth outside of that workplace and may not contribute to individuals' employability elsewhere. Then, there are workers, such as those who are self-employed, work on small business and also many older workers who hold that such certification has little or no value for them (Meyers et al. 2010).

Therefore, in considering factors and processes in relation to RPL and its enactment, we draw upon experiences within Australia and Singapore. Throughout, it is held that there needs to be frameworks and processes that are sensitive and responsive to learning arising outside of educational institutions. If the premise for assessment of individuals' learning in and through work is based only upon what experiences occur and outcomes arise in education institutions with their strong focus on prespecified learning outcomes, then there is likely to be mismatches between the kinds of learning that individuals engage in and require for that work and that which can be recognised through prespecified intents (e.g. course goals and objectives). Instead, it is proposed that processes sitting alongside, but not compromised by the norms and practices of educational institutions, need to be acknowledged, albeit progressing within frameworks that are likely to lead to legitimate and worthwhile certification. Having set out these issues, the chapter advances some propositions and practices that might be adopted to overcome these inhibiting factors and set out some basis by which such workers can have their learning recognised and certified and in ways which will serve both their needs and societal purposes. The goal here is for the content of and experiences in Singapore and Australia to provide bases for considering the recognition of these workers' skills elsewhere and in other circumstances.

16.2   Understanding RPL

The different procedures for and purposes of RPL that are enacted require consideration of how RPL is defined and, therefore, understood across different nation states with their distinct organisational infrastructure (e.g. educational and other institutions). Terminology differs from one country to another and from one sector to another. In England, for example, the term Assessment of Prior Experiential Learning is used in higher education and accommodates both assessment and learning outside of educational institutions. The term Prior Learning Assessment is used in the United States within the higher education sector (Travers 2012). In Sweden, Berglund and Andersson (2012) claim that stakeholders broadly adopt their Ministry of Education's definition: '[RPL] is a process of a structured assessment, valuing, documentation and recognition of knowledge and competences that an individual has gained, irrespective of how they have been acquired'. In the Australian context, Wheelahan et al (2003, p. 10) defines RPL as:

> RPL assesses the *individual's* non-formal and informal learning to determine the extent to which that individual has achieved the required learning outcomes, competency outcomes, or standards for entry to, and/or partial or total completion of, a qualification.

This definition unfortunately perpetuates an assumption that learning outside of education is in some ways deficit (i.e. not formal, opposite of formalised). Both definitions explain that RPL pertains to the individual; however, the Swedish definition places greater value on the individual's experience, as compared to the abovementioned definition that privileges processes and outcomes associated with educational provisions. This distinction is salient, as at the heart of the difference is the privileging of particular sources of knowledge; one the knowledge gained experientially through work, the other the knowledge of educational institutions. Ultimately, RPL needs to be seen as both an outcome (i.e. certification of learning) and a process that enables recognition of learning thereby enabling individuals' access to benefits including easier access to further education, expedited processes of lifelong education and advancement at work.

16.2.1   Approaches and Orientations

Conceptually, RPL draws on experiential learning theory (Andersson and Harris 2006) that is learning through experiences, albeit outside of experiences in educational institutions. Accompanying such a perspective are considerations of how experience is used. Reflection, for instance, is a feature of many RPL processes, particularly those involving development of a work portfolio (see for example, Pokorny 2012). Cooper and Harris (2013, p. 449) posit that RPL is perceived as a device to map one body of knowledge (e.g. working knowledge) against another (e.g. academic knowledge), 'rather than an exploration of the relationship between the two'. It is this mapping that can create difficulties as different types of knowledge are attempted to be matched. Some forms of knowledge may be unrecognisable to educational institutions, particularly that which is not easily declarable (i.e. spoken or written down), or is not directly aligned with educational purposes. Much of the RPL processes that are commonly used rely upon written and/or spoken forms (declarative knowledge). For example, the knowledge of trade unionists, which includes dispositional (i.e. values) and strategic knowledge, may not be easily aligned with the declarative-based capturing of knowledge that is common to RPL and APL processes (Cooper and Harris 2013). These authors also hold that in the recontextualisation of knowledge, there needs to be space for pedagogic agency (i.e. learners' actively construct knowledge), as these are essential to processes of learning. It is in this space that RPL may need to be enacted in particular ways and with different practices and epistemologies.

Indeed, different approaches to RPL are variously described as developmental versus the mechanistic credentialing approach (Pokorny 2012; Wheelahan et al. 2003). Wheelahan et al. (2003, p. 12) describe the different approaches in the following way:

> ... the first focuses on RPL as a *learning process* in its own right. The focus here is to use RPL for self-improvement, personal development, and self-actualisation. This is the humanist language of 'learner-centredness'. The main focus is not certification. We can describe this as the developmental model of RPL; and, the second focuses on RPL as a mechanism of credentialling. This is part of the discourse of "efficiency, accreditation, competence, access, transparency, equality of opportunity and mobility" (Harris 1997, p. 9). This is from the language of 'human capital theory,' in which individuals make decisions about their own 'investment' in their education, related to the likely returns they will receive... Both these models are valid, and one is not better than the other, as they are designed to meet different needs.

These different approaches and purposes highlight the tensions in creating single and unilateral rules for RPL. On the one hand, the educational institution awarding the RPL towards a qualification requires evidence that matches with their learning outcomes, often expressed as theoretical knowledge (i.e. declarative forms) and, albeit less frequently, if through skills assessments possibly technical knowledge (techne). Yet, as noted, dispositional knowledge (i.e. attitudes and values), as well as haptic knowledge (i.e. feel) or ways of knowing through sensory systems that are so central to many forms of work, are not easily captured through declarative forms. In addition, the practical wisdom (i.e. phronesis) of applicants is also not easily accounted for and recognised.

On the other hand, the humanist approach with a focus on learners, potentially, creates a space where the assessor works with the RPL applicant in finding ways of crossing the boundaries between these different forms of knowledge that are valued differently by different organisations. Cooper and Harris (2013, p. 15) refer to the pedagogic space as being of considerable importance to opening up pathways for those historically excluded from access to further learning and recognition in educational programmes through the design of 'diverse pedagogic interventions that are appropriate to purpose and innovative in form'. This kind of option is important for workers who for historical or other reasons were denied initial education provisions and recognition for their occupations. For instance, in a rapidly developing country such as Singapore, for many workers now aged over 40 years, there was no opportunity to access initial occupational preparation through the polytechnics or institute of technical education that current cohorts of young people now access.

Certainly, there are a number of issues associated with RPL that are referred to repeatedly in the literature, particularly the issue of quality which includes, the validity and reliability of assessment, the diverse experience of students and the issue of equivalence of RPL with those individuals (i.e. students) who have participated in formally delivered programmes. Also often mentioned is the lack of awareness of the possibility of RPL, the complexity of the process and the time it takes for both candidate and assessor (Blom et al. 2004).

A number of studies indicate that, typically, participants find the RPL assessment experience a positive one, as illustrated by reports of increased confidence and efficacy (Blom et al. 2004; Dyson and Keating 2005). However, others suggest that students' experience of the process, as opposed to the outcome, is less satisfactory (Pokorny 2012). This finding should not be surprising as the experiences of students who have participated in formal programmes are also variable. However, as RPL assumes that nonaccredited, experiential learning has the potential to be equated with formal qualifications, Wheelahan et al. (2003) argue from the educational institutional perspective that there are even skills that RPL students need to learn to be comprehensively assessed such as self-evaluation and self-assessment, career planning, 'learning to learn' and 'learning to be assessed'. While such skills are valuable in and of themselves, such as in developing increased awareness and LLL skills, they are particularly helpful in engaging productively with the RPL process. These skills can also be developed through educational interventions (Cooper and Harris 2013) as assessor and RPL candidate work together. Thus, the approach taken by assessors is important; a developmental approach is more likely to enable RPL students to generate these kinds of capacities whereas a purely instrumental credentialist approach may not provide such opportunities. Pokorny (2012), for instance, found that students who were required to adopt a more conventional academic approach to meaning-making for their assessment experienced the RPL process as disempowering and off-putting.

16.2.2   Issues of Quality

There is often doubt over the quality of the experience that lead to the recognition (i.e. credit and certification) granted through RPL. However, the issue of quality may not be that of RPL, but the tensions in matching different forms of knowledge that are not well understood or valued by different stakeholders, along with different outcomes required by different stakeholders, and perhaps curriculum and assessment outcomes that are poorly captured and expressed (Wheelahan et al. 2003). In keeping with the discussions above, Wheelahan et al. (2003) argue that many RPL applicants may not have the requisite 'graduateness' (i.e. familiarity with educational discourse and practices) that students gain from participation in formal programmes, where there is time and opportunity for peer interaction.

Using existing syllabuses and learning outcomes to assess the prior learning of candidates privileges the educational institution (Armsby 2012). The use of reflections on practice to supplement portfolios of work-based evidence is one way educational institutions address the privileging of academic knowledge. Interestingly, as noted by Armsby (2012) higher education institutions are increasingly valuing work-based projects and appreciating the nexus of theory and practice, as praxis. However, much of this is seen as augmenting or rehearsing what has been learnt in the academy rather than in recognition that particular kinds of learning arise through those experiences (Billett 2009). Ways of capturing and accrediting learning arising from experiences are not well developed and certainly not embedded in the discourse of qualifications and recognition.

Another dimension of quality is that of who administers the assessments. Citing historical examples in Australia, Billett (2005) highlights the issues involved if the assessor is a member of the workforce with all its issues of asymmetrical distribution of power, favouritism and the lack of reliability and uniformity in assessing knowledge across workplaces, the process can be invalid. Thus, he recommends the use of occupational standards and assessors from external accrediting bodies, such as educational institutions. However, this approach also has limitations such as a lack of curriculum or competence standards in emerging industry sectors, the specific requirements of small businesses and of course, the increasing nature of work that requires expertise across industry sector and disciplinary boundaries. Thus, Billett says (2005) there is a need for policy considerations that are flexible in addressing diverse occupational practices and in ways that those assessing are able to translate their assessment and certification practices to the exigencies of workplace settings. It is these kinds of practices that are discussed next.

16.3   Suggested RPL Practices

Systems, alignment of purposes and therefore approach, the development of a pedagogic space and the tools within this space are factors that require attention in the development of effective RPL. Dyson and Keating (2005), for example, offer the following suggestions at the systems level:

- RPL systems and industry- and workplace-based models need a clear purpose for implementing them.
- RPL should have clear processes that are understood and accepted by the major stakeholders.
- It is important that the key players should be fully informed and, as far as possible, supportive of the processes.
- Implementation should be cost- and time-effective, while being fair.
- Carefully planned and negotiated post-assessment processes are needed and should be fair and equitable.
- Review processes should be representative of stakeholders.

They make the point that such processes need to be clearly understood and enacted fairly. The different approaches adopted are often instantiations of distinct purposes for RPL by different stakeholders, particularly amongst employers, providers and RPL candidates all of which need aligning to create a constructive pedagogic space. The pedagogic space is not only about the approach taken but also about boundary tools in working with RPL candidates in making links across different forms of knowledge. Tools, such as valuing of practical wisdom (i.e. phronesis) and know-how craft knowledge (i.e. techne) as well as know-why (i.e. episteme), can provide spaces for dialogic conversations, thereby encouraging mutual understanding around practice (Pokorny 2012) and, therefore, its recognition.

Practical approaches such as those identified by Blom et al. (2004, p. 6) are also held to be helpful for promoting engagement with and the successful use of RPL processes. These include:

- Information sessions
- Printed information and guides for candidates
- Recognition workshops
- Provision of evidence requirements
- Provision of exemplars or guidelines for the types of evidence required
- Meetings between individual candidates and assessors
- Negotiated opportunities for recognition assessment to be undertaken

So, there are needs for practical approaches that are aligned with and support the achievement of institutional arrangements and national goals and sentiments. To explore such propositions in greater depth, an instance for Singapore is now elaborated.

16.4   RPL in Singapore and Australia

This section examines the enactment of RPL in Singapore and in Australia. Firstly, some background information about Singapore and RPL in each of the countries.

The small island nation of Singapore has developed very rapidly and in a relatively short period of time as a nation state with a strong economy and social emphasis on inclusion and engagement. Its economic development has been quite spectacular, as has the growth of its educational system and institutions. This economic development is premised upon a range of service sector strengths as well as manufacturing, distribution and logistics, all of which require a range of occupational competence, which are characterised by being dynamic (i.e. open to constant change). The significant educational emphasis and investment within Singapore is primarily focused upon its schooling system and, then, initial tertiary education through its universities, polytechnics and institutes of technical education.

However, in recent years, the need for ongoing development of worker skills has led to the establishment of a system of continuing education and training (CET). One of the key reasons that RPL stands to be important for Singaporeans is that sections of the workforce lack structured preparation and certification for their work skills. Many of these workers acquired their skills before the advent of the CET system and also have little more than school-leaving qualifications (Billett 2011). Moreover, the mix and range of occupations practised in Singapore have become quite dynamic as the economy and economic activities have developed and then been transformed and changed over the short history of this nation state. The reliance upon large numbers of foreign workers at both ends of the labour and skills market (i.e. high skill professional and low paid workers) has also led to particular patterns of skill development and utilisation. However, both the need to position Singaporean workers well within the labour market and also to promote the abilities and employ-ability of these workers are now leading to a greater consideration of processes of CET and also the recognition of workers' skills.

To support the provision of CET, Singapore's competency-based Workforce Skills Qualifications (WSQ) system was introduced in 2005. The majority of programmes within this system comprise of the standard 'train-and-assess' pathway or classroom training courses with assessments to follow (Bound and Lin 2010). Most Singapore competency programmes and assessment are undertaken in the classroom with no workplace component (Bound and Lin 2010). Despite recent changes in policy to encourage learning in workplaces as part of CET programmes, historical legacies and a range of other factors continue to see limited inclusion of and, therefore, official valuing of workplace-learnt knowledge.

The practising of RPL in Singapore is very recent. It has only been available since 2010 for the Training sector and 2012 for the Tourism and F&B sector. Therefore, it is quite novel, possibly underdeveloped and with limited application, and there remains low levels of awareness about it by both potential participants and assessors. To date, only three industry sectors have taken up the possibility of the RPL pathway. Currently, the RPL pathway is only open to those who are pursuing their Advanced Certificates or Diplomas in three out of the 31 industry-specific sets of programmes, namely, Training and Adult Education, Tourism and Food and Beverage (F&B). It is also used to meet the requirements of occupational health and safety, while avoiding employer cost in providing training. These RPL processes are managed by two training providers; one each for the Training and Adult Education framework and the Tourism and F&B programmes. To gain insights into these processes and outcomes, an assessor from each training provider was interviewed as were six RPL participants.

The Singaporean RPL practices stand in contrast to a more well-established and somewhat different approach in Australia. Dyson and Keating (2005) explain that RPL in Australia takes into account credit transfer, experiential and learning arising through work and other forms of practice. At its best, in Australia, RPL is viewed as a process (a means of self-exploration and discovery) and as an outcome with com-petence being assessed against industry-developed competency standards, leading to a qualification. RPL in Australia assists learners move through qualification levels. There are no mandatory processes, rather a range of processes are encour-aged, but RPL is intended to follow valid and reliable assessment practices and support should be provided to applicants. Qualified assessors, strong administrative and institutional processes are stipulated in guidelines. However, there can be considerable variation in practices across industries and providers.

The processes involved in implementing RPL and in accessing RPL in these two quite different national and institutional settings highlight issues of process such as:

- Workplace experiences as basis for RPL versus occupational criteria as measured by educational means (e.g. competency standards, criteria, outcomes)
- The potential of RPL as a pedagogic space
- Access to RPL processes
- Validity and reliability of assessment measures and judgements made
- The potential of RPL

In this way, these differences indicate how distinct institutional arrangements and histories and particular purposes shape the RPL processes in quite distinct ways.

16.5 Occupational, Workplace and Education Institutional Assessment

The question of should recognition be based on individuals' development, the specific requirements of a workplace or on occupational-wide criteria is one that is embedded in the following account. Many years ago, in one Australian case, the workers to be assessed were provided with the assessment items beforehand by some of their affiliates and were able to prepare to effectively respond to the recognition tasks. Even then, those who were assessing these workers reported being intimidated and as such were reluctant to make negative assessments against any of these workers. Hence, the workplace and even the workers who had benefited from these assessments came to view the process as being largely invalid. Moreover, given that some workers were assessed as being competent in tasks which were potentially risky, the outcomes were roundly judged to have made the workplace less safe and effective. As a consequence, securing bases for and enacting the fair recognition of individuals' skills needs to circumvent workplace factors and practices such as these that may attempt to thwart its validity and reliability.

While being authentic settings for judgements about performance, and the activities that are likely to be assessed, workplace environments also foster conditions that counter the reliability (i.e. comparability) of assessment processes. That is the requirements of what constitutes workplace performance are far from uniform. Moreover, as the account above indicates, workplaces are contested environments (Bierema 2001; Billett 2001b; Solomon 1999). Assessments of and judgments about performance are likely to be subject to the interests and influences of workplace affiliations, cliques, demarcations and management that can render them unfair (Billett 2001c). It follows, therefore, that when individuals' workplace performance provides bases for making judgments about occupational competence and recognition, processes need to include the kinds of measures that are common to assessment practices elsewhere: i.e. fairness, validity and reliability. Therefore, to secure fairness in the assessment and support the standing of that certification, agencies and individuals from outside the workplace may be required to conduct standard processes of moderation assessments and legitimise certification.

Just as there is a need to attend to fairness, validity and reliability of assessment within workplaces, the same is true of educational institutions. For instance, vocational educational institutions commonly use statements of outcomes (e.g. objectives, performance criteria) provided in documents (e.g. syllabuses) and educational and assessment tasks that sometimes substitute for or are remote from actual workplace performance (Raizen 1991). These tasks are used to predict individuals' performance in occupational activities in another environment – the workplace where individuals will exercise their skills. Yet, they may well be invalid measures because occupational practice and what constitutes workplace competence varies across workplaces even when the same occupation is being practised (Billett 2001a).

Conversely, because of the prevalence of classroom delivery of competency-based training in Singapore, the only models of RPL rely not on workplace assessments but on training providers as an intermediary. So despite reference to workplace experiences, educational institutional knowledge and processes are privileged in these RPL arrangements. Dyson and Keating (2005, p. 61) refer to this as the 'craft[ing] onto' course enrolment and completion rules and procedures.

However, within such frameworks, the Tourism and Food and Beverage sectors in Singapore attempt to take a developmental approach providing intensive and individualised support for candidates as subjects indicated: 'the beauty of this framework is we bring training to them' (assessor). Firstly, based on candidates' existing qualifications and experiences in their resume, the assessor will make an initial assessment and decide if the candidates can go through RPL for the various competency units within the Advanced Certificate or Diploma programmes. Then, the assessors meet with candidates individually to gather more information and evidence about how to meet the criteria of these units. For units in which candidates have no prior knowledge or skills, assessors can provide classroom training and customise a work-based project for candidates to complete. The latter involves meeting with the candidate's workplace human resources team to gain a better understanding of the trainee's current and future work, 'so let's say they have a leadership plan for them, then we probably plug in units to aid them through that'. Hence, in this sector, the RPL process is interlinked to training and development processes and is seen as a pedagogic space and process.

Although the RPL participants were generally positive about their experiences, some of them noted having their skills recognised in this way rather than attending training sessions that they missed the opportunity to learn with and from others. One suggested that

> ... you don't get to interact with your class, and learning is not just, you don't learn [in] silo but you learn with others.

For one participant, this meant that he missed out on learning new concepts.

> I could have learnt a bit more about certain theories if I were to take the lecture.

Yet, another participant suggested having sharing sessions for those who choose the RPL route as a means of addressing this problem.

Despite the concerns and practices outlined above, the informants advised that workplaces are key sites for learning and demonstrating the knowledge required for work across working lives, they present an option for the recognition and certification of work skills that can assist overcome disadvantage and also be used to maintain the recognition of skills throughout working life. They are also the places where adults spend much of their time and where their performance of occupational practice can be most validly assessed i.e. as they perform work. However, practices associated with the recognition and certification of skills learnt through work remains nascent in many countries and constrained by complexities in their organisation and enactment. It follows that understanding further how the recognition of workplace learnt knowledge might be best enacted and identifying which policies and practices can support its enactment are worthy and timely goals.

16.6   RPL as a Pedagogic Space

In the Tourism and F&B sectors, in Singapore, the key aim of RPL is to recognise and certify the work experience of employees who have been in the industry for a long time, especially as many tend to have lower, if any, qualifications. Besides certification and accreditation, the RPL assessor observed that there are other positive outcomes for workers in these sectors, including personal confidence and satisfaction, noting that, 'we have actually seen their increase of confidence when they deal with their job, even from the way they speak, after having this qualification'.

RPL processes in the Training and Adult Education sector offer different challenges, as many of these workers are adjunct/associates/casual contract workers. Candidates are assessed on a portfolio of evidence they submit followed by a face-to-face interview. Individuals gather evidence and assemble a portfolio of information quite independent of support from the assessor or awarding institution. The Tourism and F&B process is an example of assessment as learning, whereas the Training sector process is an assessment of learning. These distinctions suggest that the design and enactment of the RPL process is as important as the outcomes derived from it. All of these considerations rehearse the conception of RPL as potentially comprising a pedagogic space.

The reported strength of the portfolio approach to assessment is that it offers an opportunity for reflection on what has been achieved by the candidates. In short, it provides a pedagogic space for these adults. Such processes of reflection appear richer when the pedagogic space in which it is undertaken is collaborative, inclusive of peers and expert others who may make explicit what candidates might overlook or take for granted. However, even candidates using the portfolio process indicated that despite opportunities for reflection they regretted the missed opportunities for the learning from and with peers that is so much a part of skill development processes. In particular, because workers in the training and development sector are sole traders, they may lack the kind of opportunities for interactions which is available to other kind of workers such as those in the Food and Beverage sector. A concern associated with the lack of opportunities for learning from and with others reported by the training practitioners was concern about developing a deeper theoretical understanding. These findings prompt the question, how do recipients of an RPL qualification perceive the value of that qualification? If they do not see the value of it compared to undertaking the programme leading to the qualification, how does the industry perceive this process and, thus, the qualification? In particular, it seems that the RPL process is merely used as a means to accredit knowledge, particularly to save on the cost of participating in training programmes that such an outcome could be quite limiting of the worth of the assessment and the recognition that accompanies it.

16.7 Access

Workers whose occupational practice sits outside provisions of courses and easy certification are structurally and doubly disadvantaged. For instance, a range of workers in an Australian state-owned railway system were promised that their skills would be certified through an RPL process. However, because there were no courses for bridge building, fettlers, station managers, etc., workers in a whole range of roles were unable to have their occupational skills assessed and certified. Moreover, the kinds of occupational practices without courses and certification are often paid low and characterised as being 'low skill' and occupied by disadvantaged groups, such as women (Bierema 2001) and migrants (Hull 1997). For these categories of disadvantaged workers, finding means to legitimately and authoritatively recognise skills acquired through work offers the prospect of providing socially just arrangements, including continuing to recognise and certify their ongoing learning across their working lives. Practical difficulties arising from a lack of appropriate benchmarks against which learning could be recognised and who pays for assessment generally result in these workers not being able to have their skills fully recognised.

Questions of access in Singapore relate not only to the very small number of training providers offering RPL but also to who is considered eligible for funding support. RPL in Tourism and Food and Beverage in Singapore is only offered to individuals who are 'sponsored' by their workplaces. It is workplaces that nominate employees for this process and pay for the RPL process. In return, employees are bonded for varying periods of time. However, there is a further structural problem associated with accessing these processes because they involve the staff being away from work which is problematic because of staff shortages. The assessor explained that

> ... they can't get enough people to work; hence, they can't release the senior[s]. So that is a very big problem for us actually. It's actually a threat to us.

Unless individuals are employed and supported by their workplace in this sector, they cannot attain WSQ qualifications through RPL. The assessor acknowledged that arrangements need to be enacted for individual RPL assessments, so they are more accessible and able to be engaged with larger numbers of workers and, potentially, without their access being constrained by their employment situation.

In contrast, within the Training and Adult Education sector, the RPL process can be accessed by anyone because it is primarily used as a mechanism to secure the entry of non-WSQ trainers and/or assessors into the WSQ sector, particularly since mandatory requirements were introduced in 2011 for being a trainer and/or assessor of WSQ programmes. This requirement means that those trainers and assessors in certified WSQ programmes need to hold the Advanced Certificate in Training and Assessment (ACTA). Also, trainers who are involved in curriculum development within national CET programmes require a higher level qualification, the WSQ Diploma in Adult and Continuing Education (DACE). However, despite all of these means, the engagement with and success of the RPL process is quite modest. Since 2010, only 20 trainers have completed competency units through the RPL pathway. This low take-up can, in part, be attributed to funding, which is the same as those undertaking course work, as well as the nature of the CET work and the requirements for documentary evidence. As the RPL process is based on evidence from previous or current work roles, this disadvantages the majority of CET trainers because in Singapore they mainly work in short-term contract modes. This means they often do not have access to the kinds of documents required for the RPL process. The RPL assessor also noted that because it is a relatively new process, many workers in the sector have not been collecting the kind of evidence they require:

> … it's quite arduous, and because it is new, a lot of practitioners out there have not been very mindful in collecting artefacts from their work… I mean, they will do a bit, but not very extensively and not in a very deliberate manner.

Both assessors commented on the amount of time and effort that the RPL process often requires: 'it's actually a lot of effort for very little in return'. It is a very person-dependent and individual process, thereby also requiring considerable time and effort on the part of the candidate, sometimes their workplace, and the assessor.

16.8   Validity, Reliability and Judgement

In the Singaporean Training and Adult Education sector, assessors noted that there are usually significant gaps between the information they have and the requirements for the recognition of learning. Hence, they have to ensure that the candidate fills the gaps, 'you have to be very methodical and detailed in saying, ok this is not there, and this is there but it's not sufficient and things like that'. In addition, there is the more fundamental issue of how judgements are made. The generic standards in the competency units may not match the trainee's existing practices, but this does not mean that the latter is not effective. Judgements are made by assessors through the lens of dominant discourses about the value of educational institutional knowledge and workplace knowledge and skill. Different practices adopted by assessors in being transparent about the assessment criteria make the RPL process more or less accessible and valid. While some participants in the Training and Adult Education sector recall being given clear information about the assessment requirements, others noted that they were given examples of the kinds of evidence required, but did not have access to the actual assessment criteria, 'we are actually not exactly sure what is sufficient'.

As with any process that requires people to gather information to achieve a particular goal, the clarity of what kind of information and what kind of goal is to be achieved becomes quite central to its success. Yet, some participants commented that the process of RPL is problematic, as they are not sure what constitutes sufficient evidence to meet the required standards. This issue goes to the heart of competency-based training (CBT) systems, which are based on standards. Where standards refer to purely technical skills, there may be clear conditions that set out what is sufficient. For instance, it has been suggested that standards for aged care tend to focus very much on the technicalities of being an aged care worker yet, miss out entirely on the concept and practice of care that is so central to this work. However, in Singapore discipline knowledge and vocational and generic skills have separate frameworks and are taught separately (Bound et al. 2011). This set of situational factors places a particular emphasis on the judgement of assessors who are expected to bring to bear their expertise in the making of these judgements. The role of judgement and expertise in assessment and ensuring fairness is not endemic to CBT; these issues are an integral part of assessment processes in all education sectors. However, in echoing the reference to an emphasis on declarative knowledge referred to above, the use of standards, criteria and assessment rubrics all involve:

> ... a single-minded concentration on explicit knowledge and careful articulation of assessment criteria and standards is not, in itself, sufficient to share useful knowledge of the assessment process (Rust et al. 2003, p. 151)

Assessment processes based on standards or criteria assume that all aspects of workplace performance can be articulated and made explicit through the use of these prespecifiable declarative standards. Yet, it is the more 'invisible' aspects, such as the caring disposition that are the markers of expertise and which are more difficult to make explicit and articulate. As such, a common understanding of these standards is difficult to achieve thereby compromising easy measures of reliability. Moreover, it is perhaps not surprising that RPL candidates expressed discomfort with 'not knowing' what is sufficient to meet the standards.

RPL in Singapore relies heavily on the development of portfolios, as noted, particularly in the approach adopted for the Training and Education sector. Here again arises the issue of judgement by both the candidates when gathering their information and considering what level of recognition they should apply for (i.e. Advance Certificate or Diploma) and also the assessor who has to make decisions about the fit, completeness or absence of appropriate competence. Certainly, issues of judgement are common to all assessment processes. 'Issues of rigour in assessment of portfolios need to be addressed, but the assessor's professional judgement will inevitably enter into this assessment' (McMullan et al. 2003, p. 283). The concern here is to what degree can these judgements be supported by processes that are common to assessment practices elsewhere (i.e. reliability). These concerns include the use of moderation processes and peer validation. The fact that trainers and assessors in Singapore, as elsewhere, have expressed discomfort with making these judgements (see Bound 2010) suggesting that the wide-scale adoption of RPL processes requires that those making judgements might need to be supported by some preparation before the task is undertaken and then returned the engaging in processes of moderation. Likely, elsewhere, but clearly reported in the Singapore context, the source of this concern is situated within funding parameters and quality assurance discourses and audit processes that inadvertently encourage some private for profit providers (i.e. the dominant kind of providers in the sector) to place pressure upon assessors to pass their students as their funding is dependent on the number of successful completions. Hence, the importance of other kinds of processes provides some distance between the assessor, those being assessed and institutions which may have interests other than the enactment of a valid and reliable assessment process. Given the resource-intensive nature of the RPL process described above, the other issue is the extent by which it can be funded and who will ultimately pay for these processes.

16.9   RPL in Prospect

As elaborated across this chapter, the RPL process is not always straightforward or wholly effective. There are national, sector-particular issues and employment status issues associated with its implementation and outcomes. Issues of access are as much a part of knowing about and understanding the process and what is 'sufficient' as it is a matter of funding and determining who is selected to benefit from that funding. The recognition and valuing of RPL can be questioned not only by employers and educational institutions but also by RPL participants when they look towards formalised institutional delivery to provide deeper theoretical understandings. Yet, RPL processes can create important pedagogic spaces that can assist the development of learners' knowledge and legitimate that knowledge and its learning. It is the construction and dialogue of these pedagogic spaces that needs further investigation and consideration. It is these spaces that bridge the nexus between cognitive, academic ways of knowing and experience, practice-based ways of knowing.

Quality issues indicate the role of educational institutions, but at the same time privilege institutional ways of knowing. How knowledge is understood, valued and viewed by different stakeholders requires further investigation. Those most disadvantaged do not know how to access and engage in the process. The quality issue also begs the question, how much RPL is appropriate and desirable?

Both developmental and mechanistic approaches to RPL have been outlined in this chapter, each serving different purposes, one to ensure the issuing of a required qualification and the other placing emphasis on the processes to use RPL as assessment *for* learning. Although the approach and the complexity and requirements of the processes are linked to the question as to who wants RPL and why, it is this latter question that is the bigger question. To address the goal of using RPL as a means for greater equity in access to LLL, questions of supply, demand and funding need to be addressed but importantly too, so do the processes and accessibility to those processes.

Assessors need to be prepared and be experienced and then supported by processes such as moderation and peer engagement. Given the oft-stated value of engagement in a learning process, including the ability to reflect and consider achievements, some broader questions include: to what extent is certification valued both by individuals and the industry sector, other than as a compliance requirement for employment? Moreover, given the importance of industry standards, their use in establishing the basis for programmes as well as RPL, there are apparent inadequacies in reflecting the kind of knowledge demonstrated by those who practice. Broader kinds of benchmarks and assessment processes could be considered not only for the RPL process but also for the wider goal of promoting CET for workers such as those in Singapore. Fairness, validity and reliability are not abstract or given, but related to particular societal and situational contexts.

References

Andersson, P., & Harris, J. (2006). *Retheorising RPL*. Leicester: NIACE Publishers.
Armsby, P. (2012). Accreditation of experiential learning at doctoral level. *Journal of Workplace Learning, 24*(2), 133–150.
Berglund, L., & Andersson, P. (2012). Recognition of knowledge and skills at work: In whose interests? *Journal of Workplace Learning, 24*(2), 73–84.
Bierema, L. L. (2001). Women, work, and learning. In T. Fenwick (Ed.), *Sociocultural perspectives on learning through work*. San Francisco: Jossey Bass/Wiley.
Billett, S. (2001a). Knowing in practice: Re-conceptualising vocational expertise. *Learning and Instruction, 11*(6), 431–452.
Billett, S. (2001b). Coparticipation at work: Affordance and engagement. In T. Fenwick (Ed.), *Sociocultural perspectives on learning through work*. San Francisco: Jossey Bass/Wiley.
Billett, S. (2001c). Learning through work: Workplace affordances and individual engagement. *Journal of Workplace Learning, 13*(5), 209–214.
Billett, S. (2005). Recognition of learning through work. In N. Bascia, A. Cumming, A. Datnow, K. Leithwood, & D. Livingstone (Eds.), *International handbook of educational policy*. Dordrecht: Springer.
Billett, S. (2009). Realising the educational worth of integrating work experiences in higher education. *Studies in Higher Education, 4*(7), 827–843.
Billett, S. (2011). Promoting lifelong employability for workforce aged over 45: Singaporean workers' perspectives. *International Journal of Continuing Education and Lifelong Learning, 3*(2), 57–73.
Blom, K., Clayton, B., Bateman, A., Bedgood, M., & Hughes, E. (2004). *What's in it for me? Recognition of prior learning in enterprise-based registered training organisations*. Adelaide: NZCER.
Bound, H. (2010). *Reflexive practitioner research for professional learning in CET*. Singapore: Institute for Adult Learning.
Bound, H., & Lin, M. (2010). *Singapore workforce skills qualifications (WSQ), workplace learning and assessment (stage I)*. Singapore: Institute for Adult Learning.

Bound, H., Lin, M., & Li, S. (2011). *Generic skills: Four cases in four industries*. Singapore: Institute for Adult Learning.

Cooper, L., & Harris, J. (2013). Recognition of prior learning: Exploring the 'knowledge' question. *International Journal of Lifelong Education, 32*(4), 447–463.

Darrah, C. N. (1996). *Learning and work: An exploration in industrial ethnography*. New York: Garland Publishing.

Dyson, C., & Keating, J. (2005). *Skills, knowledge and employability*. Geneva: ILO.

Groot, W., Hartog, J., & Oosterbeek, H. (1994). Costs and revenues of investment in enterprise-related schooling. *Oxford Economic Papers, 46*(4), 658–675.

Grubb, W. N. (1996). *Working in the middle: Strengthening education and training for the mid-skilled labor force*. San Francisco: Jossey Bass.

Harris, J. (1997). *The recognition of prior learning (RPL) in South Africa: Drifts and shifts in international practices: Understanding the changing discursive terrain*. Unpublished paper prepared for the Research and Development Programme in the Recognition of Prior Learning in Higher Education (Human Sciences Research Council, University of Cape Town and Peninsula Technikon).

Hull, G. (1997). Preface and introduction. In G. Hull (Ed.), *Changing work, changing workers: Critical perspectives on language, literacy and skills*. New York: State University of New York Press.

Lengerman, P. A. (1999). How long do the benefits of training last? Evidence of long term effects across current and previous employers. *Research in Labour Economics, 18*, 439–461.

McMullan, M., Endacott, R., Gray, M. A., Jasper, M., Miller, C. M., Scholes, J., & Webb, C. (2003). Portfolios and assessment of competence: A review of the literature. *Journal of Advanced Nursing, 41*(3), 283–294.

Meyers, R., Billett, S., & Kelly, A. (2010). Mature-aged workers' learning needs and motivations for participation in training programs. *International Journal of Training Research, 8*, 116–127.

Noon, M., & Blyton, P. (1997). *The realities of work*. Basingstoke/Hants: Macmillan.

O'Connell, P. J. (1999). *Adults in training: An international comparison of continuing education and training*. Paris: OECD.

Pokorny, H. (2012). Assessing prior experiential learning: Issues of authority, authorship and identity. *Journal of Workplace Learning, 24*(2), 119–132.

Pusey, M. (2003). *The experience of middle Australia*. Cambridge: Cambridge University Press.

Raizen, S. A. (1991). *Learning and work: The research base. Vocational education and training for youth: Towards coherent policy and practice*. Paris: OECD.

Rust, C., Price, M., & O'Donovan, B. (2003). Improving students' learning by developing their understanding of assessment criteria and processes. *Assessment and Evaluation in Higher Education, 28*(2), 147–164.

Solomon, N. (1999). Culture and difference in workplace learning. In D. Bound & D. J. Garrick (Eds.), *Understanding learning at work*. London: Routledge.

Travers, N. (2012). Academic perspectives on college-level learning implications for workplace learning. *Journal of Workplace Learning, 24*(2), 105–118.

Wheelahan, L., Miller, P., Newton, D., Dennis, N., Firth, J., Pascoe, S., & Veenkerp, P. (2003). *Recognition of prior learning: Policy and practice in Australia*. Lismore: Report for Australian Qualifications Framework Advisory Board, Southern Cross University.

Index

T. Halttunen et al. (eds.), *Promoting, Assessing, Recognizing and Certifying Lifelong
Learning: International Perspectives and Practices*, Lifelong Learning Book Series 20,
DOI 10.1007/978-94-017-8694-2, © Springer Science+Business Media Dordrecht 2014

CPSIA information can be obtained at www.ICGtesting.com
Printed in the USA
LVOW10*1101170314

377730LV00005B/17/P